Writing
Children's Books

3rd Edition

by Lisa Rojany and Peter Economy

for
dummies®
A Wiley Brand

D1265389

Writing Children's Books For Dummies®, 3rd Edition

Published by: **John Wiley & Sons, Inc.,** 111 River Street, Hoboken, NJ 07030-5774, www.wiley.com

Copyright © 2022 by John Wiley & Sons, Inc., Hoboken, New Jersey

Published simultaneously in Canada

For general information on our other products and services, please contact our Customer Care Department within the U.S. at 877-762-2974, outside the U.S. at 317-572-3993, or fax 317-572-4002. For technical support, please visit www.wiley.com/techsupport.

Wiley publishes in a variety of print and electronic formats and by print-on-demand. Some material included with standard print versions of this book may not be included in e-books or in print-on-demand. If this book refers to media such as a CD or DVD that is not included in the version you purchased, you may download this material at http://booksupport.wiley.com. For more information about Wiley products, visit www.wiley.com.

Library of Congress Control Number: 2022934334

ISBN 978-1-119-87001-2 (pbk); ISBN 978-1-119-87003-6 (ebk); ISBN 978-1-119-87002-9 (ebk).

SKY10033828_032922

Table of Contents

Introduction

I f you've gone through the trouble of opening up this book, we're going to take a wild guess: You dream of writing your own children's book and getting it published. Your desire may come from a deep-seated yearning to communicate with young people or to share experiences with them. Or it may stem from an interest in a subject you think children may also delight in. Regardless of where your desire comes from, we want to help you turn that passion into a well-written, saleable manuscript.

Our goals in writing this book are to help you understand the children's book writing process and give you the tools you need to turn your children's book dream into reality. Many people think writing a children's book is child's play. Actually, it's not. It takes a lot of hard work. In fact, it can even be tougher than writing for adults. But we believe you can do it!

We know plenty of people just like you who attempt to tackle the process of writing a children's book. Some haven't the slightest idea where to start. Others have a good idea where to start, but they don't know what to do with their manuscript after they write it. Good news: We understand the process and what it takes to move through it with as little stress as possible. In the pages that follow, we provide you with the very best advice that our many years of experience have to offer.

About This Book

Writing a children's book and getting it published involves a lot more than simply knocking out a manuscript and e-mailing it to a publisher. If you're serious about getting your book published, then you need to understand the entire process of how a children's book comes into existence and how to deal with the different challenges that present themselves along the way. Where do you start? How do you get your manuscript in front of an editor at a traditional publisher? Should you consider self-publishing or maybe a hybrid publisher? Should you engage a literary agent or an illustrator? How can you use social media to promote your book? This book answers these questions, and hundreds more like them, in an easy-to-use reference that you can take with you anywhere.

Also, throughout the book, we sprinkle a generous helping of insightful, candid interviews with publishing pros who answer common questions with incredible candor and honesty — and often a great sense of humor.

We use the following conventions throughout the text to make everything consistent and easy-to-understand:

» All web addresses appear in monofont.

» New terms appear in *italics* and are closely followed by an easy-to-understand definition.

» **Bold** text indicates keywords in bulleted lists or highlights the action parts of numbered steps.

» Sidebars are the shaded boxes that appear here and there throughout the book. They contain fun facts, interesting asides, and interviews with industry experts. Of course, we hope you read each and every one, but if you're just not interested or don't have the time, don't worry about them.

To make the content more accessible, we divided it into six parts:

» Part 1: The ABCs of Writing for Children

» Part 2: Immersing Yourself in the Writing Process

» Part 3: Creating a Spellbinding Story

» Part 4: Making Your Story Sparkle

» Part 5: Getting Published and Promoting Your Book

» Part 6: The Part of Tens

Foolish Assumptions

We wrote this book with some thoughts about you in mind. Here's what we assume about you, our reader:

» You've long fantasized about writing your own children's book and getting it published.

» You may have already written a children's story but aren't sure how to prepare it for submission. You may have already had a children's book published, but you want to experiment writing a different type of children's story. Or you may even be an experienced children's book author who's looking for new perspectives on social media, publicity, and the industry as a whole.

>> You're looking for a comprehensive guide that demystifies children's book writing by focusing on the information that's most worth knowing.

>> You want to improve your writing skills and hone your craft.

>> You're willing to take the time to become knowledgeable about the conventions in the children's book world to separate yourself from the wannabes.

>> You're interested in exploring different publishing options, including self-publishing, hybrid publishing, and/or e-books.

>> You want to know how to promote and market your book to improve sales.

>> You want to know what you need to do to find an agent or publisher.

Icons Used in This Book

To make this book simple to use, we include some icons in the margins so that you can easily find and fathom key ideas and information.

REMEMBER

This icon highlights important information to store in your brain for quick recall at a later time.

TIP

These tidbits provide expert advice to help you save time, money, or frustration in the book-writing process.

WARNING

Avoid mistakes by following the sage words of advice appearing alongside this icon.

Beyond the Book

In addition to the abundance of information and guidance related to writing and publishing a children's book that we provide in this book, you get access to even more help and information online at Dummies.com. Check out this book's online Cheat Sheet. Just go to www.dummies.com and search for "Writing a Children's Book For Dummies Cheat Sheet."

Where to Go from Here

The great thing about this book is that you decide where you want to start and what you want to read. With this reference book, you can jump in and out at will. Just head to the table of contents or the index to find the information you want. For complete newbies, Part 1, where we provide you with a 50,000-foot view of all the different aspects of writing books for children, is a great place to start.

1

The ABCs of Writing for Children

IN THIS PART . . .

Step into the world of children's books.

Take a detailed look at all the different formats of children's books, from board books to chapter books to young adult novels (and much more).

Explore different genres of children's books — including fantasy, diversity, biography, and historical fiction.

Delve deeply into the children's book market so that you can find out about the institutions and people (aside from the children themselves) who make up the market's key players.

Chapter **1**

Exploring the Basics of Writing Children's Books

For many, dreams of writing or illustrating a children's book remain just that — dreams — because they soon find out that writing a really good children's book is hard. Not only that, but actually getting a children's book published is even harder. If you don't know the conventions and styles, if you don't speak the lingo, if you don't have someone to advocate for your work, or if you or your manuscript don't come across as professional, you'll be hard pressed to get your manuscript read and considered, much less published.

Consider this chapter your sneak peek into the world of children's publishing. We fill you in on the basics of children's book formats, creating a productive writing zone, employing key storytelling techniques, revising your manuscript, and getting your story into the hands of publishers who sell to the exact children's audience you're targeting.

REMEMBER

Every bestselling children's book author started from the beginning: with a story idea — just like you. Also, many of today's most successful writers were rejected time after time until they finally found someone who liked what they read or saw, and decided to take a chance. Follow your dreams. Feed your passion. Never give up. The day your children's book is published, we'll be cheering for you.

Knowing Your Format, Genre, and Audience

Before you do anything else, figure out what kind of children's book you're writing (or want to write).

Manuscripts are published in several tried-and-true formats, with new ones developed every year. *Formats* involve the physical characteristics of a book: page count; *trim size* (width and height); whether it has color or is in black and white, has lots of pictures or lots of words, is hardcover or softcover, comes as an e-book or an app — or both. Chapter 2 gives a thorough explanation of what's what in formats.

Also, your book may (or may not) fall into a lot of different genres. *Genres* are broad subjects, like mystery or adventure or romance. So figuring out your format and genre can help you determine exactly how to write and present your book. Chapter 3 has a lot of examples of genres that can help guide you in your writing journey.

REMEMBER

You need to ask yourself: Who is my audience? Believe it or not, children isn't the correct answer. Children of a particular age bracket — say infant to age 2, or ages 3 to 8 — may come closer to defining the target age you're trying to reach. But are they really the ones who buy your book? Because books are ushered through the process by grown-ups — signed up by agents, acquired and edited by editors, categorized by publishers, pushed by sales reps, shelved and sold by booksellers, and most often purchased by parents, librarians, and other adults — your audience is more complicated than you may think. In Chapter 4, we tell you all about the different people you need to impress before you get your book in the hands of children.

Getting into a Good Writing Zone

If you think you can just grab a pen and paper or handy-dandy laptop and jump right into writing, you're right! But you may also want to consider what might happen when your life starts to intrude on your writing time. How do you work around the children needing to be fed and your desk being buried under mounds of bills and old homework? How do you figure out the best time to write? In Chapter 5, we talk about the importance of making a writing schedule and sticking to it. We also emphasize finding a space of your own for writing and making that space conducive to productivity and creativity.

After you figure out how to get to work, you have to decide what you're going to write about. Coming up with an interesting idea for a story isn't necessarily as easy as you may think, which is why we provide a lot of ways to boot up your idea factory in Chapter 6. We also have ways to get you unstuck if you find yourself with an annoying case of writer's block.

As soon as you have your good idea, you need to get out there and research to make sure the idea fits your target audience. We cover the hows and whys of researching your audience, figuring out what children like and what they see as important in their lives, and then researching the topic itself in Chapter 7.

Transforming Yourself into a Storyteller

By making sure your fiction story features these key elements, you can get yourself one step closer to publishing success:

>> **Memorable characters:** Whether it's a child who can fly, a really hungry wolf, a boy and a slave floating down the Mississippi River, or a smelly green ogre, characters are the heart and soul of children's books. So how can you create characters who jump off the page and into your readers' hearts? Chapter 8 reveals how to build and flesh out great characters and how to avoid stereotyping and other common pitfalls.

>> **An engaging plot:** What exactly is a plot, and how do you figure out what constitutes a beginning, a middle, and an ending? We answer that question in Chapter 9, as well as defining conflict, climax, and resolution.

>> **Realistic dialogue:** Kids can tell when dialogue doesn't sound right. Chapter 10 features tips and step-by-step advice for writing realistic, age-appropriate dialogue for each of your characters. We also look at ways to make sure your characters sound different from one another.

>> **Interesting settings:** One way to engage young readers is to set your story in places that intrigue them. In Chapter 11, we give you some pointers on how to create interesting settings and build worlds that ground your story in a particular context and draw in your reader.

Of course, you also need to consider your author voice or *tone*. Do you want to sound playful by incorporating word play, rhyming, and rhythm (the music inherent in words well matched)? Or do you want to make youngsters giggle uncontrollably? We give you the tools you need to create your character's voice in Chapter 12. And if you're struggling with sticking to a consistent point of view, Chapter 12 can help you out there, too.

REMEMBER

Interested in writing nonfiction? Then turn to Chapter 13. It's chock-full of good advice on jump-starting your nonfiction project by choosing a kid-friendly topic, organizing your ideas into a comprehensive outline or plan, and fleshing out your ideas with all the right research.

Polishing Your Gem and Getting It Ready to Send

After you write your first (or tenth) draft, you may be ready for the revising or editing process. Revising and editing aren't just exercises to go through step by step; they are processes in which you, the writer, get to know your story inside and out. You flesh out characters, hone and sharpen the story, fine-tune the pacing, and buff and polish the writing. In Chapter 14, we guide you through the steps of revising and editing, addressing in detail how to fix everything from dialogue issues to awkward writing, advising when to adhere to the rules of grammar (and when it's okay not to), and giving you a few simple questions to ask yourself to make the process much smoother and less complicated.

And what about illustrations? Should you illustrate your book yourself, or should you partner with or hire an illustrator to create the pictures you envision to complement and enhance your manuscript? For writers wondering about whether art should be included with their manuscript, we give you the pros and cons of partnering with an illustrator. For those with artistic talent to pair with their writing skills, Chapter 15 also provides step-by-step examples of what illustrating a picture book really looks like.

In the process of rewriting and editing your story, you may find that you have some serious questions about your manuscript, such as, "Is this really final, or does it need work?" or "Is this supporting character turning into more of a distraction than anything else?" Seek out feedback from others to help you find answers to any and all questions you may be asking. You can join (or start) a local writer's group, attend book conferences or writing workshops, or participate in writing groups online. For the full scoop on all things feedback-related, see Chapter 16.

TIP

In the publishing world, first impressions carry a lot of weight. Your thoroughly revised, well-written, and engaging manuscript may fail to wow editors if it looks unprofessional. Trust us: Proper formatting goes a long way toward making your submission look as professional and enticing as possible. (Flip to Chapter 14 for some formatting tips.)

Selling Your Story

After you have a well-written, carefully edited, perfectly formatted manuscript in your hands, you're ready to launch it on its first (or 20th) journey out into the big, bad world of publishing. Chapter 17 explains

» the difference between the big, traditional publishers and smaller presses or independents

» the pros and cons of working with a hybrid or vanity publisher

» the option of self-publishing

At this point in the process, you have a few different options:

» **Agents:** You can send your manuscript to an *agent,* a person who will best represent your interests and do all query-letter writing, submitting, tracking, and negotiating on your behalf. The good ones are well worth the 15 percent they typically charge to take your career from amateur to professional. Finding the right one, getting their attention, and then negotiating your contract is a process unto itself, which we tell you all about in Chapter 18.

» **Traditional publishers:** You can submit your book to traditional publishers on your own. Finding the right match and submitting to only the right-fit publishing houses is an art form requiring in-depth research and quite a bit of sleuthing. Turn to Chapter 18 for advice on finding the traditional publisher who's looking for stories just like yours, as well as how to get what you want in your contract.

» **Hybrids:** You can go to a hybrid publisher who can help you out with the process. Chapter 19 digs deep into hybrid publishing, including what to expect and what to look out for.

» **Self-publishing:** You can opt out of the submissions game altogether and choose to publish your book all by yourself. Chapter 20 introduces you to the world of self-publishing, offering you tips, options, and guidelines about how and where to start with print or digital versions of your book.

Promoting Your Book

After you have your finished book or its actual publication date, how can you be sure anyone will ever see it or buy it? If you're working with a traditional publisher, that company likely has a marketing team dedicated to spreading the word about your book. But to be honest, the efforts that your publisher is planning on your behalf may not impress you — and may not even be enough to get the word out. So you might need to do some marketing and publicizing of your own if you want your book to sell. Don't worry, though. Publicity professionals let you in on their secrets in Chapter 21, and we give you a lot of ideas about how to get your book noticed. Marketing, planning, and promotion take you from book signing to lecture — all starring you and your fabulous children's book.

TIP

Unless you've been living under a rock, you're probably aware that social media has become a powerful force in promoting everything from products and politics to — you guessed it — children's books. Chapter 22 explains how to use social media (including blogs, Facebook, Instagram, TikTok, Twitter, and more) to introduce your book to the world, alert potential buyers to its existence, and keep it in the public consciousness long after its release date.

Improving Your Chances of Getting Published

We've worked in the publishing industry for a long time, and we have a pretty good idea of what works and what doesn't. Here are some insider tips that can significantly improve your chances of getting published. Some of these tips involve very specific advice, such as getting feedback before submitting; others provide less concrete (but just as important) tips about the etiquette of following up with publishers and how to behave if rejected:

>> **Act like a pro.** If you act like you're an experienced and savvy children's book writer, people perceive you as being an experienced and savvy children's book writer — provided you've really done your research. The children's book industry tends to be more accepting of those people who already belong to the club, so to speak, as compared to the newbies pounding on the door to be let in. So you can greatly improve your chances of getting published if you behave like you already belong. Some examples of putting yourself out there as a pro include sending a one-page query letter that addresses all the salient points, submitting your carefully and thoroughly edited manuscript, and formatting your manuscript properly. (All of these tips are discussed in Chapters 14 and 18).

>> **Create magic with words.** Writing a fabulous children's book isn't easy. A children's book editor has a very finely tuned sense of what constitutes a well-written book and what will sell in the marketplace. If you want to get your book published, your writing must be top notch — second best isn't good enough. If you're still learning the craft of writing, by all means get some reliable and knowledgeable feedback. Check out other writers' guides, as well. And you might even choose to engage the services of a professional children's book editor or book doctor to help fix up your manuscript before you submit it to an agent or publisher for consideration. Whichever avenue(s) you choose, the goal is putting your best effort forward.

>> **Research thoroughly.** To get published, your book needs to be both believable and factually correct (especially if you're writing nonfiction). If you're sloppy with the facts, your editor won't waste much time with your manuscript before deleting it from their inbox. (Chapter 7 keeps you up on the latest developments in the world of children and ways to research your topic.)

>> **Follow up — without stalking.** After you submit your manuscript or proposal, you might want to follow up with the agent or editor to whom you submitted it. Sometimes, however, you actually need to avoid a follow-up. Many publishers and agents now reply to a query with the admonition that if they don't get back to you within three to six months, you can assume that they have rejected your work. Keep in mind that agents and editors are very busy people, and they probably receive hundreds, if not thousands, of submissions every year. Be polite, but avoid stalking the agent or editor by constantly calling or e-mailing for the status of your submission. Making a pest of yourself buys you nothing except a one-way ticket out of the world of children's books. See Chapter 18 for more on when and how to follow up.

>> **Accept rejection graciously.** Every children's book author — even the most successful and famous — knows rejection and what it's like to wonder whether their book will ever get published. But every rejection provides you with important lessons that you can apply to your next submission. Take these lessons to heart and move on to the next opportunity. Head to Chapter 18 for more on dealing with rejection.

>> **Practice until you're perfect.** You can't find a better way to succeed at writing than to write, and you can't get better at submitting your manuscripts and proposals to agents or publishers unless you keep trying. Don't let rejection get in the way of your progress; keep writing and keep submitting. The more you do, the better you'll get at it — it being the elements of the writing process itself, which we discuss in Parts 2 and 3 of this book. And remember: Hope means always having a manuscript being considered somewhere.

>> **Promote like crazy.** Publishers love authors with a *selling platform* —defined as the ability to publicize, promote, and sell their books as widely as possible. By showing your prospective publishers that you have the ability to promote and sell your books — via social media; by way of workshops or speaking engagements, in traditional media such as radio, TV, and local newspapers; through your networks of relationships; and more — you greatly increase your chances of being published. (For more on promotion, see Chapters 21 and 22.)

>> **Give back to the writing community.** Both beginners and pros give back to their profession, to their readers, and to their communities. They volunteer to participate in writing groups or conferences to help new or unpublished authors polish their work and get published; they do free readings in local schools and libraries; and they advocate for children in their communities. When you give back like a pro, you improve your standing in the children's book industry, increasing your chances of getting published. And besides all that, you establish some good karma — and that can't hurt.

Chapter **2**

Delving into Children's Book Formats

hildren are as different as the many different books catering to their many different interests and desires. Because of this, children's books offer a wealth of diversity in formats, shapes, sizes, and intended audiences. In this chapter, we explain the different formats that children's books can fall into. We also show you a lot of examples of book covers so that you can get a feel for successful and representative formats that sell in various channels of the children's book market. In Chapter 3, we talk about genres, another way to group children's books. Each genre has its own conventions that you must address, as well.

Dissecting the Anatomy of a Book

Before we go dropping a lot of terminology on you, we want you to know the most basic parts of a book. If you at least kind of recognize these terms, you can more easily communicate about your book to other publishing professionals:

» **Cover:** The face your book presents to the world after it's published. You can have a hardcover book (also known as a *hardback*), meaning it has paper glued over hard cardboard on three sides (front cover, back cover, and spine); or you might have a softcover book (also known as a *paperback*), meaning it has thick bond cardstock paper for all three sides. You can also have paper over board.

  - *Hardcover:* You call a hardcover book's cover its *case.* The case is often one solid color that has the front cover and spine stamped with the name of the book and author. The *jacket* is a sheet of paper that wraps around this case and has some sort of illustration, depending on the format.

  - *Softcover:* A softcover book's front cover usually features the title, the author's name, the illustrator's name, and some graphic image. The back cover can include *sell copy* (words that describe what the book is about in brief and why it's so great), the publisher's name, copyright info, a barcode, a price, and other information that helps retailers categorize and sell it.

  - *Paper-over-board:* When a hardcover book cover doesn't have a jacket and looks more like a softcover book cover, it's called a *paper-over-board book.* The paper is wrapped around and secured to the cardboard without a jacket covering it. (***Note:*** For many board books and novelty books, the text and images begin right away on the inside front cover.)

» **Spine:** The part of the book that usually hides the binding, which is where the pages are glued or sewn together. The spine is between both covers and usually displays, at minimum, the title, the author's and illustrator's last names, and the publisher's name or logo.

» **Jacket:** A separate piece of heavy-stock removable paper that you can wrap around the cover and tuck under the front and back covers of the book. The jacket can repeat all the information and images found on the front cover. But sometimes the book's actual hardcover has only the title, the author's name, the illustrator's name (if there is one), and the publisher's logo on the spine (which often occurs in picture books and hardcover young adult novels). In these cases, the jacket provides all the images and publishing information, including the title, credits, sell copy, author and illustrator bios, and dedication.

Specifically, the front flap of the jacket usually has sell copy; the back flap of the jacket often has author (and illustrator) bios.

>> **Pages:** The sheets of paper onto which they print your story and any illustrations. Most children's books are published in *signatures* (groups) of 8 pages each because of the way that the bindery prints, folds, and then cuts the pages. For this reason, most children's picture books and leveled readers have pages in denominations of 8: such as 24 or 32 pages, 48 or 64 pages. While you move up into books that have chapters, the signatures are 16 pages long, so those book pages come in multiples of 16.

>> **Trim:** Also called *trim size;* the dimensions of the book. *Page trim* refers to the size of the book's interior pages. *Cover trim* refers to the size of the cover, which may be larger than or the same size as the page trim.

>> **Endpapers:** The double leaves of paper added at the front and back of the book before it's bound. Most of the time, endpapers are added to the book after it's printed. The binder pastes the outer leaf of each page to the inner surface of the cover (they call this process the *paste-down*), the *inner leaves* (or free endpapers) form the first and last pages of the book when bound. Endpapers are mostly of heavier-stock paper than the rest of the text pages, and they're often decorated or filled with mini-illustrations.

>> **Front matter:** The material that comes before the text or story of a book, including the title and copyright pages, a table of contents, an introduction, a dedication, and sometimes acknowledgments. Sometimes, the publisher makes the design decision to move this information to the back of the book.

>> **Back matter:** Various sections that come after the main text, mostly supporting material. For example, acknowledgements, an index, citations, a glossary, additional information about the creation of the story (if relevant), or more factual information about the story that can add to the reader's experience (though this type of back matter is less common in fiction).

>> **Spread:** The left page and the right page of an open book constitute a *spread*. For example, pages 2 and 3 in a picture book usually constitute spread 1, pages 4 and 5 are spread 2, and so on.

Grouping Types of Children's Books

You can group children's books into two overarching categories:

>> **Fiction:** Made-up stories; a big plate onto which other derivative (and delicious!) morsels may fall

>> **Nonfiction:** Writing based on real facts, people, places, or events

Within those categories, you can also divide children's books into formats based on the various ages the books serve, as well as the book's size, shape, and content. Some examples of formats include picture books, board books, chapter books, and young adult (YA) books.

Formats help publishers group their titles by *age appropriateness* (meaning where children are developmentally), physical characteristics, or both. These groupings, in turn, help children's book readers know what type of books will appeal to children in particular age ranges, or with certain interests or goals.

TIP

Always refer to your work's title and the format together — in the same sentence — when talking to agents and publishers. Say something such as, "*Alphababies* is a 300-word board book that uses photographs of babies to teach the alphabet to toddlers." With that information, the person reviewing your work can immediately identify the format into which your book falls.

REMEMBER

Many writers can't figure out their format until they actually write their story down. But other writers find it helpful to know the parameters of the various formats ahead of time. Those constraints help them make decisions along the way about plot complexity, word count, vocabulary level, and other elements that go into defining a format. Just because you know about formats doesn't mean you have to choose one before you start writing your book. You also can't squeeze just any story into any format.

Note: Publishers often release downloadable digital copies and e-book versions simultaneously with the print versions across many children's book formats. This is so consumers have many choices in how they read the book.

Illustrated Books for All Ages

What we loosely refer to as "books with pictures" describes any of the formats that focus mainly on heavy illustration and few words. Books that have pictures are therefore perfect for babies and growing toddlers, as well as in formats such as graphic novels and some middle-grade fiction. We walk you through the various formats that we consider books with pictures in the following sections.

TIP

You may notice as you read that many of the skills required to break into children's book writing for any format or age group sound alike. Well, you're right on target. In Part 3, we discuss how the same basic elements of good writing apply for any format, age group, or subject, and for fiction or nonfiction. Good writing is good writing. Period.

Baby-friendly board books

Get yourself a chunky book with a heavy stock, rounded corners, and bright, eye-catching pictures, and you've got yourself a board book (see Figure 2-1). Perfect gifts for little ones, these books are for the youngest readers — so young, in fact, that they don't even read yet! *What's Wrong, Little Pookie?* by Sandra Boynton (Little Simon) and indeed most of Boynton's books are published as board books. Fabulous picture books that are republished as board books include *Goodnight Moon* and *Runaway Bunny*, both by Margaret Wise Brown (HarperFestival), *Jamberry* by Bruce Degen (HarperFestival), and *Hug* by Jez Alborough (Candlewick Press).

FIGURE 2-1:
Example board
books.

a   b   c

a) Why Is Baby Grumpy? by Joey Spiotto. Copyright © 2021 by Joey Spiotto. Reprinted by permission of Scholastic Inc.
b) ROAR: A Dinosaur Tour © 2018 and c) CHOMP: A Shark Romp © 2019 by Michael Paul. Reprinted with permission of the author/illustrator Michael Paul, and Penguin Random House.

We fill you in on the basics of board books — and how to write a great one — in the following sections.

Beginning with the basics of board books

Board books get their name because they're made of cardboard or chipboard, which makes their pages stiffer and heavier than regular paper — and able to withstand use by small hands that don't have the fine motor development to turn regular paper pages without tearing them. Board books are perfect for kids from newborn to 3 years old.

Most board books are 10 to 14 pages long, with very little, if any, text. We're talking a few sentences at most, and sometimes only one word to a page. These books vary in size, from 2 x 3 inches to 14 x 16 inches.

TIP

Many board books are also novelty books (which you can read about in the section "Other books that have pictures," later in this chapter). *Novelty books* come with something other than just flat paper and images. Board books can have sliding and moveable parts. They come with puppets built in or touch-and-feel fabrics and papers, or they have ribbons all around the edges. Anything that can catch an adult's eye can probably also catch a baby's eye. And that's what board books do: get young children to love reading even before they can read (and really can't do much more than teeth on the books).

Writing great board books

Terrific topics for board books include early learning concepts, such as shapes and colors, and daily experiences, such as mealtime and naptime. But you don't need a lot of words to get your concepts across. Board books employ simple rhyming and repeated text and a lot of bright, colorful, engaging pictures to attract baby's attention.

To write a good board book, you need to have relatable content. To figure out whether you do, you need to research the titles already out there. Take a good look at the board books that continue to sell, and sell, and sell, such as the ones we mention in the section "Baby-friendly board books," earlier in this chapter. The best board books have a few elements in common:

>> Simple concepts or story lines appropriate for babies and toddlers.

>> Minimal text per page (often only a word or two).

>> Illustratable text (meaning you don't include any overly complex concepts). The illustrations or photographs should be clear and evocative; if the words disappeared, the images could tell the story by themselves.

TIP

Illustrators are also the writers of many board books. Often, editors at the publishing house write the actual text, based on the art the illustrator produces. The text usually takes a backseat to the pictures, which do most of the storytelling. If you want to know some board book author/illustrators to emulate, check out Sandra Boynton and Rosemary Wells.

However, because the board-book market is totally inundated with concept books and simple stories about everyday experiences, if you want to sell a board book based on text only, you have to make the text very unique indeed. To make sure your board book stands out, study what's already out there so that you can create an original concept and story.

Picture books for toddlers

Picture books, like the ones that have wildly different illustrative styles shown in Figure 2-2, are most often hardcover, heavily illustrated storybooks that cover almost every topic under the sun. They can be fiction or nonfiction, told in poetry or prose, and aimed at the literary or the mass/commercial markets. Teachers and parents who work or live with children from preschool age through early elementary years use picture books to speak to children about everything and anything the children might be experiencing at the moment: holidays, new siblings, moods, a fascination with birds or princesses — you name it, picture books cover it.

FIGURE 2-2:
Example picture
books.

a   b   c

a) Wild Colt *reprinted courtesy of Schiffer Publishing, Ltd. © 2012 Schiffer Publishing, Ltd.*
b) The Kissing Hand *and c)* Chester the Brave *reprinted courtesy of Tanglewood Books.*

One of the most popular picture book series of all time is Ian Falconer's *Olivia* series (Atheneum Books for Young Readers). This book provides a perfect example of a picture-book author/illustrator creating a fleshed-out character who looks, feels, and behaves just like the kid next door — even though she's a pig. The minimal text, limited color palette, and evocative yet restrained illustrations all work together in just the way they should in a picture book. Other bestsellers, all very different from one another, include *Knuffle Bunny: A Cautionary Tale* by Mo Willems (Hyperion), Anna Dewdney's *Llama Llama* series (Viking Books for Young Readers), *Seriously, Just Go to Sleep* by Adam Mansbach and illustrated by Ricardo Cortes (Akashic Books) (and the children's version of this duo's *Go the F*ck to Sleep,* which is definitely aimed at parents), and *Pete the Cat: Rocking in My School Shoes* by James Dean, illustrated by Eric Litwin (HarperCollins).

Pondering picture book basics

Picture books give delight to readers 3 to 8 years old (see the classic retelling in Figure 2-3). Generally, picture books have 24, 32 — or less frequently, 40 — pages and anywhere from 100 to 1,500 words. These books can capture the vastly different interests and attention spans of kids in this age range. Picture books most often measure in at 8½ x 11 inches.

TIP

Everyone in the children's book world wants to debate word length in picture books. Some editors refuse to even look at a picture book that has more than 500 words. But some nonfiction picture books go well into 2,000 words or more. Unless you're writing a nonfiction picture book that you plan to put in a 40- or 64-page book (rarer page counts), stick to the 500-words-or-less rule.

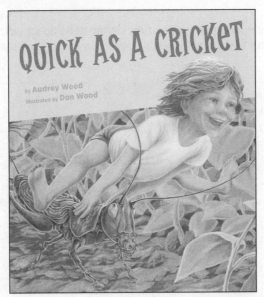

FIGURE 2-3:
Quick as a Cricket,
a picture book.

From Quick as a Cricket by Audrey and Don Wood.
Reprinted with permission of the author and illustrator.
© 2020 Audrey Wood and Don Wood. Used by permission of
HarperCollins Publishers.

WARNING

Nothing speaks more poorly of a writer than submitting a picture book of 5,000 words, even if it's nonfiction. Early chapter books can be 5,000 words.

Here's a rundown of the not-so-standard picture book varieties:

REMEMBER

>> **Licensed-character picture books:** Feature characters generally culled from popular television shows, toys, videogames, apps, and movies. Some licensed characters that have been around for a while and will probably stick around for a while more include Elmo, Barbie, My Little Pony, and SpongeBob SquarePants. According to publishing expert Jane Friedman, a third of all children's books sold today are based on licensed characters. These books are assigned authors by the publishing or licensing company.

>> **Board book adaptations of picture books:** These titles have already had successful runs as picture books, and they get a second life as board books. In general, these board books keep the same text and illustrations as the original picture books (sometimes with an editorial nip and tuck here and there, but usually not enough for the casual reader to notice).

>> **Softcover picture books:** Although the 8x8s (books measuring 8 inches x 8 inches) are the most common softcover picture books out there (see Figure 2-4), softcovers come in many sizes and shapes. In the old days, all

picture books had a first run (the first printing of the book) as hardcovers. If the hardcover picture book was successful, then the publisher would follow up with the cheaper softcover. Nowadays, publishers often release picture books initially in a softcover format (sometimes referred to as *picturebacks*). You can often find them in spinner racks at bookstores and markets.

FIGURE 2-4:
Example picture books.

a) Countdown to Grandma's House *and* b) Grandpa Lets Me Be Me *by Debra Mostow Zakarin. Reprinted courtesy of the author.*

Becoming a picture book author

REMEMBER

Although word count is a wild card, some picture books, such as Monique Felix's *Story of the Little Mouse Trapped in a Book* (Green Tiger Press), have no words. We're of the opinion that less is more. The best picture books have spare, well-chosen text and well-structured stories that complement the illustrations with zero fat (see Figure 2-5 for some examples).

To break into the picture book market, you have to write a stellar story, which involves mastering the elements of writing that we cover in Part 3. When you're done with creating your masterpiece, make sure that you do the following in your picture book:

>> **Keep it short.** Capture the essence of your story in no more than 500 to 1,000 words, the fewer the better. (If the book is longer than 1,000 words, you risk losing the attention of the youngest of the picture book audience — and hence those who do the reading to them, as well.)

>> **Make every word work really hard.** Eliminate all descriptive baggage and every unnecessary word — especially those words that the illustrations convey.

>> **Use beautiful words.** Replace ordinary words with richer, more evocative ones without getting wordy or too adult.

>> **Create a relatable main character.** Give your picture book a strong, multidimensional main character whom a child can relate to. (We talk about creating great characters in Chapter 8.)

>> **Follow a clear story arc.** Take your main character through a satisfying story arc that includes a beginning, a middle, and an end. (Chapter 9 gets into how to shape your story.)

>> **Convey concrete visual imagery.** Use this imagery in action and dialogue throughout to move the plot ahead.

FIGURE 2-5:
Example picture
books.

a

b

c

a) My Dog, My Cat *reprinted courtesy of Tanglewood Books. © 2011 by Ashlee Fletcher.*
b) Is a Worry Worrying You? *reprinted courtesy of Tanglewood Books. © 2005 Ferida Wolff.*
c) An Equal Shot *by Helaine Becker; illustrations by Dow Phumiruk. Text copyright © 2021*
by Helaine Becker. Illustrations copyright © 2021 by Dow Phumiruk. Reprinted by
permission of Henry Holt and Company. All Rights Reserved.

Other books that have pictures

Although picture books and board books seem to dominate the field in illustrated books, you can find four other players in the category — coloring and activity books, novelty books, informational books, and graphic novels. Of the four, coloring and activity books probably outdo all the others combined in terms of units sold.

THE POTENTIAL PROBLEM WITH POETRY

Most children's book editors feel pretty strongly about rhymed text. From those who despise it or merely tolerate it to those who adore it, editors are pretty picky about rhyme. Why? Because authors often sacrifice the story for the sake of the rhyme — not to mention torturing the English language to create rhymes, paying little attention to whether the rhymes even make sense. Much more often than not, amateur writers of rhyme skimp on plot and character development, throwing in extra words just to make the rhyme work. Make sure that the story and the language come first; rhyme is secondary. A good rhyming story can sell, but it has to be written as tightly as a story in prose.

If you want to write poetry, take it from us: Dr. Seuss did a fabulous job with the particular rhyme schemes he used in his books, and his books continue to sell tens of thousands of copies a year, despite the author having passed away in 1991. But if you want to rhyme, don't use Seussian meter; make up your own.

Coloring, activity, and how-to

With pictures to color and a lot of activities, including mazes, dot-to-dots, hidden pictures, word scrambles, and crossword puzzles, coloring and activity books (abbreviated to C&A books in the industry) offer kids fun — plain and simple. And you can find some educational C&A books (such as the ones in Figure 2-6).

FIGURE 2-6:
Example color and activity books.

a

b

a) Cool Yule! A Creative and Crafty Christmas! *and* b) Happening Hanukkah: Creative Ways to Celebrate *by Debra Mostow Zakarin. Reprinted courtesy of the author.*

Mad Libs (those great fill-in-the-word-blank games) can provide good, clean fun at sleepovers. Almost any arts and crafts book published by DK (Dorling Kindersley) or Klutz (Klutz Press) keeps kids busy for hours. You can find dozens and dozens of choices on the Klutz rack, including *Klutz Jr. My Cat Mermaid and Friends Craft Book, Klutz Lego Gear Bots Science/STEM Activity Kit,* and *Klutz Lego Make Your Own Movie Activity Kit.*

You can make any activity that kids enjoy spending time doing or creating into an activity or how-to book. Keep it simple and age-appropriate.

C&A books on the market today often come with innumerable and novel extras, such as punch-outs, stickers, crayons, paints, glow-in-the-dark markers — you name it. These extras actually cross-classify these C&A books as novelty books, which we talk about in the following section.

REMEMBER

C&A book authors are often in-house editors at publishing houses or established writers who have specific educational experience, firmly rooted in the publisher's stable of workhorse writers. Very rarely do new authors break into this format (although it's not unheard of if the author has a truly original concept). Another bummer: You don't always get to see your name on the front cover. Also, the illustrators for C&A books often come from studios. These illustrators either do masses of these types of books or have approval to illustrate featured licensed characters.

Novelty books

A novelty book goes beyond just words and pictures on flat pages. It's often three-dimensional and always interactive (meaning the child must engage more than just their eyes in the experience). From pop-ups to pull-tabs, from juggling balls to paper dolls, innovative novelty books can really engage the imagination (see Figure 2-7 for an example). When any type of children's book has something in addition to just flat paper and images, it moves into the novelty category.

WARNING

Printing just words and illustrations on paper has become expensive — especially if the publisher prints only a few thousand copies to start. And novelty books always go beyond simply printed and bound paper.

Once upon a time, publishers could afford to print tens of thousands of copies of a novelty title right off the bat. But when the market became saturated, it couldn't sustain all those titles. So the publishers could no longer count on economies of scale to offset the extra costs of hand-assembly or packaging the items that came with the book.

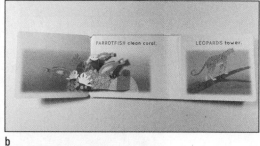

a   b

FIGURE 2-7:
Example novelty
books.

c

a) cover and b) interior from Deep in the Sea *by Susan B. Katz with illustrations by David A. Carter.*
Text copyright © 2021 by Susan B. Katz. Illustrations copyright © 2021 David A. Carter. Reprinted with the permission
of Little Simon, an imprint of Simon & Schuster Children's Publishing Division. All rights reserved.
c) interior from Hide and Seek, *reprinted courtesy of the author/illustrator David A. Carter.*

For these reasons, you find very few players in the novelty book market today. What does that mean for you? Unless you're David A. Carter (a novelty book creator who can write, illustrate, design, and engineer his own titles), Robert Sabuda (another Renaissance publishing star of multiple talents in the pop-up world), or an expert in some form of artistry such as paper artist Hélène Druvert, your chances of getting a novelty book to market are slim to none — unless you self-publish. (We fill you in on the world of self-publishing in Chapter 19.)

Graphic novels

Graphic novels are books that have a lot of pictures and fewer words, but are aimed at older readers: namely, middle-graders (ages 7 to 10), tweens (ages 9 to 12), young adult readers (12 and up), and even adults (see Figure 2-8). Not surprisingly, every page of a graphic novel boasts graphics, which can come in the form of black-and-white illustrations, color illustrations, comics, or captured video/TV/movie photos. Most often, the illustrations look more comic-book-like than full-page picture book illustrations.

FIGURE 2-8:
*Jeremy Kreep: Fang
Fairy,* a graphic
novel.

From Jeremy Kreep: Fang Fairy *reprinted
courtesy of Stone Arch Books.* © 2007 by
Andy J. Smith.

Graphic novels are, strictly speaking, novels in comic form. But they have evolved way beyond comic books. These novel–length stories feature

>> **A plethora of illustrations:** Including styles such as fine art, cartoon-like, pencil and ink, and more.

>> **Cover all sorts of topics:** From history, to memoir, to fiction, to biography, to nonfiction and anthologized works.

>> **Relatively few words:** Graphic novels have plenty of words, but nothing near the word count of a novel that doesn't have pictures.

>> **Aspects of style:** Bold, italic, underline, a lot of exclamation points, and a ton of question marks often dramatize the text. You often see word balloons and sound effects.

Graphic novels are often digest sized (5½ inches wide x 8½ inches high — about the size of a piece of paper folded in half. In the past, becoming a graphic novel writer generally required the ability to illustrate in the style of graphic novels or comics; but today, many graphic novels originate with the story and text, and the publisher hires the artist separately. If you're a graphic novel author, you can also independently pair up with someone who has the artistic talent you're looking for. (For information on illustrating your work, see Chapter 15.)

Manga is a heavily illustrated format similar to graphic novels. In fact, manga often overlaps with graphic novels. But many manga are comic books — some shorter, like traditional comic books, some longer, more like graphic novels. We talk more about manga and anime in Chapter 3, when we discuss genres.

PICKING THE BRAIN OF A CHILDREN'S BOOK EDITOR

Erin E. Molta is an editor who has worked across a broad spectrum of formats in children's publishing: from novelty books, to licensed books, to book clubs, to young adult novels — even running her own editorial service. If novelty books are your passion, she has some tips about what she looks for in novelty book submissions:

- **What formats sell:** "It's not so much the format but the author. Straight board books by Sandra Boynton sell continually, lift-the-flap board books by Karen Katz, as do classic board books reprinted from best-selling picture books, such as Eric Carle's *Papa, Please Get the Moon for Me* (Little Simon)."

- **The best formats for new writers:** "Again, the manuscript dictates a format, though we have certain formats that we consistently publish — mostly holiday or seasonal titles, like *Sparkle N Twinkle* or *Sparkle N Shimmer* series. They are holiday-based and have glitter and/or sequins on each spread."

- **What formats constantly need new ideas:** "The buzzwords these days are new and innovative. Everybody wants something different. So it can't just be a flap book, it must be a flap book with touch-and-feel, or sound, or pop-ups and foil, glitter, acetate — and it has to be able to be produced really inexpensively, too!"

- **The most common pitfalls for new writers and in what formats:** "Everybody thinks they can write for children. It's easy, right? But most people are writing as an adult to a child rather than for — or with — a child. Kids want the text to be on their level. It doesn't mean it has to be childish — just child-appealing and childlike."

- **What grabs your attention:** "New and innovative! The key to a successful format for the youngest reader is how it is integral to the text and art. If you have flaps in a book but there's no incentive to lift them — and once you do, you don't care — then that is a bad use of the flap as a technique to further the story and enhance the reading experience. I'm looking for truly interactive books, where a child can spin a wheel to find an answer or press a button, or something pops up to stimulate understanding.

"I'm looking for the perfect integration of an interactive element and lively text. Say you have animals and it's counting — and the animals are night creatures, rather than on the farm (I'm sick of farm animal books). Or you're doing a book on colors, but it's in outer space. There are zillions of books about colors, shapes, counting, and opposites, but something out of the ordinary sparks my interest!"

(continued)

(continued)

- **What leads to rejection:** "Tell me you read it to your students, grandkids, or even your very own children and they loved it. Of course they did! Would any kid say they didn't? Poor spelling doesn't help either, nor do farm animals."

- **Developing new formats:** "We get ideas for new formats from brainstorming in-house or from packagers. I usually will come up with a format and see if I have a manuscript that fits or I get a manuscript and try and come up with a format that will make it stand out on the bookstore shelves. It's very much a collaborative process — taking a little bit of what's been done and tweaking it to make it new and innovative."

For younger middle-grade readers, Dav Pilkey's *The Adventures of Super Diaper Baby: A Graphic Novel (Super Diaper Baby #1)* (Scholastic, Inc.) provides stellar entertainment. For older middle-graders, Neil Gaiman's *Coraline* (HarperCollins), originally a novella that the publisher made into a graphic novel with art by P. Craig Russell, offers creepy excitement (and was licensed into a movie of the same name). Comic books, anime, manga, graphic novels, and combinations thereof populate many shelves in the young adult section — and we go into the differences between these genres in Chapter 3. (Interestingly, female teen readers were the first, most avid readers in all of these categories.)

Working through Wordy Books

In the following sections, we take a look at books that focus more on telling a story through words than illustrations, though they often also include illustrations. This category includes easy readers, early readers, first chapter books, middle-grade books, and YA books.

Early readers

Writers and publishers develop early readers for children who are just learning their letters or perhaps even sounding out their first words. Experts in reading, teaching, learning, or curricula create particular programs around the theory of reading that the publisher has chosen to embrace, often either a phonics-based (see Figure 2-9) or whole-language-based theory.

FIGURE 2-9:
We Read Phonics, an early reader series.

TIP

Easy readers are often 32-page picture books that have simple vocabulary and sentence structure. Easy readers (or early readers) can also be 48 to 64 pages long as the reader gains proficiency. And early chapter books (which we talk about in the section "First chapter books," later in this chapter) are 48 to 64 pages long, as well. Easy readers can have as few as several hundred words to 1,500 words.

When a publishing house develops an early reader program, they create vocabulary lists and decide on parameters for story development and illustration, page counts, and more — all designed to make the child's first reading experiences satisfying and logically progressive, and to encourage more reading.

Surveying early reader basics and age levels

With anywhere from 10 pages to 64 pages, the amount of information and the word count in early reader books varies greatly, but one thing normally stays the same: the size. Most early reader books come sized at 6 inches x 9 inches. Early reader books (also known as leveled readers) usually work for kids between the ages of 5 and 9, although many series divide them into five levels, depending on the reading level of each child:

>> **Level 1:** Just getting started reading; the reader knows the alphabet and is excited about reading their first books. Sometimes labeled for ages 3 to 6.

>> **Level 2:** For readers who can recognize and sound out certain words but who may still need help with more complex words. Often labeled for ages 4 to 6.

>> **Level 3:** When a reader is ready to tackle easy stories all by themselves. For kindergarten through third grade.

>> **Level 4:** Many programs introduce chapter breaks at Level 4 for children who are ready to jump into "bigger kid" books but aren't yet ready for middle-grade topics or length. For second and third graders.

>> **Level 5:** If the program goes this far, these books are actual chapter books that have a few black-and-white illustrations scattered throughout. You can find third and fourth graders still reading these.

Writing early readers

Turning word lists into fascinating stories is no easy task. Indeed, writing truly good early reader books requires a talent for minimalism, perfect word choice, a well-honed sense of whimsy and fun, and an understanding of how to keep plot, pacing, and character development on the move with the turn of each page. We go more into the latter elements of writing in Part 3. But if you want to write well in this format, you have to research the style, tone, and contents of each publisher's early reader series and then practice. You also more often than not have to adhere to vocabulary lists. If you want to submit a book to a particular publisher, most publishers offer guidelines for their programs on their websites.

Early readers can be fiction or nonfiction and cover topics that are often found in the curriculum taught in school for particular age ranges. As nationwide testing in reading comprehension and reading skills becomes more prevalent, starting at the earliest grades, we expect even more curriculum-based reading programs to surface, supplementing what teachers are presenting in the classrooms.

TIP

If you can't find these word lists on the publisher's website, you can consult *Children's Writer's Word Book* by Alijandra Mogilner (Writer's Digest Books).

First chapter books

A first chapter book is often a child's first real foray into reading books that don't have full-color illustrations (see Figure 2-10). In this exciting time in a child's life, they get to go the section in the bookstore or library that houses the big-girl and big-boy books. First chapter books discuss more mature subject matter and have more complex stories than board books and picture books, as well as more complex characters and relationships with one another.

FIGURE 2-10:
*Nancy Clancy
Super Sleuth, Book
1*, a first chapter
book.

From Nancy Clancy Super Sleuth, Book 1,
reprinted courtesy of HarperCollins
Children's Books. Text © 2012 by Jane
O'Connor. Illustrations © 2012 by Robin
Preiss Glasser.

Most first chapter books, if they have illustrations at all, contain a few black-and-white images scattered randomly throughout. The authors of first chapter books maintain the pacing directly through story developments and conflict, rather than through illustration or subtle suggestion. Some popular first chapter book series include the *My Weird School* and the *My Weirder School* series by Dan Gutman and Jim Paillot (HarperCollins) and Annie Barrows's and Sophie Blackall's *Ivy + Bean* series (Chronicle Books).

Focusing on the basics of first chapter books

When a child moves from early readers to first chapter books, the books are longer, the illustrations switch from color to black and white, and the stories and vocabulary generally progress in complexity. Kids in the 7-to-10 age range generally read first chapter books. With approximately 128 pages, first chapter books come in hardcover or softcover digest size, which is usually around 5½ x 8½ inches. They typically contain about eight to ten chapters of about eight to ten pages each.

Writing first chapter books

Like with any other format, writing good first chapter books requires skill, and practice helps you develop that skill. First, you must read, read, read examples of the format so that you get a feel for the ways in which authors develop the characters, create and flesh out the story, use vocabulary in both speech and narrative, progress the plot, and maintain the pacing and interest at steady levels. You need an appreciation for children in the target age group of 7 to 10 years old (what they like, what they don't like, what they glom onto, and what they're likely to reject). We reveal how to figure out the inner workings of a child's mind in Chapter 7.

Middle-grade books

You probably remember reading middle-grade fiction and nonfiction books in your childhood. These books were long, detailed, and relatively complex, and they dealt with subject matter that was much more intriguing (and potentially much more divisive) than most children's picture books. Some classic middle-grade books deal with some weighty issues:

>> *Charlotte's Web,* **by E. B. White (HarperCollins):** The farmer is about to kill Wilbur, a runt of a pig, before the farmer's daughter saves him. Wilbur doesn't get lost, or hidden, or given away, but almost killed! This is big-kid stuff.

>> *The Secret Garden,* **by Frances Hodgson Burnett (HarperCollins):** Delves into death and sickness (physical and emotional), not to mention social class discrepancies.

>> *The Phantom Tollbooth,* **by Norton Juster (Penguin Random House):** Filled with word play and complex relationships.

Middle-grade books are often a child's first peek into the real world in which people die, are irredeemably bad, have to solve real problems, and even fail.

Getting down to the middle-grade basics

With an average page count that's anywhere from 96 to 156 pages, middle-grade books target 8- to 12-year-olds, and they normally come in the small $5\frac{1}{2}$-x-$8\frac{1}{2}$ size. They can be hardcover or softcover. Many get developed into series, such as the A Series of Unfortunate Events series by Lemony Snicket (HarperCollins), but just as many are *stand-alones* (meaning they're solo titles and never get developed into series).

Author Gary Paulsen's popular fiction titles, including *Hatchet* (Simon & Schuster) and *Nightjohn* (Random House Children's Books), provide good examples of the fluidity of age levels and labeling. Although many bookstores categorize his fiction in the young adult section of the store, many other bookstores shelve his books with the middle-grade books. So which format do his books fall into — young adult novels or middle-grade fiction? The answer is up for grabs. In the end, it just opens up books to more readers. The books in Figure 2-11 also offer good examples of middle-grade novels that skew toward the upper-middle grades but might not appeal as much to young adults (14 years old and older).

Writing for the middle grades

When you write middle-grade books, you can't rely on a lot of photographs or illustrations to help tell your story. Most children become aware of this distinguishing factor while they master this format: These books have few or no interior illustrations. If the book includes illustrations at all, they're often limited to black-and-white sketches at chapter breaks.

Want to break into writing for this age group? What makes good middle-grade fiction also makes good YA novels (not to mention good grown-up books):

» **Characters:** Strong, interesting, uniquely drawn characters who have a burning need or desire that drives them to action throughout the book.

» **Riveting stories:** They grab you from the get-go and don't let you go until you've turned the last page.

» **Language:** Writing that uses language to paint pictures in the mind — writing that has style (which we delve into in detail in Part 3).

» **Voice:** A truly unique, standout voice. We talk about voice in Chapter 12.

» **Cliffhangers:** Make every chapter ending leave them begging for more.

» **Audience:** A clear grasp of the audience and their concerns.

» **Perspective:** An ability to go back in space and time and put yourself into the shoes of a protagonist of that age without ever sounding like an adult or a younger child — a balancing act of the highest order.

Young adult books

Young adult (YA) books are just what they sound like: books aimed at readers age 12 and up (you can see an example in Figure 2-12). The common belief that young adults read only teen magazines and grown-up novels has fallen by the wayside, and bookstores now offer separate sections devoted to material that they believe addresses the issues, concerns, and interests of young adults, usually labeled Teen sections.

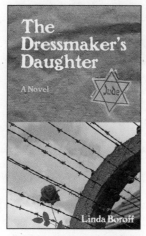

FIGURE 2-12:
The Dressmaker's Daughter, a young adult book.

From The Dressmaker's Daughter *by Linda Boroff, reprinted by permission of Santa Monica Press © 2022.*

We don't mean that bookstores and libraries never had YA sections before. They did. But the bookstores and libraries usually mixed the YA titles right in with the board and picture books — the "baby" books. Now these venues often physically separate out the books and the space to give teens their own hangouts.

» *Go Ask Alice,* by the no-longer-anonymous Beatrice Sparks (Simon & Schuster Books for Young Readers) — now in its 50th anniversary edition

» *Catcher in the Rye,* by J. D. Salinger (Little, Brown and Company)

» Francesca Lia Block's *Weetzie Bat* books (HarperCollins)

» *The Chocolate War,* by Robert Cormier (Ember)

» *Speak,* by Laurie Halse Anderson (Square Fish)

» *King of the Mild Frontier,* by Chris Crutcher (HarperCollins)

» *Forever,* by Judy Blume (Atheneum Books for Young Readers).

Diving into YA basics

Young adult books fall into two main age groups: YA appropriate for children ages 12 and up and YA for children 14 and up. Although each YA novel differs from the next, we can attribute the split in age ranges most of the time to five issues:

>> Sexual intercourse

>> Foul language

>> Drug use

>> Extreme physical violence

>> Graphic abuse

Those YA novels that overtly and unashamedly deal with these topics are aimed at the older end of the YA age range, 14 and up.

So can you find an official section or publisher designation separating these two YA age ranges? Nope. Parental guidance and a child's individual maturity level determine which books are appropriate for what ages. Do we think YA books should include age labels? Certainly not; the First Amendment is sacrosanct, labels are too infantilizing, and if a child decides they want to read or do something no matter what the consequences, adults can truly do little to prevent it.

Regardless of the specific age target (if they have one), YA novels are for those 12- to 18-year-olds who want to read novels about issues they face every day — or ones they merely wish they did.

With anywhere from 128 to 300-plus printed pages, these books usually come in 6¼ x 9¼ size (about the same size as standard grown-up hardcovers).

Young adult books are often cross-shelved with grown-ups' books, and sometimes the only distinction between the two is that the protagonists of YA novels are usually teenagers. The issues confronted in YA novels often center on

>> Coming-of-age issues of socially, economically, spiritually, emotionally, or politically marginalized kids.

   Gay teenagers, straight teens in gay-parent families, cross-gendered teenagers, pregnant teens considering their options, teens experimenting with drugs and not completely messing up their lives or dying because of it, teens falling in love with older adults and acting on it, and the like.

- » Kids who seem to live perfect lives until you look under the surface.

- » Teens in complex situations (but not always weighty or incendiary).

  Sometimes just being a teen at an exclusive prep school can present abnormally difficult situations, especially if it turns out your peers are all the walking undead.

In YA novels, the protagonists don't always win at the end. Whether they're human or not human, their issues often parallel those of human teenagers: trying to fit in; making a difference; finding love; scouting out acceptance; breaking out of their parentally imposed limitations; seeking independence; proving their worth; conquering physical, emotional, cultural, and spiritual demons; and so on. With few exceptions today, the protagonists of YA novels have lost their innocence (different from losing their virginity), but that doesn't mean they've lost hope, strength, or their ability to imagine a better life, a better self, and a better world.

REMEMBER

Some YA books are considered crossovers, meaning they can serve as both a young adult book and a contemporary adult book. An example of a crossover title is Markus Zusak's *The Book Thief* (Knopf). Although the publisher primarily designated the book a young adult novel (and Hollywood made it into a movie for kids), you can also find it in the adult section with Zusak's other books.

Writing YA books

Young adult books are filled mostly with words and rarely have any illustrations. So if you're hankering to break into the young adult field, be ready to write well for 200 pages or more. The criteria are similar to those required for writing good middle-grade fare (discussed in the section "Writing for the middle grades," earlier in this chapter), with some real differences noted:

- » **Characters:** Strong, interesting, uniquely drawn characters who have a problem — only they might not try very hard to solve it; in fact, they might wallow in it for a while.

- » **Riveting stories:** Storytelling that absolutely sparkles and makes all those apps on the young adult's smartphone or tablet nonexistent.

- » **Language:** Writing that uses language to paint pictures in the mind and writing that has style and voice (which we delve into in detail in Part 3).

- » **Voice:** A unique voice that stands out — arguably the most important element of good YA fiction.

- » **Audience:** A clear grasp of the audience and their concerns.

  Teenagers are serious about their lives, problems, and issues, and people who write for them have to treat the subject matter seriously.

Chapter **3**

Exploring the Genres

enres are the general nature of major children's book categories. They're like big buckets into which publishers throw a bunch of books that the authors wrote by using certain similar conventions. For example, mystery is a genre of fiction, as is action/adventure.

REMEMBER

When you hear about *conventions* of a genre, think customs or rules widely accepted because authors have used them that way for a long time. Basically, conventions are expectations that a reader has for a genre because that's what they're used to reading; for example, if a book falls into the mystery genre, the convention says that it has a problem that an intrepid protagonist has to solve and a solution that the protagonist struggles to figure out, finally making that crucial discovery. Sometimes you want to stick to those conventions, and sometimes you want to veer away from them to make your story more interesting. Either way, it helps to know a bit about the genres out there.

In this chapter, we explore many of the various genres in which you can find children's books. If a distinctive style, form, or content composes the very nature of certain genres, we talk about those, too. We also dip into the series pool, where single characters can take off into multi-book adventures.

TIP

If you aren't writing plays, poetry, or nonfiction, you're probably writing fiction. And you can cross, mash, or mix up fiction genres if you're confident in each of the genres you're subverting. Just make sure you research the genre (or genres) you're writing in so that you subvert in the right way.

Going Out of This World

Some children's book genres are quite literally out of this world — or at least beyond the conventional, everyday life that most of us are familiar with on this planet we call Earth. You can take a look at some of the most popular of these genres in the following sections.

Science fiction

Writers of *science fiction* can manipulate settings to fit narratives or make up out-of-this-world settings altogether. Sci-fi writers rely on the utter *suspension of disbelief,* which is a fancy way of saying that you have to believe what you read, no matter how implausible it may seem. If the writer of science fiction does their job well, they set up the story and characters in such a way that they seem to be describing something that seems familiar enough to the reader because the author bases their fictional time frame on things that already exist today. Science fiction takes existing scientific principles and theories and uses them in the plot. The author wants the reader to take this unreal setting literally, not metaphorically, and you need to make your sci-fi characters believable.

Subgenres of sci-fi include apocalypse, space travel, utopia/dystopia, cyberpunk, first contact, high tech, space exploration, space opera, speculative, steampunk, messianic works, and more. One of my (Peter's) favorite books when I was in first grade (although it's hard to find today) was Louis Slobodkin's *The Space Ship Under the Apple Tree* (Aladdin).

Writers usually write science fiction for older children, so the formats that work best for it include middle-grade books, young adult books, and graphic novels.

Fantasy

Fantasy relies on the notion that real people in real settings can encounter magical things and can often perform magic. In other words, some people have special powers, whereas others don't. Fantasy can also involve mythical creatures such as fairies and unicorns, as well as talking animals that may or may not interact with humans. Subgenres of fantasy include urban fantasy, epic fantasy, historical fantasy, paranormal romance, the supernatural, fairy tale retellings, magical realism, high fantasy, sword-and-sorcery tales, and visionary fantasy.

Fantasy is written for children of all ages from, say, three years of age and up, so the formats that work best for it include picture books (see Figure 3-1), early readers, first chapter books, middle-grade books, and young adult books, graphic novels — basically all the formats!

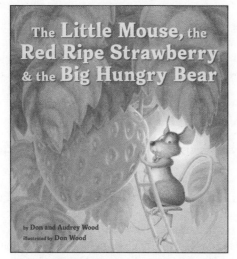

Great examples of classic contemporary children's fantasy include Roald Dahl's *Charlie and the Chocolate Factory* and *Matilda* (Puffin Books), J. K. Rowling's Harry Potter series (Scholastic Press), *Eva Evergreen* by Julie Abe (Little, Brown Books for Young Readers), and *Curse of the Night Witch* by Alex Aster (Sourcebooks Young Readers).

For recently published fantasy examples targeted at young adults, check out *Where Dreams Descend,* by Janella Angeles (Wednesday Books) and the anthology *A Phoenix First Must Burn,* by Patrice Caldwell (Penguin Books).

REMEMBER

Fantasy shares many elements with the rich array of fairy tales, fables, folktales, myths, and legends from all cultures. They come from old traditions of storytelling that you can trace to particular countries or regions. A few of the originating sources that writers mine again and again include the Brothers Grimm, Charles Perrault, Hans Christian Andersen, Aesop, Russian folk tales, and Greek mythology.

In fact, nearly every culture has a storytelling tradition that you can research for material. These stories continually inspire writers to write *retellings* and *adaptations,* stories that add to or change the source material in some unique way. Here are some excellent examples of retellings: *Ella Enchanted,* by Gail Carson Levine (Quill Tree Books), a Cinderella retelling; *Beastly,* by Alex Flinn (HarperTeen), a "Beauty and the Beast" adaptation; and *Bound* by Donna Jo Napoli (Atheneum Books for Young Readers), a Cinderella tale set in ancient China.

TIP

You can also combine fantasy and science fiction (discussed in the preceding section). Middle-grade and young adult readers especially love reading these combos. For example, Philip Pullman's His Dark Materials series (Laurel Leaf Library) has technological aspects to the plot, as well as fantasy-type characters.

Graphic novels and manga

Although graphic novels and manga are formats (flip back to Chapter 2), they're also genres.

While graphic novels can cover almost any topic, many are fantasies. Graphic novels also often cover topics such as action and adventure, comedy, romance, science fiction, sports, historical fiction or nonfiction, and detective content. Recent entries include the middle-grade series *Rise of the Halfling King (Tales of the Feathered Serpent #1)*, by David Bowles, illustrated by Charlene Bowles (Cinco Puntos Press), and *Beetle & The Hollowbones*, written and illustrated by Aliza Layne (Atheneum Books for Young Readers). Books to check out in the YA category include *Flamer*, written and illustrated by Mike Curato (Henry Holt & Company BYR), and *Banned Book Club*, by Hyun Sook Kim and Ryan Estrada, illustrated by Hyung-Ju Ko (Iron Circus Comics).

TIP

You may have heard *anime* and manga referred to as similar, but they're actually quite distinct. The difference between manga and anime is the method of delivery. *Anime* is either hand-drawn or computer animation (or a combination of both) created in Japan, regardless of origin or style, delivered as TV or movies. If the anime is produced outside of Japan but has a style similar to Japanese animation, it's referred to as *anime-influenced animation*. Anime can have original content, but it also offers adaptations of Japanese comics, novels, or video games. Depending on the content, anime can fall into many genres and target many audiences.

Horror and ghost stories

Horror stories and *ghost stories* are the creepy, goosebump-inducing stories that make you leave the flashlight on under your sheets — even when you're done reading. Good ghost stories always suck you in because they're grounded in reality. After you really fall for the characters and the setting (as if the story were about the family next door), the plot springs something otherworldly on you. For an example of good writing in this genre, check out Neil Gaiman's *The Graveyard Book* (HarperCollins), with illustrations by Dave McKean.

TIP

To break into writing horror, you need to demonstrate an appreciation for otherworldly content and hold-your-breath pacing — and you need to stick to formats for middle-graders and older.

Getting in on the Action (and History)

Who doesn't like an action-packed story that stimulates your mind and perhaps even makes your heart skip a beat or two? We know we do, and so do many other people — children and adults alike. Young readers also find history a very fascinating topic. They crave finding out more about where they and their parents, grandparents, and other ancestors came from and the experiences they and others went through in past times.

Action/adventure

With very stylized, bold covers, *action/adventure* focuses on young boys and girls who combat nature, industry, bad adults, and other evils (see the example, *The Revenge of Joe Wild*, in Figure 3-2). You can find action/adventure stories in early readers, middle-grade books, young adult books, and graphic novels.

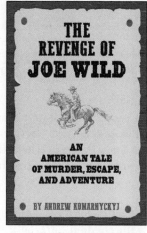

FIGURE 3-2: Find action and adventure in *The Revenge of Joe Wild*.

From The Revenge of Joe Wild. *Reprinted by permission of Santa Monica Press © 2022.*

REMEMBER

The best action/adventure stories include engaging, well-thought-out plots and a main character who's smart, self-reliant, and cunning. These stories have a true danger element and often take place in territory unfamiliar to the reader.

Subgenres of action/adventure include thrillers and espionage (usually involving a spy who must protect their imperiled country, school, or family against an enemy), mysteries, crime-solving stories, and detective novels.

True stories

Who needs to make up a story when you can find so many true stories out there simply waiting for you to transform them into a children's book? (See examples of true stories in Figure 3-3.)

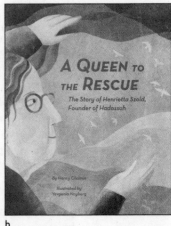

FIGURE 3-3: Example true stories.

a   b

One real-life subject that all children seem to gravitate toward is true stories about animals. One successful example is *Owen & Mzee: The True Story of a Remarkable Friendship,* by Isabella Hatkoff and Craig Hatkoff (Scholastic Press), about a baby hippo and a 130-year-old giant tortoise who adopt each other after a tragedy leaves the baby hippo orphaned.

If you narrow down the category of *animals* to dogs, cats, and other domesticated beasts (who have a lot in common with children, after all), you have another potentially winning formula. A moving example is *Marshall the Miracle Dog,* written by Cynthia Willenbrock and illustrated by Lauren Heimbaugh (The Marshal Movement), which relates the story of a horribly mistreated and disfigured dog who, against the odds, finds a loving forever home.

Many new writers swear they have an incredible tale, stranger than fiction and 12 times more lovely. Great! Go ahead and write it. Just beware that all the rules of writing good children's books apply to real stories just as much as they do to fictional ones.

Historical fiction

Who needs to look further than history to find exciting stories of heroes and heroines from all over the globe? Based on real events or on real people in history, *historical fiction* offers the best of both worlds if you write it well: exciting stories and stealthy learning. You can create great historical fiction as picture books, chapter books, middle-grade books, YA novels, and graphic novels.

My America (Scholastic), written by a variety of authors, is a successful middle-grade series in this category; see also *Lyddie,* by Katherine Patterson (Puffin Books). YA has seen an explosion of writing in this genre, including *A Great and Terrible Beauty* (Ember) and *The Diviners* (Little, Brown), both by Libba Bray. For more YA historical fiction, consider *We Are Not Free,* by Traci Chee (Clarion Books); *These Violent Delights,* by Chloe Gong (Margaret K. McElderry Books); and *The Enigma Game,* by Elizabeth Wein (Little, Brown Books for Young Readers). Teachers, librarians, parents, and children clamor for the subject matter that these well-written books cover.

Historical fiction provides the perfect genre for writing about real people that the school history books tend to overlook, such as British-Jamaican nurse and businesswoman Mary Seacole (see Figure 3-4). Historical fiction can involve presenting real characters not commonly known because of issues of race or gender, looking at the past through a new lens of diversity, or refashioning issues currently in the cultural spotlight.

FIGURE 3-4:
Mary Seacole: Bound for the Battlefield, an example of historical fiction.

Mary Seacole: Bound for the Battlefield. *Text copyright © 2020 by Susan Goldman Rubin. Illustrations copyright © 2020 by Richie Pope. Reproduced by permission of the publisher, Candlewick Press, Somerville, MA.*

To write good historical fiction, keep in mind that the time and place provide the setting for the story, but the plot and characters are still the most important elements. Don't let the setting or time period take center stage. And remember that the characters live in the time in which the story is set, so they don't remark on how different the setting is from our time period or even notice what we'd consider strange or different.

Mysteries

Good mysteries for children have been around for a long time. Children, like adults, love to piece together clues in a story to guess the outcome — or get creeped out trying to. Mysteries are here to stay, from the *Nancy Drew* series, by Carolyn Keene, and the *Hardy Boys* series, by Franklin W. Dixon, which offer mysteries for middle graders to solve, to the *Magic Tree House* series, by Mary Pope Osborne, whose protagonists solve mysteries of science and the universe. Figure 3-5 features a recently published mystery.

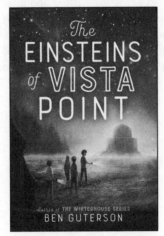

FIGURE 3-5:
The Einsteins of Vista Point, a recent addition to the mystery genre.

From The Einsteins of Vista Point, *by Ben Guterson, © 2022. Reprinted by permission of Christy Ottaviano Books, an imprint of Hachette Book Group, Inc.*

In this genre, a few conventions help authors build intriguing characters and riveting mysteries:

>> **The beginning:** The story starts with the commission of a crime (even murder in YA and adult books).

>> **The plot:** A mystery novel should solve a puzzle and create a feeling of resolution for the reader. The main plot (more on plot in Chapter 9) deals with a mystery that needs solving.

>> **The central character:** The detective or other fact-finder. The rest of the characters are usually suspects at one time or another. In the best mysteries, the central character is a quirky, humorous, offbeat, or unusual person — easy to remember and build a series upon.

>> **Suspense:** The genre uses suspense to keep the reader turning the pages.

>> **Danger:** The detective often faces danger at some point.

>> **Foreshadowing:** The author heightens dramatic tension by using *foreshadowing,* hinting at events to come or suspects' motives.

>> **The MacGuffin:** A mystery always has twists and turns, and sometimes a MacGuffin or two. A *MacGuffin* is an object, event, or device that furthers the plot and motivation of the characters, but it's irrelevant or insignificant in itself. The name was originated by Angus MacPhail, the screenwriter for a film directed by Alfred Hitchcock, king of film mysteries.

>> **Solving the mystery:** In the end, the protagonist always comes out on top, having solved the mystery.

Good mysteries, those that have a real plot and believable characters, start appearing in early chapter book series. Some mainstays are The Genius Files series, by Dan Gutman (HarperCollins), which features the McDonald twins, Coke and Pepsi, who solve mysteries; the Brixton Brothers series by Mac Barnett (Simon & Schuster Books for Young Readers), about a boy who ends up becoming the best detective by taking his cue from literary sleuths; and the Nancy Drew Diaries, by Carolyn Keene (Aladdin), in which Nancy Drew and her friends Bess and George tackle everything from sabotage to kidnapping. You can also find plenty of stand-alone titles for this age group.

Middle-grade mysteries tend to come as much in stand-alone books as they do series. Some notable newer titles are *The Amelia Six*, by Kristin L. Gray (Simon & Schuster/Paula Wiseman Books), about Millie, who discovers Amelia Earhart's goggles, only to have them disappear and then someone falls mysteriously ill and *Finally, Something Mysterious*, by Doug Cornett (Knopf Books for Young Readers), a perfect story about friends, amateur sleuthing, and a whole lot of rubber duckies.

YA mysteries are often stand-alones, unlike the many series aimed at early readers and middle graders. And the ante is always upped because YA novels can include more dangerous content and more complex issues. Many adults read YA mysteries, as well. Get the flavor of current YA mysteries by checking out some newer titles. *One of Us Is Next* by Karen M. McManus (Delacorte Press), is a truth-or-dare mystery that keeps alive the memory of a teen who died the previous year and puts its players in peril. In *All Your Twisted Secrets*, by Diana Urban (HarperTeen), six teens are locked in a room with a bomb, a syringe filled with poison, and a note saying they have an hour to pick someone to kill — or they all die.

Writing About Real People

You probably already know that people love to read stories about real people. Whether they dive into a riveting biography about someone who faced tremendous odds and beat them, or a story of first love, or the joy of having a best friend (whether imaginary or real), books about real people are evergreen, always popular. They are similar to true stories and historical nonfiction. The following sections walk you through some of the major categories within this genre.

Biography/memoir

Although many people traditionally categorize memoirs as subsets of autobiography and biography, memoirs are actually different in form, presenting a more narrowed focus. Although a biography or autobiography covers the story of a particular life, a memoir tells the story of a specific event or series of events highlighted as memorable moments in the author's life.

REMEMBER

The authors of biographies, such as the titles shown in Figure 3-6, write in the third person and do a lot of research. You can use a very literary style with biographies of historical, cultural, and scientific figures, past and present; whereas biographies of current hipsters and celebrities (both movie/TV stars and sports heroes) tend to read like *Teen People* magazine. And both types of biography have their readership. Biographies are generally written as picture books, middle-grade books, and YA — even graphic novels.

FIGURE 3-6:
Example
biographies.   a   b

a) From Sing and Shout : The Mighty Voice of Paul Robeson *reprinted by permission of the author. © 2020 Susan Goldman Rubin. The cover of* Sing and Shout *is courtesy of Calkins Creek, an imprint of Astra Books for Young Readers. b) From book covers/jackets published by Abrams Books. Used by permission of Harry N. Abrams, New York. All rights reserved.* The Eye That Never Sleeps: How Detective Pinkerton Saved President Lincoln *text © 2018 Marissa Moss. Illustrations © 2018 Jeremy Holmes.*

Great new literary picture book biographies include *The Oldest Student: How Mary Walker Learned to Read*, by Rita Lorraine Hubbard, illustrated by Oge Mora (Anne Schwartz Books) and *Drawing on Walls*, by Mike Burgess, illustrated by Josh Cochran (Enchanted Lion Books), about Keith Haring.

For middle-graders, check out biographies and memoirs such as *The Missing: The True Story of My Family in World War II*, by Michael Rosen (Candlewick); and *The Lemon Tree: An Arab, a Jew, and the Heart of the Middle East*, by Sandy Tolan (Bloomsbury USA). And for the YA audience, *Redbone: The True Story of a Native American Rock Band*, by Christian Staebler and Sonia Paoloni, illustrated by Thibault Balahy (IDW Publishing); and *Beauty Mark: A Verse Novel of Marilyn Monroe*, by Carole Boston Weatherford (Candlewick).

REMEMBER

The best biographies always reveal the most about the central figure's character and include enough details and tidbits about the character's personal life to make the reader feel like they're getting a realistic and comprehensive look at another person's life.

Memoirs are books of nonfiction narrative that are about a person's life and personal experiences. The author is the main character of a memoir, so the reader assumes the content is factual.

Although most writers are adults, not all memoirs are for adults. Many adults write memoirs for middle-graders and especially young adults. The prolific writer Nikki Grimes' *Ordinary Hazards: A Memoir* (Wordsong) recalls a fraught childhood transformed by writing. *Stupid Black Girl: Essays from an American African*, by Aisha Redux (Street Noise Books), is "an important and eye-opening contribution to conversations about global identity politics," according to Kirkus Review, a reviewing body that we discuss in Chapter 20.

LGBTQIA

LGBTQIA is an inclusive term that describes a range of sexual orientations and gender identities. It might be the reader who identifies as LGBTQIA or it might be a reader's friend or parent or neighbor who identifies as LGBTQIA. Books in this genre help all readers better understand what living these experiences is like.

The Stonewall Riots: Coming Out in the Streets, featured in Figure 3-7, is an example of historical nonfiction about being gay in the 1960s and coming out and protesting the social stigma that existed then toward gay people.

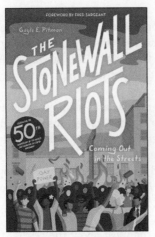

FIGURE 3-7:
The Stonewall Riots: Coming Out in the Streets.

REMEMBER

Today, children of all ages might identify as or come out as lesbian, gay, or bisexual (LGB), or they may have family or friends who do. They also need to understand other categories of gender fluidity:

>> **Transgender:** *Transgender* is the term for someone who identifies as a different gender than the gender they were assigned on their birth certificate.

>> **Queer:** Can have various meanings but inclusively offers a unique celebration of not conforming to social norms (see Figure 3-8). Includes people who identify as non-binary, neither male nor female, using the pronouns *they* and *them* instead of *she/her* or *he/him*.

>> **Intersex:** Individuals who don't fit into gender norms of boy or girl, or for those whose reproductive anatomy isn't typical

>> **Asexual:** People who don't have an attraction to either sex or who don't feel typical romantic attachment.

REMEMBER

If you aren't familiar with the LGBTQIA dynamics, all this new, possibly strange-seeming info can be a lot to digest! And some people don't understand how children can be so sure of their gender associations when they're still in their developmental stages. Possibly, children just don't know how they want to identify yet. And they may have family, friends, teachers, or classmates who fall into one of these non-binary categories, so they want to understand. For these reasons, you increasingly find these categories in picture books, middle-grade, and YA novels.

Some standouts in the picture book category include *Auntie Uncle: Drag Queen Hero*, by Ellie Royce, illustrated by Hannah Chambers (POW Kids); and the hilariously titled *The Hips on the Drag Queen Go Swish, Swish, Swish*, by Lil Miss Hot Mess, illustrated by Olga de Dios (Running Press), which takes as its inspiration the song "The Wheels on the Bus."

Middle-grade entries include *The Mighty Heart of Sunny St. James*, by Ashley Herring Blake (Little, Brown Books for Young Readers), about a 12-year-old who thinks her perfect new best friend might be someone she wants to kiss; and *The Witch Boy*, by Molly Ostertag (Graphix), about rigid gender roles with subtle trans overtones.

In YA, tons of titles exist to fuel imaginations, satisfy curiosity, and reflect a sense of identity. Figure 3-8 shows a book about two girls who must negotiate their feelings toward each other while existing in a backward-thinking town. In your research, consider titles like *The Gravity of Us*, by Phil Stamper (Bloomsbury YA); *Music from Another World*, by Robin Talley (Inkyard Press); and *We Are Totally Normal*, by Rahul Kanakia (HarperTeen).

FIGURE 3-8:
One True Way,
from the
LGBTQIA genre.

From One True Way *by Shannon Hitchcock.*
Copyright © 2018 by Shannon Hitchcock.
Reprinted by permission of Scholastic Inc.

Gender-oriented series books

REMEMBER

Gender-oriented series books are designed to appeal specifically to either boys or girls, but not both. From board books to picture books, licensed titles to novelty books, publishers develop these series to cater to gender-specific themes or characters. And although you can find many books in this genre up to and through middle-grade series — such as *Mean Ghouls: A Rotten Apple Book*, by Stacia Deutsch

(Scholastic), shown in Figure 3-9 — when we approach the YA audience, gender specificity tends to fall away.

Some of the most well-known girl-oriented titles include The Baby-Sitters Club series, by Ann M. Martin (Scholastic), which later morphed into a graphic novel series; the Nancy Drew series, by Carolyn Keene (Grosset & Dunlap), which spun off into the Nancy Drew Diaries series; and The Little House on the Prairie books, by Laura Ingalls Wilder (HarperCollins). Dozens and dozens of other series have sprouted up since Nancy Drew in the 1930s, focusing on what popular culture still considers traditional girly fare, such as pets, ponies, fairies, and the like, seeking to capture some of the avid book reading (and collecting!) middle-grade audience.

Successful entries that have a lot of girl appeal include these series by Jim Benton: the Dear Dumb Diary series (Scholastic), Franny K. Stein, Mad Scientist (Simon & Schuster Books for Young Readers), and It's Happy Bunny series (Scholastic Paperbacks).

Some stellar offerings in the nonfiction category that specifically and unabashedly target girls include nearly every title produced in the American Girl series (Pleasant Company Publications), which also includes historical fiction series that have multicultural girl protagonists across the ages. A classic to check out for girls is Louisa May Alcott's *Little Women* (Signet Classics).

Boy-centric series include The Diary of a Wimpy Kid series, by Jeff Kinney (Harry N. Abrams), the Big Nate series, by Lincoln Peirce (HarperCollins), and The Zack Files series, by Dan Greenburg and Jack E. Davis (Grosset & Dunlap). (Publishers and authors first aimed these titles at boys, but girls read them like crazy, too.)

Friendship

REMEMBER

Friendship, as a theme, runs through an enormous segment of children's books, from board books, to picture books, to YA novels. What's more important to a child than their friends? Children's books deal with questions like: Are we friends? Can we stay friends? Do they still like me? Is my old friend as good a my new one? What's it like to have a friend group? Indeed, friendship and family are the most important issues for children. (We explore family in the section "Family issues," later in this chapter.)

You need to deal with friendship issues in an age-appropriate way. Board books and picture books often use animals to stand in for people; young children generally love anthropomorphized animals, and tough issues or messages seem to go down easier if animals, rather than humans, convey them (see Figure 3-10).

FIGURE 3-10:
Friendship titles
for young
children.

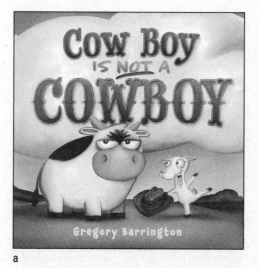
a

b

a) Cover only from Cow Boy Is NOT a Cowboy *by Gregory Barrington, Gregory Arthur Barrington Illustrated by Gregory Barrington. Copyright © 2020 by Gregory Barrington. Used by permission of HarperCollins Publishers.*
b) From Hugsby, *published by Penguin Random House. Reprinted by permission of the publisher and © 2020 Dow Phumiruk.*

Some standout picture book titles about friendship include the classic by Arnold Lobel, *Frog and Toad Are Friends* (HarperCollins); another timeless classic by Shel Silverstein, *The Giving Tree* (Harper & Row); and the bestselling *The Rainbow Fish*, by Marcus Pfister (North-South Books), which also has a board book edition.

In middle-grade fiction, friendship issues get a bit more complicated. These books weave other issues of growing up and negotiating the murky waters of middle school social interaction into the theme of friendship. Some well-done books on middle-school friendship include *Amina's Voice*, by Hena Khan (Salaam Reads/

Simon & Schuster Books for Young Readers), which is a touching story about second thoughts and the sting of changing friendships; and the classic *Harriet the Spy*, by Louise Fitzhugh (Yearling), a timeless tale about navigating friendships and social situations.

When it comes to YA books, friendships are often complicated by other issues that the author explores at the same time, such as issues of race, gender, culture, social and political themes, mental illness, abuse, relationships, family, and other burning issues of the day (or days gone by, if it's a historical novel). For example, *Ventura and Zelzah* (Santa Monica Press), shown in Figure 3-11, tells the story of teenage friendships set in 1970s suburban Los Angeles.

FIGURE 3-11:
Ventura and Zelzah, a YA friendship title.

From Ventura and Zelzah, *by J.G. Bryan. Reprinted by permission of Santa Monica Press © 2022.*

One YA book about friendship that has become a classic is Ann Brashares' *The Sisterhood of the Traveling Pants* (Ember), which was made into a movie. (You could also consider this title a crossover back into middle-grade.) Other great YA books that deal with friendship include *Not My Problem*, by Ciara Smyth (HarperTeen); *Early Departures*, by Justin A. Reynolds (Katherine Tegen Books); and *Darius the Great Is Not Okay*, by Adib Khorram (Penguin Books).

School issues

School issues can include bullying (see Figure 3-12), cliques, school friendships, peer pressure, sports, homework — so much goes on at school that it's like a world of its own. Children spend six to seven hours a day physically in school, so school makes up a big part of their lives. Every age loves books that explore school life.

Popular books about school issues include The Diary of a Wimpy Kid series by Jeff Kinney (Harry N. Abrams), and The Harry Potter series by J.K. Rowling (Scholastic), about young wizards and witches in a magical school.

A coming-of-age story often includes a school environment, though not always. *The Perks of Being a Wallflower* by Stephen Chbosky (MTV Books) is a stand-out coming-of-age story that was also made into a movie. And old standbys like *The Adventures of Huckleberry Finn* by Mark Twain (Reader's Library Classics) and *The Catcher in the Rye* by J.D. Salinger (Bay Back Books) still captivate readers today.

Developmental milestones and first experiences

From the very start, children grow and change. Kids go through so many first experiences and developmental milestones — from the first word, to giving up the binky, to learning a sport, to going through puberty. Books about these experiences abound in every format and every age (see Figure 3-13). How traumatic did you find the time-outs you had to take for throwing tantrums? You can find books about that! What about the magic of your first crush? Or the trauma of your first real friendship breaking up? You can explore anything involving developmental milestones and first experiences in a book for children of any age.

REMEMBER

Never talk down to a child about the milestones they achieve (or want to achieve) and the first experiences they have. Always treat these big events in a child's life delicately and with respect.

FIGURE 3-13:
Example titles
celebrating
developmental
milestones.

a   b

Prose poetry

REMEMBER

Prose poetry, a relatively new genre, is defined as imaginative poetic writing in prose (so most of the text doesn't rhyme and isn't metered). Prose poetry can have the effect on the reader of glimpsing into the heart of the writer in bits and pieces that manage to work as a whole. Good prose poetry blends the techniques of prose with the emotion and lyricism of poetry. Poets looking to break free from form along with prose writers seeking new means of expression may find creative freedom in prose poetry. Prose poetry is often also called "a novel in verse," even though it doesn't rhyme; see Figure 3-14.

FIGURE 3-14:
Example prose
poetry titles,
including a look
inside.

a   b   c

I Am Here Now, by Barbara Bottner (Imprint), shown in Figure 3-14, is an autobiographical look into the author's teen years. It examines what happens when you shatter your life and piece it all back again; it also looks at how an artist comes into being. *Clap When You Land,* by bestselling author Elizabeth Acevedo (Quill Tree Books), is a novel in verse about a young Latina woman and what happens when her beloved hero of a father dies in a plane crash.

Romance

REMEMBER

You write a romance for teens much like you write a romance for adults. You can choose from many subgenres (diversity, Christian, contemporary, fantasy, historical, inspirational, LGBTQIA, paranormal, romantic comedy, suspense, time travel — just to mention a few). All those subgenres have conventions that you have to fulfill; romance readers know what they want. If you're writing teen romance, make sure to read up in the genre (and subgenres) to make sure you get the tone, style, and content just right.

Giving Stories a Message

Some children's book authors write with a purpose beyond simply entertaining their readers. Some authors give their books a message, like the one in Figure 3-15, which offers a message about how we can make the world a better place working together. These books can impart knowledge or lessons to children, or illuminate religious teachings. Other books deal with current topics (such as diversity) and cultural issues, while yet others take on family issues, mental health, and dark topics such as drugs and addiction.

Learning/educational

The most skilled writers disguise learning in the most elegant manner so that the reader doesn't even know they're learning. You mostly find the learning/educational genre in board books, picture books, early readers, coloring and activity books, and middle-grade nonfiction.

Workbooks, subject-based readers, leveled readers, and supplementary school materials fill up stacks and stacks of shelves in most chain bookstores, so if you have an educational or teaching background and are a good storyteller, you can likely find work writing for children. Figure 3-16 shows two examples of nonfiction educational books.

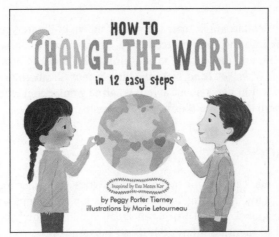

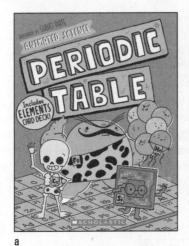 

a   b

Historical-figure biographies, activity books, and how-to books all fall into this genre. You can also find issue-based books on puberty, sex, divorce, race, adoption, understanding the LGBTQIA community, and all the cultural hot-button issues of the day for children and teens. (Although a lot of fiction also covers these topics.)

For the younger set, *What Makes a Baby,* by Cory Silverberg, illustrated by Fiona Smyth (Triangle Square), can help introduce conception, as can *It's Not the Stork: A*

Book about Girls, Boys, Babies, Bodies, Families, and Friends, by Robie H. Harris, illustrated by Michael Emberley (Candlewick).

American Girl Publications has a few great entries that deal with puberty, such as *The Care & Keeping of You: The Body Book for Girls,* by Valorie Lee Schaefer, and *Help! The Absolutely Indispensable Guide to Life for Girls,* by Nancy Holyoke (both Pleasant Company Publications). Or try *From Boys to Men: All About Adolescence and You,* by Michael Gurian and Brian Floca (Price Stern Sloan).

Educational books for children aren't limited to sex education. The environment is on everyone's minds these days (refer to Figure 3-16), so kids want to explore the subject that everyone is talking about. You can write an educational book about any topic imaginable. You just need an interest in a topic and a zest for making facts as interesting and fun as possible so that you don't lose your reader's attention.

WARNING

New writers often make the mistake of belittling the intelligence of their audience by talking down to them or preaching at them. No matter what you aim to teach your readers, make sure you keep the tone fun and the material interesting. You have to convey what you, as an author, think or expect through the information you relate and not through expressed opinions.

The publisher Treasure Bay developed a category in leveled reading called the We Both Read series (developed for the educational market but available in the mass market). In these books (shown in Figure 3-17), one page contains more elevated language for the parent to read aloud while the opposite page gives the child appropriate-leveled language to read themselves. With titles in both fiction and nonfiction, these books encourage both learning to read and parent-child interaction. We think the series provides a pretty remarkable way for parents and kids to bond over reading and books.

FIGURE 3-17:
The We Both
Read series.

Reprinted courtesy of Treasure Bay, Inc.

Religion

Religion as a genre includes stories related to the Bible, biblical characters, Christianity, Judaism, Islam, Buddhism, and any other religious affiliation and its attendant holidays, characters, or tenets. This genre permeates nearly every format of books — from board books to Bible story compilations for the middle grades. Religious diversity is also covered in school curricula, so textbooks often include excerpts from titles focusing on these issues — an added source of revenue for authors.

Books that fall into this genre include Maria Shriver's *What's Heaven?* (Golden Books Adult Publishing) and Bryn Barnard's *The Genius of Islam* (Knopf Books for Young Readers).

Aspirational and inspirational

The dictionary definition of *aspirational* involves having a desire to achieve a high level of success. In a child's world, it means hoping that you can figure out how to do something or focusing on what you want to do when you grow up. Children always aspire to achieve different things in their lives. Some want to figure out how to ride a bicycle. Others want to play a sport like a favorite sports star, or emulate a certain celebrity or social media influencer. Whatever you look forward to doing is aspirational. Figure 3-18 shows a title that delves into how creativity is something we can all aspire to.

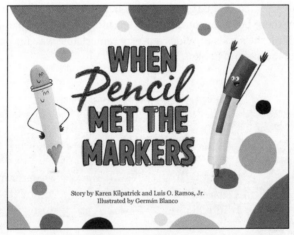

FIGURE 3-18: *When Pencil Met the Markers,* an aspirational story.

From *When Pencil Met the Markers by Karen Kilpatrick and Luis O. Ramos, Jr.; illustrated by German Blanco. Copyright © 2020 by German Blanco, Karen Kilpatrick, and Luis O. Ramos Jr. Reprinted by permission of Imprint, a part of Macmillan Publishing Group, LLC. All Rights Reserved.*

Inspirational books are usually those that have a message about how someone got to be great at something. A rescued dog who saves a child from a fire, a detective who investigates and solves crimes, a person who leads a movement — these are all inspirational topics. They inspire children to do great things in their own lives. Biographies and memoirs can often fall in the inspirational genre. Even books about religion can be inspirational. Children generally are moved by stories about people who stand out and make an impact (such as the book about women's rights in Japan, shown in Figure 3-19).

Diversity

The genre that focuses on *diversity* (formerly referred to as *multicultural* in publishing) can really pull in a child audience. Publishers want writers who have been traditionally marginalized or whose culture, background, race, or sexual orientation gives them insight into issues of diversity in a unique way. Referred to as #ownvoices in publishing, publishers want to bring the voices of writers from all over the world who've had experiences that make them the ideal spokesperson for an issue, such as the picture book and middle-grade book about diversity shown in Figure 3-20.

WARNING

You may be tempted to write about a culture that's not your own. But the controversy over the adult novel *American Dirt,* by Jeanine Cummings (Flatiron Books), demonstrates that writers can sometimes face a backlash and be accused of cultural appropriation, even if they're not writing an educational book. In Cummings' book, a *New York Times* bestseller, she wrote about a Latinx woman who has to flee Acapulco to make her way to North America. Cummings was severely criticized over the fact that she's not a Latinx writer, so she wasn't writing about experiences she herself had. Is this fair? The glowing reviews her book received across the board, and the fact that Oprah chose her for her book club, did not douse the fire.

FIGURE 3-20:
Dealing with
diversity.   a   b

If you choose to write about cultures not your own (call it cultural *appreciation*), keep in mind that people of that culture might get offended if you don't get it exactly right. So research your heart out and get a *sensitivity reader* (someone who checks the sensitive issues in the book, which we talk about in Chapter 7) in that culture or field to make sure that your book rings true.

Family issues

REMEMBER

Children don't get to choose their families, and things don't always go well in that sphere, even if only temporarily. But children don't have the same concept of time that adults do, and so issues with family can feel pressing and overwhelming. Books provide an excellent way to help children deal with such issues as different family makeup (blended families, gay families, families in which someone other than the parents actually do the parenting, and so on), divorce, siblings, favoritism, adoption, rivalries, extended family, and more).

You can find all kinds of picture books about the many faces of contemporary families, as well as middle-grade and YA books. *The Family Book,* by Todd Parr (Little, Brown Books for Young Readers), which is also in board book form, celebrates the love we feel for our families and all the different varieties they come in; and *Families, Families, Families!,* by Suzanne Lang (Random House Books for Young Readers), demonstrates all kinds of nontraditional families depicted by animals. If you look, you can find many titles out there on every specific issue that children might have with their families. Figure 3-21 includes *Babies Come from Airports,* by Erin Dealey, illustrations by Luciana Navarro Powell (EDC Publishing), which is about adoption.

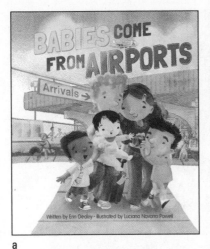

FIGURE 3-21:
Example titles addressing family issues.

a   b

Middle-grade readers also have their pick of books about families. *All About Adoption: How Families Are Made & How Children Feel About It,* by Marc Nemiroff and Jane Annunziata (American Psychological Association), covers adoption in an easy-to-relate-to manner. You can find so many books for middle-grade and YA that cover families that we couldn't touch the tip of the iceberg. Ask your librarian or local bookseller for their favorites, and they can lead the way. Figure 3-21 also shows a good YA example in the genre, *How to Live on the Edge,* which deals with a teen whose family has the gene for breast cancer.

Pets and animals

A lot of kids have a lot of love for pets and animals. Children love to read about experiences with animals, from the fascination of a child at the zoo for the first time to getting a pet. You can write a board book, a picture book, even novels about pets and animals. You can already see many of these titles on the shelves, with more coming out every season. You can write them from the animal's point of view (like in *Memoirs of a Tortoise,* in Figure 3-22) or from an animal lover's point of view.

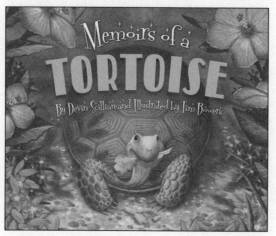

FIGURE 3-22:
Memoirs of a Tortoise.

From Memoirs of a Tortoise *published by Sleeping Bear Press. Reprinted with permission of the illustrator. © 2020 Tim Bowers.*

Cultural issues

REMEMBER

Cultural issues are generally those in which what a child experiences as a part of their culture clashes with the way that the world around them portrays that culture. Like the #ownvoices phenomenon described in the section "Diversity," earlier in this chapter, books about different cultures and writers from nonmainstream cultures can really expand children's understanding of the world and make them feel that they belong.

Some outstanding picture book entries in this genre include *M Is for Melanin,* by Tiffany Rose (Little Bee Books), an ABC book that also comes as a board book, celebrating and providing Black-positive messages. Figure 3-23 features *They're So Flamboyant,* a picture book about acceptance and stereotyping.

Middle-grade titles worth exploring include *Tight,* by Torrey Maldonado (Puffin Books), about a kid in the projects whose mom supports his laid-back nature, while his dad wants him to toughen up to his surroundings. *Marcus Vega Doesn't Speak Spanish,* by Pablo Cartaya (Puffin Books), is about a Latino boy and the estranged father whom he confronts in a trip to Puerto Rico.

Young adult books about cultural differences are, understandably for the age group, much more complicated than titles for younger children. Although many middle-grade books are a celebration of cultural differences, YA books in this genre confront more difficult issues. *The Absolutely True Diary of a Part-Time Indian,* by bestselling author Sherman Alexie (Little, Brown Books for Young Readers), is about a budding cartoonist growing up on the Spokane Indian Reservation. *American Street,* by Ibi Zobol (Balzer + Bray), a National Book Award finalist, draws on the author's experiences as a young Haitian immigrant. *With the Fire on High,* by

Elizabeth Acevedo (Quill Tree Books), covers the experiences of a young Latina teenage mother.

FIGURE 3-23: A picture book about acceptance and stereotyping.

Addiction, abuse, and mental illness

REMEMBER

Because addiction, abuse, and mental illness of all kinds are serious and scary, you find them mostly covered in YA fiction books. Authors of YA novels write about these issues in adults whose lives impact those of children, or they write about children themselves who are battling these issues. Many titles are written in the style of confessional memoirs told from the point of view of the young person.

This genre also benefits from the #ownvoices movement (discussed in the section "Diversity," earlier in this chapter). Publishers seek out writers who have their own experiences and who can translate those experiences into fiction for young adults (see the books in Figure 3-24).

YA books about addiction that you might want to check out include *Crank*, by poet Ellen Hopkins (Margaret K. McElderry), about a perfect, gifted high school student who gets addicted to *crank* (methamphetamines). *Summer of '69*, by Todd Strasser (Candlewick), drawing on the author's own experiences, talks about a young man who exists in the tuning in, turning on, and dropping out milieu of the 1960s U.S. who may be drafted to fight in the Vietnam War. The classic *Go Ask Alice*, by Beatrice Sparks (Simon & Schuster Books for Young Readers), probably one of the very first YA novels about addiction, follows a teen girl's harrowing descent into drug addiction.

Readers can find YA books about abuse harrowing and frightening, and the books' protagonists find it all the more so. Some great books dealing with abuse include *Speak*, by Laurie Halse Anderson (Square Fish), a multi-award-winning book about a girl who's abused at a high school party; *Thirteen Reasons Why*, by Jay Asher (Razorbill), about a boy who gets a series of tapes from a friend about why she committed suicide two weeks before; and *Boy Toy*, by Barry Lyga (Houghton Mifflin Harcourt), about a boy and the teacher who molested him.

The diseases that fall under the umbrella of *mental illness* involve tens of millions of children. You probably know a young person who has a mental illness. An author can explore any of these diseases creatively: attention-deficit/hyperactivity disorder (ADHD), depression, social anxiety, obsessive-compulsive disorder (OCD), eating disorders, self-harm, and more. YA novels and this genre are a nearly perfect combination. Writers who have the diseases write to inform and get across messages, and protagonists who have the diseases get through their lives with varying degrees of success.

YA novels about mental illness cover a broad range of specifics. Check out Jennifer Niven's *All the Bright Places* (Ember), about a pair of broken teenagers who contemplate suicide; *My Heart and Other Black Holes*, by Jasmine Warga (Balzer + Bray), about a girl who makes a suicide pact with a boy; and *Before You Break*, by Kyla Stone (Paper Moon Press), which deals with themes of suicide, mental illness, and abuse.

Keeping Them Laughing with Humor

Who doesn't like to laugh, giggle, smirk, chuckle, chortle, guffaw, or get a little silly on occasion? No one we know. And if you want to get a laugh out of your child (or yourself, for that matter), read them a humorous book. (See Figure 3-25 for two really funny board books.) Although some children's book genres tend to come and go, every shelf always has a place for a book that's funny. The following sections guide you through some of the most common subgenres in the universe of humorous books.

a   b

FIGURE 3-25: A couple of especially funny boardbooks.

From Night Animals, *by Gianna Marino. Reprinted by permission. © 2017 Gianna Marino.*
From Night Animals Need Sleep Too, *by Gianna Marino. Reprinted by permission. © 2020 Gianna Marino.*

Quirky characters

Some children's book characters, including people, animals, and other kinds of beings, act in odd, unexpected ways that fall outside the norm of our everyday experience. They might, for example, put their thumb in their mouth, blow hard, inflate like a balloon, and then float away with the wind. Or maybe a donkey talks and says funny things, or a dog goes to school. Whatever the case, quirky characters can really spice up your children's book. Any Dr. Seuss book is chock-full of quirky characters, such as a talking cat with a hat, a fox that wears socks, and something called a Grinch that stole Christmas.

Parody, satire, and jokes

A *parody* is a humorous imitation of an existing work. For example, *Goodnight Goon: A Petrifying Parody,* by Michael Rex (G.P. Putnam's Sons Books for Young

Readers), is a parody of the popular children's book *Goodnight Moon*, by Margaret Wise Brown (HarperCollins).

Satire pokes fun (sometimes gently, sometimes aggressively) at people, organizations, society, and more in a humorous way. *Shrek!* by William Steig (Square Fish), satirizes fairy tales and became a hit DreamWorks animated film.

Jokes are stories — often short — that end with an unexpected twist or punchline. *The Big Book of Silly Jokes for Kids*, by Carole P. Roman (Rockridge Press), contains more than 800 jokes for children ages 6 to 12.

Slapstick and gross

Pratfalls, pies in the face, slipping on banana peels, and other physical mishaps are the bread and butter of *slapstick* comedy, which is built on a solid foundation of anticipation, timing, and repetition.

And we all know *gross* when we see (or read) it. *Dog Breath: The Horrible Trouble with Hally Tosis*, by Dav Pilkey (Scholastic, Inc.), tells the story of a family dog who has bad breath that saves the day. And *Gomer the Gassy Goat: A Fart-Filled Tale*, by Hayley Rose (Flowered Press), is about (big surprise!) a goat that likes to fart.

Dark humor

Dark humor takes on painful, morbid, depressing, or rude topics in a funny way. *All My Friends Are Dead*, by Avery Monson and Jory John (Chronicle Books), is about a dinosaur whose fellow dinosaurs have all gone extinct. And *I'd Really Like to Eat a Child*, by Sylviane Donnio (Dragonfly Books), explores the dilemma of a crocodile who wants to step up his eating game from boring bananas to a real, live child.

Wordplay

Kids love to have fun with words, engaging in wordplay, which we explore in detail in Chapter 12. Whether its alliteration, assonance, parallelism, refrain, polyptoton, metaphor, simile, anthropomorphism, personification, or just making up your own words, you can engage in this form of humor in an almost endless number of ways. Most of us likely have the familiar refrain from Dr. Seuss's *Green Eggs and Ham* (Beginner Books/Random House) embedded in our brains from a very early age: "I do not like green eggs and ham. I do not like them, Sam-I-Am."

GETTING ADVICE ON GENRE WRITING FOR CHILDREN

If you want to know what it takes to stand out, listen to Doug Whiteman, former president of Penguin Books for Young Readers. Having been in the publishing business for over three decades, Doug started out as a book sales rep and worked his way to the top. Several years ago, he formed his own literary agency, The Whiteman Agency. Here's his take on being successful in genre writing:

- **Does a writer need to understand the conventions of a children's book genre and stick to what the readers expect?** "That's a really good question because we have different filters we're selling to, each of which has its own expectations. Our accounts and their buyers certainly expect things to fit into traditional molds, as do many parents and librarians. And many times, I've seen books stopped cold if they couldn't be easily classified in a traditional way. Having said that, kids themselves are looking for the truly unique and original. So the best answer to your question is: Understand the conventions and know we will have to package and position your book in a relatively traditional way in order to get past the filters, but give us some sneaky originality inside the covers to captivate the kids."

- **At the largest publishing companies what kinds of children's books are always hot?** "It seems to me that we're becoming increasingly cyclical, so there's very little that's always hot. Picture books, for example, seem to go into downturns every ten years or so. Series books are less cyclical than they used to be. And nothing is more cyclical than licensed publishing, which goes up and down like a roller coaster every few years. Probably the steadiest category is fantasy; everyone likes to think that *Harry Potter* made fantasy into a bestselling genre, but the truth is that people like Philip Pullman and Brian Jacques were selling huge numbers long before J. K. Rowling came along."

- **What kinds of books are most always not hot?** "Picture books with long texts, expensive books based on holidays that can't command high price points (like Halloween), and books that have depressing endings! I can't think of a genre, though, that's never hot."

- **What turns a one-off children's book title into a contender for a series?** "A wonderful character (or characters). People can sometimes enjoy a great book that doesn't have an impactful, memorable character, but a great character can supersede an otherwise mediocre book, leaving your readers clamoring for more."

- **Any advice for new writers?** "Do your homework and listen!"

Chapter **4**

Understanding the Children's Book Market

You may think a children's book writer would be writing solely for children; however, the children's book universe is populated by all sorts of grown-ups who essentially serve as gatekeepers, judging your book at each stage of the publishing and consumer processes and determining whether your book makes the cut and is allowed to proceed into the world of your target audience: kids.

The chain of adults whom you have to impress before even one child sees your book looks more or less like this:

Publisher/Acquisitions Editor or Agent → Marketing Pros and Sales Reps → Chain Store, Big Box Store, or Independent Book Buyer → Reviewer or Critic → Bookseller → Librarian or Teacher → Parent → Child

Of the many grown-ups who stand between you and your child audience, agents, acquisitions editors, or publishers are the first ones you must impress. An agent serves as the eyes and ears for the publishers and acquisitions editors — and all three are looking for the same qualities: a unique, well-written, absolutely worth-the-effort, *gotcha!* manuscript.

Next in line are the publisher's in-house marketing and sales reps who take their cues from the editorial team and build out plans from there. These folks are followed by book buyers, reviewers, and critics. Then the booksellers get their hardcopies to shelve after the books are published. Finally, parents, teachers, and librarians become the most powerful links in the chain.

All these adults make choices before children ever set eyes on a book. So every child without pocket change or an allowance of their own is out of your reach if you can't get these adults on your side. How do you ingratiate yourself with them? The information we share in this chapter can help you do just that.

We start by exploring these gatekeepers. We also look at your target audience — children — and what they like, what they don't like, even how you can tap into an unusual trend and perhaps write a book that rocks the ages.

TALKING WITH A SMALL-PRESS PUBLISHER

Peggy Tierney owns a successful and award-winning small publishing house, Tanglewood Books (www.tanglewoodbooks.com). In her position as owner/publisher, Peggy acquires every title on her list. We asked her how she goes about choosing books in the categories described in Chapter 2. Here are the highlights of her advice:

- **Deciding what type of book to publish when:** "I am more likely to sign something in a category that isn't glutted at the moment. A few years ago, there were simply too many picture books being published, so it was incredibly difficult to get a new title on the shelves. That doesn't mean that I won't publish a book in a crowded category, but the manuscript would have to be truly outstanding for me to consider it."

- **Choosing a format:** "As far as formats, I always publish a book in hardcover to begin with, then follow it with a paperback edition a year or two later. Sometimes a book will work in one format but not another — I always want to give a book the best chance it can have."

- **Telling the publisher who your book is for:** "For me, it's essential that the writers tell me who their audience is. It's something writers should know before they pick up a pen (or sit down at a computer). It also tells me that they've done their homework and are treating their submission like the professional endeavor it is."

- **What makes a book attractive:** "Characters that seem real; a plot that hasn't been done; great writing, which means being skilled at show don't tell; good pacing; and subtle character development."

- **What makes a book unattractive:** "A writer who clearly has not done their homework, and by that, I mean going to libraries and bookstores, studying what is on the shelves, reading everything you can. It will not only make you sound smart and savvy to your publisher, it will keep you from writing stories that have already been done — and it will make you a better writer overall."

- **Avoiding a common new-author mistake:** "As far as the writing itself, a common mistake new authors make is to try to open the book with all the background and character development. You can't wait for 50 pages to start telling the story. Character development and background have to be artfully woven in while moving the plot forward."

- **Avoiding a common picture-book mistake:** "The most common thing I see is a picture book manuscript that's too long and too advanced as far as language level."

- **Choosing from a pile of submissions:** "There are a couple of ways I decide. The first one is just taking stock of my passion for a title or lack thereof. If I love a book, I will push harder for it to be successful. And in this day and age, with so many children's books being published, a book has to be outstanding, not simply okay or even good enough. And something else I do is to send books out to kids. I have kids and teens who read for me, and they are all smart, avid readers who give me honest opinions. If a book fails the kid test, I don't publish it."

- **Thinking outside the box (or not):** "I like to do things that are different, but I know my limitations. There have been a few times when I've thought a manuscript was outstanding, but I didn't think I could do it justice. And I've referred the author to an agent or editor who might give it a better home."

- **Giving advice to beginning writers:** "They've taken a great step by reading this book! Read, read, read. Go talk to librarians and booksellers and find out what they love and why — then read it. Join the Society of Children's Book Writers and Illustrators (SCBWI) or find a really good critique group — a group that is not just there to encourage you, but to give you constructive criticism. Take a writing class."

- **Creating a great query letter:** "I would say to never underestimate the importance of your query letter. The synopsis should be a wonder of conciseness while still capturing the essence of the book and creating interest. If a synopsis is long and rambling, I assume the book is going to be the same. The writing in general should sparkle every bit as much if not more than the manuscript; I will start reading the manuscript already convinced you are a good writer. While I love to hear about a writer's passion, keep it professional and don't sound like a diva. Let me know how hard you will work to make your book a success. In other words, sell yourself to me — that helps me sell your book to others."

Getting Insight into Book Buyers' Needs

In a retail store, the *book buyers* are the people who sit down with the sales representatives from the publishing companies (or distributors hired by the publishers to handle sales) and decide which books they are going to take, for which stores, and in what quantities.

Large chains, such as Barnes & Noble (B&N), may employ an entire department of buyers who purchase, say, only fiction; others may purchase only children's books. At the other end of the spectrum, the owner of an independent bookstore with only one or two locations may also serve as its buyer, and thus may be responsible for choosing and stocking all titles in the store.

The requirements of each of these buyers may be quite different, and sales reps must adjust their selling approaches to the buyers' unique needs. For example, one buyer may be on the lookout for middle-grade fiction targeting reluctant boy readers; another book buyer may insist that every children's book have a great cover illustration and a unique hook.

A chain bookstore buyer may share some independent bookstore buyers' discerning tastes, but the chain bookstore buyer also has to consider specific sections within the overall children's book area that they have to fill, which size books will fit in those sections, which books may go well in the store's book displays, and how often they will have to replenish a section with new product to keep it from looking stale to frequent customers.

REMEMBER

The good news is that your editor will likely be very well versed in how to make your book shine no matter what kind of store it's sold in — big or small, chain or independent. But if you have your own suggestions for getting your book to stand out from the pack, don't be shy. Let your editor or agent know what you think if you're traditionally publishing. If you've chosen another route to publication, simply put those good ideas to work yourself.

The following sections offer some insight into what different bookselling venues have to offer and how they set up their product to entice their customers.

For chain and big-box bookstores

In chain bookstores such as Barnes & Noble, the children's section has a very distinct organization that is largely duplicated at every store. Most often, the children's book section separates books by the categories we explore in Chapter 2.

Although some Barnes & Noble stores still have young adult (YA) sections within the physically separate children's book section, featuring mostly classic, evergreen, and award-winning YA titles, most stores have established a totally separate YA section physically outside the children's book area, labeled Teens & YA. Barnes & Noble has made this organizational choice because teens don't want to be thought of as children. So titles and series addressing that target audience get their own special area closer to the adult sections of the bookstore.

What does this division mean for you? Specifically, as a new children's book writer, you must write your manuscript to fit one of those widely accepted and specific categories or sections.

REMEMBER

Chain-store book buyers are often concerned with more than just what's inside the book. The physical size and appearance of the book take on great importance, too. But whether a buyer is purchasing books for all the B&Ns in the country, all the Costcos in the Southwest, or one store in Los Angeles, they're looking for the best in each format for each age group.

Buyers for big-box retailers that don't specialize in just books, such as Target or Walmart, may also have additional parameters a book must meet. For example:

>> Does the book fit in the *planogram* (an aisle-long rack with tiered, face-out shelves fitting specific-size books)?

>> Is the book special enough to promote on an *endcap* (the end of an aisle)? Is the publisher willing to share the cost for this highly visible position in the store?

>> Does the book target the primary audience (the children that parents buy for)?

>> Is the book priced right to survive up to a 50-percent markdown if the *sell-through* (how well the book sells to actual buyers) is poor?

>> How will the book compete against all the *licensed books* (books based on popular television, films, cartoons, or toy characters), which comprise a large portion of the books sold in some of these venues?

Find out as much as you can about the book business because after you become a published writer, this business becomes your business, too! So get out to those bookstores, chains, and warehouse clubs, and study their offerings.

For independent bookstores

The buyers for independent bookstores may have the time to look a little more carefully at each book up for consideration. They can also exercise greater freedom in taking a chance on unknown authors and their works.

Here's how one *independent book buyer* (a buyer at an independent book store, not a big chain or a library), Jennifer Christopher Randle, defines her job:

> A buyer's job is to identify books that add value to the store — economic value and literary value both. We need to understand what our customers want, understand where sales trends are leading, be aware of which authors and illustrators are making an impact on the market, and be able to highlight the importance of different formats and genres of books for children.

> With all of that information, we then meet with publishers' sales representatives at conventions, conferences, and in-store meetings to determine which titles we will acquire.

When asked how she chooses which books to buy for different categories, here's what she had to say:

» **Infant to three:** "For the youngest, I tend to look for bright colors, familiar images, bouncy rhymes, and simple stories. At this age, the goal is to introduce a love of books to the child."

» **Picture books:** "Picture books help foster a child's imagination and wonder, helping children understand there is a bigger world out there. I was always drawn to different types of illustrators from Mo Willems to Gennady Spirin. The most important thing to me is the story — if it's good, it will be read over and over, the pictures will be closely analyzed, and a child will try to squeeze everything they can out of it. If the story is not successful, then most times even the illustrations can't save it. And yet some of the most memorable picture books are told entirely through the illustrations, which is rewarding to the reader because without the leading hand of the author, great imagination is required to appreciate the story."

» **Leveled readers:** "Leveled readers are more commonly seen in the educational/library market. They are a great way for children to feel pride in mastering each level and help grow a child's confidence in reading and reading comprehension. This is an underserved market, and I think it is also the most challenging for authors based on the constrictions. You have to use limited language, it can't be too long, and you want to tie the illustrations to the words on the page."

PICKING A BOOK BUYER'S BRAIN

Jennifer Christopher Randle, a book buyer for Daedalus Books & Music (an independent bookstore), spoke with us about what an independent book buyer is:

- **An independent bookstore buyer versus a buyer for a big store:** "For Daedalus, I purchased children's titles for one store. We were a remainder bookstore, so we had the luxury of being able to see past sales history of a title; however, we were also able to find overlooked titles that were great books but just didn't rise as high as some of the other titles. We also had a solid understanding of our customer base: a very literate, educated customer who was looking for a book to share their love of books with their children.

  "All of these factors made it easy to meet with sales representatives at the store or at conventions like CIROBE, the Chicago International Remainder and Overstock Book Exposition. We would be able to quickly go through known titles and familiar authors and illustrators, and spend more time sifting for the forgotten gems.

  "As an independent bookstore, we were not tied to marketing contracts for book placement or told how to arrange displays according to a corporate office. We could also — much more than large chain stores — take chances on unknown titles. Everybody had a say in which titles were displayed, and we constantly educated one another."

- **Changes to independent bookstores and book buying:** "Both have become more cautious and more volume-driven. Buyers are not taking as many chances, focusing their buying power on tried-and-true books. There is closer scrutiny at the sales history of authors, genres, and publishers, making for a tight market that pushes out a lot of participants. The independent bookstore is becoming an endangered species, and the enormous impact of Amazon cannot be understated. A lot of it is economically driven, yet we need independent bookstores to provide both great books and great guidance. A customer is more likely to purchase a title if a bookseller can handsell it. That means having a wide selection and an educated staff. Readers like being around other readers, and independent bookstores provide a community lacking in other venues."

- **Advice for beginning children's book writers:** "Recognize that children are smart and able to pick up on dishonesty faster than most adults. If you write in a condescending way, children will pick up on that. Don't be afraid to be honest if you're writing about a difficult subject. This is how children are able to conquer their own fears, frustrations, and sorrows. People forget that childhood is a very difficult and challenging period when you are essentially powerless amid giants. Authors and illustrators help children understand their own feelings and thoughts, expand their world past their front door, and encourage them to be curious, creative kids."

>> **Middle grade:** "Middle-grade fiction is, to me, the most exciting group of books. It is here that a reader has their first taste of genre fiction, which can grow to a lifelong passion. Give a child *The Hobbit,* and I can almost guarantee they will be reading George R. R. Martin in high school. I look for a wide assortment of titles crossing many different genres because you never know which one will be the spark that ignites a child's interest. Whether funny, scary, historical, or adventure-driven, story is king. Middle-grade fiction has little to no illustration to support it. I always ask myself, 'Can I see it?' If I can't picture my protagonist in the story they're starring in, then I would pass. I have a very active imagination, so if I can't picture your world, what chance does a ten-year-old child have?"

>> **YA:** "YA is tricky because you have to define it. Is it dumbed-down adult fiction? If it's good, should it be YA or 'promoted' to general fiction? Usually, it boils down to how it's marketed. With YA, it is important to stay informed by reading reviews, watching award lists, and reading. Story is key: You need to have complex characters with believable conflicts carrying real consequences. I think that's true of all fiction, really. The early teen years are when kids are pushing boundaries and testing limits. Reading can be an escape, a way of finding perspective, and a constant companion."

Recognizing What Reviewers Offer

Reviewers and critics come in many forms and can seriously affect how a book is received in the publishing community. Before committing to buying copies for their stores and schools, booksellers and librarians regularly review such book trade publications as *The School Library Journal, Publishers Weekly, Library Journal, The Horn Book,* the website Publishers Marketplace (which links to book reviews from all over), and all the famous newspapers that still have book review sections, such as *The Washington Post, The New York Times, USA Today,* and others.

Online reviews such as New York Journal of Books (www.nyjournalofbooks.com) also play a big role for book consumers, as do respected bloggers who focus on children's book reviews. In addition, Goodreads, Booklist Online, and Shelf Awareness give you plenty of venues to get your book noticed. The more respected a venue or blog, the more influence it has on buying choices.

TIP

Should you buy a subscription to one or more source for book reviews? Maybe — if you can't find a copy in your local library or you've got one source you want to intensively target for a review of your book. And should you pay for a review of your book? Again, the answer is maybe. When you pay for a review, you're sort of telling the world that your book couldn't gain the interest of an unpaid reviewer.

In addition, you'll need to pay for the review — potentially hundreds of dollars. Be sure to weigh the pros and cons before you sign on the dotted line.

Michael Cart is a book critic, editor, and lecturer who spends a lot of time reading and evaluating books for young adults for various publications and online venues. He is also the author or editor of 23 books, including books for YA audiences: *Cart's Top 200 Adult Books for Young Adults: Two Decades in Review* (ALA Editions). He also wrote *My Father's Scar* (Simon & Schuster), an ALA Best Book for Young Adults. In his words:

> After 60 years of avid reading, I find the things I look for more than any others are originality and freshness. Give me a story I haven't read countless times before, and I'm a happy chappie!
>
> Also, because I think it's imperative that every kid be able to see his or her face reflected in the pages of a good book — especially if that kid has been marginalized for whatever reason (race, religion, place of national origin, sexual identity, and so on) — I look for books featuring characters who have been absent from traditional YA fiction.
>
> I also look for books that are creatively venturesome, playing with considerations of structure, voice, and narrative strategy. Some recent favorites include *Switch,* by A. S. King (Dutton) and *Aristotle and Dante Dive into the Waters of the World,* by Benjamin Alire Saenz (Simon & Schuster).
>
> As for nonfiction, I look for high-interest, non-curriculum-related topics that may be offbeat but that will capture the attention of teens with limited time for reading. To that same end, I look for books with strong narrative content and also for books that are eye-catching in terms of design and visual content.

Michael recommends *Revolution in Our Time: The Black Panther Party's Promise to the People* by Kekla Magoon (Candlewick) and *Fallout: Spies, Superbombs, and the Ultimate Cold War Showdown* by Steve Sheinkin (Roaring Brook Press) as good examples of nonfiction to check out.

Discovering What Librarians Add to the Mix

Every book buyer looks at content to one extent or another, but public librarians and school librarians are among the most discerning when choosing books for their collections. The American Library Association (www.ala.org) offers a lot of reference tools on how to build a library collection, and annual ALA conferences help librarians stay current in a fast-changing field. Great library service to children and young adults assumes a close knowledge of the community and a carefully developed collection. We could attempt to explain generally how librarians make their selections, but we think you can find more value in hearing from a distinguished former librarian.

Susan Patron formerly served as Juvenile Materials Collection Development Manager at the L.A. Public Library. She also won the Newbery Medal for authoring *The Higher Power of Lucky* (Atheneum Books for Young Readers), Book 1 of what became the Hard Pan Trilogy.

At the L.A. Public Library, she concentrated on providing books to serve a large and diverse community in the city of Los Angeles. Part of this task included consideration of a huge system of satellite library branches. Each branch serves its own community and has its own budget, so although she compiled a wide monthly selection of books of all types, not every branch would buy every title.

For example, if she was considering a new book about skateboarding, she would first examine her existing collection to see whether the library system already had books that addressed the age and interest range of her target audience (meaning readers ages 5 to 11, those most likely to want to read about skateboarding) or if she could use a new book not already in the collection. Did the book that she was considering add anything — better illustrations, for example, or useful safety information?

Here are some other considerations for nonfiction:

>> Well researched, not dated material

>> Pictures appropriate for the audience

>> Contents arranged logically

>> Text readable and inviting

>> Text and illustrations well matched

>> No fictionalized dialogue in nonfiction

>> Source material cited

>> Table of contents and index

>> Author's passion about the subject

Susan says that children want a lot of variety on the page. The text shouldn't be too dense, and illustrative material should be clearly marked and ample. All ages of readers enjoy seeing illustrations or photographs that amplify and augment the text.

Additionally, trade nonfiction titles should strive for economy of words because most kids will select a thin book over a thick one. An example is *Honeybee: The Busy Life of Apis Mellifera* by Candace Fleming, illustrated by Eric Rohmann (Holiday House). This book won the American Library Association's Sibert Medal for the best informational book of the year in 2021; the list of Sibert winners and honor books is a useful one for writers of nonfiction (`www.ala.org/alsc/awardsgrants/bookmedia/sibert`).

Susan emphasized that libraries seek to maintain a balanced collection, including books on controversial topics that present a variety of points of view. Writers should not avoid subjects for fear of offending some readers — as long as the information is not sensationalized and the sensibilities of the target audience are kept in mind. For example, Susan recommended the excellent sex education books by Robie H. Harris and Michael Emberley, including *It's So Amazing* and *It's Perfectly Normal* (both published by Candlewick), as well as their many other titles for preschoolers to teens.

In terms of picture books, Susan said librarians and reviewers look for an original idea that has not been done before, or if it has, that this incarnation provides a new twist:

> A child protagonist has to solve the problem, not the adult or some magical creature, and the story should be told from a child's perspective. The pictures and words should work well together, and every page should offer enough interest, suspense, drama, or humor to keep the reader (or the person reading to the child) turning the pages. Linda Ashman's *How to Make a Night* (HarperCollins) infuses a well-worn subject — bedtime — with fresh originality and vitality and is entirely child-centered.

In terms of younger middle-grade fiction, kids are interested in subjects such as friendship, siblings, animals, fantasy worlds, and school. These themes are explored in chapter books over and over, and Susan finds that the most popular books work because they're written from the heart and have a unique voice. This audience loves humor and strong protagonists. Susan recommends as a page-turning example Helen Fox's *Eager* (Wendy Lamb Books) and its sequels about a robot who is almost human.

Susan says libraries also purchase lots of board books for babies and toddlers, including ones with flaps and die-cuts. The best board books have very few words, and the text directly relates to the very young child's experience. To facilitate access, many children's librarians actually place board books in baskets on the floor in the picture book area because they want the target audience (who may still be crawling) to be able to find them. Susan suggests that an example of a book that perfectly addresses its audience's experience is *Where's Spot?* by Eric Hill (Penguin Books for Young Readers):

> It's the perfect two-year-old's book because over and over again the text repeats a favorite word of that age group: "No!" It's funny, suspenseful, interactive, and reassuring because by the end we know that Spot's mom cares more about him than anything in the world.

> Sandra Boynton, Lucy Cousins, and Rosemary Wells also produce brilliant board books to engage babies and very young children.

Susan astonished us with the fact that her library even purchases pop-up books, which we thought would be a no-no because of their fragility. (But as we figured, the library doesn't purchase novelty books that have pieces that you can separate from the book.) Susan adds regarding novelty books:

> Even if a pop-up or novelty book is likely to be ephemeral in the collection, we will often buy it for display and story time. We want kids to see how fun, and inventive, and beautiful books can be. Well-done pop-up books, like those of David A. Carter and Robert Sabuda, are great for story time because they project to a group and can be seen at the back of the room. Plus, they are often packed with audience-pleasing surprises.

I (Lisa) donated my collection of nearly 500 pop-up and novelty titles to the Downtown Los Angeles Public Library's children's section in 2020. It was the biggest single donation of pop-up books the library had ever received. I'm glad my collection found a home where children can explore all the 3-D and paper-engineered books intended just for them!

Libraries occasionally even buy coloring books and activity books, but very selectively. For example, Susan says that if they relate to topics or information kids are asking for with school assignments, the library will provide them as supplementary material.

Susan hopes new writers will enlist the help of their local children's librarians in becoming knowledgeable and informed about the current field of children's literature:

> Public librarians can be a writer's best friend. We want books that engage and delight children, books that make them want to read for pleasure. And we love to help writers in their research — whether by tracing the source of a folktale, checking what's available on a given subject, providing tools such as recommended reading lists, or discussing what topics are of current interest to kids.

FROM LIBRARIAN TO AWARD-WINNING AUTHOR

Two years after our original 2005 interview for the first edition of this book, librarian Susan Patron became a bestselling, award-winning author (which we talk about in the section "Discovering What Librarians Add to the Mix," in this chapter). We asked her a few questions about the author experience:

- **The genesis of her book,** *The Higher Power of Lucky:* "The setting came before the story itself: I'd fallen in love with the remote, harsh, seemingly barren environment of California's Eastern Sierra high deserts, where my husband and I often traveled on vacations. I wondered what it would be like to grow up in a tiny, impoverished community there."

- **How experience as a youth-services librarian contributed to her writing:** "I learned the power of story: Well-told/well-written ones can mesmerize a group of wriggly preschoolers, transform apathetic readers into enthusiastic ones, and bring tears to the eyes of a cynical 11-year-old.

  "I discovered it's counterproductive to identify trends or write fiction that tries to correspond to what is currently popular — better to search instead for the story I was compelled to tell. I believe this is the way for a writer to find that elusive quality called voice: Write the story that's banging its hand on the door to your heart."

- **How long the writing and publication process took:** "Since I was working full time, *The Higher Power of Lucky* took over 10 years — maybe more like 12 — with various drafts submitted over those years. I was fortunate to be working with the brilliant editor Richard Jackson, who was patient and wise and kept saying, 'It's not quite ready yet.' When it was finally published, I was already focused on *Lucky Breaks,* the second book in the trilogy."

- **Transitioning from librarian to full-time writer:** "When I still had a day job, I got used to spending weekends and vacations with the novel for that long incubation period. Fortunately, I'm married to the world's most supportive husband. He understands about allowing me solitude. So our routine, in which I sit at the keyboard and stare out the window for hours at a time, is well established. Since the act of writing makes me happy — when I'm not being driven crazy by it! — sitting down every day to write is a wonderful job. Holding a printed and bound copy of a novel I have written and published is a great joy."

(continued)

(continued)

- **A book-banning brouhaha about** *The Higher Power of Lucky:* "On the first page, a dog is bitten on its scrotum by a rattlesnake. On a private list-serv, some school librarians discussed being uncomfortable with the word *scrotum,* and the conversation was leaked, eventually leading to a page-one article in *The New York Times.* This set off a tremendous national dialogue about censorship. The book was strongly endorsed and supported by the American Library Association's Intellectual Freedom Committee, the Society of Children's Book Writers and Illustrators (SCBWI), the International Reading Association, the National Coalition Against Censorship, and by many individual authors and librarians. Parents may determine whether a particular book is appropriate for their children — but only for their children."

- **Advice for prospective writers:** "Write every day. Every. Single. Day. And if you haven't already done so, join SCBWI."

Taking a Look at How Teachers Use Books in Their Classrooms

Teachers have various concerns and issues that they want books in the classroom to address. Of course, for teachers of middle school and higher, a lot depends on the subject taught, but most teachers buy books across a wide range of subjects. For example, a preschool director will buy a lot of books dealing with the behaviors, experiences, and concerns of preschoolers. *How Are You Feeling* by Erin Jang (Mudpuppy), *Sloth and Smell the Roses* by Eunice Moyle and Sabrina Moyle (Harry N. Abrams), and many of Jamie Lee Curtis's books are all good examples of preschooler-targeted titles.

We asked one of our favorite teachers — Jodi Feinstein, a mother of four — what kinds of books she looks for as a kindergarten through sixth-grade teacher. She believes the age and reading level of the child determines their book needs, and she also considers whether she's choosing a book to get a child to read or to supplement the core curriculum. For those in primary grades — kindergarten through third grade — Jodi feels that it depends on the reading level of the students, whether she's looking for picture books to read to the class or providing the first chapter/picture books they will see:

> Pictures are essential, and they must be bright and eye-catching. Humor is an absolute must because it draws in children. They love to laugh at others like them, and if the protagonist does obviously dumb or silly things, so much the better.

Jodi likes picture books that can lead to meaningful discussions in the classroom, no matter the grade level. An added bonus is if the book may stimulate the children's analytical skills. She stays away from trendy, commercial, and licensed books.

For the middle primary years — grades four and five — she says:

> The pictures are not so essential anymore, but humor is still quite important. I tell parents with reluctant readers to let them read anything you can get them to read while constantly introducing other genres of books along the way. And books with main characters their age involved in interesting and exciting adventures that fourth through sixth graders can relate to are always appreciated — especially those with sequels that extend the story, thereby piquing the child's interest and keeping them reading. On the other hand, children of this age also like to read a lot of fantasy that is completely removed from real life, but just might have the *possibility* of being possible.

And she finds that not much has changed for nonfiction books for middle-school–aged readers:

> Kids this age are invariably caught up in a world in which they are the center of the universe. They think everything in their lives generally sucks and that their life is really hard, that nothing is fair. As such, they like to read about kids who have it worse. So books such as *It Happened to Nancy: By an Anonymous Teenager, A True Story from Her Diary,* by Beatrice Sparks (Avon); *Go Ask Alice,* also by Beatrice Sparks (Simon Pulse/Aladdin); and *A Child Called "It": One Child's Courage to Survive,* by Dave Pelzer (HCI Books) are the kinds of stories they really get into: real-life, horrible things that happen to average boys or girls. I think these kinds of books actually make these readers feel better, feel they can overcome — even if just for a moment.

When the curriculum calls for supplemental reading, Jodi likes to tie in books with whatever her students are learning in history and with what's going on in the larger world, not just their world. Other teachers might assign books by topic or issue to get the children discussing subjects of relevance both in school and out in the world.

TIP

Teachers are always looking for books to supplement, enhance, and reinforce the curriculum. If you're a writer unsure of a topic, go ask a teacher what subjects they can always use more reference for. Whatever holes exist in the juvenile publishing spectrum, teachers (and librarians) are the ones most keenly aware of them. And if you're writing for the educational market, finding out the state's core curriculum can be a good place to spark an idea.

Considering Parents' Perspectives

Parents of the very youngest readers (the ones who prefer to use their books as teething rings rather than reading them) buy books that have great art, are bright and eye-catching, and are made of tasty board material. (Okay, we're joking on that last one.) So if you as a new writer are aiming to create a board book, make sure it focuses on a baby's experiences and has bright art.

It's not until a child starts really paying attention to the content of the books that their parent or parents have to be very, very, very careful of which books they buy. Because if they buy a book that they won't enjoy reading 5,000 times in a row, they only have themselves to blame. So you, as the author, really need to focus on a great story and excellent art.

While a child grows, their parents' taste in books may be less issue-oriented and more media-oriented, so a lot of licensed books (based on popular television, films, cartoons, or toy characters) might creep into the child's collection. Or not. And issue-oriented books for older children are just as important as they were back when your child was teething. This is what parents look for most: books told from a child's perspective, starring unique child protagonists who can help their own children become better people, dealing with their issues in a positive and hopeful manner.

When a child moves into the middle-grade years and beyond, they probably make more choices about what to read on their own. Whether from the school, local library, your friendly neighborhood bookstore, or online, teens like to explore books in their own time in their own way. Likely the only contribution teens allow their parents to make is monetary so that they can get their hands on the latest book they've heard their friends raving about. This fact holds true even more for nonfiction titles, which may be embarrassing for children if their parents find out they're researching subjects that they're not willing to discuss with their parents.

TIP

If you want to appeal to parents, get down and dirty — literally, get down in the sandbox and listen to what's really going on in children's minds and hearts. And then write from that perspective: what a child wants to hear, not what you as an adult feel they need to hear.

Thinking Like a Kid

Something happens to children when they grow up: They forget what it's like to have magic in their lives. They forget that an ant on the sidewalk can be a source of endless entertainment and speculation. They forget that the need to right injustices and make things fair is as necessary as breathing. They forget that most of the world has unbreakable divisions between what's right and what's wrong, what's good and what's bad, the way they looked at the world when they were little.

And most pivotally, adults forget that for children, the line between fantasy and reality is blurred. What may seem miraculous or outlandish to an adult is simply part of life to a child.

As a result of this amnesia, many new writers (and sorrowfully, quite a few published writers, although not the truly successful ones) write down to children. They write about what they think children should learn; they lecture, chide, preach, and tell stories instead of showing readers a special storybook world.

So how do you, as a new writer, write for children and not for your own peers? Keep reading. The following sections reveal a little about what children want and, of course, what they don't want.

REMEMBER

Speaking to children on their level doesn't mean speaking down to them or using baby talk. It means getting into their heads and their lives and writing about what is relevant and of interest to them.

Going after what kids like — regardless of Mom and Dad

Sometimes writing about what children like may offend adults. Stephenie Meyer's Twilight series, because it has vampires, magic, May–December paranormal love, and other (what some consider to be) dystopian or inappropriate content in it, has been banned in many areas of the United States. Yet the books in the series have won multiple awards and been made into movies.

So you have a choice: You can play it safe with topics children love (and adults don't mind), or you can take a chance with topics children love (and adults definitely mind). The choice is entirely up to you.

TIP

Here are some themes children respond to (usually at different ages), adults be darned:

>> Little people can indeed triumph over grown-ups.

>> Poopoo, peepee, tushies, passing gas, burping, underwear — all are hilarious.

>> Turning things upside down is funny — as long as those things make sense in the first place right side up.

>> Magic can occur as a logical reaction to an action.

>> Regular children can go on implausible missions regardless of what the grown-ups say or do.

>> Paranormal and dystopian realities work.

>> Having dead or missing parents makes for better adventures — as long as it doesn't feel contrived.

>> Taboo activities that older children might indulge in — cutting, drugs, sex (straight, gay, or anything in the gender-fluid spectrum), drinking, smoking, and so on — are appropriate subjects for upper-grade young adult books.

REMEMBER

When writing for children, remember this: Their world is not constrained by the same limitations and consequences as ours. In general, unless they have been abused or suffered extreme peril, children have not yet learned to be cynical or hopeless. There is always a chance for everything to work out — and that chance is lurking just beyond the next page.

Knowing what kids don't like

WARNING

We guarantee that kids don't and won't embrace the following:

>> Books that preach, condescend, or lecture

>> Books with no real story (or a plot that doesn't have a beginning, middle, and end)

>> Picture books so packed with text you wonder what happened to the editor

>> Nonfiction books so packed with text and so lacking in design and visuals you wonder what happened to the book designer

>> Books whose main characters are boring, uninteresting, or adult

>> Books with main characters who have a problem they don't actively solve, hence they don't change by the end of the book

>> Books that tell instead of show, using narrative as a soapbox and destroying any semblance of immediacy, making the story feel like old news right from the start

2

Immersing Yourself in the Writing Process

Set up your writing workspace to free yourself from distraction.

Make a writing room of your own, conducive to creativity, efficiency, and productivity.

Begin work on ideas, big and small.

Start researching both the children whom you want to read your story and the subject matter of your story.

» Figuring out your level of dedication

» Finding your best place to write

» Ignoring outside distractions

Chapter **5**

Setting Up for Success: Finding the Time and Space to Write

Guess what? Before you can revel in all those copies flying off the bookstore shelves and into online shopping carts, you have to write a book! For some fortunate writers, writing is the easy part; for others, it's like waiting at the dentist's office for a root canal.

If you're wondering how to get started and gain some understanding of how best to prepare for writing up a storm, that's exactly what we show you in this chapter. If you're a natural for the job — someone from whom the words spill out by the gallon anywhere and anytime — you may not need to pore over every section of this chapter. But if you skim through, you may find some helpful tips and tricks.

Finding Time to Write

Effective writers know when they're most productive, and they create a writing schedule around those times — then they stick to it. In the following sections, we help you pinpoint when you're most productive. We also give you some pointers on creating a schedule that makes you want to write and evaluating how that schedule is working for you.

Figuring out when you're most productive

Are you a night owl? A morning person? Are you at your best after you've had a cup of coffee and a chance to read the morning paper, or after you've run five miles? Is your house quiet for long periods of time, or is the atmosphere routinely punctuated with noise and distractions — kids running up and down the hallway or a construction project next door? The answers to these questions determine when you're most fertile and inventive as a writer.

TIP

Zero in on when you're most productive and then do the majority of your writing during that period of time. Every successful writer has a sweet spot: the time when they get the most done. Check out these tips for finding yours:

» **Try out different times.** Try writing for an hour or two at different times of the morning, day, and night. When do you feel the most creative and prolific? Be sure to give every possible time a try before you settle into a routine.

» **Work around the everyday.** Shift your writing time around specific everyday events in your life: before or after breakfast, before or after you shower or exercise, before or after you watch TV. Play with your schedule and see what feels good.

» **Write around your job.** You can accommodate your writing time and your job by taking a laptop, tablet, or pad of paper with you to work. Go into work early so you can get some writing in before your job starts, or get away to a park or cafe during lunch to work on your story.

Not all writers function the same way. Some enforce strict writing schedules and routines at the same time every day; others make sure to devote a certain number of hours daily to their craft, sneaking them in whenever they can. Yet others write only when the muse inspires them, varying the amount of time they spend writing. Whatever you choose, make sure it works best with when you're most productive writing-wise and fits into your daily schedule.

TIP

Writing once a week won't get you where you want to go; commit to at least every other day if every day is not a realistic option.

Sticking to a writing schedule

If you want to be a serious writer — and a successful children's book author — you can't leave your writing to chance. Include writing in your schedule and then do it! Unfortunately, in many ways, you may find sticking to a schedule is the hard part. Why? Because it requires discipline and focus.

Here are some reasons why you need to do what you can to make a schedule work:

» **Forming a habit:** By setting aside a specific time every day to write, you soon make writing a habit. As everyone knows, habits are hard to break (and when it comes to writing, that's a good thing).

» **Reducing stress:** After you settle into a writing routine, you take a large amount of the stress of the writing process off your shoulders. And a relaxed writer is a more effective and prolific writer.

» **Getting serious:** When you set a regular time to write, you indicate to others (family, friends, and co-workers) that this time is for you and your writing — and not to bother knocking when your keyboard is a-rocking.

» **Making a personal commitment:** Committing to writing leads to identifying yourself as a writer, which leads to more writing. Believing in yourself means taking your newfound avocation seriously.

TIP

Calendars and planners are absolutely essential tools for keeping organized and on track during the course of the day. I (Lisa) know that I have no other competing obligations where I enter writing time into my smartphone's calendar. So buy a calendar or daily planner, or use your smartphone's or electronic tablet's built-in calendar — and use it regularly.

Evaluating your commitment

Think about how your writing feels after a few weeks of sticking to your trial schedule. Are you relaxed? Energized? Distracted? Creative? Asleep? Assess your temporary schedule to find a time that works best for you.

You may sincerely want to make writing a priority in your life, but when the time comes to write, something always gets in the way — taking care of the kids, paying bills, or watching a favorite TV show. If this is the case, ask yourself whether writing a children's book is truly important to you. If the answer is yes, look for what is stealing your time and recommit to the process. Can you rearrange things and prioritize it in your life? If the answer is no, then consider waiting a few weeks or months (or even years) before you again take up your children's book. Sometimes a break can give you a lot more energy and fresh eyes for your project when you come back to it. Sometimes timing matters and it's just not the right time for that particular project.

Then again, you may just have a temporary case of writer's block, when the words don't seem to flow no matter what you do with your schedule. We reveal how to deal with writer's block in Chapter 6.

Optimizing Your Writing Environment

Just as important as finding the right time to write (which we talk about in the section "Finding Time to Write," earlier in this chapter), you need to find the right place to write. Even if you zero in on the very best time of the day to avoid distractions and focus on wordsmithing, it does you no good if you find your writing environment, for one reason or another, unsuitable for the task at hand. The following sections present some ways to find your special place and tips on how to make that place even more conducive to writing.

Locating your special writing spot

Every writer needs a place to write that's comfortable and cozy, stimulates creativity, and has the necessary writing tools. Here are some ideas for possible places to write:

>> A dedicated office in your home

>> Another room in your home, such as a den, dining room, or family room

    We strongly advise against using your bedroom as your special writing place if you have someone else who routinely occupies it with you.

>> An inspiring outdoor space

- A local library

- A coffeehouse or cafe

- A bookstore that has tables and chairs available for patron use

- A hotel lobby, fast-food restaurant, hospital, airport, train station, or bus station

  You'd be surprised how many places offer free Wi-Fi.

- A shopping mall or shopping center

- Your car or camper van

- Someone else's home: your parents', your friend's, your sibling's, or an Airbnb vacation rental space

For those who believe in feng shui, the direction you face when you write may be a factor. Some people work better facing north or east rather than south or west — or vice versa. Or west-facing in the morning and east-facing in the afternoon. These energies can make a difference!

The point is that anyplace can be your special place — you just have to keep looking until you find it. Instead of just settling at the first place you land, try a variety of different locations until you find the one that feels just right. You know that you found your spot when, all of a sudden, everything clicks and the words flow like someone just turned on the tap.

Keeping helpful references handy

You don't want to have to stop every time you're looking for a word or a synonym or a rhyme. And going online may just lead you down a time-wasting, distracting rabbit hole (Peter can attest to that!). We find that having a few hardcopy references handy can help keep your writing moving along at a clip.

You need a good dictionary, one that most publishing houses use. Get yourself the latest *Merriam-Webster's Collegiate Dictionary* — be sure to research the latest edition so you use the most up to date. You can also easily use the Merriam-Webster website (www.merriam-webster.com) or do a quick Google search, but if you're trying to stay off the Internet while you write, a good, old-fashioned hardcopy dictionary never hurts.

To find the best agents and navigate how to make submissions, you need the *Children's Writer's and Illustrator's Market* (Writer's Digest Books), by Amy Jones. It's updated annually. The book contains plenty of information for illustrators, as well as writers, including information about agents and editors — the genres of books they prefer, authors they've worked with, books they've played a role in, and how to contact them.

If you're a member of the Society of Children's Book Writers and Illustrators (SCBWI; www.scbwi.org), download a copy of *The Book: Essential Guide to Publishing for Children*. (Although it's a big book — over 300 pages — you might find it easier to flip through a printed copy than navigate the PDF.) Of course, we assume you've already joined or will be inspired to join SCBWI after you read all of *this* book. SCBWI is an invaluable resource for both new writers and experienced ones, offering tips on

>> Preparing and submitting your work — including their samples of query letters

>> Writing a great synopsis

>> Creating picture book dummies

>> Mentoring

>> Agents who are open to submissions from SCBWI members

SCBWI also has market surveys, directories of resources, and SCBWI *en español*.

Again, you probably want to stay off the Internet while you write, but you can always open a link and not wander anywhere else. RhymeZone (www.rhymezone.com) is one of the most valuable tools we've used as writers. With a simple search of a word, you can find synonyms, antonyms, descriptive words, definitions, and phrases. And as the website title suggests, you can search for rhyming words using American English accents on words; you can even search for quotations. It's a winner of a resource for writers, easily replacing the more cumbersome classic *Roget's Thesaurus* (HarperCollins).

Cutting down on clutter and getting organized

Although different people have different preferences when it comes to the amount of organization they need in their lives, many people work better and more effectively when they're organized. Consider some tips for getting organized — sooner rather than later:

>> **Clean up your desk.** The busier your life, the less time you have to clean up the old coffee cups, the wadded-up pieces of paper, the reference books, and all the other things that naturally seem to make their home on your desk. While all this stuff piles up, however, it becomes harder for you to write, not only because you have less space in which to work, but also because things start getting lost — never to be seen again.

>> **Separate obligations.** If you use your writing desk to pay bills, run your philanthropic endeavors for the children's schools, or conduct your other home business, separate out those obligations from your writing ones. Get file holders that physically keep other tasks separated from your writing so that you can move them out of the way if they prove distracting. Or you can create folders on your computer.

>> **Separate writing materials from each other.** In the same way that you don't want bills mixed in with your latest draft printout, you don't want your drafts to get mixed up with your research, your inspirational notes, or correspondence you have regarding your book. Create separate folders for each of these categories.

REMEMBER

You need even more organization after you start submitting to agents and publishers; even if you use online tools for tracking, you likely still have some paper to deal with, as well. To get ahead of the game and prepare yourself, you can create a folder for rejections so that when these letters start coming, you can reference any personalized messages or recommendations from those reviewing your work while you edit your book.

>> **Clean up your office.** In the same way that your desk can accumulate progressively deeper layers of stuff, everything from empty boxes and stacks of shoes to tossed waste paper that missed the basket and old candy bar wrappers can find their way into your office. The solution? Clean it up! And if you're feeling stuck in the writing process, taking a break to clean up your office can often get you unstuck.

>> **Revisit your office layout.** Consider where you have your desk, your chairs, your books, your computer, your filing cabinet, and anything else, and make sure it's all in the best place to support your writing efforts.

>> **Get organized now.** This tip speaks for itself. Don't just think about getting organized, actually get organized. Right now! The sooner you get it over with, the sooner you can start writing. Schedule regular organizing sessions — make it a part of your process. Schedule a regular time to clean up — say, every Saturday afternoon or on the first of the month.

>> **Eliminate distracting clutter.** Consider replacing clutter with a few items that stoke your creativity. Lisa likes to write in an environment that includes little toys and other objects that she finds ingenious or humorous, such as an iron fairy, a set of stone hands filled with tiny rocks, a clutched fist made of wax — all items that make her feel whimsical and lighthearted, the perfect mood pieces for her creative juices to flow in her hyper-organized space.

TIP

Lisa likes to research a lot of books in whatever genre she's writing at the time, including the ones that have won the latest accolades from librarians, reviews, awards, and the media. She keeps them in a neat pile, spines facing her, positioned on the side of her desk to serve as inspiration. Just seeing them there keeps her motivated and enthused.

Preventing and dealing with interruptions

Your telephone or computer can be one great big distraction that can keep you from focusing on doing the writing that needs to be done. Ignoring a ringing phone, chiming text message, or inbox full of e-mails is almost impossible. So turn off the ringer, sign out of the e-mail program, and close your browser if you can't focus when you should be writing.

If you're easily distracted by social networking sites such as Instagram, Pinterest, Facebook, Twitter, TikTok, or others, consider shutting them down while you're writing so that you're blissfully unaware of the constant stream of distractions.

If outside interruptions continue to get in the way of your writing, leave that space and find another. Or put up a sign declaring, DON'T MAKE ME HURT YOU. DO NOT INTERRUPT UNLESS THERE IS ALREADY BLOOD INVOLVED. If all else fails, reschedule your writing time for a specific replacement day — for that day only — so that you can make your writing time productive as opposed to frustrating. And plan ahead if you anticipate similar situations reoccurring.

REMEMBER

Writing is a job — an important one — and you want to make sure your writing time is respected. We seriously suggest a DO NOT DISTURB sign on the door of your writing space to alert your family, friends, and others that this is your time and they shouldn't bother you.

TIPS FROM AN AUTHOR AND EDITOR ON STAYING FOCUSED

Successful children's book writer Debra Mostow Zakarin talks about how she keeps focused on writing in the midst of a thousand distractions:

- **Whether you need a Zen-like place to write:** "After so many years of writing, I find my inspiration from life, from my children, and by just writing, writing, and writing. I've always kind of thought that an actual, physical inspirational place, at least for me, was way too contrived."

- **Setting up a special place to write:** "I have an office set up in my home — a computer, desk, and my smartphone. And, oh, my dog lies at my feet, something that really makes me feel like a writer. The space around my computer must be neat, or else I get too distracted and look for reasons to procrastinate. Also, I have learned to turn off my instant messenger so as not to get interrupted. And I make sure to log off from Facebook, Twitter, and Instagram because those are a total time drain."

- **Setting a writing schedule:** "I used to write in the late morning/early afternoon when my kids were at school. Now I have a more flexible schedule — that is, outside of my full-time publishing-director job that is immensely time-consuming. So it's mostly weekends and evenings for me; however, if I'm in the middle of writing something that I'm totally into, then I go back to my computer in the late evening, after my husband has gone to bed. My best writing, I have found, is usually done late at night."

- **Scheduling — strict or flexible:** "If my schedule were strict, I feel that I wouldn't be a creative person. I have to be flexible with my time. I try so hard to be strict, but old habits of dawdling are hard to break. If I miss a writing appointment, I try to make it up later that day or the next day."

- **Keeping writing and family life separate:** "My family is my priority, and I work my writing into my family life. Writing is my creative outlet, time just for me, my escape. I try to make sure the two do not collide by setting times for writing that are inviolate, but knowing that if my family needs me, I'll just have to try again tomorrow."

- **Advice for new authors:** "Join or start a writer's group. The feedback and support you will receive will be invaluable. Also, take writing classes, as they will really help you with structure. Most importantly, write, write, and write."

- **Pitfalls to watch out for:** "Feeling frustrated over writer's block or rejection? Just keep on going. Creativity is an ongoing process, and you have to be flexible but strict about your commitment — even when negative events occur in your life."

Chapter **6**

Starting with a Great Idea

What are some good ideas for children's books, and how do you come up with them? This chapter talks about generating ideas and starting to write. We show you how to come up with ideas by doing activities and trying to look at the world in different ways. In this chapter, you can also figure out how to use brainstorming to create additional ideas. And if you get that dreaded disease — writer's block — we help you work through that, too.

Once Upon a Time: Coming Up with an Idea

If you're like many aspiring children's book writers, before you actually begin the writing process, you may already have an idea you've always wanted to write about. On the other hand, maybe you have no specific ideas and are looking for a way to address your deep-seated yearning to communicate with children. Or perhaps you've always wanted to be a published writer, and you have this curious notion that because children's picture books are relatively short (how hard can five spreads or 32 pages be to write?), writing for children must be the easiest way to get published.

You have to decide whether your story is going to be fiction or nonfiction. Fiction is writing that comes from your imagination; it's made up. Nonfiction is writing that's based on a true event, or a real-life person or time in history, and verifiable facts. We cover the elements of writing nonfiction in Chapter 13, but nonfiction writing can certainly benefit from the basics we delve into in this chapter. If you're writing fiction, on the other hand, definitely read through this chapter.

Whatever moved you to pick up this book, having an idea starts you off in the process of actually writing your story. But guess what? Even if you don't have an idea, you can still start writing because ideas and writing go together. Ideas lead to writing, and writing can generate ideas. But writers have to start somewhere, so we start with ideas.

An idea is like a seed ready to be planted. With the right soil and fertilizers, it can develop into a strong plant, surviving many seasons and countless generations. In other words, the right idea can lead to a masterpiece of a story — one that brings joy to children for years to come.

REMEMBER

A children's book idea is just a seed, a kernel, a morsel. It doesn't need to be complicated, or long, or even developed. It just has to be a notion of something relating to children that you think you can spend a lot of time and effort working on. And even if you love an idea at first and find out you don't later, don't fret; you never have to stay married to any idea that you don't adore. You can just chuck it and move on to a better one.

But how do you come up with an idea that really moves you? One that fills you with the passion you need to skip through the writing process with anticipation and glee? We give you a few tips in the following sections.

Relying on specific ideas rather than big ones

Many new writers figure they have to have a big idea to get started writing a children's book. Big ideas are the ones you remember from high school English that involve such grand, overarching concepts as good versus evil and man (or woman) versus nature — the concepts your teacher assured you were in Shakespeare's mind when he tackled each and every one of his plays. Although you can indeed break down most ideas in the universe as simply as man versus himself, where's the fun in those concepts? How many children's books do you think sell based on the pitch, "I've written a sweeping epic poem about child versus nature in iambic pentameter"? None.

So now that you've dumped the big ideas, focus on the more specific and less grand. More specific ideas don't involve the entire universe but a narrower subset of the world. You can carefully define these ideas and nail them down in one descriptive sentence, such as

>> Six-year-old anteaters are having a hard time adjusting to life in anteater kindergarten.

>> Eight-year-old princesses can't imagine kissing a frog, much less pledging their lives to one.

You may cry, "But that subject/concept/idea has been written about so many times before! Why bother doing it again?" Good question. Someone else has almost certainly written about nearly every idea you generate. So why bother indeed?

Here's why: You can probably name dozens of books about a young boy's adventures in a magical world filled with witches, and warlocks, and talking animals. But are any of them quite like J.K. Rowling's Harry Potter series (Arthur A. Levine Books)? We don't think so, either. The way to make an old idea yours is to research the competition, make sure you don't copy, and write from the heart.

Tapping into your own experiences

You've had experiences in your life that could make great stories. It's all in the way you look at those experiences and memories. Many successful children's book authors rely on personal experiences to provide them with ideas they can develop into fun and compelling books. Dig deep into your childhood; try to recall the events and moments that were so intense the memory can still bring the feelings you had then to the forefront. For example, remember

>> When your mom told you the family was moving to another part of the city — the day after you finally found a best friend and pinkie swore to be pals forever?

>> The night your parents came home from a trip to a foreign land carrying twin babies that were now your new brothers?

>> Feeling small and scared as you hid under the sheet, convinced the monsters hiding in the closet were going to get you?

Here are some types of experiences to consider writing about:

>> **Cultural:** Do you have a unique perspective into your culture or your cultural history? Perhaps you can mine this rich trove of possibilities for something you want to write about.

>> **Family-oriented:** Families are always top in the list of issues explored in children's books. Do you want to delve into a particular family issue? Children are interested in siblings, divorce, grandparents, moving away, adoption, and many other topics. Can you mine your life for a family issue that you think children could relate to?

>> **Adventure:** Have you been on a trip or adventure that you want to develop into a story? Perhaps you've traveled to an exotic place that most children don't know about or have never visited. Or maybe you've gone skydiving, or parasailing, or windsurfing, and you think that children would thrill at the idea of those activities. Think deeply about places you've been and things you've done that affected your life in a positive way. You can share that story in a children's book.

THE HEART OF YOUR STORY: THEME

The *theme* is the subject of the story, its central core, its heart. Most themes can be expressed in a phrase or sentence at most. Common themes for children's books include the old standby, love, plus themes of overcoming problems, dealing with change, getting reassurance, reaching achievements and developmental milestones, and becoming independent. The best themes are simple, easy to understand, and applicable to most children at some time or another in their lives.

When choosing a theme, you need to keep in mind where your target audience is developmentally. To be appropriate, themes for young children have to take into account their emotional growth, interests, ability to comprehend increasingly complex issues, and limited reading ability (depending on format, which we fill you in on in Chapter 2). Themes for older children can still embrace the same issues, but you have to flesh them out with more depth and complexity.

Be sure to choose a theme that really excites you, one you can feel passionate about — no matter how many rewrites you have to go through. It's all well and good to write a story with the theme of reassurance, but if you're really more interested in writing about a child dealing with change, do the latter!

Digging through childhood mementos

Got a diary from when you were little? What about a box of old school papers? Maybe a trunk or dusty suitcase packed with art and class projects? If you can find any one of these, we guarantee that you can get ideas for stories while the memories come flooding back. Jot down whatever comes to your mind: bits of information, names of classmates or special friends, field trips or projects you found, trouble you got into — you can potentially develop whatever flows into your mind into a book.

Flipping through a photo album

Looking at an old photo album can help you come up with good ideas by reminding you of childhood experiences. Your own baby or childhood photo album is a good start.

Peruse the photographs until you find one that strikes you as compelling. Then ask yourself some of these questions about the child in the photo, writing the answers while you go:

>> Who is the child? (If you don't know their name, give them one that seems to fit.)

>> When and where do you suppose the photo was taken?

>> What are they doing at that moment? (If the surroundings in the photo don't give you any clues, make up something.)

>> How do they feel about what's going on? (Does their body language or facial expression suggest anything right away?)

>> Why are they feeling that way? (Are they scared? Happy? Put off? Proud? Unsure?) What could have caused their reaction?

>> Is there someone else in the photo who's affecting the child? What did that person do that may have caused the child's expression?

Looking at an old picture of herself, Lisa came up with these answers to the preceding questions:

> That's me! I look about three years old. I'm sitting on a blanket at the beach. I'm holding a bucket up to the camera as if to say, "Look at this!" I seem to be very excited. I don't recall what was in the bucket, but perhaps something alive, like a sand crab. The only other person with me is the one who is taking the picture, and that must have been my dad because my mom detests the beach.

What idea did that photo generate? Lisa can recall when she was young feeling very strongly about protecting all animals, no matter how small, and sensing it was a very important job only she could be trusted with. Perhaps she could use that recalled emotion to write about a child who goes to the beach and discovers a bunch of sea creatures who can speak. They tell her their world is endangered and they need her to save it. They try to get her to follow them to an undersea kingdom only children can see. When she follows them and her feet touch the water, the entire world changes, she develops a fin where her feet used to be, and she finds herself breathing underwater like a fish. Having this new talent allows her to explore where children have never been before — and the story goes on from there. It may not be the most original idea in the world, but it's a totally viable story idea, which serves as a warm-up to more story ideas.

Drawing from other children's experiences

Perhaps your memories of childhood are so fuzzy they're practically nonexistent — or you just wish they were. You certainly don't have to limit your-self to your own childhood experiences. You could write a scenario the way you *wish* it had happened. If, as an adult, you've had experiences with children and you think those experiences are important and interesting, you can use them for ideas. Maybe you're acquainted with a child who's dealing with a particular issue, such as the death of a sibling or a divorce, and you can't find a book that addresses their problem in a way you like. What a great idea for a book! Or maybe you know a child who's a fascinating character and simply must have adventures written around their unique personality.

Pulling ideas from the world around you

Open your eyes. Look around you. Really pay attention to your life. What do you see? What's going on with children today that you find interesting? What have you read or seen about children that grabs your attention?

Do you know of an issue you want to explore? Perhaps you think a political, soci-ological, or historical issue would make a great children's book. Do you think something going on in the world today needs addressing? If so, good — because many books that deal with world issues make it onto the bestsellers lists. Can you find a way to get into an issue that children care deeply about?

When you read magazines or newspapers, read with the intent of finding ideas for children's books in the content. When you watch TV, search for stories that have kid appeal. (We take you into a child's world and help you figure out what may appeal to children in Chapter 7.) Start looking at the world with writer's eyes — eyes that see everything as an idea or a possible subject.

For example, Lisa once read an article about how researchers think the teen brain grows and develops. While Lisa read, a thought popped into her head: What if a teenager re-created Mary Shelley's Frankenstein monster in robot form from used computer parts? Lisa understands the impulse many teenagers have to gain control of their lives in one way or another, so she likes the idea of a teenage scientist attempting to create a robot monster to wreak havoc on their world. You may say that Lisa's idea has nothing to do with the article and has been done before, but those facts don't matter. One day, Lisa might use the idea to write a fresh story based on it. And even if she doesn't, at least she's generating ideas — one of the first critical steps in the writing process.

TIP

When researching ideas for children's books, read other books in the genre that you love, but don't rely on the books you read as a child. Find books published in the last five years that have sold well. Ask your librarian or a local bookseller about titles in that genre that have captured the imaginations of today's children. If you get stuck, you can always check out *Story Sparkers: A Creativity Guide for Children's Writers* by Debbie Dadey and Marcia Thornton Jones (Writer's Digest Books). This reference book is an oldie but a goodie.

Stumped? Break through with Brainstorming

Brainstorming is a creative technique in which you freely express random thoughts and ideas on a subject in the hopes of coming up with a creative solution. It's a process that takes your brain's inventive energy, focuses it on a subject, and then lets it open up so that ideas can flow out of you.

REMEMBER

The key to brainstorming is gathering as many ideas as you can in a relatively short amount of time, withholding judgment about their merits until later. When you're brainstorming, focus on the quantity of the ideas you're generating, not the quality. You want your imagination to be as free as a child's — and children's imaginations are unfettered by judgment because they aren't bound by the constraints adults live by.

The purpose of a brainstorming session, whether you conduct one by yourself or with others, is to amass bits of information you can then cull down into usable ideas at a later time. The best brainstorming sessions are ones in which you allow yourself to think thoughts as crazy, outlandish, far-fetched, and miraculous as possible. When you don't constrain your thinking by what you know or think is plausible — instead allowing yourself to go wild, cross boundaries, and turn the world upside-down — you're using brainstorming for what it can truly offer: interesting information to morph into great ideas somewhere down the road.

The following sections provide helpful brainstorming ideas to get you started.

Doing it all by yourself

Do you have a ritual that you follow when you want to come up with new ideas? For Peter, the best solo brainstorming occurs when he's in the shower. That's where his very best ideas come to him. Something about hot water pouring over his head — the sound, the heat, the steady pulsing — simultaneously focuses and frees his thoughts, allowing his brain to roam and generate ideas. Lisa gets ideas while trolling huge gift shows and toy fairs. All those knickknacks somehow get her brain going, and she always fills up a notebook with a lot of notes about what she sees and what she imagines creating.

Follow these steps for a simple approach to brainstorming by yourself (don't try this in the shower; electronic tablets tend to dislike water):

1. **Find a quiet place.**

   You need a spot where you can be free of distractions for at least 15 minutes.

2. **Grab a timer plus something to write on.**

   You can use either a big pad of paper and a writing tool, a tablet with a Notes app and a stylus, or your laptop's document creator.

3. **Set your timer for 15 minutes, and then start writing down every story idea you can think of.**

   TIP

   If you have trouble getting started, picture a child and try to take that child on a trip to experience as many different things as you can imagine.

   Your ideas may be similar to stories you already know, or they may be totally new. Don't judge an idea; just write it down and move on to the next one.

4. **When your 15 minutes are up, stop writing and look at your ideas.**

   Although many of your ideas may not prove usable for stories in the long run, chances are you have a gem or two hidden in the pages generated by your brainstorming session.

When you go back to your lists (we hope you make time to engage in brainstorming every so often in order to have multiple lists), you may find one of the ideas has potential. You know an idea is worth pursuing if reviewing it inspires in you ways to expand it, if you can't stop thinking about it, or if it ignites some sort of passion in you. That's when you know you can write about that idea in a heartfelt and sincere manner.

You have to care about an idea to make the act of expanding it into a story fun. No matter how uniquely fabulous an idea may seem, if you don't care about it, you can't work with it. The writer next door might be able to use it, but not you. At least, not at the moment.

Giving free association a whirl

One way to brainstorm about a particular subject is to free associate, meaning writing down all the words you can think of that are even randomly associated with a starting word or phrase. Free association works great when you have a very vague idea that you want to solidify. Say you want to write about a bunny rabbit. To free associate, you write down all the words you can think of related to bunny rabbit. You can write them in a column or write bunny rabbit in the center of a piece of paper and use arrows to point to the words radiating out from it like spokes on a wheel. There are also apps you can use to do this on your smartphone, tablet, or laptop.

Off the top of our heads, we can free associate the following from bunny rabbit: toothy, furry, fluffy tail, fast, a lot of sisters and brothers, jumpy, hoppy, long ears, twitchy nose, timid, whiskers, long paws, jackrabbit, hare, white, brown, lop ears, claws. You can also list as many opposites to those words as you can think of because a lot of the drama of a story later comes from conflict, which is often generated from opposites clashing in some way (you can find out all about conflict in Chapter 9). Some opposites we might list include: toothless, bald, tailless, slow, fierce, only child (well, only bunny).

The more free associating you do, the more your vague idea forms into a solid idea. Later, when you're ready to write, come back to your lists and see whether any of these words help you with character development (more on creating your characters in Chapter 8).

Taking up journaling

Not all solo brainstorming is done in one session. Sometimes, idea brainstorming is done over time. A very popular and common way to record your ideas as they come to you is to engage in journal writing. Why? Because journaling is a great way to free up your mind and create a living record of your life that you can go back to again and again to mine for ideas.

Brainstorming in journals falls into a few categories:

>> **Free-form journaling:** Writing for the sheer joy (or pain) of writing. No agenda, no exercise, just translating thoughts into words that you put onto screen or paper. Some folks like to begin journaling by writing about whatever prevailing emotion is driving them at the moment. Others like to record dreams and use them as problem-solving devices — attempting to decipher hidden meanings and possible connections to waking life. Others like to use a journal as a listening post. The point is, there's no structure to what you do, no rules — anything goes. Whatever you decide to write about, free-form journaling helps you develop ideas and get used to writing on a regular basis.

REMEMBER

Regardless of your approach or topic, you must follow one rule about free-form journaling: Thou must not judge thyself, nor even reread what thou hast written, until thou art done for the day. This writing is intended for only your eyes to help you come up with ideas for your children's books, so feel free to let yourself go. Writing in a journal can be a joyful experience. And before you can discipline yourself as a writer, you need to feel the freedom of writing for the joy of writing.

>> **Structured journaling:** Are you the type of person who prefers structured activities? Some writers like to take a formal approach to journaling, keeping a journal restricted to just one area of interest. Start with a specific theme, an exercise, a writing prompt, or a goal, and write to expand on it. For example, they may keep a food journal, a dream journal, a journal written only when it's raining — or a journal of ideas.

TIP

Aside from helping you get into the habit of writing, structured journaling leaves you with a potential treasure trove of ideas to draw from during your long career in writing children's books. Who knows? One day, a children's book starring a toothsome, slow, only bunny looking for a mother figure may bear your name on its cover. (And join the shelf alongside Bunnicula and P.J. Funnybunny!)

Companion journaling: If you're really brave and have a trustworthy colleague or writing partner, share a journal, leaving a space after each of your entries for commentary or companion entries by your writing partner. If you want to make it really easy, you can keep an online shared journal. (Google Docs is a free and easy tool for sharing and collaborating on writing projects.) With the idea that two heads are better than one, companion journaling is a good way to brainstorm with a friend. At the very least, you may be surprised at what you read.

Buddying up to the buddy system

Brainstorming with writing buddies is a fun way to generate ideas. You and your buddies agree to come to a meeting prepared to discuss current events, trends, changes in the world — whatever you want — with the understanding that these issues should all revolve around the lives of children. Then steer the conversation toward coming up with ideas that may lead to stories or books for children.

In a round-robin fashion, each person gets to bring up their first topic of interest and present it to the group for discussion. So if we were playing the brainstorming game, it would go something like this:

LISA: I really want to write something about fairies, but I can't think of anything new.

PETER: Will your fairies fly? Will they have magical powers? Will they speak?

LISA: Maybe they've forgotten how to fly. Maybe they're like children who've lost the ability to have fun. Or maybe they're just uncoordinated and can't get their wings to work.

PETER: Where do they hail from? And how exactly are they magical? How are they different in terms of the magic they can do versus what the magic trolls, gnomes, elves, and other creatures of that ilk can do?

LISA: Or maybe fairies aren't the only ones who have forgotten their magic. Maybe the entire world of these creatures is in crisis. I really like something about getting their magic back — maybe bringing in other creatures. I like gargoyles. I'll add those to my list.

PETER: I had a particular idea in mind. I wanted to write about children who stay in afterschool programs. I wanted to start with a group of kids who are sort of abandoned between the time school closes and the time their parents pick them up, and they go on all sorts of adventures related to learning.

LISA: Be careful not to make the learning part too obvious or preachy. Maybe the adventures involve magic in the sense they can travel to space or to foreign countries or inside an acorn or whatever. But I wonder what they have to do to get there? Is there science involved in the travel part, or do they just magically arrive there and then the particular adventure begins?

PETER: I don't know yet. I'll write that down. And maybe they have to solve problems set way back in time, going all the way back to the dinosaurs. They could explore age-old questions we all wonder about, such as how the dinosaurs disappeared and what made ice ages occur.

LISA: Sounds like The Magic School Bus series! I really like those ideas. Everyone finds time travel intriguing. Maybe these kids each have special powers that help them look at things differently, like scientists do.

PETER: Yeah. I like that. Okay, we've both got something to start with!

Brainstorming by going back and forth between you and your writing buddies can generate and hone ideas, helping you develop them much faster than most writers can accomplish alone. Also, if your writing partners are as brutal as ours are, they tell you when your ideas are lame and underdeveloped, and they encourage (or bully) you into going back to the drawing board. After you get an idea that you feel strongly about and that your partner(s) thinks rocks, you can get started writing your children's story — or at least you can go to Chapter 7 and discover what to do next.

Asking the advice of classmates and writing professionals

Writing classes can really help you hone your writing skills in many ways, including giving you access to an expert in the field who can tell you if, idea-wise, you're headed off into a place you probably shouldn't go. Writing teachers are great resources.

You can also brainstorm with your classmates to get ideas, and then go over those ideas with your teacher, who can help you figure out which ones work better for you. Or you can brainstorm alone with your teacher and have them help you work out which ideas have the most promise in terms of uniqueness and interest to you. (You're the one investing a lot of energy to make the idea come alive as a story, after all.)

Online children's book writing courses attached to major universities can also give you some great experience and knowledge. In an online course, you can get individual interaction with a teacher without ever having to leave the comfort of your ergonomic desk chair.

Check out these resources before you invest any time or effort in them, making sure they offer what you need and involve experts who can really help you reach your goals as a writer.

TIP

If you're not taking a class that gives you easy access to a writing teacher, see whether you can pay a professional writing teacher for an hour of their time. Just make sure they know the specific purpose of the session. Also, come prepared so that the meeting is productive and you get the most for your money.

At writing conferences, you can get ideas and hone them into an actual book. Writing retreats, usually in bucolic and restful settings, are a great way to develop your ideas and shape them into a viable manuscript. Get feedback and nurture your creativity through writing workshops, which you can find online or at some universities (or you can start your own workshop by using SCBWI's lists of regional chapters or the Authors Guild Discussion Groups pages). You can even get mentorship for your completed manuscript at Pitch Wars, which we discuss in more detail in Chapter 17.

Seeking help from your audience

Children themselves are a wonderful resource when it comes to ideas. Brainstorming with them, however, needs to be directed because many kids love every idea you present to them (bless their hearts).

If you're visiting a classroom, consider bringing a list of ideas and generating discussion based on these topics. Brief the teacher beforehand by sharing your list and reiterating the purpose of your brainstorming session. We guarantee that if the children are verbal enough to carry on a conversation, and if you can get the teacher to facilitate based on your list of topics, you can find out stuff about your topics that you never even considered.

A typical session of brainstorming picture book ideas with a group of four-year-olds may sound something like this:

LISA: So I was thinking about writing about little sisters and brothers and how you get along.

CHILDREN: (Silence; no response.)

LISA: Like, if you have a little brother, how you manage to get along with him.

CHILDREN: (Silence; no response.)

LISA: (Getting a little desperate, trying not to let it show.) For example, what would you think if I wrote a story about a little brother who disappeared, and his older brother had to find him?

CHILD 1: You mean his big brother would save him?

CHILD 2: Like a hero?

LISA: (Relieved.) Yes! Exactly. Would save him —

CHILD 1: (Interrupting.) — from a mean fire-breathing dragon? Who would melt the little brother because he took toys from you and broke them?

CHILD 2: And you didn't have enough time to save him before he got scared some by the dragon. So he would drop the toys he stole from your room?

LISA: Yes. And maybe there would be a princess —

CHILD 3: I like princesses!

CHILD 1: As long as they aren't wearing dresses because you can trip on dresses when you're climbing the tower to save your little brother.

LISA: Then maybe the princess could be a brave one who can help you find your brother. But first you have to find the magic key.

CHILD 3: The key to the castle? Or to mom's car? Because sometimes my little brother takes the car keys and drools all over them.

CHILDREN: Eeeeew!

Cross our hearts and hope to die, you can't ever leave a classroom without at least one great idea that makes your fingers itch to get writing.

HOW BARNEY SALTZBERG GETS HIS BEST BOOK IDEAS

Whatever exercises you choose to help you generate ideas and get started writing, you need to put pen to paper (or fingers to keyboard) and just go. Take it from Barney Saltzberg, acclaimed creator of children's songs, as well as successful children's book writer and illustrator. He tells it like it is about ideas and writing:

- **How Barney gets his best book ideas:** "There's no formula. If I had one, every book I write would be a hit! Ideas come to me in many different ways. Sometimes, I'll hear something and say, "That's a great title for a book or a song," and that's how it begins. One of my favorites is my Neal Porter Holiday House book, *One of These Is Not Like the Others*. It is based on my reaction to the old *Sesame Street* video and song, "One of these things is not like the others. One of these things just doesn't belong." The notion always intrigued me. Yes, three noodles and a paintbrush are different, but rather than point that out (which is obvious), I wanted to find a way to connect these different things. An example: three pigs and a wolf. The pigs, at first glance, look a little timid, looking at a wolf. The page reveal is they are in a band together making music. One of these is not like the other — and that's the way we rock! The book is published in six languages, so clearly the sentiment struck a chord. We need stories that model connection."

- **Brainstorming with others (or not):** "I try to brainstorm with other people from time to time, but personally, I find that I need to sit with whatever I'm working on and brainstorm by myself. It works the best. It's not a bad idea to get someone else's viewpoint, but you really have to trust them to have the same way of thinking as you do, and that's nearly impossible in my case."

- **Starting with the format or the book idea:** "I begin with an idea and see which format it fits into later."

- **Recording and evaluating ideas:** "Sometimes I find myself making notes on scraps of papers, napkins, or on my computer. It depends where I am when the idea hits me. I always think they're good ideas. It's only when I've worked on them for a long time that I know if they will truly work or not."

- **Developing an idea you feel good about:** "Since I'm a writer and an illustrator, my working habits are different from writers who only write. Sometimes I'll be writing and then find a piece of paper and start drawing the characters I'm writing about. The body language and facial expressions of those characters sometimes color how the written story develops. Mostly, I just force myself to sit with my computer and write and write and write."

- **The dreaded writer's block:** "Unless you're talking about a neighborhood full of writers and that's where you live — on the writers' block — I personally think there's really no such thing as writer's block. Only a writer who's avoiding writing. I guarantee that if you sit down and just write, things will happen for you! Will everything you write be great? Absolutely not. But you're writing."

- **Advice for coming up with great ideas for children's books:** "You have to start writing. Write from within yourself, as a child. It sounds corny to say, 'Write from your inner child.' But that's where the voice is. Don't set out to write an entire book. Just make short sentences, blurting out anything and everything. Eventually, something will pop out. Recess. Homework. Walking home from school. Playing in the yard. The neighbor next door. Something will trigger a flood of memories from which to start a story."

For more sage advice from Barney Saltzberg, flip over to Chapters 7 and 15.

Going to the source

If you haven't recently spent any time around children, why not head back to school? You could be there in an official capacity, perhaps as the coach at a community center or a nearby school, or even as a teacher at your local church, synagogue, or mosque. Many volunteers give their time and expertise for altruistic reasons, and you can, too. For more insights on classroom observation and interaction check out Chapter 7.

REMEMBER

The more time you spend around children, the more your ideas reflect their world — and the more your writing speaks to them.

Or perhaps you prefer to take the backdoor approach. If purposefully trying to generate ideas instantly freeze-dries your brain, some other unrelated but enjoyable creative endeavor may melt down your resistance. Consider taking a class in painting, pottery, drawing, woodwork, beading, gardening, cooking — any art or craft class that may interest you. Using your hands and eyes in creative activities other than writing can actually help your creativity, which in turn helps you think of good ideas, which in turn helps your writing — even if you can't make the connection right away. (Bonus: It also relaxes you enough to help you come up with new ideas.)

TIP

Check out websites like skillshare.com, thrivecreativecommunity.com, writingandwellness.com, or createtv.com. These are great resources to peruse and encourage creativity as a lifestyle choice.

Checking the "best of" book lists

"Best of" lists offer a great way to see what's generating interest and accolades out there. And current ones can help you get ideas for *comps* (comparable books) to make sure your idea hasn't been recently written about.

For recently published books that kids like, try the IRA/CBC (International Reading Association and Children's Book Council) Children's Choices list at www. cbcbooks.org. For librarians' "best of" lists, try the Notable Children's Books list on the ALA (American Librarians Association) website, www.ala.org. And booksellers keep track of what's cool, too, so check the American Booksellers Association's Book Sense lists at www.bookweb.org. Even Goodreads offers best of lists every year in every format and genre of children's writing.

Twice yearly, Publishers Marketplace comes out with its Buzz Books lists for the upcoming spring/summer and fall/winter seasons. You can download these lists for free at Amazon (www.amazon.com) after Publishers Marketplace releases them. You can preorder some of these books, or you can keep an eye out for them and pounce on their publication dates. Alternatively, you can try to get them at your local library.

Fighting Writer's Block

Picture this: You have a great story idea that has kept you writing for days. On the fifth day, you're happily writing when the doorbell rings. You answer it to discover a package delivery. You sign for the package and return to your desk, and then you realize that you've completely lost your train of thought. Minutes pass. Then a half-hour. Then you notice dust in the corner of the room you hadn't seen before, so you grab the broom. Next, you're at the kitchen sink washing dishes. Finally, you return to the computer, but you realize your writing has come to a crashing halt. You're paralyzed in front of a computer screen that seems to be actively mocking you. And no matter how many times you straighten up your desktop and change the pretty background pictures, you can't seem to write a word.

REMEMBER

Getting stuck is something that all writers — no matter how skilled they are or how much practice they've had — experience from time to time. The writer's brain is like a mighty river — usually it flows along smoothly, but sometimes a 40-foot barge sinks right in the middle, causing the river to back up and the words to stop flowing.

If you get stuck long enough, you can experience those two little words guaranteed to strike fear or dread in the heart of anyone who has ever faced a deadline or had to earn a living from their words: writer's block.

Based on some research, we found out that not everyone believes in the existence of writer's block. (See the sidebar "The psychology of writer's block," in this chapter, for the counterargument.)

Other people even think that psychologists created writer's block to take advantage of writers' insecurities and make piles of dough from those writers.

We think writer's block does exist (sort of, but in a way that you can resolve immediately). It's simply a condition that requires one of two remedies:

>> **Take a break.** Give yourself permission to get away from the pressure of writing for a while until the urge to write strikes again — but not indefinitely. If the urge doesn't strike within a few days, try the following remedy.

>> **Do some writing exercises.** Use writing exercises to get your writing juices flowing again. For example, simply write down anything that comes to mind about anything in your life. It doesn't have to relate to your story at all. And don't edit, just write freely. This exercise is just a little ruse to get you back into writing itself. Surprisingly, the simple act of just writing can bring you back to where you need to be: working on your children's book. (We go over a lot of ways to get writing in the section "Stumped? Break through with Brainstorming," earlier in this chapter.)

If you find yourself plagued by writer's block, flip to the writing exercises in Part 3.

Consider making ideation part of your writing process, which helps prevent writer's block in the first place. Doing these exercises regularly keeps your writing fresh and fun. Not every idea that is generated is worth turning into a story, but every idea is worth keeping. An Idea Box is a great place to keep your lists, creative notes, and sketches — keeping one in your writing space can be very inspirational. It's also a good way to track your progress and development as a writer. The more you do this, the better you'll get at discerning a good story from a so-so story.

REMEMBER

Do writing exercises for fun. For laughs. For the sake of doing them. Writer's block has two parts: losing the urge to write and being unsure about what to write. So exercise your imagination — a very important muscle in getting over writer's block and finding out how to master the process of writing.

THE PSYCHOLOGY OF WRITER'S BLOCK

Ever wonder why your brain gets stuck? We have (more than once or twice), so we did some research on writer's block. Much to our surprise, writer's block is not the result of watching soap operas on TV (which is very good news for Peter) or of eating too many carbs, or from our enemies sticking pins into twin voodoo dolls crudely designed in our images (though we're still a bit suspicious about that one).

According to the folks in white lab coats who spend their working days and nights researching this phenomenon, writers actually get stuck when a temporary disconnect occurs between the brain's frontal lobes (located behind your forehead) and temporal lobes (located behind your ears). Among other tasks, your frontal lobes act as your writing organizer and editor, and your temporal lobes control your understanding of words and come up with those fabulous ideas sure to capture the interest of your publisher.

When your frontal lobes take charge — pushing aside the ideas set forth by your temporal lobes — you quickly find yourself stuck (bad). When your temporal lobes take charge, the words flow unimpeded, fast, and furious (good). So can you do anything to help your brain move through the occasional slow spots?

Bang your head against the closet door really hard. (Just kidding!)

Pay attention to what kinds of events in your life or environment seem to lead to writer's block — and what kinds of action make it go away. Then do less of the former and more of the latter. (Yeah, yeah — we know that solution sounds ridiculously easy, but remember: Not everyone believes in writer's block anyway. And how much do you want to bet that those who don't believe in it don't suffer from it, either?)

Chapter **7**

Researching Your Audience and Subject

The best children's books have some grounding in a child's reality, and the best way to discover what that reality is — rather than what you imagine it to be — is to get out there and explore. In this chapter, we take a look at some of the best places to find out more about kids and about the people standing between your manuscript and the children you're trying to reach: how they think, how they act, what they like, what they think is gross versus what they think is cool, and what proves perennially popular.

We also touch a bit on researching your topic itself. If your subject falls into the nonfiction realm, you have a lot of facts to get straight. But even if your subject is fictional, you may choose to ground certain aspects of it in reality — maybe a reality about which you don't know much, such as Victorian England or the civil rights movement of the 1960s. Or perhaps one of your characters is a beaver, and you have no idea what beavers eat or where they live. In this chapter, we also give you some strategies to dig into the secret lives of children. You must go even further when it comes to presenting the facts, which have to be right on target. This chapter helps you get there.

Hanging Out with Kids

REMEMBER

If you're writing about kids and the issues that they deal with in everyday life, you want to make sure to write from their perspective. Many new writers make the mistake of writing from a grown-up perspective. As a children's book writer, you need to keep in mind that the children you're writing for want entertainment, not parenting. You need to capture their imaginations and bring them into your world, not teach them lessons about right and wrong. No one likes a lecture — especially not children, who are probably already getting more than their share of lectures at home and school.

Of course, you also have to remember that children likely are both your target audience and the subjects of the book you're writing, which means the information, the descriptions, and the language have to be accurate. If you want your child characters to be believable, you need to know how children talk, what they wear, what they do, and how they go about doing it. Every detail matters.

If you're panicking right now because the only thing you can remember from your childhood is that you wore smaller clothing or loved peanut butter and jelly sandwiches, never fear. You can gain perspective on kids simply by hanging out with them. The following sections offer a few ideas for how to do just that.

Going back to school

For at least nine months of the year, Monday through Friday (in most parts of the world), from approximately 8 a.m. to 3 p.m., children attend (some may claim are held prisoner in) school, which therefore happens to be a great place to go to do your research. Lucky for you, many teachers are open to having writers come into the classroom. Just be sure you check in with the front office before you start wandering the halls. You may need to sign in, and you may need a school representative to accompany you.

However, health, safety, and security protocols may make getting into the classroom tricky. These days stricter entry is more the norm. Most likely free reign in a school setting will not be granted. It might take some negotiating and more involved discussions with the school administrators about what you are trying to achieve in order to gain access.

If you are able to spend some quality time in a school setting, it can be the perfect research venue. You can make the experience active by leading a project or volunteering for an arts and crafts activity or game, or you can simply lurk passively in a corner, watching and listening. How do the kids dress? How do they interact with one another? What do they say to one another? How do they handle conflict? What toys or games do they prefer, and do the boys play or act differently than the girls do? Is there a time set aside for art? What kind of art do kids create at different ages? What about during lunchtime? Is there gender segregation, and if so, why? If the day includes a rest period, how do the grown-ups make the little beasts adhere to the rules? Do children behave differently upon arrival than they do upon departure?

GET BY WITH A LITTLE HELP FROM YOUR LITTLE FRIENDS

Want to observe thinking, busy, creative children in action inside a preschool or kindergarten classroom? Don't just visit a school empty-handed. Take along all the fixin's for a bookmaking session! You just need

- Five sheets of white construction or card stock paper per child
- One sheet of colored construction or card stock paper per child (not such a dark color that art doesn't show up on it)
- A single-hole punch
- A ball of yarn
- A children's story, either your own or one whose subject matter is similar to yours but that isn't extremely popular (so the kids probably don't know it already)
- Crayons or markers, one complete set per five children or per table

Have each child fold the five white sheets of paper width-wise to create the interior of the book. Then have the children take the colored sheet of construction paper and wrap it around the interior pages. To tie the sheets together (the binding), you are going to punch holes on the left side of the book. Punch the first hole about an inch from the top and 1/4-inch in from the outside folded edge and punch the second hole about an inch from the bottom and 1/4-inch in from the same outside folded edge. Take two pieces of yarn about 8 inches long each and loop one piece through each hole, tying the ends. Voilà! You have a blank book.

Next, read your chosen story aloud to the children. Then tell them you need their help to figure out what happens to the characters next. (Some writers like to leave out the ending in order to fire up their listeners' imaginations.) Together, as a classroom, each child writes the next five spreads (or ten pages) of the book to create either the ending or the sequel to the story. Every child gets to pick a number out of a hat, and you can use those numbers to solicit answers to the questions you want to ask them to get the story going. (The numbers help keep the chaos of many willing participants in check by giving each child a turn in order.) Tell younger kids not to worry unnecessarily about getting the words just right; you want them simply to draw the pictures for the characters.

With older children, do they seem to roam in packs? How are those packs differentiated from one another? Is how someone dresses a big deal? How can you tell? Are the alphas overtly apparent? What do kids have in their lockers? How do they behave with and speak to one another or their teachers?

All this information and more gives you a peek into the lives of real children — the ones that you want to read your book after it gets published. And if you're privileged enough to have your work end up in their hands, you best make sure you haven't misrepresented or miscast them.

Becoming a storyteller

If you want to understand how children in your target age group think, read a book to them and then have a question-and-answer session. You can do this with children who are as young as three or four years of age, depending on how verbal they are and how accustomed they are to speaking in front of other kids. Preschoolers are ideal for this kind of exercise because they love to raise their hands, give their opinions (often in great and meandering detail), and listen to themselves speak to an adult who actually cares to hear what they have to say. Or you can pick older children, such as tweens or teenagers. Whoever you think your target audience is, get information from the actual bodies that fall into that age range.

Regardless of where you go to get the attention of children, make sure you're prepared to present a truly captivating read (trust Lisa, there's nothing more humiliating than reading to an audience that couldn't care less because you can't grab their attention or hold onto it after you get it). Don't just read any random old book — make sure it has a similar subject matter or topic to the book you want to write. Get familiar with the book before you come in to read it to the kids so that you can ask some really good questions afterward.

Also, make sure the kids aren't hungry, tired, or waiting to embark on a bus for a field trip to the observatory or zoo — believe us, you can't compete.

TIP

You don't have to do the actual reading. Bring someone else to do it. Writers who really want to get the most out of the time spent with children turn the time into a partnership of sleuthing. (Peter is Holmes to Lisa's Watson.) When you read out loud, you're probably so engaged in the acts of reading, turning pages, and trying to sound interesting to a child that you can't make adequate observations. That job falls to your partner. Just follow these steps to work as a story-time sleuth:

1. **Seat yourself next to your partner, but off to the side a bit.**

   You need to see the faces and bodies of most of the children listening.

2. **Have your partner read the book aloud while you take notes.**

Be sure to note the following:

- *How the children respond:* At what point in the story do they lean forward in anticipation? Do their faces ever show fear, amazement, or sadness?

- *When the children start fidgeting:* Perhaps the timing or pacing of the story lags at that point, or maybe something about it isn't appropriate for your audience.

- *Where they interrupt or ask questions:* Maybe something in the story isn't clear.

- *What their body language says:* Do they seem interested or bored? Maybe they don't think the story is as great as you originally did.

3. **After you write down everything you can and your partner finishes reading the book, start asking your audience questions.**

What do the children think about the main character? Does your audience like or dislike them and their friends? Do your listeners like the chosen subject? What do they want to hear more of? Do they not like anything in the book? Do they wish they could change anything about the book? Why?

The answers to these questions can tell you a lot about how children of that age approach the subject you want to write about, as well as what issues are relevant to them — and what issues aren't.

TIP

To make the most out of any question-and-answer session with children, formulate good questions that can yield the kind of detail you need as a writer. Questions that result in yes or no answers and don't provide room for elaboration are sucky ones. For good questions, you can start out with the reporter's trusty six, detailing them to your particular needs and concerns:

» **Who:** Ask questions that focus on the main character. Can you (the children) tell me more about this character? Who are they, exactly? What kind of person (animal or object) are they? Are they a good person? A bad person? Do they have any problems? What are those problems? Do they solve the problems? How? How would you suggest the main character solve their problems? What about the supporting characters? What are they like? Do you find them appealing or not? Why?

» **What:** What's the story really about (what is its core or central theme)? What's the main problem that the main character has to solve? Does the main character have good ideas about how to handle themselves in every situation? Why or why not? What happens to make the story interesting or boring? What do you think happened to the main character or their friends after the story ended?

For nonfiction, you have a few more "what" questions to ask. What did you discover about the subject that you didn't know before? What do you find most interesting about that new knowledge? What do you want to find out more about?

>> **When:** When does the story take place? If it happens in the past, could that story happen today? Why or why not?

>> **Where:** Where does the story take place? Is the setting a real place or a pretend place? How can you tell? Could that story have happened where you live? Why or why not?

>> **Why:** Why did you find the story interesting? Why do you think it's important for children to read or hear?

For nonfiction, you can ask: Why do you think children should know about the main character or subject?

>> **How:** How does the main character solve their problem? Can readers use the same solution to solve a similar problem? Why or why not? How do the issues brought up in the story affect you and your friends today?

MONSTERS DON'T TOUCH

I (Lisa) learned one of my most valuable lessons about writing for children of picture book age during a reading. Early on in my career, I had written a story about monsters. These were your run-of-the-mill kind: the ones hanging out under the bed, outside a darkened window, and in the closet. The story's protagonist had to figure out a way to make them all go away so he could get a good night's sleep. The story had been edited by a professional editor friend, vetted by a teacher, and was all ready to submit. But I wanted to see and hear what children might think about monsters, in general.

So I brought two stories about monsters with me on the train. One was written by a famous author. The other was mine. While reading my story aloud to a trio of small children on the way from Providence to Boston one morning, I realized that monsters are allowed (even expected) to be scary, mean, smelly, and generally odious — but they must never, ever actually touch the child protagonist or someone they love. When that happens, the story becomes too scary and makes children cry. At this point, I also realized that children crying on a train echoes in a loud and disturbingly public manner. Now, whose story do you suppose made that horrible faux pas? (Hint: It wasn't the famous author's.) As you can imagine, I have never forgotten that particular lesson — and it has helped guide my writing ever since.

The answers to these questions help you as a writer in so many ways. You get to see how children process information. You get an inkling of what they focus on and the issues that they see as of paramount importance (you may be very surprised). You get to hear about the way they deal with fears or excitement. And, if you're very lucky, certain audience members may veer completely off subject and give you some unexpected but very valuable insider information that you can then use in your writing.

Borrowing a friend's child for a day

Do you feel like you know how your target audience really thinks? Do you consider yourself an expert in children's speech patterns and interests? Unless you work with children on a daily basis or live in captivity with some of your own, you probably don't know how their sinister little minds really work — and you may not be as good at picking up on how they talk as you could be.

Do your writing a favor and make some grateful parent or guardian (very) happy at the same time: Borrow a child for the day to test your theories. Don't just take the kid to a movie, where you can't really observe much of the child's reactions and opinions in the moment. Take them to a museum, a park, a meal — or all of the above. Start a conversation about something the child shows interest in. Engage the child's senses. Then observe and listen.

You can't always get children to open up easily, but you shouldn't have to do any hair pulling. Make your queries about some information you need, such as, "I was wondering, do you know how a bee makes honey? Want to go to the bookstore/library and find out?" You want to engender discussion, getting children to talk about their lives and their feelings, which gives you more information to write about in your book.

TIP

Here's a good trick: Build a comparison between your ridiculous childhood and theirs. For example, "When I was a child, we had to wear orange ties and purple top hats to school every single day. Isn't that silly? What happens at your school that you think is silly?"

When you come home from what we're sure will be an interesting — albeit exhausting — day of research, try to write down everything you can recall about what happened. Then when you go back to developing your idea, you can see how what you discovered adds to or changes the direction of your story.

HOW AUTHOR BARNEY SALTZBERG RESEARCHES BOOK IDEAS

Barney Saltzberg (www.barneysaltzberg.com) is a successful author, illustrator, and children's music performer. Through his varied careers, he's spent plenty of time with children, and he continues to discover more about them with each encounter. Here he explains what he has learned from interacting with children.

- **Insights from visiting children at school:** "Life as a child isn't always as fun as I sometimes remember. Traveling around the country, I've seen children going to school hungry and who don't have any books at home. I find that no matter where they come from and how they live, when we sit down together, they want to sing, and draw, and laugh, and that they all have stories they long to tell."

- **Using the web for research:** "I Google a lot. Sometimes for images, when I need to draw something. Other times, I'll Google a title I think up to see if it's out there already. If it is, I'll look up the book or song and make sure I'm not stepping on someone else's toes. If it's not out there, then I run with it. When I finished a book called *Cornelius P. Mud, Are You Ready for Bed?* (Candlewick Press), I found tons of websites where parents talked about all the things they do in order to put their children to bed at night. It was very helpful in developing my story."

- **Keeping topics (and the book format itself) relevant:** "People are still people. A good story is a good story. You may be blasting aliens on a handheld device, but if a story has soul and speaks truth, readers will be captivated."

- **Guiding writing students when it comes to research:** "I suggest they go to children's bookstores and libraries, find the picture books — and read, and read, and read. When they're done reading, read some more!"

- **Researching at conferences and book conventions:** "I think any place you can go to gather information is great. You'll never use everything you hear and see, but any way you can get information about publishing and about the writing process can be invaluable. Also, it helps to meet other people who are doing what you are doing so you can learn from the authors and illustrators who have made it. It's also helpful to meet your peers, people at your particular level of writing. People like yourself, who are trying to find their way in this field. You'll have plenty of stories to share."

For more words of wisdom from Barney Saltzberg, see Chapters 6 and 15.

Dipping into Popular Culture

Whatever the latest trend, whether it's related to food, fashion, music, toys, games, cartoon characters — you name it — you can bet that kids and their friends will be the first to know about it, if not actually the ones who create it themselves. Why? Three reasons: First, children have an insatiable curiosity and desire to know about the latest and greatest gadget, toy, trend, and so on. Second, advertisers that produce products for children target them mercilessly through television advertising, programming, movies, apps, video games, and more. Third, many children have smartphones today.

Take a dip into pop culture yourself with the information we provide in the following sections. We guarantee you can make your story all the richer with your efforts.

WARNING

No one can spot a faker faster than a kid. Just because you're aware of pop culture and know all the right words, songs, or fashions doesn't mean you can pass for a child. Be sure to not take your pop culture familiarity too far. And that goes for writing dialogue, as well, which we cover in Chapter 10. Using current slang (which may not be current by the time your book comes out) is generally a no-no unless you're writing a book that includes dialect of a certain culture.

Watching kids' TV shows and movies

For a quick way to dip your toes into the prevailing popular culture, watch cartoons — specifically, the recent hot cartoons. Many of these cartoons (think *PAW Patrol* and *The Loud House*) have created their own popular culture (and generated millions of dollars in spin-off toy, game, and app sales in the process). You can find out all about the latest cool animations by scouring entertainment magazines (such as *Entertainment Weekly*), perusing online TV guides, or simply turning on the TV. If you can watch along with children, so much the better.

Kids have access to animation 24/7 through YouTube, apps, and free streaming devices. Also, teens watch animated shows, too, so for the older kids, FX, AdultSwim, and FOX or Nickelodeon have offerings later in the evenings. Netflix and Hulu are also great categorizers of genres and can be good places to dive down the research rabbit hole to find edgier cartoon content like *Rick and Morty* or *Big Mouth.*

Speaking of Disney, it has all those live-action TV shows that have tween audiences — especially girls — mesmerized. What about these characters and story lines prove endlessly entertaining? If you don't know, find out. Disney+ is interesting because you can use it to track the development of content over the decades to see how things have changed and notice directions and risks that are being taken.

Don't forget about animated movies. They've evolved way beyond the Disney fare that you grew up on. Although those old favorites are still out there and going strong on streaming services, today's kids can also find a plethora of fabulous animated movies and *anime* (Japanese animated movies and TV characters). These movies spawn toys, which then spawn more films, which then spawn TV shows and apps. It's a pop-culture wheel that just keeps on spinning.

When you watch children's cartoons or films, pay attention to the lines that generate laughs. Are they verbally subtle, do they bang the audience over the head, or are they largely physical slapstick? In what ways do they suspend reality or bring fantasy into the story line? Which cartoons and films are the most popular? What about them do you think generates this popularity? Also, notice when the adults are laughing versus when the kids are laughing; they can be very different.

Playing kid-focused digital games

The digital age brings kid-friendly games into even the tiniest of hands. In fact, many children growing up today have likely teethed on some electronic handheld device — literally and figuratively. Traditional video game systems that hook up to your TV still exist (think Sony PlayStation, Wii, and Xbox), but you can also find handheld gaming devices such as the Nintendo Switch and the Nintendo DS series, as well as smartphones and tablets that offer hundreds of thousands of apps for kids to play and explore.

Virtual reality (VR) headsets, such as Oculus, are gaining ground as well. Headsets can stand on their own as well as a crossover between phones, tablets, and monitors to include more players into the gaming experience. They are also on the leading edge of next-generation technological expansion and setting the ground for the "metaverse" — the emerging online network of 3D virtual worlds. Believe it or not, kids know about this stuff.

When you watch children play these games (or better yet, when you jump on in and play for yourself), pay attention to the worlds created therein: the characters or avatars that the players create themselves (what they wear, what they do, and what their attitudes are about each other, what are their superpowers), the setting (real, imagined, outer space, a juxtaposition of all three), the story lines (it's not all warfare out there), the music, the gaming goal. (Here's a good one: For what games will children pay out of their own pocket to buy extras such as tokens or virtual currency.) All of these factors give clues about what children are really into, how they think, and what really grabs their attention.

For the older kids, pay attention to who they want to invite into their game and why. Do they want so-and-so for his strategy tactics? Or what's-her-name for her dexterity with utilizing a certain weapon? Or with another guy who has already beat the next level which they want to skip over ASAP because the level beyond that is more interesting. Super valuable information.

Also check out gaming companies like Activision Blizzard and Take-Two Interactive Software to find out what is in their products pipeline to be released over the next 12 months. Check in on a gaming recycling store that specializes in selling used games such as GameStop and see what the best sellers are, what flies off the shelves before they can even tag them?

Reading parenting and family magazines and blogs

Parenting and family magazines and blogs can help you dip into pop culture. Within their pages and on their sites, you can find all sorts of articles and commentaries that tackle topics of concern to parents and children. Whether they talk about how to deal with a teenager who idolizes pop singers (and who wants to bare her belly button at school or wear a dress constructed of raw beef just like her idol) or discuss which licensed-character piñatas are hot (and which are not), you can find plenty of thoughtful references to children's issues.

Major parenting and family magazines (each with an accompanying website that's chock-full of content) include *Family Circle, FamilyFun* (now part of *Parents* magazine), *Working Mother, Today's Parent,* and *Highlights.* While you flip through some of these magazines, note the advertisers and the types of products that they're selling or talking about. This is how kids are hooked into wanting to buy.

But in terms of research, reading parenting and family magazines and blogs allows you to glean details about what parents are really talking about, the issues that concern them, the new objects or trends children are introducing their parents to, and the like. Kids torture their parents daily with all the new information and gadgets they bring home, and if you want to know about those newfangled things, read about parents trying to wrap their brains around it all. You can find this type of research insightful — and often hilarious. And then when you go to write your story, the details about what's offered in all these sources that you choose to include can help you create a more realistic world. Conversely, the details you choose to leave out can also make a big statement about the world you're trying to create, be it reality- or fantasy-based.

Perusing pop culture magazines and blogs

What better place to get instantly steeped in popular culture than by buying and reading a stack of magazines that worship at the altar of all things celebrity and pop? If you want to get a quick course on pop culture, you can't go wrong with *Entertainment Weekly, People, Paste, Star, Wired, Seventeen,* and *J-14.* Children are the early adopters of most new technologies, trends, attitudes, and patterns of speech. If you want to see what your tween and teen audience members wear, read about the music they're listening to, find out about the celebrities they're obsessed with, become familiar with the TV shows and movies they're raving or ranting about, get inundated by the same advertisers that are after their dollars — these magazines can get you the lowdown.

Many blogs cover pop culture. Research them online to find the ones that you think best reflect the current trends, and then read to your heart's content.

Look for items that have relevance to your topic. Are you writing about a female main character? Research what girls of that age are playing with, wearing, and talking about. Thinking of writing a relationship story for teens? Look for articles that focus on what relationship issues between modern teens really involve. Those personality and love quizzes in teen magazines are great for clues into this arena, by the way! And while magazines like *Seventeen* may reflect an aspirational approach rather than one based on the reality of high school, it still offers useful information.

Surfing the web

Whether you go to the massive website of *Entertainment Weekly* magazine (www. ew.com) or a one-page online sales brochure for an obscure cartoonist who could soon become a household name, the web is loaded with pop culture.

There are numerous gaming websites targeted to children in different age brackets. Some of the most popular include

- » PBS Kids (http://pbskids.org)
- » Miniclip (www.miniclip.com)
- » Steam (www.steampowered.com)

Most of the pop culture magazines listed in the preceding section maintain their own websites. And you can find many more websites specifically devoted to popular culture in all its glory. Here are a few examples:

>> NPR Pop Culture (www.npr.org/sections/pop-culture)

>> popculture. (www.popculture.com)

>> PopMatters (www.popmatters.com)

Last but not least, keep an eye on major pop culture events, such as annual popular arts conventions put on by San Diego Comic Convention (www.comic-con.org), annual music festival Coachella (www.coachella.com), and others.

Browsing bookstores

Browsing bookstores — particularly independent bookstores devoted to children's books — can help you find out what's new and exciting in popular culture. Here are some great examples of independent children's bookstores:

>> A Whale of a Tale in Irvine, California (http://awhaleofatale.indielite.org)

>> Children's Book World in Los Angeles (www.childrensbookworld.com)

>> Books of Wonder in New York City (www.booksofwonder.com).

You can also search through the often huge and inviting children's book departments in big stores such as Barnes & Noble and Costco. Amazon (www.amazon.com) and Powell's (www.powells.com) are great places to browse online (unless you live near Portland, Oregon — in that case, get yourself to Powell's in person!). You can get a much better sense of what a book is about if you hold a children's book in your hand, especially books that have a lot of illustrations or unique packaging, so the online route may not give you the info you really need.

If you want to know what children are reading, sit down and read. Read books from every section and every shelf — at least a few pages or a chapter. Haunt the section that features the format you're concentrating on so that you can know intimately what's out there. A lot has changed in publishing in the last ten years, and you should be aware of what the formats that we describe in Chapter 2 really look, feel, and read like. After you truly immerse yourself in these formats, you can then further hone your idea, taking clues from approaches that you like and those that you don't.

TIP

While you browse, keep the 50/25/25 rule in mind. If you're writing a children's picture book, read and research (at minimum) 50 published picture books. If you're writing a children's middle-grade book, look at a minimum of 25 books in that category. And if you're writing a young adult (YA) novel, you need to check out at least 25 published YA titles. Get immersed!

For instance, if you want to write a picture book about pirates, do you want to take the pseudo-real-life approach like the one taken by Melinda Long in *How I Became a Pirate* (Harcourt Children's Books)? Or do you want to teach children about pirate life in a whimsical, rhymed fashion like Kathy Tucker in *Do Pirates Take Baths?* (Albert Whitman & Company)? Perhaps you prefer to answer questions about pirates in a more encyclopedic (and purposely ridiculous) fashion, the way that Tom Lichtenheld does in *Everything I Know About Pirates* (Simon & Schuster). All of these fictional picture books about pirates target the same audience, and they all approach the subject in a unique manner. By studying them, you can invent yet another different and exciting approach.

REMEMBER

Be careful not to clone your idea directly from the latest smash-hit bestseller — you can bet that as a result of the popularity of that particular book, every publisher has been swamped with hundreds of manuscripts for knockoffs. Be different and stand out from the crowd — regardless of what's currently popular.

TIP

Be sure to acquaint yourself with comics, graphic novels, and manga. Children are really into these formats and the genres they cover. More and more early-reader books are formatted like comics or graphic novels. Don't sell yourself short by not researching these genres. You may find good ideas or even good storylines that you want to explore.

Visiting children's stores online or in person

Toymakers are always ready, willing, and able to leverage the latest kids' trends by designing and selling products that tap into those trends. If a trend is hot, you can almost certainly find a doll, action figure, video game, costume, playset, app, or some other toy devoted to it. Although nothing quite compares to wandering the aisles of your local toy purveyor to steep yourself in a world that's uniquely oriented toward children and their tastes and desires, you can let your fingers do the walking by doing some online toy browsing. A popular website to check out is Hamleys (www.hamleys.com), which is associated with a British chain of toy stores.

Visiting toy stores and places that cater to children's lives and activities can help you get in the kid zone. By *kid zone*, we mean that when you're surrounded by what kids are surrounded by and you get to see what kids like and don't — in other words, when you stand in their shoes — it helps you approach your story more from their perspective. For example, maybe your idea involves writing about a kid who loves to build things. You go to the toy store to see what kinds of building sets are popular today. Surprise! Toy makers have invented tons of new building toys and materials since you were a kid. Does that change what your character does? Maybe!

Studying kids' fashion trends

Clothing and fashion are reflections of the prevailing pop culture. What did today's aspirational pop idols wear on last night's episode of *American Idol*? You can bet that clothing manufacturers around the world are gearing up production of whatever fashion the big names wear within hours of the show hitting the airwaves. Whatever the trend — from surfing, to hip-hop, to goth, to nerd gear — clothing stores can show you what's hot.

Try Claire's, Tilly's, The Limited Too, Justice, or Abercrombie. If you can't find any dedicated children's clothing boutiques in your area, be sure to check out the children's clothing departments in large retailers such as Target, Macy's, Kohl's, and Nordstrom. And don't forget children's or tweens' or teens' vintage or second-hand clothing stores or consignment shops. The owners can be great sources of information on what kids are wearing and looking for — it's a bonus if customers are in the store while you are there as that can yield great dialogue reconnaissance opportunities.

Again, standing in children's shoes (or their clothes, for that matter) helps you get a feel for what children appreciate and what they don't. Fashion and clothing trends especially affect tweens and teens, so if they're your target audience, it behooves your writing to develop a familiarity with this part of their world, too. For instance, if you're writing about a tween girl who wants to be just like her bigger sister, when you have her steal her sister's clothing, what is she going to steal? Probably not the saddle shoes, cashmere pullover, and pleated skirt from some people's childhoods.

Eavesdropping where kids hang out

Want to know how kids speak and act today? If you don't have any of your own children (I [Lisa] pick up a lot just driving my kids around and eavesdropping on their conversations in the back seat), you can make some very useful observations by hanging out in kids' spaces. Just situate yourself in a corner, stay as invisible as you can manage, and listen. If you're a brave sort who doesn't mind the loud noises of video games and kids yelling, try out a local rock-climbing gym, parkour court, or a laser tag/paintball location. Or go to your local mall's food court and take a seat near a group of kids hanging out. We guarantee you'll be surprised (maybe horrified) about kids' interests and the way they discuss them. (If you're a male, doing this discreetly can be the difference between amiable eavesdropping and stalking if you're not careful. Just sayin'.)

Researching Your Nonfiction Topic

Although you can play fast and loose with some facts in a fictional work, you don't have that luxury when you're working on a nonfiction book. Inaccurate information in your nonfiction book not only potentially risks your reputation with publishers and book buyers, but it can lead to disillusioned children when they discover that their favorite nonfiction author is a fraud. And you don't want to disappoint all those children, do you?

Also, many educational publishers and publishers of nonfiction require that they can verify all information and find documentation of all attributed dialogue. Your audience probably assumes that everything in a nonfiction book is 100-percent true, so your responsibility for verifying your facts is acute.

So how do you make sure that what you're presenting as facts are really true and not just the latest urban legend floating around the Internet? You research, you research some more, and then you research your research.

REMEMBER

By trebling up on your research, you're following the *Rule of Three:* If you can find three trustworthy references or resources, you can feel confident that your research is accurate. Go for already published sources that you can hold in your hands and choose sources from three different publishers. Never rely on Wikipedia entries for facts; anyone who's interested in the topic can write and edit those entries, so you don't know whether the information contained there is accurate or prone to errors (the writer could be just a dilettante with an opinion).

Outlining the research process

The amount of research you need to do, where you do it, and the depth of your efforts very much depend on the exact genre of nonfiction children's books you want to write, how deeply you want to cover the topic, and the sophistication of your audience. A board book on firetrucks — with fewer than 100 words — requires far less extensive research than a nonfiction middle-grade reader on the life and times of Rosa Parks.

So how do you go about researching your nonfiction children's book? Just follow these steps:

1. **Choose a topic.**

   The topic you select greatly impacts where and how you do your research.

2. **Outline your book.**

   How do you know what research to do if you don't know what topics you want to cover in your book? Here's the short answer: You don't.

3. Create a research plan.

The plan should include the sources you intend to look up (newspaper and magazine articles and books), places you intend to visit (libraries, museums, research institutions, historical sites), and people you intend to interview (experts, researchers, celebrities). If, for example, you're writing a nonfiction book about farm animals, your plan might include visiting a local library, spending some time on the Internet, sitting in at a 4-H club meeting, conducting interviews with children who live on farms with animals, and (of course) visiting real working farms. And don't forget to include in your plan the images you might need to create or acquire permission to use along the way.

TIP

If you take a picture that you want to use in your book (unless it's at a public park or of a national treasure), or you conduct an interview with someone and want to quote them, you probably need to get written permission. Publishing houses have entire departments that deal with permissions. And you can find online legal permissions forms for your subject(s) to sign. The publisher of this book, John Wiley & Sons, Inc., has a standard release or permission form available to use at `http://authorservices.wiley.com`. You can never be too cautious — cover your butt by using these forms in case an issue comes up later.

4. Put your plan into effect.

Get out there and start researching your topic. Many writers find researching almost as fun (and in some cases, more fun) than the actual writing process. Peter once wrote a book about New York City's Orpheus Chamber Orchestra, which required him to accompany the orchestra on an all-expenses-paid concert tour through Germany, Italy, Spain, and the Czech Republic to do his research. It was a tough job, but someone had to do it.

5. Organize your results.

Transcribe interviews, organize articles, compile facts, and credit sources. Be sure to triple-check your facts — when in doubt, check it out again and then one more time.

TIP

To make sure you get all the information you need from each source or reference book — before you place that source back in the stacks and forget where you found it — avail yourself of copies of two of the best guides for writers of nonfiction: *The MLA Handbook for Writers of Research Papers* (Modern Language Association) and Kate L. Turabian's *A Manual for Writers of Research Papers, Theses, and Dissertations* (University of Chicago Press). Both of these tiny (but mighty) books can guide you on how to attribute and credit sources properly and completely. Make sure to get a recent edition. Copies from ye olde college days will surely date you.

Getting around locally

Depending on the topic you're researching, plenty of local resources (and their websites) can help with your research. Some of these resources include

- » Local newspapers
- » Libraries
- » Government offices
- » Company headquarters
- » University research labs
- » Planetariums
- » Census records
- » Museums

Going far afield

You're not limited to doing your research locally: You also have the option of doing your research long distance. Check out these additional resources (and their websites) for doing your research:

- » Library of Congress (www.loc.gov)
- » Smithsonian Institution (www.si.edu)
- » The National Archives (www.archives.gov)
- » National Geographic Society (www.nationalgeographic.org)
- » National magazines
- » YouTube interviews
- » Podcasts
- » Khan Academy (https://www.khanacademy.org/)
- » TED Talks (https://www.ted.com/)
- » Out-of-town small newspapers
- » Associations and societies
- » National experts
- » Research institutes

- » Universities and colleges
- » Government offices
- » Foreign embassies
- » Businesses

Using the power of online telephone directories and the Internet, you can track down a phone number or URL for even the most remote resource pretty easily. Don't be shy — most of these organizations field questions like yours all the time. And most experts are happy to help by guiding you to the next step, foisting you off on someone else, or stepping up and sharing some expertise.

Visiting the web — a lot

The Internet offers you all kinds of things —entertainment, information, up-to-the-second news, and fun. But although much of what shows up on the web is presented as fact, too often these facts are actually fiction.

WARNING

Sadly, the Internet is chock-full of falsehoods, half-truths, and outright lies. When you use the Internet to do your research, keep your guard up against so-called experts who really aren't. Anyone can put up a website promoting themselves as an expert on any topic.

TIP

To separate Internet reality from Internet fantasy, keep these tips in mind:

- » **Be skeptical.** If it sounds too good to be true, suspect that it probably isn't true.
- » **Find good sources.** Identify trusted online sources of information on the Internet, such as online encyclopedias, national newspapers and magazines, or other long-established, reliable media.
- » **Beware of blogs.** Remember that blogs are particularly notorious for playing fast and loose with the truth. Consider them sources of opinion, not necessarily fact.
- » **Confirm your information.** Use reliable, published sources to confirm what you may have found on a site.
- » **Challenge the information mongers.** E-mail them and ask for links to their sources. If they can provide those links, great. (Research those sources, too.) If they don't give you their sources, suspect that they're not telling the truth.

3

Creating a Spellbinding Story

Tackle the exciting — and daunting — task of writing the first pages of your children's book.

Put together your thoughts and basic ideas.

If you're writing fiction, create and develop characters, figure out the plot, establish the setting, and work on dialogue, point of view, and voice.

If you're into nonfiction, do some research and find a way to make the material different from what's already out there and interesting to young readers (and parents, teachers, and librarians, too).

Chapter **8**

Creating Compelling Characters

Your main character is the soul of your story. Flawed or perfect, full of love or temper tantrums, your protagonist must be memorable and must evolve. Think of all those great characters you remember from your childhood — they're great for the very fact that you can recall them so many years after reading about them. They must have had something special about them. What magic potion do you add to a name and a face that makes a character come out so well?

It's not magic at all, actually. In this chapter, we tell you how to create memorable characters. We advise you on how to keep those characters real — not stereotyped or boring — and we show you how a character arc can help you check up on your character to make sure that they do the growing and changing that they need to do within the course of your story. At the end, we add in a few character-building exercises for practice.

REMEMBER

What makes a character great is the way they see the world and interact with it. Not just the way they talk (although that's very important), but also the way they walk, the look on their face, the tics that they exhibit when nervous — in other words, the manner in which they do everything that they do. Their actions tell your reader who your main character really is — the narrator doesn't.

The Secret Formula for an Exceptional Main Character

Kids read children's fiction to encounter characters who are exceptional, not mundane. They want their main characters to be prettier or uglier, more evil or sweeter, nobler or meaner, braver or more fearful than real people. Even if the characters are boring, kids want them to be exceptionally, hilariously, fabulously more boring than the average bore. That doesn't mean the characters should be unrecognizable as human (or animal, if you're anthropomorphizing), but they should embody just a tad bit more of everything than a person (or an animal) could in real life. Give them big doses of the curious, silly, funny, awkward stuff. Adding a little extra highlights the personality quirks that are important to the story and make the character more memorable.

REMEMBER

But here's the catch: Whether they're real people or anthropomorphized creatures, you have to make the characters believable. No matter how extraordinary they are, they still need to be motivated by the same wants and needs as the readers in your target audience.

So, how do you go about creating a character who's three-dimensional and real? You figure out what makes them tick, and you flesh that out. We explain how to do both in the following sections.

Defining your main character's driving desire

Sometime at the beginning of the writing process, you need to ask yourself just what makes your main character move and groove. What do they really want that they simply can't do without? What propels them to do what they do throughout your story? What burning desire lights them on fire and keeps them motivated from the first time we meet them until we bid adieu? Pretend you had to define your character in one sentence. How would you describe their distinguishing attribute, the one that sets them apart — the one that makes them memorable?

REMEMBER

Every main character needs to have a goal or something that they want very badly. This is the character's core; just like an apple without a core would collapse in on itself, a character without a discernible core is hollow and forgettable. If the term core is too obtuse, call it the character's want. From the moment you introduce your character to the last page, you focus on what your character wants: how they get it, what's in their way, how they overcome those obstacles to get closer to what they want, how their want changes them in the end. All these driving questions revolve around what your character wants.

You have to make a character's want attainable, such as wanting to be someone's best friend. It can seem unrealistic, but so are many people's wants — that doesn't mean they stop wanting that one thing. And that person can still reach that unrealistic goal (like turning into a gryphon); after all, didn't most people believe many of the most remarkable achievements were impossible until someone made them real?

For example, in the Brothers Grimm fairy tale Snow White, a story everyone's familiar with, the queen wants one thing: to be the most beautiful in the land. When her mirror informs her one day that she's no longer the fairest one of all, she completely loses it. She decides that she wants to be the prettiest so badly she will stop at nothing — not even murder — to make sure she eliminates her rival. When all her spectacular efforts fail to make Snow White disappear forever, she hires a hit man (the hunter) to finally realize her dream, her desire — her want. In the end, she fails to get what she wants. But that's okay. Failing just means a character hasn't yet accomplished a want.

The entire story of *Snow White* revolves around the queen's want. Her want banishes Snow White from the castle, then from the kingdom. Her want makes her dress up like a witch and try to kill the princess herself. Her want causes the conflict. And it's her want that nearly drives her to madness. That's true desire, and that's what your character needs.

Show, don't tell: Fleshing out your main character

So, how do you let the reader know about your character's driving desire? Well, continuing with the Snow White example from the preceding section, you can spell out this desire in a straightforward, narrated manner by telling the reader: "There was a queen who wanted more than anything to be the fairest in the land." But you shouldn't. After all, where's the drama in that?

What you should do is opt for the more subtle approach in which the reader discerns the protagonist's core by observing how they behave and interact with others. Your readers find figuring out the protagonist's driving desire for themselves far more captivating.

In other words, show the queen in action while she flaunts her hatred by arguing in dialogue with the mirror. Show her dressing up like a witch, hunting down Snow White, and then, with gnarled fingers, offering her the poisoned apple. Finally, show the interaction between the queen and the hunter when she orders him to kill Snow White.

Don't tell readers the queen is driven by her desire; show how she acts in order to fulfill that desire. Have them hear her argue aloud with the mirror. Get them in that dungeon laboratory while she transforms herself into a witch. Make them smell the fresh crispiness of the apple she offers Snow White.

You can help your readers discover your main character's desire by going through the fleshing out process. You need to give your main character a set of physical attributes, but you really fill out a great character with all the quirks, desires, and emotions that comprise a human being. In creating a character, *fleshing out* involves taking the want (the skeleton) and adding the body (the muscles, ligaments, skin, and all the rest) to bring your character alive on the page.

When you flesh out your character, you make that real, just like the Blue Fairy made Pinocchio a real boy. You build a character bit by bit, making them real by planting clues throughout your story about how the character thinks and feels, by letting the reader hear what they say and how they say it, and by allowing the reader to watch as they interact with other characters to reach their goal.

REMEMBER

Fleshing out is all about what your character does. The old adage "what you do shows more about who you are than what you say" holds true here more than ever. It's all well and good if your friend says, "I'll be loyal to you forever"; it's quite another to watch them defending you by raising their fists, actively taking your side by stepping over to you, acting loyal by the things they do. Readers need to see your characters doing. What your characters do makes them memorable.

TIP

To flesh out a character, you need to have them lead the way through the basic plot or the action of your story, which we cover in Chapter 9. But if you don't know them well enough to do that yet, you can do one of two things: You can practice having them talk to another character (see the following section, as well as Chapter 10), or you can make a character bible (see the section "Compiling a Character Bible," later in this chapter).

Getting to Know Your Characters through Dialogue

Use dialogue to get to know your main character better. But don't have your character talk and talk ad infinitum in your story. Instead, use dialogue between characters to reveal who they are, how they feel, how they think — to flesh them out verbally. For instance, the narrator can write, "Jon was as dumb as a doornail." But you can make the reader privy to actual dialogue in which what Jon says (or doesn't say) illustrates just how clueless he really is.

Also, make sure each bit of dialogue has a purpose. It must either

» Develop a character (flesh them out a bit).

» Move the story forward (add to the plot).

» Provide a moment of conflict to heighten the drama and quicken the pacing. Get readers turning the pages because they simply must find out what happens next.

Purposefully use dialogue in your story. Don't include every single "Hello" or "Nice to meet you." The dialogue you write must contribute something meaningful to the story. Don't use dialogue to recap action we've just witnessed in narration or vice versa; that's redundant and the perfect way to lose your reader.

Don't have characters repeat each other's names in dialogue. Characters use each other's names usually only when one character is introducing another, when one character wants to get another character's attention, or when someone is upset with someone else — for instance, a parent with a child. (Do you remember your mother using both your first and middle names when you were in trouble? And if she used your last name, too — boy, then you were really going to get it.)

Some writers like to have their characters speak to one another in dialogue form just to get a better idea of who those characters are — to literally write out an exchange between two characters to bring them alive in the writer's mind before the actual story writing begins. Chapter 10 discusses the ins and outs of getting your characters to talk to each other, so we give you only a short discussion here of how developing a dialogue between two characters defines them.

Take two characters you're thinking of using in your story and write a dialogue between them. This exercise can help you jump-start the story from the idea stage to actually writing and developing the main character. Don't worry about how good your dialogue is right now — just let the characters talk to one another.

Have your characters start chatting about your theme (the subject of your story; see Chapter 6) to flesh it out a bit, and have the characters argue about it. For example, perhaps you can have a supporting character challenge your main character on your story's theme:

BUNNY RABBIT: I think my mom is gonna return me for a new bunny.

MOUSE: What do ya mean? You're broken? Sometimes my mom returns broken stuff.

BUNNY RABBIT: No, I don't think so — but the other day, I heard her say the new bunnies were on their way.

MOUSE: Oh.

BUNNY RABBIT: And when new bunnies come, what happens to old bunnies?

MOUSE: Oh, I see what you mean. What'll she need old bunnies for if she's got new ones? Like shoes. When you grow out of the old ones you give 'em away.

BUNNY RABBIT: Yeah. I wonder who she'll give me away to? You think I'll get recycled or something?

MOUSE: No. 'Least I don't think so. We better come up with a plan to show your mom you're not really broken. And quick!

TIP

Notice the use of contractions, truncated sentences, and incomplete sentences? This is the way people speak in real life. If you have a character who doesn't speak this way, that character sounds stilted, wooden, and just plain odd, which you want to avoid — unless the character is supposed to be a very erudite British professor, of course.

Keep your characters talking to each other until you get a real feeling for who these characters are. Already, you can see here that Bunny is a sweet, sensitive, and naive little tyke. Also, with the help of their friend, they can become a take-charge sort of bunny. Plot-wise (more on that in Chapter 9), this dialogue shows you that Bunny has misunderstood what they overheard and is in for a big change in their life (although not the one they expect) and that Mouse is going to help them try to solve their problem. This dialogue fleshes out Bunny, Mouse, and their problem. It helps the writer better understand the roles of both characters, their particular personalities, and how they can participate in the plot development so far.

TIP

If you can read the meaning of a bit of dialogue in two ways, either rewrite it for clarity or show what the character is doing when they say it. Body language can be very telling. For instance, when a teenager says, "Sure, Mom," it can be taken many different ways:

>> "Sure, Mom." The teenager's smile lit up their eyes.

>> "Sure, Mom." The teenager rolled their eyes and stomped off into the living room.

>> "Sure. Mom?" (This version has the teenager answering a question in the affirmative and then getting Mom's attention to ask another question.)

Compiling a Character Bible

A great way to really build a character, attribute by attribute, is to create a blueprint of them, which folks in the know refer to as a character bible. A character bible is a type of character outline in which you lay out everything about your character in one place so that you can find answers to many questions about the character's personality and desires. A character bible can help you achieve consistency throughout the manuscript.

We suggest starting a document that's separate from your story, in list or prose form, so that you can refer back to it and amend it while you get more into your writing. Your character bible can even include visuals if you're a doodler or illustrator. Some really good questions your character bible can answer include the following:

>> What's their name? Whom were they named after and why?

>> How old are they?

>> What colors are their hair, eyes, skin?

>> What's their ethnicity?

>> What do they look like (tall, thin, short, round, gangly)?

>> Where do they live? Where were they born? If not the same place, when did they move, and did it affect them in any way?

>> How would you describe their personality?

>> What are your character's physical quirks (bites nails, blinks when nervous, brushes hand through his hair, sniffles a lot)?

>> What do they want more than anything?

   This question answers your main character's *want* or *desire,* which propels the entire plot. (See the section "Defining your main character's driving desire," earlier in this chapter, for discussion on your character's motivation.)

>> What are their character weaknesses or flaws?

>> Do they behave the same way around their friends as they do around adults? Why or why not?

>> Are they smart? Not so bright? In what do they excel? In what do they fail?

>> Are they talkative or more introverted?

>> Are they athletic? If yes, what are their favorite sports? If no, why not?

>> What small details set them apart from others?

Do they wear a special totem hidden under their shirt? Do they speak only in a whisper? Do they always have an earbud in one ear?

>> Do they have brothers and sisters? What are their names and ages?

>> Do they have a best friend? Name and age, please.

>> What's their big secret that they keep from everyone?

These questions incorporate the emotional, social, and physical — all aspects that contribute to making each one of us who we are. And because someone can answer these questions about every person in the world, you should be able to do so for your main character.

Surveying a sample character bible

Here's an example of a character bible from a middle-grade novel in progress, modeled off of the questions in the preceding section:

>> **What's their name? Whom were they named after and why?** Barnaby H. Lee. He was named after his granddad, Barnaby Hollis Lee, the man who invented a time machine, then disappeared on the day Barnaby was born.

>> **How old are they?** Barnaby is nine years old, but he seems wiser than his years. Not in a geeky way, but in the way he expresses himself and how he speculates about complicated social and emotional issues.

>> **What colors are their hair, eyes, skin?** Barnaby has platinum blond hair, big green eyes, and translucent skin. He looks a little otherworldly.

>> **What's their ethnicity?** Barnaby's parents are both olive-skinned, of Mediterranean descent. Barnaby looks like no one else in his family.

>> **What do they look like?** He's tall for his age, slender, almost jellylike in his flexibility — it seems as if his limbs kind of flop around when he walks, like they're barely attached.

>> **Where do they live? Where were they born?** Barnaby lives in Dead Oak Village, a suburb of a big American city, where he was born and where his family has lived for five generations or more.

>> **How would you describe their personality?** Barnaby is a dreamer, but he's also very smart. Unlike most boys his age, he is very sensitive and aware of emotions and feelings. He often has premonitions that turn out to be true, but he hasn't told anyone about them. He likes to be around people but often seems not present when he is, as if he's listening to a conversation happening in another room. Barnaby is the first to comfort you if you're hurt; he's also the first to defend you if you need it.

»» What are your character's physical quirks? Barnaby's eyes are weird: Even when they focus on you, you can't really get a fix on what's in them or on his expression. Barnaby's most noticeable characteristic is that he looks up to the left often, like he's listening to a conversation you can't hear.

»» What do they wish for more than anything? Barnaby wishes he could talk to his granddad. The old man has something important to say to him, and Barnaby has no idea how he's going to figure out what that is.

»» What are their character weaknesses or flaws? Barnaby has the courage of his convictions. He won't ever shove them down your throat, but he won't back down, either. This makes him a great friend to have, and an exasperating one, too. Barnaby came out of the womb knowing right from wrong; however, when Barnaby gets an idea in his head, he does whatever he needs to so that he can go where he wants and get what he wants. He never means to hurt anyone, but someone always seems to get hurt by accident.

»» Do they behave the same way around their friends as they do around adults? Why or why not? Barnaby is interested in everyone — from the smallest baby to the elderly. He acts the same around everyone (polite, well-mannered, not at all hyperactive or pushy).

»» Are they smart? Not so bright? In what do they excel? In what do they fail? Barnaby is smart and excels at school. He's not so good at group activities because he tends to disappear in them; he's not that outgoing.

»» Are they talkative or more introverted? Barnaby can talk up a storm on issues he's interested in, but he's generally more introverted. He's not shy; he just doesn't offer up of himself.

»» Are they athletic? If yes, what are their favorite sports? If no, why not? Barnaby is a great wrestler. Even though he weighs next to nothing, his flexibility allows him to outmaneuver everyone in his weight class, even heavier wrestlers. He's good at track and other solo outdoor pursuits, but he has to be careful in the sun because of his paleness.

»» What small details set them apart from others? Barnaby is set off from others by the way he looks, the way he's so seemingly ethereal, and his maturity. In a conversation, Barnaby's words seem to precede his thoughts, making him ahead of himself somehow. But he's wistful about it, not a know-it-all.

»» Do they have brothers and sisters? What are their names and ages? Barnaby has a sister and a brother. His sister Natasha is older, age 16. She adores Barnaby but rarely has time for him. His brother Ryan is 14 and also has little time for Barnaby, but Ryan's not mean to him like many older brothers might be.

>> **Do they have a best friend?** Name and age, please. Barnaby's best friend is a girl named Phoebe. She's 10 and lives next door. Barnaby and Phoebe have been best friends since they were three months old.

>> **What's their big secret that they keep from everyone?** At the end of the first chapter, Barnaby finds the map of his own house, which leads him to the blueprints for his granddad's time machine.

Now, you don't need to develop every character to this extent for every story in every format. But even in a picture book in which you have a very limited word count, knowing a lot of details about your characters can't hurt. Character enrichment involves adding layers of complexity by using bits of description, a lot of action, and just the right dialogue. The more you flesh out a character, the more real you make them (or it) to your reader — and the more memorable they become.

Creating consistency

REMEMBER

Whether a story is real or not, the characters must always be believable and consistent. First, figure out who your characters are and flesh them out (see the section "Show, don't tell: Fleshing out your main character," earlier in this chapter, for tips on creating your character). Give them enough interesting traits so that you don't make them one-dimensional, predictable, or boring. Then, make sure they stick to who they are. So if you have a character who's afraid of heights, then suddenly that character decides to go mountain climbing, you have a little problem — unless the character is doing that flip-flop as a ploy to disguise what they're really doing (rather than going mountain climbing). Of course, your characters can have qualities that make them seem odd or bizarre — bring them on! — but you need to make them consistently odd or bizarre.

Every time your character is involved in any sort of action, interaction, or dialogue, think about how you can either add some new fleshing out details or reinforce a character trait you've identified from your character bible.

TIP

When you come to a point in your story at which you have to make a plot development decision about something your character is about to do or not do, ask yourself this: Would they really do that? If not, what would be their motivation to do something that seems out of character? Keep your character bible handy and refer to it when you can't come up with the answer on your own.

How do you know when you've made a character real? If you find yourself referring to them as you would your children, your spouse, your best friend, or your partner, they have become real for you. The challenge is making sure they become just as real to your readers.

To make your character really stand out (as opposed to being forgettable), you need to focus on how they're special and different from every other character you've read about before. We assume you've read at least 50 books in your genre if you're writing a picture book or 25 if you're targeting either middle-grade readers or the young adult (YA) audience. What has all that research shown to you? Each main character is probably different from all the other characters in some important ways. Make those differences unique and interesting in your main character. Don't rely on stereotypes — and certainly don't copy a character already out there. Create a character that children want to relate to because that character is so cool and different! Keep in mind that there are 7 billion people on the planet — that's lots of characters. There is no need to repeat; there are infinite character possibilities to work with.

Writing Stories with Two or More Main Characters

Many beginning children's book writers are told never to write a story that has two or more main characters unless they have a lot of experience doing so. Although we think that's sound advice for some writers, we don't think every new writer needs to feel constrained by this dictate. However, we do suggest the following tips to make sure that your characters stay distinct and different from one another:

>> **Create a character bible for each main character.** Flesh out attitudes, manner of speaking, and any other small details that set each character apart from the others.

>> **Write out how each of your characters would behave when faced with a tough choice.** Make the options things that compromise the character, no matter what they choose — then use this example to continue fleshing out your character.

For example, what if Main Character #1 is caught with a forbidden item in their locker that isn't theirs, but they know whose it is? What do they do? If they tell, they lose their best friend. If they don't tell, they get expelled. Whichever option they choose, they suffer — but their choice tells us more about them.

>> **Limit your story to two main characters who are clearly different.** Maybe you have one girl and one boy; or you could have one snake and one turtle. These differences can help you draw differentiations and flesh them out while lessening the chance that they start sounding or acting alike.

Don't feel like you absolutely can't have more than two important characters; but if you do, one or two of those important characters have to take center stage as the main characters, while the rest appear as the supporting cast.

>> **Make the background of one of your main characters very different from the other.** For example, if Main Character #2 is a recent immigrant from India, their cultural background and experiences inform not only their actions, but also the way they speak. Or what if one of your characters is a foster child, raised by many different families, attached to no one? Add something to make them really distinct to differentiate them in your writing.

>> **Put up a picture of each character so that you can really picture them in your mind.** If you aren't the best artist, try cutting out photos from magazines or other sources that inspire you. You can even assign an actor or a celebrity to each of your characters.

>> **Use people from real life as inspiration.** Your best friend, a close relative, a co-worker, someone you like or dislike — use that person as the framework for your character. You may even want to use that individual's name in the manuscript until your very last editing, when you change it to protect the innocent — or not so innocent.

>> **Make sure that when each character speaks, they don't sound like every other character.** For example, if you have one character who's talkative to the point of never coming up for air, make sure your other characters don't possess this particular attribute.

Don't use character names that sound alike or that start with the same letter or phoneme — unless, of course, you're okay with your reader being very confused. Also, avoid alliterative names (Ginger Goose, Doug the Dog, Zed Zebra); it's been done to death and now comes across to an editor or agent as less than professional (the work of a dilettante, not a seasoned writer like you).

Choosing Supporting Characters

When you decide who else to add to your cast of characters, ask yourself who you need in addition to your main character to tell your story. "Who does my main character need around them to make them believable, as well as to help them carry out their destiny?" For example, in 99 percent of stories, the main character needs at least one other character to speak to and interact with (and have conflict with), no matter the subject or length of your story.

Enter supporting characters. They help to convey the context of the story. For example, if your story takes place 150 years ago, supporting characters could show

how life was back then: blacksmiths, butchers, street cops on horseback, teachers at one-room schoolhouses filled with children of all ages, and the like.

Additionally, supporting characters can be

>> Catalysts in the plot, causing events to occur or information to be shared: If your story is about a boy like Barnaby (whom we developed a bit in the section "Compiling a Character Bible," earlier in this chapter), who's looking for some hidden information, perhaps your supporting character tells him a story about their grandmother, showing Barnaby a photo album that gives him a clue as to its whereabouts. Or maybe your supporting character unwittingly leads the enemy right to your main character's secret hideout.

>> Dissimilar to the main character to highlight the main character's assets or flaws: Perhaps your main character is an introvert. Their best friend, your supporting character, is an extrovert. The outgoing one puts your main character in a situation causing them extreme discomfort, which in turn leads them to do something completely out of character or perhaps something to totally mess up their life.

Unlike main characters who have to push the story and plot further (more on plot in Chapter 9), supporting characters don't have that limitation. So you can make them colorful, silly, super-brave, or even magical. Literally, they support the main character's journey, whatever that journey is. Think Tinkerbell in Peter Pan and Donkey in the movie Shrek. Whomever you choose for your supporting cast, make them three-dimensional and avoid stereotypes.

REMEMBER

Develop supporting characters when you need them in your story, which becomes apparent when your plot calls for someone for the main character to interact with to pull the story forward. You can ask many of the same questions about the supporting characters that you do about the main character in order to develop them, but you needn't go into quite as much detail. (See the section "Compiling a Character Bible," earlier in this chapter, for a list of character questions.)

TIP

Here are some tips to help you develop supporting characters:

>> **Decide the function of the supporting character in your story.** For example, are you including this character so that you have someone who can serve as an obstacle or challenge between your main character and their goal? Or is this supporting character's job to serve as the conscience of the group, reminding them of the correct path to take, while they insist on going the other way?

>> **Figure out the supporting character's function in relation to your main character.** In other words, how does this supporting character support (or inhibit) the development of the main character? Children might need parents or adults (or someone who assumes that role) around them to highlight their uniquely childlike perspectives.

Never make your book's main or supporting character an adult (unless you're writing a story about a parent/child relationship). Even if you are telling the story of Nina and her mom, make the child character the main focus. Kids don't care about how the adults in their lives act and feel as much as they do about their peers — whether they're friends or enemies.

>> **Flesh out the supporting character by adding in details.** Create a character bible (discussed in "Compiling a Character Bible," earlier in this chapter) just like you would for your main character.

>> **Figure out how your supporting character's differences from the other characters help them fulfill their function regarding the plot.** If you have an introverted main character like Barnaby (from the section "Surveying a sample character bible," earlier in this chapter), perhaps the function of his best friend Phoebe is to serve as the one who reaches out to others, who gets things done in the real world, while Barnaby is living inside his head.

>> **Step into the supporting character's shoes.** When you're writing this supporting character, imagine yourself inside that person's head: What are they thinking right now? What do they see? What impulses or emotions do they show or suppress? What do they notice while another person is talking? What is their mood? All these markers can help you make them real — which you need to do to create a real-seeming character, no matter how minor a character they are.

No matter how minor a role, if you mention a supporting character by name, that character warrants your attention. They have a point of view, an attitude, particular behaviors, a personality — even if we only glimpse a bit of these attributes. Whether they help convey the theme of your story (more on themes in Chapter 6) or move the action forward at a crucial point, they add to your story's flesh and bones.

Calling All Character Arcs

A character arc is just a simple visual tool to help you chart out your character's development. Make their driving desire clear from the start. Draw into this arc the changes that your main character makes in their life. Use this arc to see how they drive the action when the story starts, then when something occurs that requires action, then when their plight reaches a climax, and finally when they head toward resolution.

You use a character arc by assigning different points of your character's development to the different dots; this helps ensure that your character goes through enough changes and struggles to make them and their story compelling. Here's a summary of the steps that characters tend to face. Take the old-fashioned story of Cinderella and apply it to the arc in Figure 8-1:

>> When we first meet your main character, we see their driving desire (the ascent begins). Cinderella is a happy, well-adjusted girl living a privileged life when her father remarries and brings a stepmother and two stepsisters into her life — all three of whom detest her. Show Cinderella as sweet and trying to cope, a girl who is confused but still has her father watching her back. Make clear her desire to be considered an equal and equally beloved member of the family.

>> They have something happen to rock their world/challenge their reality (steeply ascending). Cinderella's father dies, leaving the poor girl at the mercy of the merciless stepmother and stepsisters, a veritable black sheep. Cinderella tries to stay her course but fails to move these women whose abuse of her escalates.

>> And they have to deal with it (ascending further). Cinderella still uses her same old way of coping (being sweet and working hard to avoid the reality of her situation), but the abuse gets worse.

>> They fail (peak): Cinderella fails to stand up for herself, and she ends up a scullery maid in her own home. Time for a change, but is she strong enough?

>> Then they try some more and fail (dips, then peaks even further). Cinderella and everyone else in the household are all excited over the upcoming ball and are getting ready to attend. Cinderella again resolves to put a happy face on her situation, but she is thwarted and can't attend the ball.

>> They hit a seeming stalemate (flatline, but not for too long): The fairy godmother helps her attend the ball. Cinderella rises to the occasion, dazzling all attendees, including the prince, but she has to run out of the ball at the last minute, leaving a slipper. So she's back to where she started: in rags, with no prospects.

>> Then they figure it out (begins descending). Cinderella decides that she wants a chance to try on that slipper, no matter what her stepsisters, who may suspect her involvement with the prince, say or do.

>> They hit a bump, but instead of reverting back to old solution(s), they try out a new one (further descending). Cinderella gets locked in the cellar when the prince arrives, but instead of accepting her fate with a smile and cleaning even

harder, Cinderella alters her driving desire, gets wise, and fashions a way to break out in time. Eventually, she gets hitched — thus fulfilling her desire to be loved, but creating a chosen family instead of the stinky one she inherited. Wiser and back to her old position and privilege, we have to see how she uses her power.

» And they end a changed and ideally better person after all (fully descended). Although she could have her stepmother and stepsisters thrown into a dungeon from where they would never escape (or worse), Cinderella opts to take the higher road and allows them to live their lives.

REMEMBER

A character arc just gives you a fancy way to make sure your character has grown and changed throughout the course of the story.

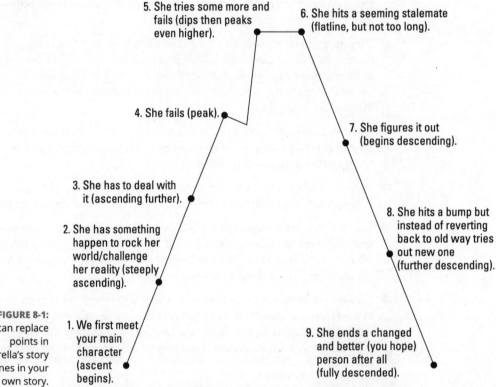

5. She tries some more and fails (dips then peaks even higher).

6. She hits a seeming stalemate (flatline, but not too long).

4. She fails (peak).

7. She figures it out (begins descending).

3. She has to deal with it (ascending further).

2. She has something happen to rock her world/challenge her reality (steeply ascending).

8. She hits a bump but instead of reverting back to old way tries out new one (further descending).

FIGURE 8-1:
You can replace points in Cinderella's story with ones in your own story.

1. We first meet your main character (ascent begins).

9. She ends a changed and better (you hope) person after all (fully descended).

Character Don'ts — and How to Avoid Them

Just as important as what you do with your characters, you need to know what *not* to do with them. The following sections take you through some of the most important writing no-no's and reveal how to avoid making character-killing mistakes.

Steer clear of stereotypes

WARNING

Stereotyped characters are ones who are too familiar and thus wooden: the smart geek, the airhead cheerleader, the mean beauty queen. When you meet every expectation a reader has about how a character will end up, you create a stereotyped character. When your reader finds no contradictions or surprises related to a character throughout the story, that character is in trouble.

You can avoid stereotyping your characters by combining traits that the reader doesn't expect to encounter in one character. So if that mean beauty queen turns out to be moonlighting as a janitor at a homeless shelter to pay for her uniforms while conjuring up spells to cure ailing pets at the local animal shelter, then you have a potentially very interesting character.

Another way to avoid stereotyping involves using a character bible to spell out unique traits and combinations of traits. (We explain how to create a character bible in the section "Compiling a Character Bible," earlier in this chapter.) What exactly makes people unique? Here are tips for creating interesting characters:

» List the memorable people you've known in your life. Don't list just the ones you know really well who made a difference in your life. Also list the ones who were so quirky and enigmatic you just had to find out more about them. List the ones you would have joined doing ordinary things such as errands all day long — just because they were so different.

» Try to identify what makes those people so memorable. For example, here are some things that can make a person truly unique in the world:

- Do they constantly point out things about the world and other people that no one else seems to see or care about?

- Do they rarely offer anything up unless someone asks them — and then, whoa!

- Do paradoxes in their personality set them apart? Say that someone has compassion for the plight of all animals and insects great and small, but they wouldn't share their afternoon snack with another human, even if you threatened to rip out their fingernails one by one.

>> Consider whether your character(s) can include one or several of these characteristics. Instead of labeling a character as smart or dumb, athletic or not, decide what those labels really mean to you. For example, instead of developing a character as smart, why not develop one whose abilities allow them access to secret and special information that others don't know about? Rather than creating a beautiful character, what about developing a character who's unattractive by choice in their quest to find a partner who appreciates them for more than their looks?

When you think of memorable people, think about the ones who

>> Really moved you: The coach who came to a neighbor child's house every day for a week after school to make sure the child mastered skills in a sport, thus allowing the child to compete in that week's game.

>> Made you laugh: The child in the classroom who had to add their two cents to absolutely everything the teacher said, regardless of what it was, and always had something compelling to add (believe it or not) because of the strange way they looked at the world.

>> Perplexed you: The miserable grandma who smiled only when the grandchildren left and she could play with her cats. Don't feature the grandma as your main character, but consider her from the kids' point of view — or maybe the cats' perspective. (You can find more on point of view in Chapter 12.)

Try to take some of the characteristics you describe in the mental exercises in this section and see whether you can use any of them to build your main character (or a great supporting character).

TIP

If you want an actual exercise to help you develop interesting, non-stereotypical characters, check out the section "Developing Characters through Writing Exercises," later in this chapter.

Don't tell us everything

Don't underestimate the power of motion. As a matter of fact, you probably know this phrase (maybe from writing classes or a writer's group): Show, don't tell. But what exactly does that mean?

Showing involves getting the character

>> Interacting with another character, using dialogue, body language, or physicality

>> Actively going from one place to another

>> Interacting with the world around them; getting involved in some active, hands-on, and personal way

Telling involves narration, where you describe all the getting, going, and interacting, but you never actually demonstrate the character in the act.

Showing (and not telling) equals action; here's an example of telling versus showing.

This passage tells the story instead of showing it:

> Olivia felt bad. She wished she could call up her best friend and tell her how much she wanted to take back what she had said, but by the time she actually did it, it proved too late. The friend had already left. So Olivia sat and pondered what she could do. In the end she called up another friend.

This passage tells us Olivia feels bad, when it should show you by dramatizing Olivia expressing her feelings. Then it tells you about a phone call to a best friend instead of showing Olivia making the phone call so that you can see how she goes about it.

Here's a version of Olivia's story that involves showing:

> Olivia wiped the tears from her eyes and picked up the phone. "Is Genevieve there?" she blurted.
>
> "No, she's already gone home for the summer."
>
> "But — but — I never got to tell her — "
>
> "Sorry, hun. She'll be back in September." A dial tone filled Olivia's ear.
>
> Olivia stared at the phone. She punched in a different number. "Hello, Chloe? It's me. I've got an idea."

We discuss dialogue more in Chapter 10, but suffice it to say that writing out what a character says rather than telling us about it in narration is a lot more compelling.

TIP

When your main character appears in your story but doesn't engage in dialogue or get involved in some action within a few paragraphs of their appearance, then you're probably telling, not showing.

WARNING

Beware of dumping tons of background information in successive paragraphs, known as a data dump. Character development must be more subtle and oblique, not hitting the reader over the head with gobs of information all at the same time. Data dumps also qualify as telling instead of showing. Add character development bit by bit throughout your story. Let the reader discover who these characters are and build their own connections to them.

Toss out passivity and indefinites

Don't overuse the passive voice ("to be" verbs) if you want to keep your characters interesting, your plots active (more on plots in Chapter 9), and your writing strong:

» Cut out "to be" verbs. Strong, direct writing eliminates passivity and "to be" verbs. For example, instead of writing, "The sound of the shot could be heard from Annabella's house a mile away," write, "Annabella heard the shot from her house a mile away."

» Get rid of the passive voice whenever possible. Passive voice makes characters and plot boring:

- Passive: There were a lot of people in the square.

  Active: Tons of people packed the square.

- Passive: The reason she felt so bad is that she had a bothersome pain in her leg.

  Active: A sharp pain shot up her leg. "Ouch!"

TIP

Search for the phrases there is, there are, and it is (or their past tenses) in your story. When you find these phrases, cut them out completely and rewrite the sentences. Same with the words it and thing. Do a universal search of your manuscript and eliminate them mercilessly. And if you can do the same for that and *which* without destroying your meaning, out they go!

In the same way, indefinite prose (writing that ultimately says nothing and adds nothing useful because it's so nondescript) is colorless, tame, and ultimately timid. Write like you mean it. Instead of meandering into what you want to say, jump right in:

» Indefinite: She was not sure that going to that school really made any sense for her life.

  Definite: Going to school was a total waste of time.

>> Indefinite: That story is really not defined in spots. The plot does not have any real climax, the main character seems listless, and the writing could use a little spicing up.

Definite: The plot couldn't be any more lifeless. And does the main character feel anything? I wonder if the writer of this piece is even breathing.

We can't stress enough how important positive, strong, direct writing is in character development — as well as in every other aspect of your writing. For more on writing style, see William Strunk, Jr., and E. B. White's classic *The Elements of Style* (Pearson).

Don't rely on backstory or flashbacks

Backstory is the account of your character's birth to the day before your story begins. Backstory may include historical references, family connections, allusions to other parts of your story, psychological setup — you name it. It's basically all the information about how your character came to be the person they are in your story before the action begins. In longer works, you can drop in hints of backstory here and there. Even in picture books, you can make allusions to the past if they're definitely relevant. But most backstory doesn't belong in your book.

WARNING

Use backstory only as an immediate and clearly necessary development tool for the character or the plot of your story. If the fact that your character has lived in foster homes before they win the scholarship to boarding school really informs your story, let your readers know — but only if doing so moves the action forward. If mentioning their backstory causes you to spend a lot of successive paragraphs explaining the character's past, readers probably don't need to know all that. A long backstory brings the action of the story to a grinding halt. If you want to let out details in a character's backstory, show it in the way they act.

A flashback is a literary device used to reveal information about some past event by having the character, in their mind, literally flash back to the past, recalling some event so that the reader can experience it, as well. Flashbacks can interrupt the flow of a story. If you must use a flashback, do so only briefly, once in a while, and if you absolutely have to (meaning if you didn't use one, the reader would be truly lost and wouldn't comprehend what happens next in the story).

Yes, we know *The Catcher in the Rye,* by J. D. Salinger (Little, Brown and Company) is arguably one of the most successful children's books in history, found on every high school YA reading list and told almost entirely in flashback. However, Salinger's book, like many classics, is an exception to the rule — meaning it's something a new writer should almost certainly not attempt. Why? Because a flashback happens entirely in the past and is often referential only, meaning the author includes it only to explain something in the present that the story is really about.

Developing Characters through Writing Exercises

Children are wild creatures at heart. That tendency to revel unrestrained in their lives allows children to experience events and emotions very deeply. Incorporate that kind of open emotionality into children's books to make your character more interesting.

But we, as adults, have often forgotten what it means to have emotions right at the surface, to care about someone so deeply and unselfconsciously that you notice everything about them and take it all in.

REMEMBER

Exercises can help you develop and strengthen general and specific writing muscles. You can use each exercise that we introduce in the following sections not only to get yourself writing, but also to come up with themes to write about. You absolutely must write memorable characters — and you can't write memorable characters unless you know them really well. For further practice, prompts, and inspiration look up masterclass.com in the writing section and learn what some prominent literary masters have done to keep their sparks flying and their characters growing.

Describe your first best friend

For a children's book writer, writing memorable characters is the single most important skill for you to master. But sometimes you may have trouble coming up with a good idea for a character. You can get a head start by writing about your first best friend.

Devote an entire single-spaced page to everything you can remember about your first best friend. Use each of these descriptions to paint them as the substantive character they were:

>> Their appearance

>> Their clothes and style

>> Their favorite color

>> Their family members and what they were like

>> Their favorite food or treat

>> Their favorite activity that you two did together

>> Their favorite activities

>> The secrets you shared

>> The things about them you envied or tried to emulate

>> Their way of walking, talking, or eating that set them apart

TIP

Writing about someone you knew well as a child is the perfect way to develop your ability to create good child characters. Ultimately, you can change a lot of attributes about a character to fit your story (and to protect the innocent), but this exercise can help you figure out how to build a unique person out of words on paper. Long after you forget exactly what happened in Louise Fitzhugh's *Harriet the Spy* (Penguin Random House), you still remember Harriet. Years after reading Roald Dahl's *Charlie and the Chocolate Factory* (Puffin Books), you may not recall the plot, but you do recall Charlie, the Oompa-Loompas, and the inimitable Mr. Wonka (a better childlike adult character has never been written!).

Borrow your favorite children's book characters

Pick up one of your favorite books and write down the names of the main characters, the ones who made you fall in love with the book. Now, take those characters and write them a new adventure in your own voice. (Quite a few children's books have successfully used existing literary characters from books that are in the public domain.)

This exercise allows you to write by using someone else's ideas and characters that you know well (so you don't have to come up with your own) while allowing you to take those characters on a totally different adventure that you write in your own voice.

You might think that exercises like this one are unrelated to the task at hand (writing your children's book), but we promise that it's directly related. It helps you hone the skills you need for your writing, allowing you to practice before you commit to the real thing.

Revisit a painful or joyful experience from your childhood

Everyone was a child once. You may not remember all that much about your childhood in detail (unless you're one of those rare people with prodigious memories of childhood). But you can remember some particular painful or joyous experience that really elicited emotion. Many books dedicated to the craft of creative writing suggest this psychological approach to writing: Write from memories that pained you or filled you with elation.

So go back to the beginning of your development as a human. Pick out a painful experience that you can remember from when you were young. Write from that child's experience:

>> What exactly happened? What brought it about?

>> Why was it painful? How did the pain feel in your body?

>> How did you express your pain, if you did? If you didn't, why not?

>> How has the event reverberated throughout your life, if it has?

>> Why would you never wish the event on another child?

Writing from these painful memories can bring you right into a child's head.

On the other hand, consider writing about a wonderful experience that happened to you as a child. Write about an event that so filled you with joy that you can remember it today (even if it's something as simple as getting what you wanted for your birthday):

>> What about it made you so happy?

>> How did you express that happiness? If you didn't express yourself, why not?

>> Why would you like to see another child have an experience like yours?

Mining the little glorious moments in your life as a child can help you create a child character who is similarly joyous — even if it's just at the end of your main character's story.

Chapter **9**

The Plot Thickens: Conflict, Climax, and Resolution

Most writers aren't exactly sure what a plot is. Is it the story line itself? The action within the story? The steps that the main character takes while they progress from beginning, to middle, and through to the end? The answer is yes — to all of the above.

Plain and simple, *plot* is what happens. In particular, it's what happens to your main character — all the connected events involving the protagonist that lead up to a climax. Your main character drives the plot of the story, directing its forward motion from the very beginning to the very end.

To be convincing, a plot has to unfold in a believable way, regardless of whether the characters are animals or the story takes place in the future. In this chapter, we help you create believable and engaging plots. Because your main character is so critical to your story's plot, we concentrate on showing you how the events and actions involving the main character make up a plot. We also introduce you to drama and pacing, two important storytelling components that can make or break your plot. And because we know you're eager to apply what this book shows you, we walk you through the process of outlining your plot and preview some common plot problems (and how to avoid them).

Plot: It's All about Action

Plot revolves around what your character does, how they walk the talk, how they interact with others, and why. In children's books, plot and character are king; stories that children really like always have action and a main character who ends up in a satisfactory place.

REMEMBER

Action isn't description. Action is where your character's feet take them and what they literally and figuratively bump into on their way there.

Action involves showing what happens in the here and now, not relating what happened in the past, when the event's already over. Even if you use the past tense to describe what's already occurred, relate the story by conveying the action in an immediate way.

Here's an example of telling what happened (the action) after it's all over:

> She went to the pet store, but all the monkeys were sold out. So she decided to liberate one from the zoo.

Try this instead:

> She slipped into the pet store. After searching row after row and finding only empty cages, she walked up to the counter. "Excuse me, but do you have any monkeys?"
>
> "Nope. All sold out." The clerk turned away from the counter, busying himself with paperwork.
>
> *Rats!* she thought. *It's not like I can go to the jungle and invite a monkey to come over and play.* Then a wonderful idea occurred to her: *Why not liberate one from the zoo?* She was sure the monkeys hated it there anyway, all locked up and lonely.

The second example is still told in the past tense, but the story puts the reader in the main character's shoes, walking where she walks — even listening in to her thoughts. That's how you show action.

TIP

Kick off your plot with your main character almost immediately in a situation of conflict. In other words, give them a desire to fulfill or a challenge to overcome. Then give them something that gets in the way of that desire or makes it difficult to complete that challenge. Your story can detail that problem; add to its complexity; move along to your climax, where the situation gets worse; and then resolve everything.

Centering on the Story

In a successful children's story, the plot and the main character are closely intertwined, which means you flesh out your protagonist by showing readers how they react and what they do at each point in your story; however, a plot that narrates events is very different from a plot comprising meaningful events involving characters who change as a result of their actions. The latter is a *story*.

A plot that narrates a sequence of actions, one after another, doesn't provide much meaning, even if you have the main character involved at every step. Consider this basic plot:

> A sheltered young girl's wealthy father remarries a woman who has two daughters. The father dies. The stepmother enslaves the girl, treating her badly. The girl grows up as a maid in her own house. A prince holds a ball to find a bride. With a bit of magic, the girl is able to attend but must leave at midnight. The prince falls in love with the girl. The girl runs from the ball right before she would have been reduced to rags. The prince searches all over the kingdom for her, but can't find her. Many would-be wives scheme to get his attention. He devises a way of ascertaining the girl's true identity. She figures out how to get noticed. At last, they're reunited. They marry, and the girl no longer has to be a maid. The princess employs her stepmother and her stepsister in the house but does not mistreat them as they did her. The prince and the princess live happily ever after.

Even though the preceding example gives a narration of events, you know instinctively that it isn't a story because you don't care about these characters. You don't see the main characters, the prince and Cinderella, in action. You don't watch Cinderella getting ready for the ball. You don't hear the prince's agitation at her disappearance. As a result, you don't care about them or what happens next.

But if you show the emotions that the characters feel, revealing those emotions through their actions and reactions to events, you have the beginnings of a real story. And if you show what the main characters do that shapes, changes, and molds them throughout the story — going through conflict and struggling to get to the other side — you really get your readers' attention.

Giving Your Story a Beginning, Middle, and End

Every good story has a beginning, a middle, and an end. The beginning reels you in, the climactic middle keeps you going, and the end satisfies you with resolution.

REMEMBER

Keep these pointers in mind to make sure your plot engages readers from start to finish:

» **Hook readers from the get-go.** Your plot needs a beginning in which you introduce your main character and hook readers into the action by introducing the character's driving desire, creating conflict right away. Consider the story of Cinderella. At the beginning of this tale, Cinderella's dad dies, leaving her at the mercy of a cruel stepmother and dreaming of a better life.

» **Direct the conflict to its natural climax.** You then have to build the conflict to a point where the main character is really in trouble, and the story could go either way — the conflict reaches a climax. In the middle of Cinderella's story, she meets a partner who can help her escape her terrible life, but he can't seem to find her.

» **Resolve your story with a conquered conflict and a changed character.** Begin to shape your ending by providing an opportunity for your main character to face the conflict, overcome the worst of it, and become a different — perhaps better — person as a result of all they have gone through by the end of the story. Cinderella's story ends with her decision to escape and try on the slipper, thus ensuring a better life. And she fulfills her driving desire to belong to a family — her chosen family, not the one she inherited.

Propelling Your Story with Drama and Pacing

After you decide on a beginning, middle, and end to your story, you need to incorporate enough drama, using pacing, to keep the reader interested. *Drama* is struggle, conflict, emotionality, and turbulence. *Pacing* involves keeping the drama at a more heightened speed than you would find in real life.

You can create a good story and memorable characters by focusing on what your character wants (their burning desire, which we help you find in Chapter 8), the actions they use to achieve their goal (plot), and the conflicts that get in their way (drama), plus the anticipation and uncertainty of whether they can get to the goal line (pacing). The following sections talk about the keys to incorporating drama and pacing in your plot.

WARNING

If you have scene after scene in which no real change occurs, you don't have a plot. Each plot point (action point) must somehow involve the main character and their main desire. It must fall somewhere on the character arc that we describe in Chapter 8.

Drama: A reason to turn the page

If your character experiences strong emotions due to the events of the story, you have drama. Likewise, if the turbulence of those events tosses your character around, such that their life is changed or their way of life is threatened, you also have drama.

TIP

To make sure you have enough drama in your story, ask yourself whether your character is struggling at each major plot point. Think about the tale of Cinderella. Is she suffering? Is she challenged? Is something threatening what she wants? Are the events in her life turbulent enough to keep people interested? If not, you have work to do.

Pacing: How you keep the pages turning

Pacing is the force that keeps the reader turning the pages, wanting — no, needing — to find out what happens next. In your story, each major plot point has to keep readers guessing about what may happen next.

Because your audience likely has grown up on TV, video games, and smartphone apps that present rapidly moving story lines, children's books offer quicker action than in the past. What does that mean for you as a writer? You need to know when and how to pick up the pace in your story.

TIP

Here are some tips for creating good pacing in different types of children's books:

>> **Picture books:** Keep the story going at a good clip by drawing out conflict evenly throughout and writing tightly and well. (For a practical tip on how to check picture book pacing during the editing phase, head to Chapter 14.) Illustrations can go a long way in perfecting the pace; make sure the images are pulling their weight with plot, drama, and pacing.

- **Younger children's chapter books and middle-grade books:** End the chapters with cliffhangers that leave the reader with a question. Literally, you can end with a question: Would Amanda figure out a way to get enough oxygen before the flooding waters completely engulfed her? Or figuratively: Amanda watched the flood waters rise, wondering when she would be forced to take her last breath. Just beware: Don't use a cliffhanger with every chapter, or you lose the element of suspense.

- **Young adult novels:** Have chapters end on a high note, in the middle of a scene, at a tense moment so that you can keep readers turning the pages, but you don't have to be quite as heavy handed about it as you do when writing for younger readers.

Outlining to Structure Your Plot

Structure is simply the bones of your story upon which you lay the skin and organs: drama, pacing, effective transitions, and strong point of view. You hear a lot of talk about structure in writing circles, and structure truly is the key to a good story. To give a story structure means you use your main character to propel the action through beginning, middle, and end. That way, the plot proceeds apace.

You can turn your story's plot structure into an outline pretty easily. Outlining your story allows you to pinpoint what your main character wants, what they do to get it, and how conflict intermittently challenges them. If other characters become important, you can expand your outline to include them, too. Regardless, use your outline as a repository for the who, what, when, where, why, and how of each of the three parts — beginning, middle, and end — of your story. From there, you can easily flesh out the details. The following sections explain how to create an outline to help you solidify your story's structure.

REMEMBER

Plot and character are closely intertwined because the protagonist drives the plot. Character and plot are so connected that they proceed neck and neck on the same schedule. When the plot hits a bump, so does the main character (or vice versa). When the conflict in the plot approaches resolution, so does the main character's desire. And when the ending results in a changed character and a wrapped-up plot, the reader feels like the journey was worth it.

DEFEND YOUR PROSE — OR LET IT GO

Make sure your entire book's structure works by doing an action outline for every single part.

If you're writing a picture book, for each and every paragraph, ask yourself Lisa's Three Hallowed Action Questions:

1. Does this paragraph move the plot forward? How?

2. Does this paragraph develop my main character by showing them in action? How?

3. Does this paragraph introduce drama through conflict and thus make the story proceed at a nice pace? How?

If you can answer "yes" to at least one of these questions — and if you can defend how you did it in front of a hanging jury — you can keep that paragraph. If you answer "not really" or simply "no" — cut the paragraph.

For chapter books and longer books, ask yourself these very important questions for each chapter. If a chapter has one of these purposes, then it can stay in. If nothing really happens and you can't point to exactly the sentences that give you an affirmative answer to any of these questions, guess what? Out it goes.

TIP

Sometimes, you may find visualizing what plot structure looks like challenging, even with an outline. Fortunately, if you created a character arc for your main character, you already have a plot visual handy. Refer to the character arc for Cinderella in Chapter 8. Notice how the beginning is illustrated at the bottom left of the arc, the middle/climax is at the top, and the resolution moves on the down slope. If you can take apart your own story and plot it out on an arc like that one, you probably have your basic plot laid out.

Creating a step sheet

A *step sheet* (also referred to as an *action outline*) is a useful tool for keeping track of plot points. It can also help you keep track of the beginning/middle/end of your story, pacing, and character development. You can make your step sheet as detailed or as thinly written as you feel you need.

Here's what the beginning of a step sheet may look like, using the story of Cinderella as an example. We've cut out a lot of the steps in the plot and left just a few key examples for you to look at. Your step sheet, on the other hand, should have a bullet point for every single action that takes place:

» The beginning:
- **Plot point:** A spoiled young girl's wealthy father remarries a woman who has two daughters.
- **Character development:** Show Cinderella in action trying to befriend her mean stepsisters.
- **Pacing:** Show the emotion behind the growing dejection that she feels.

» Also the beginning:
- **Plot point:** The father dies.
- **Character development:** Show Cinderella's grief.
- **Pacing:** Show the stepmother and sisters plotting to take over the house and grounds.

» The middle:
- **Plot point:** A prince holds a ball to find a bride.
- **Character development:** Show the entire town excited over the event, Cinderella depressed at not being able to participate.
- **Pacing:** Show the prince in action as an adventurer, a romantic — a definite catch.

» The end:
- **Plot point:** The prince and the princess live happily ever after.
- **Character development:** Show the rightness of the good guys winning.
- **Pacing:** Slow down into the final ending.

TIP

Make your main character the focal point of your step sheet, but you can add secondary characters if they affect the main plotline. Just make sure you wrap up their fates at the conclusion of the story, too.

Fleshing out your outline

A step sheet is a bare bones outline that helps you clearly see your plot structure. Some writers like a more detailed outline so that they have a sort of blueprint from which to write. A more fleshed out outline can provide a separate place for you to add notes about details that you want to incorporate when you get to that point in your story. It can also provide highly left-brained people with a literary to-do list, highlighting specific steps to check off after you accomplish them.

REMEMBER

Use outlines as organizing tools. Don't treat them like holy words carved in stone. If, in the course of writing fiction, you find yourself veering away into some interesting but unforeseen place, follow your characters to see where they lead you.

Now suppose you choose to write your Cinderella story as a middle-grade chapter book. Now you can create a full outline of the story, starting with the journalist's trusty six questions:

>> **Where:** Setting

>> **When:** Time

>> **What/how:** Plot point

>> **Who:** Character development

>> **Why:** Drama, pacing, and character motivation

So the start of your outline may look like this:

>> Chapter 1:
- **Setting:** A castle and its grounds.
- **Time:** Medieval Europe.
- **Plot point:** A spoiled young girl's wealthy father remarries a woman who has two daughters.
- **Character development:** Show Cinderella in action trying to befriend her mean stepsisters.
- **Supporting characters:** Father, stepmother, stepsisters, house staff.
- **Pacing:** Show emotion behind Cinderella's growing dejection.

>> Chapter 2:
- **Setting:** Same, but widens to include the town, church, and burial ceremony.
- **Time:** A few months later.
- **Plot point:** The father dies.
- **Character development:** Show Cinderella's grief.
- **Supporting characters:** Introduce Cinderella's best friend, Jude.
- **Pacing:** At the end of the chapter, show the stepmother and sisters plotting to take over house and grounds.

» Chapter 3:

- **Setting:** Same castle, but show Cinderella going to town.

- **Time:** A week later.

- **Plot point:** The stepmother enslaves the girl, treating her badly.

- **Character development:** Show Cinderella facing up to her tasks with good cheer, determined to survive despite the conditions.

- **Supporting characters:** Further develop the relationship between Cinderella and Jude. Show the townspeople watching her degradation from upper-class to working class.

- **Pacing:** Show how her stepmother begins plundering Cinderella's father's assets to feed her own vanity and greed.

TALKING WITH MICHAEL GREEN, FORMER PRESIDENT AND PUBLISHER OF PHILOMEL BOOKS

For the real scoop on plotting, pacing, and drama — and what they all mean after you get your manuscript to a real-live children's literary publisher — check out what Michael Green has to say. He was president and publisher of Philomel Books, a division of Penguin Books USA. Here's his perspective:

- **The first thing that captures your attention in a new manuscript:** "I take an uncommon interest in someone's opening sentence. A weak one doesn't necessarily signal a weak manuscript, but a strong one announces a writer and does tend to bode well for what lies ahead. I also listen for a writer's voice. Before plot or characterization has the chance to take root, voice can take root."

- **The one thing that can cause you to immediately pitch a manuscript:** "Nothing earns a rejection slip faster than an overwritten first paragraph. It never bodes well. There is a time and a place for character description or exposition, and the story's opening is never it."

- **How to tell whether a main character works:** "The main character should take life unto itself. It should speak, breathe, and react on its own — that is when an author knows the character comes across as real."

- **The most important elements in a well-constructed plot:** "A well-constructed plot is a bit like an open umbrella. It forms an arc that envelopes and reaches out toward all characters and plot points. It unifies and gives purpose to everything that touches that arc."

- **Dramatic pacing:** "Picture books and novels are separate beasts. A picture book will always have a sense of pacing, a sense of movement. A good part of that movement is owed to the artwork, though, which needs to move along the story on its own terms.

  "Within the spacious boundaries of a novel, dramatic pacing and characterization are vital. An author needs to be careful, however, of not forcing the issue. Quiet, subtle moments in Chapter 2 might very well be setting up an earthquake in Chapter 5; the contrast between the two will help the tension pop when it finally arrives."

- **Tricks to drama and pacing:** "Watch for the unusual when reading other writers' books. Different writers play different games with pacing and drama; be attentive to what works for you as a reader. Also, pay attention to how chapters close. Chapter closing lines should be tiny jewels that close a door on one scene while tempting a reader to tear open that door and burst through the other side to see what happens."

Knowing when to circumvent an outline

If you think the issue of an outline seems absurd or overkill, it probably is — for you. For example, you probably don't need an outline for a board book. Most picture books don't get written with an outline unless the writer gets stuck and needs help figuring out why. If you apply the advice in the sidebar "Defend your prose — or let it go," in this chapter, for every sentence of a picture book, you always end up with a tighter manuscript.

Additionally, some writers simply can't work with an outline at all, preferring to just get writing, and then working on (and reworking) the written pages without an organizational tool to fall back on.

Preventing Plot Problems

Not all plots are the same, but some common plot problems can creep into your story when you're not looking. Fortunately, we can help. Here are a few guidelines about approaches you should avoid so that you don't muck up your plot:

- » **Action with no actor:** When you're writing a scene, make it clear who's doing the action. Don't make your reader hunt around previous or successive paragraphs to figure out who is the star of the scene. The same goes for dialogue, which we discuss in Chapter 10.

- » **Actor with no action:** Don't go on and on about a character — any character — without making sure they do something relevant to the plot. In other words, if you find yourself mired in a lot of description, backstory, or pages of dialogue without any narrative action, your character and your plot aren't moving forward.

- » **Scene it once, scene it twice, but never thrice (or more):** Although some writers like to write from different points of view (POVs, see Chapter 12) in alternating chapters, don't repeat a scene just so the reader sees it from another character's POV. They got it the first time. Now move on.

- » **Not-so-lovely loose ends:** Remember that character you introduced in the second chapter? The one who was giving your main character a hard enough time for you to mention them by first — and maybe even last — name and spend an entire chapter on them? Make sure you let us know by the end of the story what happened to them. Don't leave any of your plot points without some kind of closure, either. Believe us, plenty of readers out there notice — and hate it. Conversely, don't go on and on, belaboring the ending. Make it short and sweet.

Writing Your First Draft

Don't expect to sit down and craft a perfect children's book from start to finish, even if you've fully outlined your characters and plot. Writing isn't just about putting your first thoughts on paper and being ready to publish. Instead, writing is about writing, revising, and revising some more.

The only way you can write freely is to turn off your inner critic and just get going. Travel as far as you can with your character bibles and step sheets (discussed in the section "Creating a step sheet," earlier in this chapter), and then just stop. Don't worry about character arcs, plot steps, pacing, or even drama. Just let your main character go. Find yourself blathering on? No problem. Just keep going until you reach the end. When you do get to the end, pat yourself on the back! You have an official first draft done — which no one is ever going to see.

The only element that you must make sure you have in place before you start writing is your character's burning desire, which drives your story. (See Chapter 8 for info about crafting your characters.)

After writing your first draft, you have some options:

>> Go back and work on your second draft, using the tips and techniques in this chapter.

>> Read all the chapters in Part 3 — and then go back and start work on your second draft.

In between each draft (or every few drafts, if you're writing a chapter book or longer work), print out your story and reread it with a pencil, just like many editors did in the old days. For many people, reading printed matter on paper makes it more "real" than reading it on a screen. Reading it aloud also offers a good way to check whether the writing flows or whether it's awkward or incomplete. It's also a good idea to sleep on it in between drafts. Give yourself a breather and celebrate your accomplishment. This gives your brain time to rest and refresh. After you have your story polished to a shine, you can dive into the dirty work of editing, covered in Chapter 14.

» Adding speech to your character bible

» Reading dialogue aloud

» Making your dialogue mistake-free

» Exercising your dialogue writing muscles

Chapter **10**

Can We Talk? Writing Effective Dialogue

Dialogue is a form of action; you can use it to develop character and plot. It can enhance pacing and drama. And it can increase a book's readability by transmitting necessary information while breaking up passages of narration and description. Writing good dialogue isn't the same as writing realistic dialogue. Realistic dialogue is boring as all heck to read if you write it out in the way that it actually occurs. To write good dialogue, you must develop a keen ear and translate what you hear into a wittier, smarter, more meaningful version of itself. So, in order for your characters to sound good, you first need to write the way people actually talk — and then make it better.

In this chapter, we help you figure out when to use dialogue. We also discuss the functions dialogue must serve within your story and your characters' development to make it worth including. We talk about how good dialogue requires drama and tension and how to get in the groove of putting words into children's mouths by listening and paying attention to some actual, living owners of those mouths. We show you how your character bible can help you define each of your characters, making them sound different from one another, and how you can check your dialogue by listening to it read aloud. We also take you through some of the most common dialogue mistakes and help you hone your skills with a couple of handy exercises.

The Fundamentals of Good Dialogue

Writers are like jugglers. They have to keep many elements going at the same time: character development, plot construction, establishing setting — the list goes on. You can use dialogue to develop everything from characters and plot to setting, drama, and pacing — but only if you know how to incorporate dialogue effectively.

The first step in writing good dialogue is to figure out when you should use it at all. Although we can't give you a rule of thumb about when to use dialogue (mostly because each children's book format differs, as does each writer's style), we can tell you to use it whenever you have a lot of descriptive or narrative paragraphs that you need to break up. You can also use dialogue to help develop a character or characters in your reader's mind, showing the characters interacting in order to reveal who they really are. Dialogue can also help move the plot forward, when you need a character to take the reader to that next part of the story.

Of course, good dialogue also has drama. It creates emotion and inspires action. We tell you more about this, as well as the different functions dialogue can play in your story, in the following sections.

WARNING

If you can't spell out exactly why a piece of dialogue exists, that dialogue probably doesn't belong in your story. For example, small talk or simple greetings between characters don't pass muster if they don't add anything concrete to your story. Dialogue needs to have a true function (such as giving information, developing characters, or moving your story forward), and the reader needs to find it interesting (in other words, it needs to have drama).

Dialogue has a function

REMEMBER

Although dialogue gives you a great tool for enriching your fiction (and your nonfiction), it's not the same as talking. *Talking* is two or more people exchanging words — meaningful or not, boring or not. *Dialogue* has a function, a job to do.

You use dialogue in your story only if it performs at least one of the functions that we cover in the following sections.

Giving information

You have to write narration and description, unless they incorporate action, in a somewhat static way, by *telling* rather than showing. Dialogue gives information in a direct way, *showing* the reader what's happening, rather than telling the reader about it in description. When you use dialogue to convey information, you add spice and emotion, personalization and action, interaction and character development. Consider the following example of how dialogue gives information:

> JANE: Didja call him?
>
> NELLY: Yeah. But he wasn't home. Let it ring and ring. Called a bunch of times, too. I think he never came home last night.
>
> JANE: C'mon. I bet I know where he is!

In this exchange, we find out that the person whom the girls are discussing is missing and that they want to go find him. The narrator could have revealed this information in prose, but it's not as interesting:

> Jane called Nelly to find out if Nelly had contacted their friend James. Nelly revealed she had tried, but James had not answered despite repeated attempts. So Jane dragged off Nelly in search of the missing boy.

Developing characters

Instead of describing who a character is and how they behave in a specific situation, use dialogue. In the following example, dialogue develops characters:

> "Do you mean that you think you can find out the answer to it?" said the March Hare.
>
> "Exactly so," said Alice.
>
> "Then you should say what you mean," the March Hare went on.
>
> "I do," Alice hastily replied. "At least — at least I mean what I say — that's the same thing, you know."
>
> "Not the same thing a bit!" said the Hatter. "You might just as well say that 'I see what I eat' is the same thing as 'I eat what I see'!"
>
> "You might just as well say," added the March Hare, "that 'I like what I get' is the same thing as "I get what I like'!"
>
> "You might just as well say," added the Dormouse, which seemed to be talking in its sleep, "that 'I breathe when I sleep' is the same thing as 'I sleep when I breathe'!"
>
> "It *is* the same thing with you," said the Hatter, and here the conversation dropped.

In this exchange from Lewis Carroll's *Alice's Adventures in Wonderland*, we learn that the March Hare and his cohorts are a bunch of semanticists, picky regarding specificity, especially when it comes to their beloved pastime of talking in riddles to Alice, whom they accuse of fast and loose treatment of the language. While the dialogue continues, we also find out that her companions quite easily puzzle Alice, which we take to mean that Alice (in this exchange, as a character) is not as smart or as quick-witted as the others — even though the exchange is fairly ridiculous.

We could have accomplished the same character development in prose, but you wouldn't have half as fun reading it, nor would you understand the characters' personalities, quirks, and thought processes as clearly.

Moving the story forward

Dialogue is action through interaction; therefore, good dialogue moves plot points in your story ahead. Check out this example of how dialogue moves the story forward:

> "What's the matter, Mother?" he said.
>
> "Oh, Diamond, my darling! You have been so ill!" she sobbed.
>
> "No, Mother dear. I've only been at the back of the north wind," returned Diamond.
>
> "I thought you were dead," said his mother.
>
> But that moment, the doctor came in.
>
> "Oh! there!" said the doctor with gentle cheerfulness; "we're better to-day, I see."

In this exchange from George MacDonald's *At the Back of the North Wind* between the main character, a boy named Diamond, and his mother, we find out that Diamond doesn't realize that his journeys with his friend, the North Wind, leave him sicker and sicker. Reading the text, we realize also that Diamond has no idea how long he has been gone or that he leaves his body behind when he travels with her. The dialogue not only moves the story forward to Diamond's recovery in the world inhabited by his family, but it also adds information, characterizing the journeys he goes on as somewhat otherworldly.

Again, the author could have put this dialogue easily into straight prose narrative, but prose just doesn't have the same drama.

Dialogue has drama

Dialogue needs to be dramatic. It should create arguments, strong emotions, or conflict between your characters. That conflict should lead to some new action on the character's part (and move the story along). Good dialogue is short, potent, and meaningful.

Say you're at a point in your story where you need to move the plot forward. You could do it in narration, or you can accomplish it in dialogue. Often, dialogue conveys more drama and much more emotion, while revealing more about the characters' personalities, than prose can. Take this example:

> Jane nearly tripped over Nelly as she approached the train door. There he was. "I don't believe it," she muttered to herself, feeling her heart start to race. James saw her and stopped, causing those behind him to grumble and shove in their hurry to get past him. "I was sure you wouldn't be here," she whispered.
>
> He grinned, raising an eyebrow. "I just lost a bet, too."
>
> "With *who?*" Jane demanded.

In this short exchange, we move the plot forward by discovering James's whereabouts. We also glean important information: that James, whom Jane and Nelly want to find, has just come back from a trip somewhere. We find out that Jane feels more for James than just platonic concern, based on the depth of her emotion, her heart racing, her speaking in whispered tones, and her instant jealousy at his mention of a bet with an unnamed person (perhaps a rival for his affections). And we also find out that this funny, confident boy shares some of Jane's feelings because of his happy-go-lucky grin and his raised eyebrow. All these little actions, expressions, and body language show instead of tell. (We dive into showing versus telling later in this chapter.)

This exchange could have proceeded completely differently. James could have stuttered and blushed, indicating that he's not confident or happy-go-lucky. Jane could have attacked him verbally, demanding to know where he was and why he hadn't contacted her or Nelly. Written that way, the dialogue would tell us different things about the characters themselves, and it would have moved the plot forward differently and given us different information about the relationship between Jane and James.

You can work in dialogue at the beginning of a scene to introduce it in an active way. Try writing the entire scene in dialogue, and then just in narrative. Then take the best of the prose parts — those that add to the setting, the actions, the indicators of tone of voice or body language, the expression, the characters' movements, the short descriptions — and merge them together. Between the two versions, you should come up with a fleshed-out scene that actively moves the plot forward, sustained by characters who make it all come alive by what they say and how they speak.

Listening to Real-World Dialogue

Training yourself to listen and really hear is the first step to writing dialogue that sounds like real people speaking to each other and not like a writer trying to simulate real people talking to each other. One time-tested universal tip about dialogue is that in the real world, children sound very different from adults — and children must sound different in your writing, as well. Consider the following sections your primer into how kids talk versus how adults talk.

How kids talk

Go to any park or classroom filled with children the age of your audience. Listen. You encounter the following:

>> **Contractions:** For example, *it's* and *can't* versus *it is* and *cannot*

>> **Stuttering and hemming:** A lot of *uh, yeah, um, well, hmm, like, you know?,* and all their incoherent relatives

>> **Incomplete sentences:** *If you wanna* versus *If you want to go, you may exit stage right*

>> **Nonverbal communication:** A chin nod or a headshake in reply, rather than actual words

>> **Body language contradicting words:** Crossed arms signaling a specific attitude, even if the words contradict that attitude

Just ask the parent of a teenager if you don't understand this example.

>> **Shortcuts:** Forms of communication such as slang

If you write your dialogue without at least a few of the above, it comes out sounding as tedious and wooden as a court transcript. You can't write dialogue exactly the way you hear it in real life, but you can get close. Here's an example of how an actual conversation between two teenagers may sound:

KID A: Didja hear what happened to Sarina?

KID B: No. What?

KID A: She got totally narced on.

KID B: By who?

KID A: Dunno. That blond girl? Maybe that other — you know.

KID B: No way.

Notice the shortcuts and the incomplete sentences. Pay attention to how body language says a lot because not much information is actually conveyed in this dialogue, despite the number of exchanges.

To make this dialogue really work for you, by developing a character and moving plot forward (see Chapters 8 and 9, respectively), you'd have to rewrite it to something like this:

> KID A: Didja hear what happened to Sarina, that new girl who was, you know, trying to hang with the popular kids?
>
> KID B: No. What?
>
> KID A: She got narced on. Someone told about her shoplifting. Ya know — some full-on freetail therapy.
>
> KID B: Yeah. But who told?
>
> KID A: I dunno. Maybe that blond girl, the leader. Or whoever she showed the stuff to. The price tags were probably still on.

This version tells you a lot more about who the players are, what happened, and what's really at stake in terms of the plot. We didn't change it much, we only tweaked it a little to make it better than it was, while still retaining the tone of the teenagers' original speech.

How grown-ups talk

Grown-ups, for the most part, speak like children do in terms of shorter sentences mixed in with longer ones, interruptions, crossing over each other's speech, incomplete sentences, contractions, and more. Here's the major difference: In their dialogue exchanges, grown-ups can (depending on the situation) swear, use big vocabulary words (sparingly and in context), use less slang, and generally sound more mature.

TIP

Yes, we all know adults who sound like kids (maybe they're trying too hard to be cool, right?) and kids who sound like adults (read: Poindexter alert!), but unless you have a definable purpose for these two instances, try to avoid them. Otherwise, you're like a person pretending to be a writer who can actually write good dialogue. We can't have that. We want you to write the real thing — the good stuff!

Adding a Speech Section to Your Character Bible

In Chapter 8, we discuss creating a character bible that really lays out who your character is in terms of personality, looks, history, family, quirks — all the elements that contribute to making up a person. A character bible functions to help you get to know who your character is and to help you differentiate between characters.

A great addition to a character bible identifies how your character speaks. Consider the following characteristics of speech and lay out where each of your characters falls as far as these attributes are concerned:

>> How articulate are they? (We're referring to characters who are old enough to be articulate, of course.) Are they educated, and does their speech reflect that education?

>> Are they not a native English speaker? What's their native tongue? Does their English sound like they got it from a book? Or is your character a younger child apt to make grammatical mistakes, such as mispronouncing words?

>> What's the quality of their voice? Is it hoarse? Loud? Soft? Squeaky? High? Low?

>> Do they have any verbal anomalies, such as lisping or stuttering?

>> Are they direct in their speech or shyer, more obtuse?

>> Do they use swear words or slang, jargon, or street talk?

>> Are they loquacious or terse? Abrupt or apt to talk your ear off?

>> Do they answer every question with another question?

Although you can't (nor should you) answer all of the preceding questions for every character, questions like these can help you find your character's particular voice and keep that voice consistent and differentiated from the other characters in your book. Plus, your character bible's speech section helps you avoid the problem of having your teenage protagonist sound the same as their mother.

Testing! Testing! Reading Dialogue Out Loud

REMEMBER

To test whether your dialogue works, listen to someone else read it back to you. When you hear your dialogue read aloud, pay attention and ask yourself

>> **Do the child characters sound like children?** If they consistently speak in complete sentences or use strings of huge words, you probably have your English professor in mind and not a child. Shorten sentences. Add a mild stutter. Fill in some information about the character by using brief descriptions of telling body language and facial expressions.

>> **Do the characters sound different from one another?** If not, you need to listen to how various people speak and try to capture those differences. And revisit the speech section in that character's character bible to see whether you're remaining true to your original idea of how they actually speak.

>> **Is the speech wordy or to the point?** If it's wordy, you probably have too many adjectives and describe too much in your dialogue. Shorten. Hone. Tighten. Make better, more precise word choices.

>> **Is the emotion clear from the words you use?** If not, choose your words more precisely, making each one count; keep RhymeZone (www.rhymezone.com) open on a tab in your browser to find synonyms. Go back to your character bible. Between important speakers' lines, add occasional, brief descriptions of their revealing facial expressions or body movements.

>> **Does your main character have a strong voice?** Do they sound interesting and unique? If not, you may want to reexamine their personality and see what special speech patterns or tone of voice may make them more compelling. Perhaps you need to get to know them better. Try some of the exercises described in the section "Improving Dialogue by Using Writing Exercises," later in this chapter.

>> **Why does each piece of dialogue appear in your story?** Does it move the story forward or further embellish a character? If it doesn't, *sayonara,* baby!

A new writer almost always struggles with dialogue. But with practice and determination, you can write great dialogue. And when in doubt about a particular piece, leave it out.

REMEMBER

When you write dialogue, you have time to craft the ultimate witty comebacks, astute questions, and on-target answers (unlike in real life). On paper, you can make your characters sound better than the rest of us lugheads. So, for all those times you went home cursing yourself for failing to deliver that perfect retort — the one that came to you on your way home — consider writing books as your revenge. Make those characters talk pretty.

Avoiding Common Dialogue Mistakes

People really do speak in fits and starts, but that doesn't mean your characters should — it simply takes up too much valuable space to include all those hems and haws, pauses, and incomplete sentences — unless you can fill them with meaning, and that takes practice. In speech that you hear, you get all the nonverbal nuance and inflection. Speech that you read, on the other hand, loses those cues, so your words have to work extra hard.

You have to practice listening, writing, and editing to become a good writer of dialogue. You also need to be willing to make some mistakes, at least in your drafts. Of course, writers who have come before you have made some mistakes so commonly that you don't have to make them yourself. Check out the following sections for the scoop on these mistakes and how to avoid them. These sections feature scenes with Jane, James, and Nelly, who make an appearance in the section "The Fundamentals of Good Dialogue," earlier in this chapter.

Failing to have conflict or tension

Dialogue that just delivers information or develops a character without, in itself, containing any hint of drama or tension isn't very interesting. That doesn't mean your characters have to get into a fight or speak meanly to one another. But they should actively move the story forward. For example, here's our short scene from the section "Dialogue has drama," earlier in this chapter, written without any tension:

> Jane and Nelly approached the train door. James appeared a moment later. "There he is," she said. He saw her and stopped, causing those behind him to mutter and shove in their hurry to get past him. "Good, you're here," she said.
>
> James hefted his backpack over his shoulder. "Yep, I'm here."
>
> "Okay, let's go, then," Jane said.

Repeating information: Showing versus telling

REMEMBER

Many beginning writers feel they have to introduce the dialogue with an explanation of what's to follow (or conversely, to follow up the dialogue with a recap), essentially repeating the same information in narration. Don't waste the reader's time. Choose one or the other, not both. And remember to choose *showing* (actual dialogue and action) rather than *telling* (recapping or narration) whenever possible.

The following scene illustrates the silliness of repeating information that you've already given readers in the narrative:

> As they made their way out of the train station, Nelly wanted to find out where James had been, so she asked him.
>
> "Where'd you go?" Nelly asked, trying to act casual now that they had left the bustle of the station.
>
> "I went to see my uncle," James replied. "And he told me — "
>
> Nelly interrupted him in a rush. "The one in prison? The — the murderer?"
>
> "Yep. And boy did I find out — "
>
> "You went to visit a murderer? Are you crazy?" Nelly nearly shouted.
>
> Jane had to get her to quiet down so they could hear James speak.
>
> "Will you please shut it?" demanded Jane. "I wanted to hear what he found out."
>
> Nelly sniffed, looking at the ground. "Fine. But I still think it was dumb."

Describing dialogue

Some beginning writers forget that they can use dialogue, so they describe verbal exchanges between characters instead of just giving us the exchange in dialogue. Case in point:

> Once they had steered clear of the train station, Nelly casually asked James where he had gone. He told her that he had gone to see his uncle. Nelly, shocked, interrupted him, demanding to know if he was talking about his uncle the murderer. James admitted that that was indeed the uncle that he saw and tried to explain, but Nelly interrupted him again. Finally, Jane had to tell Nelly to be quiet so James could tell them all about what he found out.

Putting this exchange into dialogue rather than just reporting about it makes the story much more immediate and engaging.

Using too many speaker references and attributions

Believe it or not, your characters don't need to use each other's names in each leg of your dialogue. And you also don't need to identify each speaker by name each time with an *attribution* ("he said," "she replied," "he asked"). However, if you have three or more speakers in one exchange, you might choose to use attributions for clarity.

See for yourself how unrealistic dialogue can sound when you use too many references and attributions:

> "Hi, Nelly," began James.
>
> "Hi, James," replied Nelly.
>
> "How are you, Nelly?" asked James.
>
> "Oh, doing fine, doing fine, James," stated Nelly.
>
> "Hey, Nelly, how is Jane?" enquired James.
>
> "Jane is fine, James," added Nelly. "How is your Uncle Bob?"

People just don't talk that way, whether they know each other or not. Besides the overuse of names and attributions, notice the unrealistic lack of contractions (*How is* rather than *How's*). And instead of using words like *began* and *stated*, try just using *said* to declutter your dialogue.

WARNING

In real conversations, people never repeat each other's names every other line — or even every once in a while. As a matter of fact, you often say someone's name only when they can't hear you, so you have to say it to get their attention; or if you introduce someone to someone else, you probably mention their name. Using a person's name over and over suggests one of the following:

>> The person who uses a person's name over and over looks down on the other person to get their attention.

>> The person mentioning the name is in a position of power over the named: for example, "Peter Michael Economy! Get your butt over here before I — " said Mrs. Economy. You get the gist.

Creating heavy-handed and unrealistic dialogue

People talk in shorthand, using contractions and body language to convey meaning. So don't load up your dialogue with a lot of information that people wouldn't include in normal conversation. For example:

> "Your uncle is in prison for a reason. He stole all that money from your grandfather with that no-good best friend of his in 2018, killing that poor nurse from Kentucky in the process. The bullet went straight through her heart, which we all considered symbolic, considering he broke your grandmother's heart, not to mention ruining the family name when your family history was dragged through the papers, revealing your illegitimate birth and your grandfather's sketchy past," said Jane.

> "Yes," agreed James, "he is in prison for a reason. But that reason is not what you think. That reason is wrong. He was wrongly convicted because he was not holding the gun when it went off and he did not even want to go into that bank in the first place!"

The preceding example gives narrative disguised as dialogue. Young people would never actually say these words, especially in the way they're written. The amount of detail is unrealistic for the context; too much information is packed into each speaker's turn. Make dialogue simple and to the point, not encumbered by tons of background information and backstory or flashbacks (more on those in Chapter 8).

Filling space with unnecessary dialogue

Don't use dialogue to fill up space on the page or accomplish things that you could convey in a sentence of narrative. For example, when characters introduce themselves, you probably don't need to do it in dialogue — not unless something else important happens during the introduction that gives it a clear function in the story:

> "Hello, Mr. Sloan," said Nelly.

> "Hello, Nelly," said Mr. Sloan. "And who have we here?"

> "Mr. Sloan, I'd like to introduce you to my friends, Jane and James," said Nelly.

> "Hello, Mr. Sloan," said James, extending his hand to Mr. Sloan.

> "Hi, nice to meet you, Mr. Sloan," said Jane, smiling at Mr. Sloan.

NIT-PICKY DIALOGUE PROBLEMS

Some of the mistakes people make when writing dialogue seem pretty minor. But when you see them again and again, particularly in a short children's book, they only get more annoying. Sure, the following list may read like pet peeves to you, but now that we mention them, we bet you start to see them everywhere, too (if you haven't already!):

- **Writing long speeches, lectures, or monologues:** In these passages, one character goes on and on, uninterrupted, for paragraphs. Yaaaaaaaawn.

- **Using *said* tags:** Writing action or body language into the dialogue can move things along. Complex dialogue tags ("she muttered," "he interjected," "they enquired," and so on) slow things down. Use them sparingly when you have to, but when you do, use them only with one character in the spoken exchange. And use only *said* and *asked,* rather than all the other options. The more elaborate tags get heavy-handed, and using them falls into the same category as using too many adjectives and adverbs.

- **Relying on adjectives and adverbs:** Make the words of dialogue that you put in the character's mouth specific and well-chosen enough to convey the emotion without requiring clarifying phrases or adverbs (such as *happily, sadly, tearfully,* and *angrily*).

- **Using semicolons:** Don't use semicolons in dialogue.

- **Indicating a pause in conversation with a comma:** Use an ellipsis (. . .) in dialogue to signal speech trailing off and an em dash (—) to signal an interruption.

- **Using phonetic spellings of dialects:** Use dialect or regional accents in dialogue only if you're very familiar with the dialects. Do it flawlessly and consistently — or don't do it at all, because bad dialect can be seen as offensive to those who use it.

This exchange is much better off in narrative, short and to the point:

> Nelly walked into the office of Mr. Sloan, her father's lawyer, and introduced her friends.

Improving Dialogue by Using Writing Exercises

To write dialogue well, you need to develop a good ear and do a lot of practicing. But you may be better at it than you think. The writing exercises in the following sections can help you get in the practice of regular writing and give you the chance to rehearse writing dialogue without the pressure of having to make it good.

Talking on paper

You can make letter-writing (or e-mails, texts, and instant messages) as free-form as you want. You can write like you speak. You can be trivial and funny, and you can even use bad words. And you can write ungrammatically, in truncated sentences, using shorthand and even emoticons or Internet slang (think LOL or IMHO) to get your meaning across. So sit down, fire up the old laptop, and start talking on paper.

Write letters to anyone, about anything. Have a friend whom you owe a call? Surprise them instead with a handwritten page or two about what's going on in your life. Haven't been in touch with that friend from college? Pretend they're on the phone and carry on a conversation. And to get some practice with dialogue, instead of writing it all in narrative, relay some conversations you've had recently with others (or overheard others having) — and feel free to make your replies more witty and to the point than they really were.

If you really want to increase the usefulness of this exercise, write a letter to a child whom you know: your own child, your friend's child. Keep the subject matter appropriate, but write whatever comes into your head. Kids love to get mail; really little ones can't even tell whether it's well-written — and they don't care.

Introducing your first best friend to the love of your life

Want to try an approach that can really bring characters to life through dialogue? Simply choose two people you know (such as your best friend and your significant other — see the exercises at the end of Chapter 8) and begin a dialogue between them on paper, imagining them talking with one another face-to-face.

A famous writing teacher, who guided many aspiring novelists to fame and fortune, always had her writers begin her workshops with this exercise, a fictional dialogue between two people you know well. Now that I (Lisa) run my own workshops, I also have new writers try it. I always tell them that if nothing else happens, they now have some interesting character studies that they can auction off on eBay when they become rich and famous children's book writers.

IN THIS CHAPTER

» **Establishing context, and doing it right**

» **Putting all your info into a context bible**

» **Knowing when you don't actually need to set a scene**

» **Engaging your readers' senses**

» **Writing your own smellography**

Chapter **11**

Setting the Scene

M any books about writing don't talk about setting, but whether you're writing fiction or nonfiction, your characters need to do whatever they do somewhere, right? And you need to set up that particular somewhere for the reader almost the same way you set up a character — only much more subtly and much more briefly — so that the reader gets a picture in their head about the places where all the action in the story occurs.

In this chapter, we show you how to set up scenery to give your stories and characters context, creating a much more interesting and believable children's book in the process. We share exactly when to include scenery and context and how much of it to include before giving you a demonstration of how to use one of your senses to create context.

Giving Context to Your Story and Its Characters with Scenery

The most important reason for setting up scenery is to give your story and characters a context in which to do what they do. For example, when your adventurous main character comes from a house in a city, you can't just name a city, real or imagined, and leave it at that. You need to give that city character, imbue it with a sense of uniqueness so that it adds to who your protagonist is when they're in that place. Why? Because you're shaped positively or negatively by the places where you live. These places contribute to who you are.

How many times do you hear about people who left home and never looked back? That's indeed interesting, but we need to know more: What's the character's hometown like that made them want never to return? Describe the aspects of the town that create emotions in your character. You can then use these contexts to shape your characters. In addition, a well-established context gives the reader a starting point from which to dive into the action.

TIP

Context, environment, venue, place, scenery, somewhere — we use all of these words pretty much interchangeably in this chapter. And you absolutely must get right the contexts in which the main character — and the characters who get in their way — spend the majority of their time.

Creating a Context Bible

You need to ground every story that you write. You create that grounding or foundation when you develop a context. A *context* gives a character a place to begin, a place to set their feet, and then a place to either jump into or away from when the action indicates. Although you almost always want to begin a story right away with the main character in action (which we explain in Chapter 9), sooner or later, that character needs to go somewhere. Where is that somewhere? And is that somewhere important? The amount of context that you develop in the story answers those questions for the reader. And to help you figure out the details of your context, you need to develop a context bible.

You create a context bible very much in the same way that you create a character bible (which we show you how to do in Chapter 8). The context bible does pretty much the same thing for context that the character bible does for a character: It helps you develop, know, and evocatively describe a component of your story. In the case of the context bible, you create all the different places where the action occurs. A context bible keeps all the location information in one spot.

To create your context bible, you need to ask some fundamental questions about the environment in which you want to place your character. These questions help make a place come alive, much like a well-developed character does. Create the context so well that a reader can place themselves there and actually imagine what it looks like, how it feels to live in or visit that place, what different parts of that place smell or feel like, and what characterizes its tone, style, and inhabitants.

Here are some questions you can ask to develop an environment for your story:

>> What is the place called? Where did that name come from?

>> What part of the world is it in? What's the weather like? Is it near water? Mountains? Plains? How does this location establish a tone to the place?

>> What is the ethnic makeup? If mixed, is it blended or segregated? How many people live there? How many people are just visiting?

>> Is there a central area where people congregate and tourists visit? Does it have a landmark unique to the place?

>> What does it smell like?

>> What different noises or sounds do you hear when you walk down a street?

>> What's the place known for? How does that affect its character?

>> What's the first thing newcomers notice when they arrive?

To create and develop a context, you don't necessarily need to include paragraph upon paragraph of description in your finished story. Exactly the opposite: Developing a context means knowing a place well enough that a few well-chosen sentences can evoke for the reader a feeling or tone for the place.

Often, you read books starring characters that come from real cities. The author drops the name of the city and leaves it at that. What a rip-off. The reader may not know what they're missing — and that's the writer's fault. For example, Lisa comes from Los Angeles, California, which isn't just a huge city, but a huge county with many different cities inside it, each with its own character. People generally assume that if you live in a particular one of these cities, you share in the character of the place in which you live.

Knowing When to Include Scenery and Context

A reader who doesn't get enough information about a main character's whereabouts probably can't tell you that's the reason they're not enjoying your book. But they feel a certain lack of connection to the character — which is the kiss of death. If a main character doesn't engage the reader, children put down the book and never pick it up again. If you don't explore contexts at all, your reader may feel lost, as if the characters are floating around, homeless, groundless, foundationless — because even a homeless character or a character on the run from home has to come from somewhere, pass through somewhere else, and be headed somewhere.

With middle-grade novels and longer books that involve many different scenes and chapters in which the main character moves from place to place, you need to make sure your readers know something about where the characters are at any point in the story. When your story begins, make sure it takes place somewhere and that you give the somewhere at least one fabulously descriptive sentence within the first few paragraphs of the book. While your book progresses and the main character moves from place to place in each scene, make sure you have at least one descriptive sentence about each new context.

Here's an example of a middle-grade setting we wrote that works:

> Barden Woods was haunted. Everyone knew the story about Barden, the famous wood carver. He had spent his days among the giant redwoods, surrounded by children, whittling toys, tiny furniture, even treehouses. One day, not long after The Great Fire destroyed part of the woods, Barden disappeared. The villagers whispered that he had been carried off by wood spirits. Barden Woods became a place forbidden to children, a scary, dangerous place. It still was.

Board books, picture books, and other formats for the youngest readers don't necessarily require descriptive sentences establishing context because the illustrations usually do that job for you. In these cases, you can simply identify setting (home, school, the park, and so on) with a word or two. You can include scene-building sentences or phrases, but you don't need to go into great detail.

How do you know when a scene needs scenery description or contextual establishment? The next sections help you out.

If your book doesn't have pictures to tell readers where they are, and if your setting is similar to any of the examples in the following sections, you need to craft a description of the scenery and include that description as part of the storytelling.

When place figures prominently

Every story needs living, breathing characters — people, animals, or anthropomorphized objects such as the dancing teapot and candelabra in Disney's *Beauty and the Beast* — to create reader interest and move the action forward. But sometimes, the place in which a story occurs can be almost as important to the story (think Harry Potter's wizardry school) as the characters that inhabit it — and therefore it deserves a level of description that provides complete context and scenery.

For example, a mystery story that involves the inhabitants of a haunted house requires a meaningful description of the house. In the same way, a story involving a character who is an explorer means you need at least a brief description of each place explored. Consider the important role that context and scenery play in historical fiction, such as the American Girls Collection series of books (American Girl Publications), which are set in specific years and places. For example, *Meet Kirsten*, by Janet Shaw, opens with Kirsten's first view of the United States from the vantage point of a ship in the ocean, moving — along with the main character — to New York City and finally to Minnesota.

When place plays an important role

The setting of your story is far from incidental when it's not just a starting place for the character or an ending place in the action. In the following passage, the setting isn't nearly as important to the plot as the character's personality:

> Nina left for school every morning at seven o'clock. And she returned home promptly at three in the afternoon. At noon sharp, she sat down for lunch and after school she allowed herself a snack at 3:15 on the button. Nina was a very punctual person. So when Nina did not show up for her first class right on time, Mrs. Feinstein knew something was wrong.

Nina's punctuality is the subject of the passage, and to describe her school would both interrupt the flow of the prose and fail to add anything interesting that readers need to know. However, if the passage reads like the following, the story needs a description of the school:

> Nina left for school every morning at seven o'clock, dragging her feet the entire way. With each step, she thought of recess at ten, lunch at noon, and, best of all, the end of classes at three. With her shoulders slumped, Nina barely managed to get to her first class on time, no matter how hard she tried. Today was no exception. As she heard the first bell, signaling three minutes left to get to class, Nina lifted her eyes and increased her pace. The tall, red-brick facade soon came into view, its disheveled eaves and broken windows looking like a face that had barely survived a car accident. She slipped into Mrs. Feinstein's room just as the last bell rang.

The subject of the preceding passage is the main character's reluctance to go to school. Because she's reluctant to go to a specific place, the reader wants to know the reason; show them that reason.

When description of place doesn't interrupt flow of action

Sometimes, you can interrupt the flow of the story you're meticulously crafting by tossing in a description of the place where the action is occurring. When you interrupt the flow in this way, your reader may become momentarily confused or disoriented, or they may simply lose interest in your story — outcomes that you don't want as an author.

Suppose your main character is plummeting down a mineshaft, mere seconds away from certain disaster. This is probably not a good time to describe what California in the year 1849 looked like. It is, however, a good time to describe the thoughts going through your character's head while the bottom of the shaft fast approaches.

Or suppose a giant squirrel is chasing your knight in shining armor through the woods, teeth bared and saliva dripping from its furry mouth. Stopping the action to describe the verdant soil, the softly swaying flowers, and the gentle pollen-filled breeze would certainly interrupt the story — distracting the reader and ruining the moment.

TIP

How do you know whether your description of a place interrupts the flow of your story? A sure sign is if you feel like putting it in parentheses — or if you find yourself moving it around because you're not sure where it really should go. Our advice? When in doubt, leave it out.

When you must mention an exotic locale

We don't mean to sound America-centric or xenophobic, but the great preponderance of readers of books written in English do come from North America, Great Britain, Ireland, Australia, and New Zealand. Consider your probable audience when you drop in a reference to an exotic locale. If, for example, you're writing in English and you mention a place like Borneo or Tierra del Fuego, consider it exotic to most of your readership and let them in on what it's like there. For an example of an English-language children's picture book that does a great job of describing a foreign country — in this case, Kenya — check out *Ndito Runs*, by Laurie Halse Anderson and Anita Van Der Merwe (Henry Holt & Company).

When you mention a specific place at the beginning

You've probably read a zillion books that start off with a lovely description of a place in the first paragraph or two, and then plunge right into the action. Authors write this initial description for a couple of good reasons:

>> When your reader encounters your reference to a specific place, you pique their curiosity — they want to know more about it.

>> Setting the scenery and context at the very beginning of a longer story quickly transports the reader out of the day-to-day reality of their current environment and into the fantasy world created by the book's author. Indeed, part of the magic of any well-written book involves transporting readers to new places, where they can meet new people and see new environments.

Consider the first words of L. Frank Baum's book *The Wonderful Wizard of Oz*:

Dorothy lived in the midst of the great Kansas prairies, with Uncle Henry, who was a farmer, and Aunt Em, who was the farmer's wife. Their house was small, for the lumber to build it had to be carried by wagon many miles. There were four walls, a floor and a roof, which made one room; and this room contained a rusty looking cookstove, a cupboard for the dishes, a table, three or four chairs, and the beds. Uncle Henry and Aunt Em had a big bed in one corner, and Dorothy a little bed in another corner. There was no garret at all, and no cellar — except a small hole dug in the ground, called a cyclone cellar, where the family could go in case one of those great whirlwinds arose, mighty enough to crush any building in its path. It was reached by a trap door in the middle of the floor, from which a ladder led down into the small, dark hole.

Can you picture Dorothy's home in your mind? Did you forget where you are right now because you moved to a different place? Although your book doesn't need to begin with a description of the scenery or context, you can take this approach to immediately bring the reader into the world of your story, especially in longer books.

When you use place to transition to a new scene

Not every story stays in the same place for the duration of a children's book. In fact, more than a few stories start in one place, and then move to one or more other places during the course of the action. When you end a chapter or scene in one place and start the next one in a new place, you need to tell readers where you've taken them. If you don't set the scene, they feel lost and frustrated.

The following description from Lewis Carroll's *Alice's Adventures in Wonderland* ends a chapter and marks Alice's arrival at a new scene — at the March Hare's house (which happens to be the location of the Mad Tea-Party, which commences at the beginning of the following chapter):

> She had not gone much farther before she came in sight of the house of the March Hare: she thought it must be the right house, because the chimneys were shaped like ears and the roof was thatched with fur. It was so large a house that she did not like to go nearer till she had nibbled some more of the left-hand bit of mushroom, and raised herself to about two feet high: even then she walked up towards it rather timidly, saying to herself, "Suppose it should be raving mad after all! I almost wish I'd gone to see the Hatter instead!"

Providing the Right Amount of Setting

You can develop the skill of knowing how much to describe scenery or context while you become a more experienced writer. But in the meantime, follow this simple rule about how long or involved to make a description in a children's book that doesn't have pictures: You need only one well-constructed sentence per new place, except where writing more adds significantly to plot or character development.

WARNING

When you write an early chapter book, a middle-grade novel, or a YA book, don't think that just because you have more space and higher word count, you should feel free to devote entire pages to scenery or place descriptions. Keep it short. Make your words work hard for you. Consider more than a paragraph describing the most important place/context in your novel long — perhaps too long, in many cases.

Consider this brief mention of the town of Cardiff Hill early in Mark Twain's *The Adventures of Tom Sawyer*:

> Cardiff Hill, beyond the village and above it, was green with vegetation and it lay just far enough away to seem a Delectable Land, dreamy, reposeful, and inviting.

Does Twain need to say any more about Cardiff Hill? (We think not!)

Engaging Your Readers' Senses

A good sentence or description of scenery, of place, of context evokes a strong image in the reader's mind. Getting someone to see what you want them to see by reading words that you've written requires careful writing. To help create a vision for your readers, engage their senses. You engage their sight when they're reading your words and looking at any accompanying pictures, but to engage the mind's eye, you need to help them use their imagination. The best contextualizations about a place describe the way it tastes, feels on the skin or to the touch, sounds, smells, and looks.

WARNING

Don't spend too much time on the way a place looks. You want your readers to be able to see the place in their mind's eye, to imagine how it looks; but show them by using words that develop a sensory experience that focuses more on the other senses. That way, you don't get too caught up in *telling* (a no-no) versus *showing* (a yes-yes).

You can probably imagine how to describe a place by using most senses, but how can a place taste? The following example uses the reader's sense of taste to evoke an image in their mind's eye:

> The house reminded her of a sour lemon on a hot day, both refreshing and surprising. Flanked by traditional white houses with blue trim, it was light yellow with screaming purple trim and an enormous orange front door.

The following description uses the reader's sense of sound to convey the terror the main character feels:

> From somewhere deep within the school came screams of fright, groans of pain. Staring at the dark windows and boarded-up doors, Roxy could not move a muscle.

For real examples of how writing can engage the senses, check out C. S. Lewis's *The Lion, the Witch and the Wardrobe* (Scholastic) for the tastes of Turkish delight, the bitter coldness of Narnia, and the sounds of footsteps and carriages approaching. Also read Natalie Babbit's *Tuck Everlasting* (Scholastic) for the bristly, itchy grass; the heat of the noontime sun; and the deep, damp mattress of leaves on the ground. Finally, read Frances Hodgson Burnett's *The Secret Garden* (HarperCollins) for the wailing of cholera victims and the sweet taste of wine.

REMEMBER

The best writing gets the reader's senses fired up, alongside the heart and mind. Whenever we experience an event, our senses record it right along with our hearts and our minds. As a result, most people have years and years of stored experiences trapped inside them that you can access by reawakening those sense memories. And engaging your senses, your emotions, and your fertile imagination brings you closer to a child's world.

Knowing When Not to Make a Scene

You have a lot of reasons to include scene development or description of scenery. But you also have reasons to not include those descriptions. Often, writers include a context description that fails to add anything measurable or meaningful to the story. To tell whether something is meaningful or measurable, ask yourself whether it has a purpose that you can articulate if someone asks you to do so. The following list reveals scenarios when setting the scene can do more harm to your story than good:

» **Scenes that have no characters:** Does the sentence or paragraph you're including involve your main character or an important character? Does it provide a place in which that character does something or experiences something meaningful to the story? If you can't answer yes to these questions and explain it to yourself, then out it goes!

» **Scenes that don't advance the plot:** Is the description you're including essential to the action occurring in or around that place? Does it move the story forward by taking us somewhere involving conflict or drama? Is the place related to the main character's compelling desire or want? If you can't answer yes to at least one of these questions and explain it to yourself, then it's not worth adding.

» **Scenes that tell rather than show:** You probably find writing narrative description fun and easy. And writing scenery often falls into that category. But you can end up *telling* and not *showing* really, really, really (did we mention really?) easily. *Telling* involves giving readers events occurring in the past, as opposed to the present (even if the entire book is written in the past tense); removing immediacy from the story, slowing down the pacing, and boring the reader in many cases. *Showing* is writing that moves the character's feet, propels the story forward, increases conflict or drama, and focuses on action. Does your text show rather than tell? If not, then rewrite it!

Exercising Your Nose through Smellography

Some new writers find setting the scene for readers scary. You often have to do some research. And if you base your scene on a real place, you must make your scene detailed and authentic; otherwise, readers who know the place dismiss your story outright. As we note in the section "Engaging Your Readers' Senses," earlier in this chapter, to create a meaningful context — a foundation from which your character starts, to which your character goes, or in which your character ends up, you need to make readers feel, smell, taste, hear — really experience — the place you're developing. To really immerse your reader in your story, engage their senses.

You can most easily engage the sense of smell, which is also one of the most powerful senses. Have you ever smelled an old tub of cocoa-butter sunscreen or a vial of flowery, fragrant perfume and been instantly transported back to that precise moment when you smelled it before — years or perhaps even decades ago? Smells often lead to memories and emotions, which you can translate into great ideas and powerful writing.

To uncover memories you may have forgotten, give the following exercise a try. It's so easy that you won't even feel as if you're working on your context-giving skills. Just follow these steps:

1. **Set a timer for 15 minutes and start it up.**

2. **Think of the first smell you can remember.**

   How far back can you go? Maybe you remember the smell of the strawberry shampoo your mom always got for you.

3. **Start writing a simple smellography.**

   A *smellography* is a chronological record of your smell memories, as many as you can think of until you reach the present day.

   Set aside enough time to really think back deep into your past. For example, here are some of the smell memories from the beginning of Lisa's smellography, starting with her very first memories and working toward the present day:

   - My hands after playing with modeling clay

   - Toe jam from tube socks

   - My wet dog at the lake

   - My grandparents' freshly mowed lawn

   - Freshly ground coffee for the grown-ups and hot cinnamon rolls after dinner

4. **Choose one or more of the smell memories, and write a short story about it/them.**

The exercise works if it gets you writing. Don't worry right now about the shape the writing takes, how the story unfolds, or which particular words you choose. The object of this free-flowing, stream-of-consciousness exercise? Just write.

» **Playing with words and making them funny**

» **Creating magic with voice, style, and tone**

» **Giving your voice a makeover**

» **Using pretending to find your voice**

Chapter **12**

Finding Your Voice: Point of View and Tone

E very story is told from some point of view (POV for short), and that POV indicates who's telling the story and what limitations they have to contend with. When you write, you must do so from a consistent point of view. In this chapter, we help you choose a POV and figure out how to keep it consistent.

Choosing a point of view is just one of the decisions a writer has to make when they develop a writing style best suited to the tale at hand. Along the way, you're also choosing which words you use to convey your own style and the tone of the story. Words, the basic building blocks of a story, help to draw pictures in the reader's mind, bringing the reader into your make-believe world. Words give a character a voice, develop a point of view, and elaborate on a plot.

But words serve other purposes besides providing a basic foundation; they also give life to your writing. By using words in creative and innovative ways, writers can evoke all kinds of emotions in readers, from wistful nostalgia, to wild hilarity, to bite-your-fingernails suspense.

In this chapter, we also explore the nuances of how to use words to make your prose come alive, to evoke strong emotions in your readers, and to give your writing a tone of its own.

Building a Solid Point of View

Point of view (POV) is the perspective from which a book is narrated, the position or vantage point from which the author presents the story to the reader. You use point of view to show readers through whose eyes (and in whose mind) they're seeing the world of the story. In the following sections, you can find out about the different types of POVs, how to pick the right POV for your story, and how to choose the tense that best supports your chosen POV.

Reviewing POV options

The primary POV decision you have to make before you can write even one sentence is *person.* Third-person stories are told by a narrator who isn't part of the story, whereas first- (and usually second-) person stories are told by a narrator who's also a character. Here's a breakdown of the POV persons:

>> **First person:** First person entails the author outright telling a story, perhaps their own, by writing as if they're the main character, narrating the book by using the pronoun *I*. Your character (usually the protagonist) is telling the story through their own eyes. First-person POV means the teller of the story can't be *omniscient* (all-knowing) because regular people can't be omniscient; as such, the teller of the story can report only what they can realistically know. For example, they can't know someone else's private thoughts or what will happen in the future. Here's an example:

> I could not believe my eyes. There she was. Standing there in the outfit that we both admired yesterday at the mall. Neither of us had the money to buy it then, so how had she come to be wearing it now?

> "Hi," she now said, all cheerful and bright. "Like it?" She shimmied a little and laid a big smile on me, oblivious.

> It was clear to me now. In this new school, I was clueless about the rules of right and wrong. I'd learn soon enough.

A new writer can struggle with first-person POV because it requires truly establishing a unique voice and not getting caught up in your personal reality. Although you may enjoy experimenting with various voices, most writers try to get plenty of experience writing in the third person before moving to first.

>> **Second person:** This perspective allows the writer to address the reader directly, using the pronoun *you.* You use second-person POV when you want to distance yourself from involvement in the story.

Few published novels use second-person POV. In fact, we can only think of a few successful examples, including Jay McInerney's *Bright Lights, Big City* (Vintage) and *The Missing Girl* by Norma Fox Mazer (HarperTeen). Stories told in second person require an extremely skilled facility with voice and language; you really can't sell it if you don't make it nearly perfect. You may feel your story warrants it, but we suggest waiting until you've had a lot of practice writing before you tackle this particular beast.

>> **Third person:** Third-person POV is the author telling the story using the pronouns *he, she,* or *they.* Three types of third-person POV exist:

- *Limited:* In this type of third-person POV, the author gets to read the thoughts of only one main character.

- *Multiple:* Although this type allows you to tell the story through multiple characters' viewpoints, most of the main action viewpoint is still reserved for the main character. E. L. Konigsburg's *The View from Saturday* (Atheneum Books for Young Readers) is told in third-person multiple POV, with quite a few main characters (Noah, Nadia, Ethan, and Julian) all contributing to the telling of the story.

- *Omniscient:* This type of third-person POV comes from the viewpoint of a narrator who knows all and sees all — kind of like God. As a totally omniscient author, you act as God for your characters. You can go into the mind of any character; report on anything that's happening anywhere with anyone in the story at any time (even the future!); interpret any character's actions or thoughts; reflect, judge, and reveal truths.

The main difference between the three types of third person is the amount of omniscience the author chooses. For the record, most children's books use the third-person limited POV; it's also the easiest to master.

Picking your POV

So how do you know which POV to pick for your story? So many variations of nuances go into every story, so we can't tell you in which situation you should choose which POV. But here are some general situations in which the choice becomes more transparent:

>> **You're an in-your-face writer and know your main character as well as you know yourself.** Then the first-person POV may work for you. Just know that it has its limitations, just like us real-life characters: You can use *dialogue only* to reveal the motives, thoughts, and feelings of characters other than the narrator. You get to play God, but only with half a deck of cards.

WARNING

When you write in the first person, you need to have your main character involved in the story from beginning to end, and everything in between. But that character can't read other people's minds or foretell the future.

>> **You want to make yourself, the writer/narrator, an actor in the drama.** If you're an experimental person who likes to put themselves to the test, the second-person POV may be the ticket for you.

WARNING

In the days when oral storytelling was all the rage (before books were common household possessions), the storyteller would often interrupt their tale and directly address the listener, like using "Dear Reader" — asking questions or making personal commentary — before going back to their tale. The writing world calls talking directly to the reader *editorializing* or *authorial intrusion.* Unless you're writing an instructional book, talking directly to the reader isn't something we recommend. It's disruptive to the narrative, not to mention annoying to the reader who gets thrown off track and jolted back to plain old reality.

>> **You like to take the path well traveled.** Try writing in a third-person POV — also known as the most common way of telling a story. You need to determine how much omniscience you need and with how many characters in order to choose between third-person limited, third-person multiple, or third-person omniscient, but we can help you with that:

- *Your story is about one main character.* Such as in Ian Falconer's *Olivia* and *Olivia Saves the Circus* (Atheneum/Anne Schwartz Books). Choose third-person limited because you need to get into the head of only one character.

- *Your story involves two or more main characters.* All of these characters have a different take on the story and contribute equally to the telling of that story, third-person multiple POV probably works best for you.

- *You're writing an epic story in which you cover many generations or many characters over an expanded period of time.* If you feel that you may need to read every character's mind (telling the reader everything about everyone), go with third-person omniscient.

REMEMBER

After you choose a viewpoint, you have to stick to it. When writing short books, such as board books or picture books, you definitely need to stay with one POV. Don't change the POV in books this short.

If you're writing a relatively long book that has chapters, you may choose to write one chapter from one character's POV and the next from another's POV, like Natalie Babbitt does in *Tuck Everlasting* (Farrar, Straus & Giroux Books for Young Readers). However you choose to organize the narrative, don't change POV within a scene or chapter. And be consistent; if you choose to alternate POV in every other chapter, stick to the rhythm and don't deviate.

Matching tense with POV

Part of choosing a POV includes choosing a tense to write in. When writing a kids' book, you have two main tenses to choose from:

>> **Present tense:** I write, you write, he/she writes, they write, we write

>> **Past tense:** I wrote, you wrote, he/she wrote, they wrote, we wrote

Present tense is the tense of choice for stories told from a first-person POV due to its immediacy, its intimacy, and its now-ness. Putting a first-person POV in the past tense simply doesn't emphasize the *now*. Second-person POVs also benefits from the present tense, which allows you to more directly address your reader while you take them through your story.

Past tense works best if you plan to tell your story using any of the third-person POVs. In fact, most classic children's stories are told in the past tense, using a narrator who relates what transpired.

STORYTELLING VERSUS STORY-SHOWING

We think storytelling should be called story-showing. Why? Because storytelling is a throwback to the oral tradition of passing on tales face to face around a campfire or through the grapevine. Today's stories are active, focusing on what the main characters do where, showing all the aspects of the story in the here and now (even if it takes place in the past or future tense) by using action and dialogue — and to a much lesser extent, narrative description. Storytelling implies a relaying of information or events that happened long ago and often includes authorial intrusion (as in *The Canterbury Tales,* written in the late 14th century, in which the narrator often jumps in to comment on and interrupt the story he's relating).

Having Fun with Words through Wordplay, Rhyming, and Rhythm

For many writers of children's books, having fun with words is the best part of the writing process. You might find playing with words, creating word pictures in your readers' minds, and building rhymes out of thin air more fun than a barrel of monkeys. In the sections that follow, we take a closer look at the many different ways you can play with words, including rhyming and rhythm.

Engaging in wordplay

Words are fun. And what better way to have fun with words than to write a children's book? You have far more freedom to play around with words when you write children's books, compared to writing other kinds of books. The sky is truly the limit.

Use some of these common methods to have fun with words:

>> **Alliteration:** Making the initial consonant sounds of words two or more times in a line or sentence creates a rhythmic component to the writing. For example, "She stewed in her soft and simple shoes."

Assonance is similar to alliteration, but uses vowel sounds instead of consonant sounds. For example, "Ho! We go 'til I say no!"

WARNING

New writers often fall into the trap of using alliteration or assonance in naming characters, which is amateurish. It screams, "I am new at this and think it's so cute!" For example, Billy Bully. If Billy is a bully, *show* him bullying, don't just give him a label to make your reader see that he's a bully. Just say no.

>> **Parallelism:** Repeating similar thoughts in two different phrasings. You can find variations on the theme:

 • *Antithetical:* When the second phrasing is the exact opposite of the first: "The good boy did his homework and cleaned his room; the bad boy threw his homework in the trash and dumped his dinner on the floor."

 • *Synonymous:* When the second phrasing is almost identical to the first. "The warm sun warmed the faces of the children at play; the children's faces glowed with the first rays of the sun."

Be careful not to use parallelism to repeat yourself or insert redundancies into your writing. For example, "The good boy did his homework on time; completing all his tasks in a timely manner." This is unnecessary repetition because both sides of the semicolon relay the exact same information. That doesn't add any fun; that verbosity needs to get cut. Choose one and lose one.

>> **Refrain:** Repeating a line or group of lines throughout a story. Consider the following lines, repeated throughout Dr. Seuss's *Green Eggs and Ham:* "I do not like green eggs and ham. I do not like them, Sam-I-Am."

>> **Polyptoton:** Repeating the same word in different forms. "The ogre was strong, and he revealed his full strength as he toppled tree after tree in the forest, headstrong to the very end."

>> **Metaphor:** Comparing two unlike things by using any form of the verb to be. "The color blue is a cold, winter's day — snow forming drifts on the sides of the road and icicles hanging from the roof of the house."

>> **Simile:** Comparing two unlike things, using *like* or *as.* "His anger was like a summer's storm — arriving quickly and without warning, then soon passing without a trace."

>> **Anthropomorphism:** When human motivations, characteristics, or behavior appear in inanimate objects, animals, or natural phenomena. For example, Thomas the Tank Engine, from The Railway Series, by Rev. W. Awdry (Egmont), is an anthropomorphized train that has a human face, feelings, and emotions. He's always getting into all sorts of trouble.

>> **Personification:** When human qualities appear in an animal or object. "Flowers danced in the field."

Some children's book writers make up words. Dr. Seuss (whose real name was Theodor Geisel) was a master at this; his made-up words were understood because of what was happening in the story. Lewis Carroll, author of *Alice's Adventures in Wonderland* as well as other stories and poems, ranks up there with the very best, making up words that were evocative because of the particular context in which he used them, allowing the reader to envision what they meant. We used to advocate making up words, but we've found that 90 percent of the time, this tactic doesn't work for beginning writers. Usually, made-up words are a sign of laziness (unwillingness to find the right real word or combination of words) or an attempt to insert humor that ends up feeling forced (your idea of a funny, made-up word does not necessarily jibe with a child's). So steer clear of wordplay that involves making up words.

Taking different approaches to rhyming

Rhyming is an essential tool in many children's books, especially those written for younger readers. In general terms, words *rhyme* when the last stressed vowel and the sounds that follow it are the same — for example, *blue* and *zoo*, or *horse* and *Norse*. Rhyming introduces a repetition of sound patterns that makes your words more interesting to listen to or read — and easier to remember. Rhyming, when done well, also gives words a rhythm that can approximate music when you read them aloud. You can rhyme with sounds or create rhyming patterns, which we talk about in the following sections.

TIP

If you're a writer who wants to rhyme, check out the resource RhymeZone (www. rhymezone.com). If you're stuck on rhyming a word, you can enter that word into the RhymeZone text box, then click the Search button to see a list of the words that rhyme with your word. They provide rhyming word and phrase options from one syllable all the way to eight syllables.

Rhyming sounds

When playing with rhymes, you usually start with sounds. Take a look at these different rhyming schemes based on sound:

>> **Perfect rhyme:** When the vowel and final consonant match exactly, like with *mute* and *pursuit*.

>> **Partial rhyme:** When a rhyme is close, but not perfect, like with *fought* and *fault*. Partial rhyme is also known as *near rhyme, off rhyme,* or *slant rhyme*.

>> **Half rhyme:** When the final consonants match exactly, but not the vowels, like with *rats* and *hits*.

>> **Eye rhyme:** When words rhyme in sight, but not in sound, like with *cough* and *tough*.

>> **Masculine rhyme:** Words in which one syllable rhymes, such as *pop* and *stop*, or *soak* and *poke*.

>> **Feminine rhyme:** Words in which two or more syllables rhyme, such as *jeepers* and *creepers,* or *torrid* and *horrid*.

WARNING

Young, beginning readers (not those who still only have an adult reading to them) may not be sophisticated enough as readers to understand or even properly sound out partial, half, or eye rhymes. Eye rhymes definitely don't belong in children's books because this particular rhyming technique may tend to confuse young readers who are still working out the right and wrong ways to spell and pronounce words. And eye rhymes don't work when you read them aloud, the best test for whether your rhyming really works the way it should in a children's book.

Rhyming patterns

When it comes to rhyming, sound is important, but so are the patterns of the rhymes you use. Two of the most common rhyming patterns are

>> **End rhyme:** When words at the end of successive lines or sentences rhyme, such as

"The more she ate the more she grew,

until she reached five foot two."

>> **Internal rhyme:** When words rhyme within a line or sentence, such as "The old man on the moon sang his weary tune."

Keeping your story moving with rhythm

In the same way that music depends on *rhythm* — a recurring pattern of notes or beats — to propel it forward, the written word can depend on rhythm. This rhythm in the written word is often called *meter*. When you read your story aloud and something doesn't sound quite right, your meter probably is off, meaning it's not consistent. To check meter, you actually have to count the syllables and keep the same rising and falling tone and the same accented words in the same place for each line.

The most basic unit of rhythm is the syllable. A *foot* (plural, *feet*) is a unit of stressed and unstressed syllables. You can build a rhythm throughout your work by repeating any of the five most common feet:

>> **Iamb:** One unstressed syllable, then one stressed syllable (da DUM), like in, "I *do* not *like* greens *eggs* and *ham*."

>> **Trochee:** One stressed syllable, then one unstressed syllable (DA dum), like in, "*Pe*ter, *Pe*ter, *pump*kin *eat*er."

>> **Anapest:** Two unstressed syllables, then one stressed syllable (da da DUM), like in, "'Twas the *night* before *Christ*mas and *all* through the *house*."

>> **Dactyl:** One stressed syllable, then two unstressed syllables (DA da dum), like in, "*Hick*ory, *dick*ory, *dock*."

>> **Spondee:** Two stressed syllables (DA DUM), like in, "One fish, two fish, red fish, blue fish."

To figure out whether your rhymes work, find someone who rhymes well (like a poetry teacher, a published writer of rhyming poetry, or even a songwriter) and have them look over your work. If you don't have access to these talented individuals, then try the method we like to call "pounding on the table." Identify your rhythm, and pound it out to your words to make sure you have an even and consistent meter. Better yet, have someone who doesn't know your rhyme read it out loud while you record them speaking. Listen to them reading your story and notice where the reader stumbles over the meter. Also, don't force the meter by assuming the reader will stress a normally non-stressed syllable to make it fit into the meter of the surrounding lines.

WARNING

Thou art not allowed to torture, mangle, or otherwise beat up proper English in an attempt to make your rhyme work. You need to make your lines comprehensible as regular, unrhymed prose before you attempt to rhyme them. If you're in doubt: Just say them aloud. If you've never heard anyone in this century speak like that, we feel confident that your English is all wrong. Precisely 99 percent of editors agree that nothing's worse than writing that sacrifices understandable English simply to force a rhyme to work. Regarding Dr. Seuss, do not use Seussian meter. Seuss did it over and over, and his books continue to sell. Seussian meter belongs to Seuss. Leave it be. Make up your own.

WARNING

A final caution about writing in rhyme: The rhyme must be incidental to the story. The text still needs well-developed characters; a plot with a beginning, middle, and end; no unnecessary words; good pacing; and so on. The rhyme should be the last consideration, simply adding another level of whimsy to the book — not your first priority as a writer. In other words, don't manipulate the characters and events of the story or add unnecessary words just because they make the rhyme flow.

TIP

Also, don't assume that you have to write in rhyme. Rhyming is a very tricky technique to do well and can make or break a solid story with engaging characters, both of which kids care more about than whether the story rhymes or not.

Using Humor to Your Advantage

Perhaps the quickest way to a child's heart is through humor. Children love to laugh, and after you get them laughing, you've truly captured their hearts (and their minds, for that matter). In the following sections, we take a close look at what kinds of things kids find humorous and share how to incorporate outrageous (and even gross) ideas into your writing.

Figuring out what kids consider funny

Before you can start writing funny children's books, you need to understand the kinds of things that kids tend to consider funny. And although you may not see a rhyme or reason for exactly what children find humorous, research shows that children go through different stages of humor development.

According to humor researcher (no, we didn't make that up) Paul E. McGhee, Ph.D., you can expect the following developmental changes in preschool children's humor:

» **Stage 0 (Age 0 to 6 months):** Laughs, no humor. During the first six months of life, children laugh not because they find something funny, but because something physically arouses them — like bouncing the little tykes on your knee or tickling them. To tickle this age group's fancy, write your story in a way that requires the actual reader (parent, sibling, or care provider) to do something funny, like read in a funny voice or make unexpected physical movements or gestures. The content doesn't matter — how it's presented does.

» **Stage 1 (Age 6 to 12 months or so):** Laughs with or at parent or caregiver. During this period, children begin to find humor in the behavior of a parent or other significant people in their lives. Making silly faces or odd sounds can get a laugh from kids in this age bracket, as can a funny game of peek-a-boo. Write these kinds of actions into your story so that the parent or caregiver can act them out.

» **Stage 2 (Age 12 months or so up to 5 years):** Pretends that a particular object is something it's not. You've witnessed the power of pretend if you've ever seen a child sit in a big, cardboard box, making noises like a gasoline engine (pretending the box is a race car); inviting their favorite dolls to an elaborate tea party (pretending they're real, live people); or turning a folded-up piece of paper into a jet airplane (pretending it is coming in for a landing). Use the power of pretend in your stories to tap into this source of humor.

» **Stage 3a (2 to 3 or 4 years):** Plays with the names of common objects or actions. At this age, while language skills improve, kids begin to find humor in misnaming common objects. You can plumb this source of humor by calling a shoe a boat, turning a dog into a cat, a strawberry into a raccoon, and so forth.

» **Stage 3b (2 to 3 or 4 years):** Misnames with opposites. This form of misnaming — particularly attractive to many children — involves stating the exact opposite of a particular word. Cold is hot, up is down, over is under, fast is slow, wet is dry. Every adjective has an opposite — consider the possibilities!

>> **Stage 4a (3 to 5 years):** Plays with the sounds of words. At about three years of age, children begin to play not just with word meanings, but with their sounds. A common word such as *turkey* springs forth any number of variations including *wurky, jerky, perky,* and so on. Children alter words for the humor of doing so and begin to create their own nonsense words to be funny. Use word sounds to create humor in your story.

>> **Stage 4b (3 to 5 years):** Uses nonsense word combinations. Most three-year-olds begin to put real words together in combinations that make no sense. Examples of these kinds of humorous combinations include "I want some monkey juice" or "Give me that mushroom spoon." What nonsense word combinations can you insert into your story?

>> **Stage 4c (3 to 5 years):** Distorts features. While children increase their command over the real names of objects, people, or animals, they find humor in distorting some aspect of them. They do this by adding features that don't belong (putting a fish's head on a dog's body); by removing features that do belong (a house with no doors); by changing the shape, size, location, color, and length of familiar things (a person with a grapefruit head); and by ascribing impossible behavior to people or animals (a cat that talks).

>> **Pre-riddle stage (5 to 7 years or so):** Discovers riddles and jokes. Sometime during this period, most kids discover the joy of jokes and riddles, and the verbal humor shared by older children around them. The ubiquitous knock-knock joke is an example of this kind of humor. ("Knock knock." "Who's there?" "Orange." "Orange who?" "Orange you glad I didn't say 'knock knock' again?")

If, however, you want to aim your writing more toward older kids, it helps to understand their unique sense of humor:

>> **Early elementary:** Children at this age love broad physical humor, such as getting a pie in the face, pants falling down to expose underwear, slipping on a banana peel, and so on. Children find it especially funny if a "serious" character (such as a parent or teacher) unwittingly takes part in this slapstick.

>> **Older elementary:** Witness the popularity of the Captain Underpants chapter books for ages 7 to 10 by Dav Pilkey (Scholastic). From about second grade on, kids begin to appreciate verbal humor (witty banter, sarcasm, irony, and so on in dialogue) and have the patience to allow the author to set up a joke over several scenes.

TIP

When you get more experienced incorporating humor in your writing, you can try branching out beyond specific humor stages. Tons of books achieve many levels of humor, thus appealing to many different ages. Even adults enjoy reading them again and again (imagine that!). Dr. Seuss books fall into this category, as do Sandra Boynton's Little Pookie board book series (Little Simon).

A CHILDREN'S BOOK AUTHOR WHO WRITES FOR ALL AGES

Leslie McGuire, author of hundreds of children's books — ranging from board books to picture books, from easy-to-reads to middle-grade novels — is a talented writer with a very quirky outlook on life that often finds its way into her prose. Here's her take on writing for children:

- **What role does humor play in your books?** "I don't always use humor, but when I do, it's usually a way to make children think. After all, laughter is really a shock reaction. Something unexpected gets said or done, and it's enough to get your diaphragm in your chest fibrillating — and that's what a laugh is — physically at least. That's what makes a good joke. The punch line is quite unexpected."

- **How do you use words to engage children in your books?** "Again, I use the unexpected, especially in descriptions of things. In one book — which wasn't funny — I described a baby owl's view of a Luna moth as "A delicious, pale green moth." That makes children think about the eating habits of owls, and what may seem yucky to you might actually be gourmet-style wonderful to an owl. You could always describe a fancy sweater that has a feather boa trim around the neck and sleeves as "A bicycle accident with an ostrich." Language is so very powerful, it's a true shame that most writers for children (and everyone else, I might add) tend to rely on clichés or just boring exchanges. That's dreadful, especially when you consider that in a children's book most of the descriptions are in the picture, so unless you have something interesting to say, you really should avoid saying anything at all."

- **How do you make sure your rhyming works?** "Although this isn't as pompous as it sounds, I like to fall back on Gustave Flaubert at times like those. It took him seven years to write Madame Bovary because he yelled every sentence out loud until the music of it was correct. I don't yell it, but I say each sentence or sing it rhythmically until it has the correct meter. Not all that easy, I must say. Even worse, considering what I write, Flaubert would probably be horrified."

- **What are your tried-and-true ways to make your books fun to read?** "The trick is just to avoid overblown words — and when you must use one, define it right away. Not only does that upgrade their vocabulary, it's a comprehension thing. Part of using humor is injecting an engaging way to make children think about what they just heard or read, and that's an opening for reading comprehension that's actually fun."

(continued)

(continued)

- **How do you vary your writing style for different age levels of readers?** "When writing for each age group, you have to see the world through their eyes, not through your own. Become a five-year-old. Become an 11-year-old. If that's too hard, then imagine a child of the age you're supposed to be writing for, one that you know, and tell that child the story as if that child were sitting right there with you."

- **What pitfalls should would-be authors watch out for?** "Low self-esteem. That's the worst. Don't let it get to you. If you love what you wrote, then someone else will, too."

Turning to the outrageous and the gross

You might be surprised to hear that kids love ideas and concepts that are either outrageous, gross, or both at the same time. Well, it's true. A number of books — including *Oh, Yuck: The Encyclopedia of Everything Nasty*, by Joy Masoff (Workman), and *Grossology*, by Sylvia Branzei and Jack Keely (Price Stern Sloan) — have tackled a wide variety of formerly taboo topics, much to the delight of young readers everywhere. Some of these topics include

>> Barf, burps, boogers, poop, and farts

>> Internal animal parts: eyeballs, hearts, and brains

>> Acne, skin bumps, or other itchy red spots

>> Leeches and worms

These topics tap deeply into the spirit of young people for the following reasons:

>> Kids haven't yet been fully conditioned to pretend that these everyday things and events don't exist.

>> These topics get a rise out of adults whenever kids mention them.

>> They're just plain fun to read about.

If your story merits the inclusion of something gross, then by all means, don't hesitate.

REMEMBER

Adults continue to debate about whether using gross and outrageous topics and words is bad form because it teaches kids to use those words, or whether everyone should acknowledge and celebrate these words. The message from kids, however, remains loud and clear: Bring it on!

The Mojo of Good Writing: Exploring Voice, Style, and Tone

After you figure out how to set your scenes (see Chapter 11), write scintillating dialogue (see Chapter 10), and inject so much humor that even you can't stop laughing (see the section "Using Humor to Your Advantage," earlier in this chapter), you still need to get a grasp on a few more aspects of good writing. And unfortunately for writers everywhere, these aspects nearly defy instruction.

For example, when you read a particular author and find yourself drawn in by everything you're reading — so much so that you savor every last page and hate for the book to end — then you've fallen for the writer's mojo (magic). Instantly addicted, you search frantically for other books by the same author. You even order their books in advance so that you can get them the second they come out. You're falling prey to mojo. And if you know this kind of addiction — in your every cell, every nerve ending — you know that mojo is pretty heady stuff.

So where can you get some mojo? Well, we don't know any dealers — and we wouldn't recommend them if we did — so you're just going to have to develop your own mojo as a writer, just like your favorite writers have. And they do it with three things, which they keep consistent throughout a story:

» **Voice:** The communicative and cumulative effect created by the author's way of writing. Successful authors write the best books with a voice that's strong enough to make the protagonist — and the book as a whole — memorable.

» **Style:** The panache with which the writer manipulates the conventions of modern language. In other words, *style* is the way the author adds his own particular twist to *diction* (word choice), dialogue, sentence structure, phrasing, and other aspects of the language. Style can be sparing and minimalist, outrageous and flowery, terse and evocative, or crisp and formal.

» **Tone:** The attitude the story conveys toward its subject matter. For example, a story may convey an attitude of humor or sarcasm toward its characters and events, signaling to the reader that they should take the material with a grain of salt. Then again, the story may convey an attitude of sincerity and earnestness through subtle content and language manipulation, thereby telling the reader to take it seriously.

Capturing your mojo and suffusing your words with your particular tone, style, and voice takes a lot of practice. Beginning writers have so many aspects of writing to ingest and master that developing these other qualities in their writing doesn't always come easily. While you write more and more, becoming increasingly comfortable with your abilities and skills, you most likely find that your mojo starts sneaking into your writing without you knowing it.

REMEMBER

Regardless of what you experience, promise yourself to never try to copy someone else's style or self-consciously force a voice on your writing — those kinds of cop-outs cheat the world of the unique voice buried deep within you, just waiting to come out.

The following sections explore the elements of voice, style, and tone in more detail so that you can begin to create your own.

Finding your story's voice

To determine your voice, start by identifying the voice of your favorite authors. While you're reading, ask yourself this question: What kind of person does the narrator sound like? Search the narrative and pay attention to the dialogue for the answer.

TIP

You can express voice strongly in dialogue, when you make the way the characters speak and express themselves so unique that you conjure up portraits of what the characters would look like if they suddenly appeared in the room. We give you tips for creating stellar dialogue in Chapter 10.

Although we can't excerpt huge passages from other books to demonstrate what a strong voice is, here are some titles to check out:

>> **Picture books:** Anything you read in the Olivia series, by Ian Falconer (Atheneum Books for Young Readers), or the Llama Llama books, by Anna Dewdney (Viking Books for Young Readers)

>> **Early chapter books:** The series of Ivy + Bean, by Annie Barrows and Sophie Blackall (Chronicle Books)

>> **Middle-grade books:** Diary of a Wimpy Kid series, by Jeff Kinney (Amulet Books)

>> **Young adult (YA) books:** Hunger Games series, by Suzanne Collins (Scholastic Press), and Mike Mullins's Ashfall series (Tanglewood Books)

Some older titles you may recognize that offer up a powerful writerly voice include books like S. E. Hinton's *That Was Then, This Is Now* (Penguin Books for Young Readers); and E. L. Konigsburg's *Silent to the Bone* (Atheneum).

In all of the books that we mention, the author's voice calls to you from the first page, drawing you into the main character, into the setting, and into the drama. If you want to develop a unique voice and improve on it over time, write from your heart and develop an attitude and a worldview that permeates your writing.

Voice embodies the writer's quirks, their good ear for subtle differences in dialect and accent, their ability to observe a person and steal that person's unique mannerisms, the way they express their sense of humor — in other words, their personality and the way they interject it into the narrative. You can make your voice serious and calm, harsh and judgmental, incredibly funny and wry — you name it.

For additional help finding your voice, see the section "Helping Your Voice Emerge by Playing Pretend," later in this chapter.

Writing with style

Somewhat hard to define, *style* involves the unique way talented writers put together their words. You need to read writers who have style to really understand how they achieve it. One stylist extraordinaire is Francesca Lia Block, the writer who burst upon the YA scene with her Weetzie Bat books a few years back (HarperTrophy). Read any of her books, and you immediately feel like this airy personage — half real, half fairy — has invaded your consciousness and drawn you into a world that you recognize but that has somehow become expanded to include magical possibilities.

With style, just like with clothing, you get to choose it and present it however you want. All this freedom sounds great, right? Well, you have to choose a style you can stick with and feel comfortable with before you can pull it off successfully in each manuscript. Sure, blending plaids and polka dots makes a statement that others may not soon forget, but can you wear it consistently for six months or a year? Will you still believe in the statement you want to make a year from now? Ask yourself these questions before you choose your voice and attempt to make it real in your writing.

Have you found your style yet? If not, then experiment and have fun!

Taking the right tone

Think of how you use tone of voice to convey your real meaning when speaking with a friend. Tone can change the meaning of the declaration "It was so moving that I nearly cried" in many different ways. Depending on the way you say something, the inflection you place on certain words and the vocal range you use — not to mention your body language or facial expressions — your conversation partner can take that sentence seriously, sarcastically, hysterically — it all depends on tone. The same goes for writing. How you present your words changes your tone.

Ian Falconer's Olivia picture books (Atheneum/Anne Schwartz Books) have a very matter-of-fact tone: Olivia is a crazy little pig, but make no bones about it: She is who she is, and she ain't ashamed of it. Barney Saltzberg's picture book *The Problem with Pumpkins* (Gulliver Books/Harcourt) has a juvenile tone, getting right at the level of its preschool participants and helping them figure out who gets to be the pumpkin on Halloween in a straightforward manner.

You can take many tones with your words and toward your characters, but the right ones seal the meaning of your story and make your writing memorable. And, for any writer, you can't do much better than making a lasting impression on your reader. Experiment! Enjoy your writing!

Knowing When You Need a Voice Makeover

If your story suffers from blandness, if one character blends into the next, or if your protagonist seems like every other character in your story, you probably need a voice makeover. The following list reveals some other clues as to when your voice needs some work.

>> **You have more than one POV in a scene:** A changing, inconsistent POV confuses the reader. In one sentence, we're in one person's head. and in the next sentence, we're in another's. How do readers know you've changed POV? They figure it out because something is off. Even if you indicate you've made the POV change with a dialogue tag — such as "thought Harry" — right after you get into Dana's head, your reader's still going to pause. Your reader finds that nanosecond pause jarring, and they can fall out of their suspension of disbelief. And then you may lose them for good.

   So, if you choose to read ten Dr. Seuss books in order to get in the mood for rhyming or the entire The Hunger Games series, by Suzanne Collins (Scholastic Press), to spark your imagination while you write your YA fantasy novel, make sure that what you write immediately afterward doesn't mimic the other writer's style.

>> **Your omniscient narrator battles a character for voice:** If you choose to write from the POV of the omniscient narrator and find that one or more of your main characters seem to keep butting in and taking over the story with their voice, pay attention. Perhaps this character (or group of characters) is strong enough to carry the story in their voice. Try putting your story in the first-person POV with that character doing the narrating.

- >> **Your story sounds monotonal:** If your story sounds like the droning of a finely tuned engine, no sputtering or stuttering, you're in trouble. This problem occurs most often when every single one of your sentences is about the same length, has the same rhythm, carries the same structure (for example, subject + verb + object), or repeats the same words in too close proximity (such as in the same or a nearby sentence).

TIP

Here are some tips to help you address common voice issues:

- >> Don't change the POV in a scene or in the same chapter if you're writing a chapter book for any reading level. But if you must change POV, use a new chapter or a scene break to get the job done.

- >> If one or more of your characters keep jumping up and down to get your attention, give it to them. They may just turn out to be the star of your story.

- >> Fix a monotonal voice by varying sentence structure and length, word usage, rhythm, and word choice.

Helping Your Voice Emerge by Playing Pretend

Ever wonder what it's like for a child to experience something for the first time? When the boundary between fantasy and reality is transparent — like it is for most young children — you have a high probability of magic occurring while you walk down a street. Being a child is so amazing because of this acceptance of magical possibilities — and most adults seem to forget it. You don't need to spend any time explaining in a picture book why something magical happens because a child can easily imagine magic. As a matter of fact, much of what adults see as explainable may appear magical to a child. Get into this mindset to become a really great writer of children's fiction.

Next, we give you a writing exercise designed to help you find your voice and fire up your imagination by getting you into the place where children spend most of their free time: their minds.

Pretend to be someone (or something) else

Standard advice to writers is to write what you know. Writers.com (www.writers. com) wholly disagrees. They write, "The best creative works force both the writer and the reader to consider new perspectives and learn something new; writing from a new point of view makes for a great exercise in expanding your creative limits."

In light of this advice, pretend that you're someone you know intimately, such as your significant other or best friend. Write for 15 minutes in that person's voice. Don't judge, just write. What is your subject's morning routine? Do they drink coffee? What kind — homegrown, Starbucks, or McDonald's? Do they read the newspaper? Which one — the paper version of *The New York Times* or online? Does your subject go to work, or do they have a secret rendezvous scheduled in a local shopping mall? How do they get there — carpool, bus, train? Who do they meet when they get there? What do they do together? Let your mind wander freely.

Here are some suggestions to start your perspective adventures:

>> **Two different perspectives on the same story:** For example, you could write from both people's perspectives of a quarrel.

>> **A historical figure or a celebrity who fascinates you:** Imagine what their voice would be like and write from their perspective.

>> **An object:** Consider perhaps a vacuum cleaner, a sculpture, or the TV looking out at you like Big Brother.

>> **A person you don't really like:** Get into their head and write in their voice. You can really have fun revising history or re-imagining a real-life person's perspective — no matter how odious and, perhaps, inspiring.

This fun exercise can help you get a handle on how it feels to write in your book character's POV. When you're stuck in your head, try writing from someone else's!

Chapter **13**

Writing Creative Nonfiction Books

As any writer who writes both fiction and nonfiction can tell you, writing nonfiction books is quite different from writing fiction. Although fiction allows you to pick any topic and create a unique universe around it, nonfiction doesn't give you the same leeway; it must be factually correct. If you're writing nonfiction about Harriet Tubman, for example, you can't ascribe superpowers to her. Although she may have been fit and strong, she probably didn't possess X-ray vision or the ability to fly.

With that thought in mind, we dedicate this chapter to discussing everything you need to know about writing nonfiction children's books. We talk about some major similarities and differences between writing nonfiction and fiction. We consider how to choose fun and fascinating topics, and we take a look at how outlining your nonfiction story can really help you stay on track. We also share some common mistakes when it comes to children's nonfiction (and how to avoid them, of course), as well as a few writing exercises that you can try to hone your nonfiction chops.

The Nonfiction Children's Book World at a Glance

A *nonfiction* book is one based on facts. You can write historical nonfiction, focusing on an event (such as the September 11, 2001 attack on the World Trade Center in New York City) or a person (think tennis great Serena Williams). Or you can hone in on a topic such as dinosaurs, machines, or oceans. Biographies are nonfiction, as are autobiographies and how-to books (which explain to the reader how to do something). The available subjects and topics for nonfiction are nearly endless, which is why we help you find a topic that inspires you in the section "Choosing a Great Nonfiction Topic," later in this chapter.

The different elements that go into nonfiction books are often the same as in fiction; only the contents are different. For instance, for visuals, nonfiction books often use *photorealistic illustrations* (illustrations done in a style that approximates photographs), photographs, line drawings, and simple diagrams, maps, and charts. You have to really balance the ratio of text and visuals so that you don't overshadow the images with the text, cluttering up the page with too many words. (A pet peeve of many book buyers — see Chapter 4.) The design of a nonfiction book may have to juggle many more elements per spread than a book of fiction; for instance, if the book has main text, main visuals, charts, factoid boxes, text bubbles, and other visually stimulating graphics, the publisher has to lay them all out to encourage the reader to peruse all the content without feeling overwhelmed.

NONFICTION FOR THE FICTION LOVER

A nonfiction style that reads like fiction is called *narrative nonfiction*. It uses fiction techniques such as narrative, dialogue, and a story structure that has a beginning, middle, and end — but everything that happens in the book is true. Biographies can be narrative nonfiction, as can memoirs or books about events in history. Books that have narratives focusing on the main character's diary entries fall into this genre, as do *epistolary books,* in which the narrative consists of protagonists who wrote letters back and forth to one another. All the letters and correspondences in these books must be real documents — although verifying whether the writers of these documents were telling the truth about their lives would probably constitute a completely different book on the topic. Examples include *Heads or Tails: Stories from the Sixth Grade,* by Jack Gantos (middle-grade memoir; Square Fish), or *The Boys' War: Confederate and Union Soldiers Talk About the Civil War,* by Jim Murphy (young adult history; Clarion Books).

Nonfiction plays a very important part in the spectrum of children books. Teachers use nonfiction books in their curricula from preschool to high school. You can find nonfiction in board books, Young Adult (YA) books, and everything in between. And nonfiction lends itself perfectly well to the parameters of all the formats you can read about in Chapter 2. The only major difference is that although fictional picture books target ages 3 through 8 and max out at a word count of 1,500, you can aim nonfiction picture books at audiences up to age 12, and the text can feasibly run over 1,500 words.

The Eyewitness Books series (Dorling Kindersley) provides a great example of a nonfiction series appropriate for ages 9 through 12 that beautifully balances many different visual elements with the right amount of text. Each title, written by a different author or team of authors, offers an in-depth look at one subject — such as pirates, horses, or insects — and spends about 56 to 72 pages really digging into the aspects of the chosen topic, which kids really care about. (For more about idea development and what your audience wants, see Chapters 6 and 7.) Instead of reading like dry reference books, these books give the reader mini encyclopedias — fascinating and packed with information.

TIP

To help you figure out a topic for your nonfiction book that might get picked up by schools, research your state's core curriculum. Although the U.S. doesn't have a set national curriculum, school districts and national associations do require or recommend that schools follow certain instruction standards. Visit the U.S. Department of Education's website (www.ed.gov) for more information.

Writing Toward a Nonfiction Masterpiece

You write nonfiction differently than fiction in a few ways. Although you may not have a main character (unless you're writing a biography or autobiography) or a plot tied to that main character, your topic is essentially your main character. And you need to make some decisions early on:

>> **Theme or subject:** The book's main idea or concept. What's your subject? See the following section to help answer that question.

>> **Characters:** Do you have a main character? What about supporting characters? (If your book doesn't focus on a particular person or group of people, or if you're writing a how-to book, you usually don't really have any characters.) See Chapter 8.

>> **Plot:** What happens in your book. You may not have a plot in nonfiction, but you still need to set up your work with a series of intertwined actions that progress from a beginning, through a middle, to an end in order to keep it moving and interesting to your young reader. Your outline can help you create and track this structure, as we explain in the section "Outlining Your Creative Nonfiction," later in this chapter.

>> **Setting:** Where does the subject take place, or is the place your subject? Many nonfiction books explore many settings. (Flip to Chapter 11 for more on setting.)

>> **Point of view:** Except for many biographies (and, of course, autobiographies), you usually write nonfiction and how-to books in the third person. (To find out more about point of view, see Chapters 7 and 12.)

>> **Format and target audience:** Although you don't absolutely need to know what format and what audience you want to write for when you begin writing your book, that information certainly helps you focus your efforts. (We cover formats and audience in Chapters 2 and 4 and researching your audience in Chapter 7.)

After you make the decisions in the preceding list and begin writing, you still have to make other choices that don't apply when you write fiction. For example, in nonfiction, you have to make sure that all dialogue is factual and verifiable — many publishers require complete and documented accuracy. Will your book need a table of contents? What about an index?

You have to give credit where credit is due:

Aside from the visuals, how do you plan to keep your text engaging? If you're writing about an event in history and don't have a single historical figure you want to use as a main character, how do you plan to keep readers engaged? Suspense, humor, and romance all still have places in nonfiction — and you, the author, still must provide them. (Chapter 9 gives ample tips about pacing and drama that you can easily apply to nonfiction writing.)

Just like with fiction, after you come up with a great topic and nail down the basics, you need to go out and make sure that kids today find your topic relevant, up-to-date, and interesting. But then you jump into researching your topic. Although you don't need to do research for all fiction, you absolutely must for nonfiction. And the vast majority of nonfiction writers, unlike most fiction writers, use outlines to organize their thoughts and help them flesh out their ideas. After you write the first draft of your nonfiction book, your rewrites and edits involve the same sort of painstaking and careful attention to detail you used when initially writing it — if not more.

HELPING SHAPE YOUR NONFICTION CHILDREN'S BOOK

Librarians and booksellers tell us that the design and layout of a nonfiction book are paramount to their buying decisions. They probably won't buy books that have too much text and not enough pictures, or books in which the design is cluttered, illogical, or hard to follow. Although the publisher designs the interior of a nonfiction book, you can do much to encourage good design:

- Research well-designed nonfiction books and note the elements they use to add extra information to the primary text. For example, say that a book intersperses little, interesting factoids throughout the text by using talk bubbles and cartoons; but you want to use photorealistic illustrations. Just write text for these illustrations and include them in your manuscript. Or maybe you like this book's sidebars and icons (the Tips and Warnings, for example). Consider putting something similar to these elements in your own nonfiction book. You don't strictly need these elements to convey the basics, but they add interesting and beneficial information to the main body of the text.

- If you have a lot of terms to define on each page, write them out separately as an addendum for the designer, including page references, so that the designer can figure out a cool way to incorporate those terms into the overall design.

- If text blocks seem to work better in your mind's eye (and in the competition), then create actual text blocks in your manuscript. (***Warning:*** Some publishers prefer that you simply add an addendum that describes what you have in mind if you're submitting the manuscript.)

- When you sell your masterpiece, you can even try to negotiate input in the design phase of the book — although, unless you have other titles under your belt, this might be an uphill battle with the publisher.

TIP

Authors sell a great majority of nonfiction books, even the short ones, via a proposal. We cover the basics of writing a nonfiction book proposal in Chapter 17.

Choosing a Great Nonfiction Topic

In the sections that follow, we consider how to choose a topic to both delight the children who read it and excite you during the writing process. We also take a look at sources for nonfiction book ideas and great places to test your ideas before you spend all your time and energy developing them.

Looking at topics that get kids' attention

When it comes to fictional topics, you probably already have a pretty good idea of what gets children interested in reading: stories about wizards, flatulent canines, heroes with superpowers, princes and princesses, talking fish, cats with hats, Martians, girls from Kansas with ruby slippers, and many more. But what about ideas for nonfiction children's books? What topics float kids' boats? Here are just a few:

>> Pets

>> How bodies work

>> Sports

>> History and culture

>> Dinosaurs and other exotic animals

>> Biographies

>> Backyard nature

>> How things are made

>> Science and technology

>> Strange, terrible, gross, interesting facts

REMEMBER

Choose a slant to the topic that makes your approach unique and interesting to the intended audience. Younger kids (preschool through first grade) like topics presented as they apply to the kids' lives. For example, how to find and study bugs in your backyard. Kids in second grade and up often use nonfiction books to write reports at school or do research, so think about how your topic can tie into the curriculum. And you always want to add humor whenever possible, through the text, illustrations, or both. Consider the example of a nonfiction book in the picture book format for kids up to age 10 called *It's Disgusting and We Ate It! True Food Facts from Around the World and Throughout History,* by James Solheim (Aladdin).

WARNING

Anthropomorphism (attributing human characteristics or behavior to an animal or object) and *personification* (attributing a personal nature or human characteristics to something nonhuman, or representing an abstract quality in human form) don't usually work in nonfiction books because this pushes them into the fictional realm.

Finding topics that interest you

When we say you should choose a subject that floats your boat, we mean choosing a subject that you have a strong personal interest in. Although ultimately your reader has to find the topic you choose interesting (otherwise, why buy it?), you have to find it interesting first. If you're not into it, your writing reflects that. Also, the publishing process can take quite some time. Choosing a topic that interests you can help sustain you during the ups and downs of the writing-publishing cycles. To decide which topics float your boat, use the following indicators as a guide:

>> **Choose a topic you know a lot about.** If you know a lot about a particular topic, not only does that indicate you probably like it, but it also means you likely have plenty of background knowledge to get you off to a smooth start.

>> **Choose a topic you're curious about.** Perhaps you've been wondering about a particular topic for a long time — maybe years — but you've never yet taken the time to find out more about it. You may, for example, have a fascination with sharks — a topic about which you know little beyond what you learned from watching the film *Sharknado* years ago. This fascination may drive you to research the topic thoroughly — to the point that you become expert at it.

>> **Choose a topic that you're passionate about.** Passion for something — an idea, a thing, a person — can really motivate you to achieve great things, including writing a great story. Tap into the emotion, energy, and inspiration that your passion releases by choosing a topic that you're passionate about.

>> **Choose a topic that has personal meaning to you.** If you, your parents, or your grandparents immigrated to this country from, say, China or Mexico, why not choose a topic that allows you to further explore your own roots and your cultural heritage? Maybe you can write a book based on Chinese New Year or Mexican festivities for the Day of the Dead.

REMEMBER

Life is too short to waste your time writing books for which you have no passion or feeling of connection. Leave those books to someone else while you focus on finding the topics that work best for you. Use the word *should* as a test. Do you think, "I should write a book about this topic?" That perspective isn't as powerful as saying, "I can't wait to write a book about this topic." If you see your topic as a *should*, drop it until it becomes a *can't-wait-to* or until a different *can't-wait-to* topic comes along.

Branching out into the real world

Beyond finding topics that interest your potential readers — and that interest you personally (see the preceding section) — look at the real world and real topics going on today or from the past. A glance through the pages of almost any newspaper or magazine can reveal a wide variety of topics for you to consider.

Checking out the hot topics of the day

Kids are connoisseurs of all things current and hot. If something new has appeared out there, kids probably already know about it. Whether you want to find out about the latest hot singer, the edgiest fashions and trends, or the coolest electronic gizmo — kids are likely already way ahead of you. Older kids are also paying attention to current events that affect them, such as school shootings, local and national elections, and so on. Be sure to check out Chapter 7, where we devote an entire section to dipping into the popular culture for ideas on what's hot.

Delving into broad topics that need more coverage

Topics such as dinosaurs or firetrucks don't really lack coverage in the children's book market; however, you can find other, overlooked topics — such as American citizens of Japanese descent forced into relocation camps during World War II, or great women astronomers, or the impact of population growth on fragile ecosystems. Consider asking the following questions while you search for a subject that needs more coverage:

>> Is the person, event, or thing historically significant?

>> Is the person, event, or thing relatively obscure?

>> Would a book based on the topic have a measurable and positive impact on its young readers?

>> Are there other books on the topic? Do they leave certain issues unaddressed (which you can address in your book)?

>> Do you simply need to tell this story because you see it as particularly unique, timely, or compelling?

If you answer a number of these questions in the affirmative, you have a compelling case for writing about that topic. So don't just think about doing it, do it already!

Testing Your Topic

After you pick out a nonfiction topic (which we help you figure out how to do in the section "Choosing a Great Nonfiction Topic," earlier in this chapter), how can you figure out whether it's a good one? By testing it. And who should test your ideas? We suggest getting feedback from kids, teachers, and librarians.

Seeking feedback from kids

What better place to get feedback about your idea than straight from the horse's mouth? Kids can help you quickly determine whether your idea is a winner or something that belongs on the back burner. Here are some questions to ask your potential audience to get the feedback flowing and to ascertain whether you're on the right track:

>> Do you like this idea?

>> What about this idea do you like?

>> What about this idea do you dislike?

>> What would you do to make this idea more interesting?

>> What idea would you like better than this one?

>> What did you already know about this idea? What was new for you?

Be sure to check out Chapter 6, in which we discuss going to kids to generate ideas for your stories. Many of the same suggestions we offer about generating ideas apply to testing out your ideas, too.

Seeking feedback from teachers and librarians

After you select your topic, get a second opinion. And get that second opinion from people who spend more time with eager young readers than most anyone else on the planet: librarians and teachers.

Librarians and teachers are on the front lines of every youthquake and megatrend that passes through their libraries and classrooms. If the kids like something, librarians and teachers probably know about it weeks — perhaps even months — before you do.

You can also find out whether a topic covers the right ground by looking at the public school curriculum for different grades or for specific grades in the age range for which you want to write. Look for the appropriate state and federal educational guidelines and curricula online — you can even find word lists for each grade. Most school districts also have their curricula on their websites. Ask teachers who teach a grade you want to target whether they see a need for more books on certain topics for use in the classroom.

Outlining Your Creative Nonfiction

Many nonfiction writers rely on outlines to help develop and organize their stories. A good outline displays, at a glance, all the topics that the book needs to cover in the order that it should cover them. And an outline helps avoid chronological or topical holes. Because an outline must cover the selected topic from beginning to end in a logical and sequential way, it essentially serves as your road map, telling you where you are right now, where you've been, and where you're going.

We help you develop an outline for your nonfiction book in the following sections.

Starting simple

An outline guides you, the author, while you write, but it also helps with the planning process. A simple outline has three main parts:

» **Title:** The title of your book.

» **Headings:** Major points you plan to address in your book. In the finished book, they may become separate chapter titles, or they may remain headings.

» **Content:** Text that elaborates on the topic named by each heading (or chapter title).

Say that you decide to write a children's book about megalodons, those gigantic, ancient sharks that roamed the seas from about 25 to 1.6 million years ago. Your outline for this topic may look something like the following, using the title *Megalodons: The Real Story:*

» What is a megalodon?

- Ancient shark (name means *big teeth*)

- Existed from 25 to 1.6 million years ago (Miocene and Pliocene Epochs)

- Looked like a really big present-day great white shark

- >> How big were megalodons?

  - Estimated at 40 to 100 feet long

  - At least three times larger than present-day great white shark

  - Jaws could open 6 feet wide and 7 feet high

- >> What did megalodons eat?

  - Mostly ate whales

  - Also consumed squid

  - Maybe enjoyed some sushi? (throwing in some humor never hurts)

- >> What about those big teeth?

  - Largest fossilized teeth discovered to date are 6 inches long

  - Had three to five rows of teeth in mouth

  - Didn't chew its food, it gulped it down whole or in large chunks

- >> What happened to megalodons?

  - The impact of global cooling

  - The great population crash

REMEMBER

A number of different approaches work when it comes time to create your outline. You can type it out on your computer or write it out by hand. Or you can write each of your headings on an index card and write out a paragraph describing its content underneath. You can also use sticky notes on a blank wall (just keep the windows closed; wind is not your friend).

Whatever approach you take, we promise that the time you put into creating an outline for your nonfiction book pays you back many times over when it comes time to write your manuscript.

Fleshing out your ideas

After you draft an outline (discussed in the preceding section), you have a choice: Either start writing your book from the outline as it stands or continue to refine the outline, adding more material to flesh it out. Although it may seem like unnecessary extra work, the more fleshing out you do, the closer you actually bring yourself to the finished product. And every step closer to the finished product brings you closer to accomplishing your goal: creating a children's nonfiction book you can be proud of.

You can flesh out the ideas in your outline in a couple of different ways: either starting at the beginning and strictly working your way to the end or jumping back and forth between different sections of the outline, working first on what interests you most and dealing with more challenging sections later. You don't need to follow any one particular approach to fill out your outline; just adopt the approach that works best for you.

Here's an example of how a fleshed-out, researched outline may look (if you're writing *Megalodons: The Real Story*, that is):

>> What is a megalodon?

- A megalodon was an ancient shark that may have been an ancestor of the present-day great white shark. Megalodons churned widely through the oceans, off the coasts of large parts of the Earth — North America, Europe, South America, India, Oceania, and more. The name megalodon means *big teeth* — the largest megalodon teeth found to date are about 6 inches long.

- Megalodons glided through the world from 25 to 1.6 million years ago, and they are now extinct. Megalodons lived during the Miocene and Pliocene Epochs.

- Megalodons looked like a really big version of a present-day great white shark. They had many of the same features as modern-day sharks, including gill slits; front and rear dorsal fins; a pectoral fin, pelvic fin, and mouth; nostrils; and so forth. Their skin was rough and gray in color and had sharp scales.

Enhancing your outline by using visual aids

Like the old saying goes, "A picture is worth a thousand words." Some people simply better internalize and play with information when they see ideas presented visually rather than via the written word. If you're one of those people, try drawing out your outline so that you can really visualize it.

TIP

A *storyboard*, for example, is simply a series of drawings that represent events occurring in sequence. You can use a storyboard to outline a single chapter or an entire book. If you're an extremely visual person, you may find a storyboard helpful while you outline your book. Some writers buy cue cards, put their salient topics on them, and arrange them on a corkboard. Others who write picture books or board books paste the outline topics on actual pages to help them visualize the progression of the book and the word count they must keep in mind. Still others draw pictures, making dummy books that include illustrations or sketches to show on the page what the words must express.

You may also find other visual aids quite useful, too, including presentation software or even a simple paper-based flip chart that flips through the action in the sequence you plan to write it.

TIP

If you're more of a visual person, you can try out a *mapping wheel*, as Lisa calls it, by following these steps:

1. **Write your topic in the center of a piece of paper.**

2. **Write your planned chapters or headings around the main idea.**

   Space them out so that you have room to write around these chapters or headings.

3. **Add lines from the topic to these chapters or headings.**

   The lines should look like spokes on a wheel.

4. **Add facts and factoids around each chapter or heading.**

5. **Draw lines from each chapter or heading to the appropriate facts and factoids.**

   Include information that you want to address in your writing.

From this mapping wheel, you can see the skeleton of your book laid out before you.

Common Creative Nonfiction Mistakes (And How to Avoid Them)

A variety of mistakes can occur when you're writing a creative nonfiction children's book. Here are some of the most common mistakes, along with some quick fixes for them:

>> **You don't know your stuff.** Remember, you need to have your facts straight when you write nonfiction. If you're not sure about something, then look it up!

>> **The book is out of date.** Many nonfiction books — especially about fast-moving topics such as technology — are timely today and out of date tomorrow. Keep up with the latest-and-greatest news on your topic, and make sure your book reflects it.

>> **The story is boring.** Because creative nonfiction is, by nature, nonfictional, you may find it challenging to push the creativity button hard enough to avoid writing a boring book. You can avoid this trap by having fun with your writing — be creative!

TIP

To make sure your writing isn't boring, have fun writing it. If you can convey your own excitement and wonder about a topic onto the page, the fun you're having comes across in your word choices, varied sentence structure, exciting transitions, and wonderful factoids or interesting asides that relate directly to your chosen topic.

Writing Exercises for Creative Nonfiction

Yes, writing nonfiction children's books means you have to get your facts straight, but it doesn't mean you can't have fun doing it. At its heart, writing creative nonfiction focuses on presenting factual information to your readers in a way that they enjoy. The following writing exercises can help you develop the nonfiction chops you need to make your work shine.

Pretend you're a newspaper reporter

Newspaper reporters masterfully present factual information in an engaging, concise, and accurate way. The best newspaper articles draw you in with a captivating title and opening first sentence or two (what news organizations call the *lede*), and then they tell you five important things about the story: Who, what, when, where, and why.

So, what better way to practice writing creative nonfiction than to pretend you're a newspaper reporter? To begin this exercise, first imagine that your editor has just given you an assignment to write a short article about some person, thing, or event. You can make the assignment local in nature — perhaps a construction crew recently uncovered an intact woolly mammoth skeleton at a building site — or you can choose something national or even international. Research the story to gather the facts; then write your article.

Don't forget to make your article not just factual, make it engaging and fun — be creative. Keep an eye out for the unusual — facts that your readers will find interesting and entertaining. If the subject of your article has a large collection of bugs in their garage, organized by size, color, and wingspan, then by all means, report that. If the new Ferris wheel in your city is the tallest in the tri-state area, then make sure you write about that, as well as about any interesting factoids that you uncovered in your research, such as how many boxes of popcorn stacked one on top of the other you would need to reach the top of the wheel.

Try writing at least three newspaper articles — more if you're particularly inspired by this exercise. Try varying the age of the audience. How would you change the article for elementary, middle grade, or high school readers?

Create a funny five-step procedure to wash a dog

A large segment of nonfiction writing falls into the category of how-to guides. The book you're holding in your hands right now is a proud member of that segment of nonfiction writing — it shows you how to write a children's book and get it published. Regardless of whether the creative nonfiction children's book you plan to write is a how-to book, you can sharpen your creative nonfiction writing skills by writing a how-to procedure.

In this exercise, write a five-step procedure for washing a dog. Now, we don't want you to write just any five-step procedure. We want you to write one that's as factual as you can make it, but that's also as funny as can be. While you detail each of your five steps, think about at least one funny thing to help you illustrate the step. For example, if you decide one of your steps involves placing your dog in a bathtub in your home and lathering it up with doggy shampoo, imagine what happens to your bathroom walls (and you!) when the dog suddenly decides to vigorously shake off all the soap suds? Or when it leaps out and escapes the bathroom, running down the hall pell-mell? You get the idea.

More short exercises to get you writing

This exercise is a one-pager. Imagine you're in a time and place of great danger. For example, imagine you're in Germany in 1939; or stuck in a polar ice field in 1915; or huddled underground waiting out a dust storm in 1934 Kansas; or escaping the fire in San Francisco in 1906. (You get the idea, but we run with 1939 Germany for now.) Write down what you know was going on in that place at that time. Write about the place as you imagine it was back then. Describe

>> What the place looks, smells, and feels like when you walk around

>> What the people wear and how it's different from today

>> How desperate people are emigrating from Germany

>> Why these people feared for themselves

Bring a sense of danger and drama to your writing, even if you're guessing half of what you write.

In this two-paragraph exercise, write about a wonderful food that you love. Describe it with all the verve and creativity you can. Employ your senses. That's paragraph one. Then in paragraph two, take the opposite approach and describe how you can't stand that smelly, nauseating food. Consider using meat as your food for this exercise: First you describe it from a meat-lover's point of view, and then you describe it from a vegetarian or vegan's point of view. Repeat this exercise with other things you love: a book, a flower, a picture, an animal, an appliance or tool.

Use the mapping wheel described in the section "Enhancing your outline by using visual aids," earlier in this chapter, to create a story about a celebrity. In the middle of the wheel, put that celebrity's name. Then, like spokes radiating out from the center of the wheel, connect words that describe that person. Go for everything from hair, eyes, teeth, and clothing choices to every salacious detail you know about their life (confirmed or not). Sit back and look at your map. Could you write a biographical paragraph about that person? If so, go for it!

INTERVIEW WITH SUSAN GOLDMAN RUBIN, AUTHOR

Susan Goldman Rubin, a children's book author extraordinaire, has regularly wowed her readers with well-researched and captivating nonfiction books. We asked her some questions about writing nonfiction for children:

- **Why did you start writing children's nonfiction books?** "I turned to nonfiction because I loved art and wanted to share my enthusiasm with young people. My first nonfiction book was a biography of architect Frank Lloyd Wright. It came about when my husband and I were going to take our kids on an outing to Hollyhock House, one of Wright's buildings in Los Angeles. When we told the kids where we were going, my 10-year-old stepson (who had visited many museums) said, 'Frank Lloyd Who?' That's when I knew I had to do the book. I published it with Abrams, a house known for their splendid art books. One project led to another. Sometimes, my editor invited me to do a book for young readers in conjunction with an upcoming exhibition. Along the way, I began to write about Holocaust themes. This, too, came from the heart."

- **Why is it a mistake for would-be children's book authors to ignore the nonfiction genre?** "When I teach or speak at a writers' conference, I strongly encourage would-be children's book authors to try nonfiction. I urge them to choose a subject that greatly interests them and find an approach suitable for a particular age group. About half of all published children's books are nonfiction, and there is a real need for fresh, new material. Chances for breaking into the market are greater with nonfiction."

- **What about writing nonfiction children's books excites you?** "I love research. Finding out secrets and gathering information about real people and actual events thrills me. The process is like a treasure hunt. One clue leads to another, whether I'm looking for text information or for photos and art to use as illustrations. When I wrote *Toilets, Toasters and Telephones: The How and Why of Everyday Objects* (Harcourt Children's Books), for instance, I spent hours on the phone looking for a photo of an early Egyptian toilet seat dating from 1370 BCE. I called Cairo and wound up on a first-name basis with an Arabic-speaking phone operator as I searched for The Egypt Exploration Society. Finally, I found that it was located in England, and the society provided me with the picture I needed — gratis!"

- **How do you select a topic to write about?** "I select a topic from the heart. Something that I feel passionately about, that I must do, even if I think it may have limited sales. Perhaps the subject has never before been presented to children and I feel compelled to write about it. This happened when I stumbled upon the story of artist Friedl Dicker-Brandeis, an unsung heroine of the Holocaust. The true story gripped me. I put aside another book project under contract and, with the permission of my understanding editor, focused on *Fireflies in the Dark: The Story of Friedl Dicker-Brandeis and the Children of Terezin*."

- **In what ways is writing a nonfiction children's book more challenging than writing a fictional children's book?** "The challenge of writing nonfiction is to show, not tell, and use narrative techniques of dramatization with action and dialogue. However, scenes have to be based on reliable sources. A nonfiction writer has the responsibility of being accurate and truthful. Quotes can't be made up. Finding words that were actually spoken that will be clear and meaningful to young readers presents a difficult challenge."

- **Describe your research process.** "When I begin a project, I read everything I can get hold of on the subject. I read books and articles geared for adults as well as those written for children. I especially want to know what the competition is so that I can come up with something fresh. I watch videos on the subject. I interview people who can give me new information and quotes."

"Travel gives authenticity to nonfiction writing. When I wrote the book about Friedl Dicker-Brandeis, I managed to go to Terezin, the ghetto/concentration camp near Prague where she had been imprisoned. If I've taped interviews, as I did for that book, I play them back at home, transcribe the words, then incorporate the best quotes for my purposes into the narrative."

(continued)

(continued)

"I write the book chapter by chapter, getting feedback from my supportive but critical writers' group. I keep going over the manuscript, tightening and brightening, until it's ready to show to my agent and editor as a well-edited first draft. Even then, there's more research to be done when my editor and the copy editor give me their comments and queries."

- **What advice do you have for prospective nonfiction children's book authors?**
"My advice for prospective nonfiction children's book authors is to follow your hearts. Write about subjects that truly excite you. See what else has been published and how recently. Maybe it's time for a fresh look at an old topic. Or perhaps in today's world, it's appropriate to introduce very young readers to a subject formerly offered only to older children. Come up with a catchy working title. Find a unique angle. One of my editors says, 'If you've got the hook, you've got the book.'"

4
Making Your Story Sparkle

Turn your rough stone into a polished diamond.

Visualize what you want your children's book to look like when you finish it, and then shine it and buff it until it sparkles.

Explore how to rewrite and edit your book.

Take a look at how to format your text, whether to illustrate it, and how to get feedback from others.

Chapter **14**

Editing, Revising, and Formatting Your Way to a Happy Ending

E ven the best, most professional, writes-for-a-living type of writers can't create absolutely perfect books or stories the first time around. In the real world (that place where we hope most of you live), writing is a repetitive, iterative process during which you first input some words, then you make some changes, then make some more changes, add or delete a word (or paragraph, section, or chapter) here or there, and correct some misspellings or grammar issues — then you start all over again. In short, you revise, edit, and polish again and again. Any great author needs to become familiar with revising and editing, which can turn a lackluster manuscript into a compelling, award-winning book.

TIP

Don't edit or revise until you have your complete first draft done. You need to write your first drafts freely, mistakes and all, capturing your imagination and creativity without a little devil editor on your shoulder telling you something's not right. Get down the draft and then you can contemplate editing.

Some people consider editing and revising the same process. But for our purposes, we separate them as follows:

>> **Revising:** The fixing process you do when you go back to check whether all the major parts of your book work (like the parts we cover in Part 3)

>> **Editing:** The fixing you do after you're pretty sure you've finished the major parts; you're just working on fine-tuning.

>> **Formatting:** The fixing you do to make sure your manuscript is in the right font, that the paragraphs are spaced appropriately, and that headers and margins are all correct.

Seasoned writers know that the revision process is just as important to the final result as completing that first draft. In fact, you may find good revisions and edits often more important than the first draft. So don't fear the revision, embrace it. It's a natural part of the writing process. Look forward to it. Trust us: A good revision is every writer's best friend.

We, therefore, dedicate this chapter to arguably two of the most important parts of the process of writing a children's book: revising and editing.

Your Revising Checklist: Getting Major Story Elements in Order

In the revising phase, you make sure that you have the major elements of your story in order — specifically theme, characters, plot, pacing and drama, setting and context, and point of view. The following sections walk you through how to examine each of these major elements in the course of revising your book.

TIP

If you're revising a manuscript that you suspect has major issues, follow our advice to keep track of what you want to work on: Each time you go through the manuscript from start to finish, attempt to tackle only one issue at a time. So, if you're ready to revise your characters to make sure you've properly fleshed them out, take one character at a time from start to finish. Then, go back to the beginning and do it all over with another character. Repeat this process until you go through your manuscript for each of the characters you want to work on. When you finish, move on to the next issue. This structure keeps you from going crazy wondering what to focus on while you work your way through.

Just be sure to take a break after completing a pass through your work. Each time you check an issue from start to finish, take a breather of at least a few minutes — even a day, if you can. If you go back to your manuscript the next day and you don't see any improvement from the changes you made — or worse, that you only created more problems for yourself — then stop revising. At this point, you're ready for some serious feedback. We help you find resources in Chapter 16.

REMEMBER

A lot of the points you need to check for in a revision of fiction also apply to non-fiction. Perhaps they don't have an exact correlation, but the major issues are more similar than not. The one main difference is that in nonfiction, you have to check and recheck facts while making sure to provide for a balance in the text and other ways of conveying information (we talk all about nonfiction in Chapter 13).

Theme

Theme is the main idea that flows through the narrative and connects the components of the story together. If another reader (such as a friend or someone in your writing group) can't describe your theme in a word or two (maybe a sentence), perhaps you need to better home in on one. If so, you might need to revise your story with theme in mind.

Make the theme apparent at the start of the story by introducing the type of problem the character needs to solve. For example, if your story's theme is reassurance, put your protagonist in a situation in which the solution leads to them finding reassurance. Then, insert reminders to the theme throughout the story in the form of *foils* — issues that get in the way of your character's main desire or need. Furthering the example, show your character feeling insecure. Maybe even show other characters playing upon their insecurity to create conflict. And in the end, make sure that character finds the reassurance they've sought — or achieves an equally valuable replacement.

Characters

Your primary goal as a writer is to create unforgettable characters. Why? Because if your characters are dishrags, your manuscript may as well be, too. In 99.9 percent of children's books, the characters make or break whether you have on your hands a single title or a book that has series potential. If you poorly develop the character in the text, no amount of magnificent writing or perfectly crafted plotting can save you. A memorable character mostly comes from the marriage of complementary illustrations (when appropriate to the format) and an active story line. (In board books, you use so few words that you may conclude you make the characters memorable by the illustrations alone — and in most cases, you're right.)

REMEMBER

What makes a good character great is the way they see the world and interact with it. The character's quirks and preferences, the way they talk, the way they move, the actions they take, the way they deal with conflict, the reactions they demonstrate — all the characteristics that bring the written character alive make them seem like they exist in real life — as a human or otherwise. Seeing characters in action shows the reader who they are. You can read all about creating memorable characters in Chapter 8.

You must flesh out your main character and their supporting cast to make them interesting. They also need to sound their age. Additionally, throughout the book, your main character must actively change from who they were at the start of the story — preferably as the result of their own actions and choices. If you're writing a picture book, make sure the main character appears in every important scene. If you're writing a chapter book, make sure that in each chapter, you further develop the main character in some way, no matter how small. You can use plot events, dialogue, conflict, or interaction with another character to create these developments.

Plot

Plot is the action that drives a story forward. Every story has a beginning, middle, and end, and when an author handles these plot elements clumsily, the resulting work exhibits major problems. Although huge surprises and plot twists can work well in children's books, you may find yourself with a disjointed mess unless you tie up loose ends very carefully.

Ask yourself these questions about your plot:

>> Have I made what happens in the story from start to finish pretty clear?

>> Can I point out the beginning, middle/climax, and end/resolution?

>> Does my main character have enough conflict with the primary issue they have to resolve?

TIP

If you haven't created an action outline (also known as a *step sheet*; see Chapter 9) to help you determine answers to these questions and give you something concrete to check off, you might want to do so to help you revise. If you need to reconfigure your plot for more dramatic, engaging impact, the action outline can help you keep track of what action leads to what reaction, and which conflict leads to which consequence.

Pacing and drama

Pacing and drama are intrinsic to a well-written plot, particularly when you're writing for children — an audience not known for its patience. To maintain the interest of your reader, your story needs to move along briskly and hold your reader's attention. When your pace or amount of drama lags, you quickly lose your reader to other pursuits (such as a more engaging electronic device or a TV show.)

TIP

To judge the pacing in your book, simply ask yourself whether the action moves at a fast enough rate to keep the reader wanting to turn the pages. Flip back to Chapter 9 for all the details on drama and pacing.

In older children's books, make sure each chapter ends with a cliffhanger or an unresolved conflict. That way the reader has to keep turning the pages.

To check the pacing of a picture book, create a quick-and-dirty mockup of your book:

1. Divide your manuscript into separate book pages.

Create about 26 pages for a 32-page book or 36 pages for a 40-page book (leaving one page for the title page, the back of that page for the copyright information, and two pages for endpapers).

2. Write each page of text onto a separate sheet of paper.

3. Staple the papers together along the spine like a book.

Staple the pages back to back, like they would appear in an actual book.

4. Read your newly constructed book.

The first page of text should be a right-hand page, the last a left-hand page.

5. See whether a different action appears on each pair of facing pages (also known as a *spread*).

You want the illustrations to differ from spread to spread.

6. Make sure something exciting happens on the right-hand page of each spread.

Make the reader want to turn the page to see what happens next.

Note: Make up this division of text solely for your benefit — don't send your picture book to an editor like this. (For proper submission formatting, see the section "Formatting Basics: First Impressions Matter," later in this chapter.)

To gauge the drama or compelling action of your story, ask yourself or an early reader friend whether the story has enough *OMG!* or *Oh, no!* moments to keep it compelling — and whether you or your friend can verbalize why. These moments are also called *twists* or *buttons*. Refer to Chapter 9 where we discuss conflict, climax, and resolution.

Setting and context

When you write about a particular place or *setting,* you want the reader to picture it, meaning they can feel the wind blow, smell the pine trees and cedar on a high mountain peak, or sense the grainy sand under their soles and between their toes. If the reader can't picture a particular setting after reading about it, then you, as the author, haven't done a good enough job of describing it. Find all the tips and tricks about creating a scene with setting in Chapter 11.

REMEMBER

To develop a simple context that's interesting and different, don't write a *data dump* (running on and on) about a place, describing every little leaf and crack in the sidewalk. Ground your story in a place so that readers know where the character is coming from or going to. The reader needs to understand what sets this place apart from all of the rest — and you introduce your setting little by little while you proceed from place to place.

When you revise your manuscript, ask yourself whether the reader knows immediately where they are at the start of the story. Have you provided any contextual information, setting the story apart from real life? For example, if the story takes place in a mining town in 1849, does the reader know that right off the bat? Have you elegantly intertwined the setting and contextual clues in the action, or does the reader have to slog through long descriptive passages to get the information? Go through and check each instance where the place and/or time changes, making sure you clearly draw the setting and make efficient and effective word choices.

Point of view

The point of view, or POV, you choose reflects how your reader experiences your story. Have you chosen a POV and stuck to it consistently? If you're writing a picture book, your story should have only one POV — period. If you're writing a chapter book for older children or a YA novel, you may choose to alternate POVs, but you shouldn't alternate them within a single scene or chapter.

You can check whether your POV is consistent by reading your story and noticing from whose viewpoint you're seeing the events. If you get confused, your reader probably does, too. For more on point of view, check out our discussions in Chapter 12.

CONCISE, CONSISTENT, AND COMPELLING WRITING

As any English major can tell you, you can find enough rules for how to write well to fill more than a book or two. But all you really have to do is keep the Three Cs in mind:

- **Be concise.** Never use 50 words when just 5 can accomplish the same goal. Your publisher doesn't measure the value of your book by how many words you write; you make your book much more powerful when you have a clear and unfettered message, without any flowery, vague, or otherwise superfluous language. Pare your story to its barest essence.

- **Be consistent.** Keep plots, characters, chronologies, and story lines consistent, and develop them logically from page to page and from chapter to chapter if you want your reader to follow along. Take time to look at the big picture to ensure consistency throughout your work; you may even want to chart plots, chronologies, and the like to be sure that your story hangs together. (We explain how to chart your story's plotline in Chapter 9.)

- **Be compelling.** The best stories seem driven from within; they pick you up and move you along on an exciting journey to some new place you've never been before. Use action words to draw your reader into your story and to keep their interest after you get it.

When revising your book, make sure that the main character is well-established, that the plot involves action and movement, that the character has a problem to resolve, and that you offer a satisfying resolution. You need all these key ingredients in your recipe for a great story.

Fine-Tuning Your Text: Editing Important Areas

Sometimes, your manuscript has something wrong with it, and you simply can't identify that something. When you're editing your work, you need to know not only how to recognize the problem, but also how to fix it. Most likely, if you address the major issues in your revision, one of the smaller (yet still mighty important) issues we describe in the following sections is off. Don't worry. In addition to outlining some of the most common problems writers face, we also hand over tips from professional editors for conquering them.

Strengthening your opening

You need a strong opening sentence. This advice may sound like a no-brainer, but it's really quite important. Just like when you're watching a movie on TV, if the plot or characters don't grab you right away — click! — you're on to the next channel, looking for something that can hold your attention.

To hook your reader right away, give your opening lines some suggestion of conflict, apprehension, suspense, or at least a promise of such. Tricks for creating good opening lines include starting off with a bit of dialogue or a conversation that piques the reader's curiosity, offering a glimpse into some very dramatic event, then pulling away before that event's conclusion to set the mood of the story; or describing the main character and their problem in one short sentence:

> Now Kathryn Camille had a big, fat problem, and if she didn't solve it by eight o'clock that night, she was dead meat.

With a chapter book, you can spend an entire paragraph setting a scene. In a picture book, you have to jump into the action ASAP. Don't worry if it takes a while for a strong opening sentence to come to you. Many writers leave that task until the very end.

Keeping your dialogue tight and on target

Are your characters' personalities reflected in their speech pattern, tone, or the content of their dialogue — or do you have a five-year-old character who speaks like a teenager or a mad scientist who has trouble articulating even basic scientific concepts? Dialogue that doesn't match the characters you create makes your writing seem implausible and confusing, wooden and lifeless, or painfully contrived. For example, this kindergartener's dialogue sounds like a teenager's: "Yo, dude! I gotta majorly big news. She's hot. Smokin'." Pretty ridiculous, huh?

Go through all your dialogue and make sure each character sounds appropriate for their age and what you have them in your story to accomplish, plot-wise. Also, check that the characters sound different from one another.

Another issue involves excessive use of dialogue. Have you ever heard someone talking and instead of finishing what they're saying, they end their sentence with, "... and blah, blah, blah"? In general, *blah-times-three* acts as shorthand to indicate that whatever followed in the dialogue isn't worthy of the time it takes to say it. When you use too much dialogue in children's books, the readers' minds automatically switch into blah-times-three mode. They start skipping what's on the page to get past all the blah-blah-blah.

Characters who talk to themselves or spend too much time wondering aloud aren't effective characters. Dialogue must involve interaction that moves the plot forward in a meaningful, measurable way.

Check out the discussion about writing realistic dialogue in Chapter 10 and then pass through your manuscript, reading your dialogue aloud to see if it rings true for each character, further develops that character, moves the plot forward, heightens drama or pacing — or if it's just plain blah-times-infinity.

Transitioning effectively

When you're talking with your best friend, you can jump from subject to subject without confusing them. Your hand gestures, body language, tone of voice, and history together can all add to your story, allowing your friend to follow you without getting lost. But in a book, you must help the reader move from scene to scene, from place to place, from character to character. How do you do that? Simple! You use transitions effectively.

Transitions are passages that connect one bit of your story to another. They move you forward in time without getting you lost, and you need them when your character changes locations, activities, conversations, or time frames, or when your story alters its focus. You can make a transition as brief as one word or as long as a sentence.

Here's a trick: Use one word from the last sentence of a paragraph in an obvious way in the first sentence of the next paragraph to indicate change while promoting continuity. For example:

> Mary was trying on a pair of glittery pink shoes when the ceiling fell in. *Miraculously,* she escaped unscathed. Brushing herself off, Mary left a twenty to pay for the shoes and scooted out of the rubble.
>
> "Speaking of *miracles,*" Mary said into her cellphone as she left the store, hopped on her scooter, and headed for home, "can you believe . . ."

The word *miracle* allows Mary to change venues without leaving the reader confused about the fact that one minute she's trying on shoes, then disaster occurs, and the next minute she's motoring around town with bits of plaster in her hair. That's a sneaky but effective transition.

When you manage to put together all the little pieces into the coherent whole that makes for a great story, check that all your transitions are present, accounted for, and effective.

Trimming wordiness

Many would-be writers think that because children's books are short, you can write them really easily. We wish! Writing shorter works is actually more difficult. When you have a lot of words to work with, you don't have to make your word choice as focused. You can beat around the bush, decorating your words with pop-corn strings and colorful lights and butterfly wings — all manner of ornamenta-tion. What's an extra word here or there when you have thousands to work with, right? When you have a limited word count to work with, though, every single word counts.

But even if you're writing a novel for children, your words still need to work hard. For example, instead of writing your paragraph like this:

> The orphanage was a gray place, with gray walls, a gray ceiling, water-stained gray floors, gray furniture, and even a sort of grayishness floating in the air. The children themselves, possessing a gray pallor, seemed to emanate an unhappy gray mood.

You might want to consider writing it like this:

> The orphanage and its inhabitants were gray as rain. The floors, the furniture, even the children seemed muted and colorless.

Although the first example explains the dismal context, setting a mood and letting readers know that even the orphans themselves (the characters) are unhappy and gray, it's too wordy, using 41 words to say and accomplish what half do just as well (if not better). You keep that rewritten, tightened sentence in the book because it sets up the context where much of the plot takes place; therefore, it contributes to plot development. The writer can justify it because they have a spe-cific, defensible reason for it — so it gets to stay.

TIP

Children's books have typical word counts for each format. Because of these word-count expectations, the shorter the work, the more carefully you have to build your plot and your characters. Whatever excess verbiage you have must go. Here's a trick we use: If you find yourself overwriting because you can't seem to express exactly what you mean, sit back, say what you mean aloud to yourself, then try writing it again. Another trick involves reading your work aloud; often, hearing the words can help you tell whether the writing works.

Additionally, check overuse of adjectives and adverbs, and eliminate long, descrip-tive passages. Go through every sentence of your book with a fine-toothed comb, always seeking to tighten, to replace a weak word with a more evocative one, to eliminate redundancies. Make it a fun writing challenge for yourself to see how many words you can tweak or cut. Taking the time to do this task well at this point in the process can help you end up with a much stronger manuscript.

TIP

I (Lisa) have my own quartet of Rules for Revisions. A sentence or paragraph doesn't deserve to stay on the page if it doesn't

>> Flesh out a character.

>> Build a plot through action.

>> Develop a context.

>> Add to the pacing/drama.

Out it goes. Goodbye.

Keeping your chronologies in order

Time is a constant. But when you violate sequential timelines by not providing any clear and apparent milestones, or when time becomes unclear or loses its grounding in reality, then readers get lost. And a lost reader is not a happy reader.

For example, if you had your main character speaking to his teacher before he goes to school that day, you have your chronology of events out of order. An action outline like the one we describe in Chapter 9 can really help you make sure that your beginning, middle, and end (and all the important plot events in between) are in order.

Formatting Basics: First Impressions Matter

If your manuscript doesn't make a good first impression, you likely receive one of those dreaded rejection letters. Or, more likely, your manuscript falls into the black hole of the trash, never to be seen again, without receiving any further acknowledgement whatsoever. (See Chapter 17 for advice on dealing with that nasty but inevitable part of a writer's life.) The key to a good first-millisecond impression? A well-formatted manuscript. Editors see a gazillion manuscripts every day, and the sight of certain common errors makes them sigh with impatience. With so many resources available to writers of children's books, it seems crazy to submit anything other than a clean and well-edited manuscript.

Although all publishers and agents have specific submission guidelines that you must seek out and follow for your manuscript, some guidelines more detailed and specific than others, publishers and agents expect some generally accepted formatting. We walk you through this standard formatting in the following sections.

WARNING

One surefire way to irritate editors — and sentence your submission to the scrap pile — is to use fancy fonts or typesetting. Avoid colors, bigger letters (known as *drop caps*) on the first words of a new chapter — all that fun stuff you see in finished books. Page designers and art directors make these decisions at a later stage. Right now, this formatting only distracts from the story you're trying to tell. Your submission may look plain — perhaps even homely — to you, but your unadorned, fully edited, and deftly polished manuscript looks simply beautiful to the publishing pro who receives it.

Including the proper information on the first page

Every manuscript you send must go out with complete contact information on the first page, as well as the title of your book and the word count (see Figure 14-1). The number of words, combined with the information in your query letter (which we explain how to craft in Chapter 17), immediately indicates to the editor or agent whether you're submitting an entire picture book or the first three chapters of an epic YA novel.

Whether you're writing a board book, a picture book, or a chapter book, center the title of your book and format it in all caps. Place two line spaces (or one double space) between the title and the first line of text. And speaking of the first line of text, make it flush left. The only difference between a board book or picture book submission and a chapter book submission is that you add a centered chapter header below the title on the first manuscript page and on the first page of every subsequent chapter.

Following other children's book formatting conventions

Ready to become a formatting pro? Pay close attention to the following children's book manuscript conventions:

>> If your agent or editor requests a hard copy, print your manuscript on 8.5-x-11-inch regular 20-pound white printer paper and use black ink only.

>> Use 12-point Times New Roman or Arial font (unless the publisher's submission guidelines indicate otherwise).

Lisa Rojany

1234 Some Street West

Some City, California 90000

310.555.1212

Editorialservicesofla@gmail.com

Words: 10,000

THE VAMPIRE HARE THAT ATE ROOM 35

Chapter One

Blah blahdeb lahblah blahdeblahblah blahdeb lahblah blahdebl ahbl ah blahdebl ahblah blahdeb lahblah blahdebla hblah blahdebl ahblah blahde bla hblah bla hde blahb lah.

"Say what?"

"Ditto that. Huh?"

Yet more blahdeblahblah blahdeblahblah blahdeblahblah blahdeblahblah blahde blah blah blahdeblahblah blahdeblahblah blahdeblahblah blahdeblahblah blahdeblahblah blahd eblah blah blahdeblahblah blahdeblahblah blahd eblahblah blahdeblahbla blahdeblahblah blahdeblahblah blahdeblahblah blahdeblahblah blahdeblahblah blahdeblahbla blahdeblahblah.

FIGURE 14-1: A sample first page of a manuscript submission.

- » Double space.

- » Make sure that the first line only of story text on the first page — and of every new chapter or scene break — is flush left, not indented. Every new paragraph thereafter gets indented. Don't use your spacebar to make these indentation spaces.

- » Format your text area's page margins so that they have 1-inch margins all around (top, bottom, right, and left).

- » Begin your headers on page 2.

- » Make sure that your manuscript uses continuous pagination by creating automatic page headers starting at the top of page 2. Don't use your footers for any content whatsoever.

  Choose the same font that you use for the manuscript for both the text and the numeral in the header. Your header, starting at the top of page 2, should look like this:

BOOK TITLE/Your last name only	2

  For example:

THE VAMPIRE HARE THAT ATE ROOM 35/Rojany	2

  Put the title in all caps, no spaces around the slash, followed by your last name starting with an uppercase letter and then all lowercase. End the line with the page numeral flush right.

  Make sure you have a line space at the bottom of your header so that you have space between the header and the top of your story text.

- » Don't *justify* your text (which spaces your words so that all margins form clean, horizontal lines) because editors prefer ragged right, the words appearing as they do naturally at the end of a line. The design team justifies text in finished books; you don't need to do it for manuscripts.

- » Don't add art directions to your text unless you're illustrating your own book. (*Art directions* are notes to the illustrator that indicate what illustration accompanies particular text and where to place the illustration in relation to the text.) Your words need to stand on their own, evoking strong images in the reader's mind without any prompting. If you need to explain what the editor or agent should be seeing in their mind, then your words don't work.

  Are you wondering whether you should include images in your board or picture book submission so that editors get the meaning of your text? We help you figure that out in Chapter 15.

Not to Put Too Fine a Point on It: Checking Basic Grammar and Style

Although many publishing houses have their own in-house style or grammar guides stipulating how to treat serial commas, ellipses, or em dashes (don't panic yet, we cover these elements in the following section), the general guidelines that we offer in the following sections guarantee that you have a manuscript clean enough to impress any nit-picking editor — even if they later change it to reflect the publishing house's style choices.

TIP

For more detailed advice on writing style and grammar, check out the short (but absolutely right-on) classic *The Elements of Style*, by William Strunk, Jr., and E. B. White (MacMillan Publishing Company). Notice that the second author of this seminal work is the very same one who wrote the children's classics *Charlotte's Web*, *Stuart Little*, and *The Trumpet of the Swan*. You can be both a very creative writer and a formatting and grammar pro.

Punctuation

Punctuation consists of periods, commas, apostrophes, question marks, quotation marks, ellipses, dashes, and all manner of little doohickeys too numerous to list here. We're just going to throw in a few of the most common punctuation types (and how to use them properly):

» **Watch your commas.** Use a comma only to separate two complete sentences joined into one (called a *compound sentence*) or to make meaning clear when you can't do so with a rewrite. Don't use commas just because you paused in your typing, you took a breath, or you just feel like it. A complete sentence's structure looks like this: subject + verb + object. This compound sentence separates two complete sentences from each other: *Little Bear ate a lot of honey, and he went to sleep soon after.*

» **Use single quotes only inside double quotes.** For example: "Did you hear her say, 'Little Bear is never, ever, ever getting any more honey'?" American English doesn't use single quotation marks for anything else.

» **Put ending punctuation inside quotation marks.** Whether your sentence ends with a question mark, an exclamation point, or a period, they all fall inside the ending quotation mark when you write dialogue. One of the only exceptions is when you're quoting a quote and exclaiming about it or questioning it. For example: "Did you hear her say, 'Little Bear doesn't deserve any honey'?" She actually asked him a rhetorical question! A two-year-old bear!" However, if a quotation ends with a semicolon or a colon, you place these marks after the quotation mark. For example, "Let me quote from Peter Economy's poem, 'Why It's Great to Be Greek':"

>> **Use the correct ellipses.** Ellipses indicate pauses, usually in dialogue. An ellipsis should look like this . . . with spaces evenly throughout. The period, exclamation point, or question mark at the end of a complete sentence doesn't count as part of the ellipsis. Here's an example of an ellipsis in action: *"She couldn't have. Or could she? . . ." he said, surprise rendering him speechless.*

Style

Style is simply how you write. Style involves issues in which you have choices in both your approach and your execution.

>> **Stick with closed-up em dashes.** *Em dashes,* which are the length of two dashes, indicate interruption and upcoming lists. Keep your em dashes close to the text instead of adding spaces. For example, say *All those animals — Chloe's house was packed with them,* rather than *All those animals — Chloe's house was packed with them.*

Even though publishers often don't use spaces around an em dash, each publishing house has its own style guide. This book's publisher, John Wiley & Son, Inc., puts spaces around em dashes, which is why you see that convention throughout this book.

>> **Indicate a range of numbers by using en dashes.** An en dash is longer than a dash and shorter than an em dash. Here's an example of it in use: *Everyone who would ever matter on Planet V was born 1964–1970.*

>> **Stick to hard text breaks in a chapter book manuscript.** *Hard text breaks* are actual page breaks from one chapter to another. You have to manually insert them according to your word-processing software's specifications. Don't rely on hitting the Enter or Return key until you cross over into the next page to get the job done because every time you make an edit, the chapter break will move.

>> **Follow the rules for numbers.** Spell out numbers under and inclusive of ten and use numerals for 11 and up. Don't mix both in one sentence. And if you have a bunch of numbers in a sentence, the majority wins: If more of the numbers are under ten, spell 'em all out; if more of them are 11 and over, use numerals. Dialogue is an exception to this rule. Always spell out numbers in dialogue, no matter how large or small they are. And never start a sentence with a numeral.

- » **Pay attention to hyphenation rules.** Only hyphenate numbers that modify a following word (for example, don't hyphenate *one hundred* unless it's modifying another word, such as *one-hundred feet*). Similarly, don't hyphenate time references unless two numbers represent one numeral (so that's *two thirty*, not *two-thirty*; but you would write *two thirty-five*).

- » **Use serial commas.** A *serial comma* is the comma that appears in a string of three or more verbs, adverbs, adjectives, nouns, or parallel phrases. For clarity in children's books, use serial commas to separate more than two objects in a list and to help children keep things straight. For example: *Mrs. Montgomery leaned over Genevieve's desk, picked up the pencil, tapped it on the desk until the child awoke, and then turned away in a huff.*

REMEMBER

Consistency is king. If you choose to put spaces before and after em dashes, do so throughout the entire manuscript. Same goes for spelling out numbers and using serial commas. With so many differences in style guides and house styles across publishers, there's no one correct way to style a manuscript.

Miscellaneous

Here are some additional tips to help you avoid common mistakes:

- » **Don't mix up *which* and *that*.** Use *which* in a sentence that has a modifying phrase that you could delete and still leave the sentence's meaning intact. If you can take away the modifying phrase and still give the same amount of information, use *which* (and put a comma before it). Otherwise, use *that* — but only if you have to. Using *that* too often can sound clunky.

- » **Eliminate lazy words and passive words.** Vague words such as *it* and *thing* don't really do much for your story. Neither do *to be* verbs (*am, are, is,* and so on). Get rid of as many of them as you can.

- » **Delete said tags.** *Said tags,* such as *she said* and *he said,* tell the reader who said what. You may think you always need them, but you really don't unless you have more than two speakers in a scene of dialogue. Trust us. (But if you do need said tags to keep speakers clear, then use only *said* and *asked.* Refrain from all the other possibilities. You want to keep your text uncluttered.)

- » **Don't start every other sentence with *but, and,* or *however*.** Editors hate overuse of these words, and the literati — or at least, those who fancy themselves as such — don't yet acknowledge this American English usage. You can use these words to start sentences every once in a while, but don't overdo it.

- » **In dialogue, indent for a new paragraph each time you switch speakers.** Each speaker gets their own indent, no matter how short or long their speech. And if you have to use a speech tag or describe body language, join it up in the same paragraph as the speaker's dialogue.

- » **Always spell check your document.** Be sure to run your word-processing software's spell-check feature — even though it isn't always correct. When in doubt, find a good online dictionary or thesaurus. Never wing it if you don't know for sure. That's just plain silly and makes you look like a bear of very little brain.

- » **Vary the rhythm and length of your sentences.** Mix up long and short ones. Break up description with dialogue. If you use the same monotonic pattern — *First I did this. Then I did that. Then she did this. Then we did that.* — your manuscript reader gets bored and turned off by the lack of spark and variation.

- » **Address parents and other adults with titles such as Mr., Ms., Dr., and so on, as appropriate to their elevated station above children — at least, in age.** To do otherwise puts parents and children on the same level, which is inaccurate in children's books. When you refer to parents in particular, use a capital letter when you reference the relationship in lieu of a name and use a lowercase letter when preceded by a pronoun. For example: *Mom is an expert quilter. Everyone knows my mom spends her weekends quilting up a storm.*

REMEMBER

  In kids' books, children are the stars, the main characters, the ones we want to get to know on a first-name basis. You confuse your reader if you throw out first names for adults like you do for children. Adults can speak to each other using first names, but don't make kid characters use an adult's first name because it indicates lack of respect — unless the child is breaking a social taboo.

- » **Don't rely on shortcuts for emphasis.** If you find yourself **bolding,** *italicizing,* USING CAPITAL LETTERS, or lots of punctuation!!!!, then your words aren't doing their job. You need to choose your words more carefully so that your word choice indicates any emphasis!

- » **Don't use names that sound alike in one manuscript.** As a matter of fact, don't use names that start with the same letter, letter sound, or diphthong. And don't switch from a proper name to a nickname and back again willy-nilly. Readers get easily confused — and so will editors.

- » **Don't just jump from one scene to the next without a transition indicating a change in place or time.** How would you feel if someone you were engaged in a deep conversation with at work on Wednesday were to simply disappear (poof! gone!) in the middle of speaking — and show up three days later in your bedroom to continue where they left off? Don't put your reader in this kind of situation.

>> **Watch tense changes.** If you're telling a story in the past tense, stay there. You absolutely can't switch tenses in books for readers 12 and under; and only do so at your peril for young adult readers. It requires significant skill to alternate different points of view in different time frames. If you're a first timer, leave the tricky stuff for your sophomore effort.

Hiring Help: Working with an Editor or Editorial Service

After you do your best to revise and edit your story, you may need a professional editor or editorial service to check overarching elements of your story (such as plot, character, or structure) or to address smaller, but no less important, issues (such as word choice, grammar, and formatting) to ensure you're ready to submit your manuscript to an agent or publisher.

An *editor* is someone who corrects, finesses, and polishes a work at different levels of complexity to prepare it for publication. An *editorial service* can simply constitute one editor's business, especially if they offer many different services (such as proofreading, line editing, and ghostwriting), or it can be a business composed of several editors who have expertise in different areas.

Before you can choose someone to work with, you need to know exactly what kind of service you want. Here are the different types of services you may be interested in:

>> **Developmental editing:** Editing the larger issues of a book including plot, pacing, characterization, and dialogue to help the writer make sure these areas are all working in the manuscript. Does not include editing for grammar, style, spelling.

>> **Line editing:** Going through a manuscript from start to finish and editing every line for every issue, from grammar, spelling, and style, to drama, pacing, characterization, and anything in between.

>> **Copy editing:** Mostly fact and grammar checking; usually used for nonfiction books.

>> **Read-through and evaluation:** A general, overall reading of the work for its literary merits (or lack thereof) that points out the major flaws that you need to address without necessarily telling you exactly how to go about fixing them.

- » **Ghostwriting:** When an editor or writer writes or thoroughly revises an original manuscript from start to finish and isn't credited on the book, but does get paid and often shares in the royalties — or gets a nice flat fee.

- » **Proofreading:** Checking an edited version of a book against an earlier version of an edited manuscript of the book to make sure the proof doesn't have misspellings, isn't missing anything, has images that correspond to text, and contains all the edits indicated in the edited version. Side by side, the two versions should mirror one another after a proofread. Usually done at the publishing house.

- » **Literary consultations:** A seasoned writer can consult with an editor to determine the literary merits of a work in progress. These can range from a read-through of the work and a citing of general impressions, to more involved editing for character development, to complete line editing.

- » **Writing coach:** Service offered by an editor who acts as editor, teacher, and mentor to the writer throughout the entire writing and publishing process. A writing coach may work one on one with the author, or they may lead a writing workshop. Unlike a critique group, in which every member participates equally, the workshop leader may do most of the critiquing.

The following sections help you find potential editors or editorial services that you can work with and help you narrow down the editing field with the right questions.

REMEMBER

Ultimately, you want a fun and informative experience with an editor or an editorial service. You want to walk away from the process with specific ideas and methods for making your manuscript the best it can be, secure in the knowledge that the money was well spent — regardless of whether the manuscript ultimately sells. A good edit gives you the type of information about writing and editing that you can use again and again.

Finding a good editor or editorial service

When you're in the market for a professional editor, do some homework before you hire someone. Just like financiers perform their due diligence on companies that they may want to buy or invest in, you need to do your own research regarding your choice of editors.

To check whether an editor is on the up and up, you can try The Science Fiction and Fantasy Writers of America's Writer Beware page (http://sfwa.org/other-resources/for-authors/writer-beware); or visit the water cooler of the writing world, where folks discuss everything and anything about writing: the Absolute-Write Forum (https://absolutewrite.com/forums/index.php).

Sites like these can let you know whether you've found a good editor (or agent) or a bad apple (according to other people's experiences). Like with many online discussion boards, don't get caught up in the gossip on these sites, and take the information you find there with a grain of salt.

TIP

Consider these issues to get the most out of your editorial experience:

» **Find a professional children's book editor.** Children's books have different requirements than adult books. Find someone who has at least ten years under their belt as a children's book editor at a reputable children's book publishing house. Do they have published books that contain Library of Congress numbers, books that sell in bricks-and-mortar bookstores, and books that you can locate in a public library?

Children's book writers can find a list of freelance editors who have been verified for professionalism at the Society of Children's Book Writers and Illustrators website (www.scbwi.org).

» **Ask whether your editor has written and published their own children's book or two.** If so, you can assume that they have experience on both sides of the line: editing and being edited. An editor who's also a published writer knows what it's like having words critiqued and may carry this sensitivity into their work with you.

» **Find out what the editor's clients and colleagues say about them.** Look for quoted accolades or awards on their website or on the Internet. You want someone whom at least a few industry professionals speak highly of. Reach out to these professionals by e-mail for verification of their opinion. (For more on referrals, see the following section.)

» **Inquire about your editor's education.** Although university education shouldn't make or break your decision (a few self-taught editors or those who have been mentored by the best in the business can provide valuable assistance), knowing that your editor has a passing familiarity with quality written material through the ages can provide a writer with a knowledgeable edit.

» **Find out how much the editor charges.** Some editors charge a per-word fee, some charge a per-page rate, and some charge by the hour. Others charge a flat-rate minimum to start and then add on more money, depending on how many pages your manuscript contains. Some charge a per-project fee, specific to the length of the manuscript and the manuscript's current stage of writing or editing. Some offer professional discounts for repeat customers, published authors, or members of certain professional writers' organizations. As you can see, the possibilities are nearly endless. Ultimately, however, only you can determine the kind of editing you need, how much you can afford, and what price is fair.

Give your manuscript to the editor before they quote you a rate. Not all manuscripts are alike, even if they have a similar word count. The writer's writing style, previous experience, and formatting all affect how much time the editor needs to edit a manuscript. So the editor needs to peruse your manuscript before giving you an accurate price quote.

REMEMBER

Most editors don't require contracts (an e-mail exchange can suffice), but they often do require up-front payment in full with the understanding that they return any *underages* (money they don't use) with the manuscript. You can expect a call or e-mail from the editor to approve any *overages* (more money required to complete the job, either because of an unintended miscalculation on the part of the editor or the writer's decision to add more services to the tab).

WARNING

Some editorial services list one editor's credentials to bring in business and then send out the work to some other editor. Check to make sure you're getting the services from the person whose credentials you approve and that the service isn't farming out your work to a subcontracting editor without your knowledge. Or if they tell you that they plan to subcontract it out, make sure you have the right to approve the subcontractor.

Asking the right questions

Asking the right questions before you hire an editor or editorial service helps ensure that your experience goes more smoothly and that you don't run into any misunderstandings about the work that you want done. Here are some essential questions to ask the editor or editorial service that you plan to hire:

>> Do I get a written evaluation or critique letter, along with manuscript comments? (These formal written critiques offer guidance about how to make the changes suggested by the editor on the manuscript itself, but critique letters also add to the cost.)

>> If I have questions, do I get to talk with you for free after you send back my edited manuscript? (Usually, the answer is no.) If not, can I e-mail you questions (preferably in bulk, as opposed to one e-mail at a time) regarding issues I may not fully understand?

>> Do we correspond by e-mail or phone? (Most likely, the editor wants to communicate via e-mail to avoid the dreaded game of phone tag or the headache of scheduling across coasts — or across continents.)

>> Do you charge for a pre-editing phone consultation or a face-to-face meeting? How much?

>> Can you work digitally with track-change edits and commentary? What if I want edits by hand on a hardcopy printout?

>> How much do you charge for reviewing my revisions?

>> Can you provide a client list or a few referrals that I may contact by e-mail or phone? (A must when a writer is performing their due diligence on an editor.)

>> Do you give any discounts for members of professional writing organizations, published writers, need-based clients, or repeat customers?

Whether the answers to the preceding questions satisfy you depends on the services you need.

The editor should also specify what *formats* (types) of children's books they've been paid to edit in the past. (Refer to Chapter 2 for more on formats.) If an editor indicates a preference or a predilection for editing a particular format, such as middle-grade books or picture books, consider that information in your decision-making process.

WARNING

Whatever you do, don't send out an NDA (non-disclosure agreement) to an editor to sign before you send your manuscript for an estimate. Professional, accredited, respected book editors don't steal ideas; they help articulate those ideas and make them better. (If you're worried about copyright protection, see Chapter 17.) Do your homework on your editor so that you feel confident they're trustworthy. They probably don't have the time, much less the inclination, to steal ideas because what would they do with your ideas? Submit them and risk getting caught and destroying their reputation and thus their entire business? Seriously, it's like using a nanny cam: If you feel the need to set them up all over the house, you haven't found a person trustworthy enough to care for your children. So move on and select someone else.

Digital versus hard-copy editing

Most editing today happens digitally by using the Track Changes feature in Word, the Edit function in Google Docs, or the simple editing tools in Adobe Acrobat for PDFs. The editor can do universal fixes, make all the changes they deem necessary, and provide explanation or guidance (preferably both). For example, by using the Comment feature in Word, the editor can add text in the right margin of the document that you can easily see.

Not many editors do *hard-copy editing* (actually printing out a manuscript and working on real paper) anymore, but some people prefer working on paper because they find all the dotted lines, regular lines, color marks, and marginal comments in digitally edited manuscripts hard to read. Some people like hard-copy edits because reading their manuscript on paper makes it feel more like a real book than just text on a computer screen. In a hard-copy edit, the editor uses proofreader's marks (easily found on the web for reference) and edits right on the paper. With a hard-copy edit, the writer has to then input all the little changes themselves into the manuscript. Regardless, be sure to submit your manuscript exactly as the editor (or agent or publisher) requests it, electronic or hard copy.

EDITORS DON'T AGENT, AND AGENTS DON'T EDIT

Many new writers think that their professional editors should *agent* them (represent or sell their book to publishers) after the editing process or refer them to a particular agent or publisher.

In our opinion, charging a client for an edit with the promise of a referral to an agent or publisher is unethical. If an agent charges a client for an edit prior to or as part of representation, this practice is also unethical. Although many editors may have a list of professional agents to which they refer clients, and agents may choose to refer new clients to certain respected editors, no money should change hands between the agent and editor — it's called *double dipping,* and the Association of Authors Representatives, Inc. (AAR, www.aaronline.org), to which many agents belong, largely frowns upon it. (See Chapter 17 for more about agents.)

An independent editor and an agent are two separate but equally important parts of a writer's life — and should remain separate because their jobs are distinctly different. Use the Society of Children's Book Writers and Illustrators website (www.scbwi.org) to research agents. Membership in this organization allows writers access to a list of agents willing to take on SCBWI-member clients. Do your homework because some agents don't accept all formats, may be on hiatus regarding new clients, or may specialize in a format different from yours (fiction versus nonfiction, young adult novels versus picture books).

Chapter **15**

Creating Pictures from Your Words: The World of Illustrations

As an author, how do you get your book illustrated? Should you get illustrations before you send the book to an agent or publisher? If you're not an illustrator, how do you find the right one for your book? And if you are an illustrator, how do you get considered for illustrating jobs?

This chapter gives you answers to those questions, even providing a detailed interview with an experienced art director and book designer. But here's the bottom line: If you aren't an illustrator, don't illustrate your book. Simply said, bad or amateurish illustrations turn off editors and agents in a big way. And turned-off editors and agents don't want to represent you or buy your story. Even if you have a well-written story that might very well be the Greatest Children's Story Ever, it might get rejected solely because of the recipient's reaction to subpar art.

In this chapter, we talk about illustrating or not illustrating, as well as the steps of illustrating from sketch to final color art for both hand-drawn and computer-generated art. And if you plan to go the self-published route, we have you covered there, too, with advice for hiring someone to illustrate your book.

To Illustrate or Not to Illustrate

Nothing surprises new writers going for traditional publishing more than this bit of advice: Unless you're an artist who has a lot of artistic talent, don't illustrate your own manuscript. Also, don't bother paying or contracting with someone else to do it. Period.

Seriously. We're not joking. Amateurish illustrations make your manuscript look unprofessional. They also distract from the words. And if the editor likes the words but absolutely hates the illustrations (or vice versa), they're likely to reject both because they assume the writer and illustrator come as a package deal and ripping them apart would invite a host of complications best avoided.

If you're a talented illustrator, as well as a writer, congratulations. But are you really as talented an illustrator as you think you are?

A writer trying to break into illustrating, too, can struggle to figure out whether they have the requisite talent and skill. If you're already agented, get feedback from your agent — trust us, if you are indeed good, the agent stands to make plenty of money off of your endeavors, so they'll give you an honest, experienced opinion. But if you're not agented, how do you figure out whether you're good enough to risk submitting your art with your manuscript?

Three words: Get. Professional. Feedback. You can't answer this question on your own. Professional feedback doesn't mean paying someone to pat your back or run away screaming in horror. It means getting your work in front of art directors, designers, and editors at children's book houses via portfolio reviews at book conferences before submission. (For more on this tactic, see the section "Getting Your Art Seen by the Right Folks," later in this chapter.)

Recognizing Why You Shouldn't Hire an Illustrator

Editors like to pair up authors with their own choice of illustrators. They choose someone they believe can add yet another dimension to your words by creating just the right images, truly complementing and completing your work. Your editor may choose to pair you, an unknown writer, with a known and recognized illustrator to help sell the book. Or perhaps they want to pair you with a newbie illustrator who has just created a style they think will take the world by storm. Maybe they've been waiting for just the perfect writer to pair up with their most favored and beloved illustrator. Whatever their decision, it's theirs to make.

LEAVE THE ART TO SOMEONE ELSE

Glenn Murray is co-author, with William Kotzwinkle, of the bestselling series *Walter the Farting Dog* (North Atlantic Books), a book that took a lot of detours before it finally found a publishing house. Glenn recommends that you leave the illustrations to the publisher if you aren't an artist yourself:

- **What have you noticed about how most publishers' work when it comes to illustrations?** "One thing I notice is that many writers of children's stories are unaware that most publishers don't want you worrying about the artwork. Publishers have editors, and art directors, and designers in-house to handle the images and do not necessarily want or need your input as the writer. Publishers also often choose experienced illustrators who understand the process as well as page design, formatting, and all that. I have found that most authors and illustrators have never met or talked — all arrangements were made through the publisher's art department and the editor in charge of the project.

  "Editors seem to like it this way, but most novice writers don't understand this. Novice writers feel they need to submit a whole package [text and art] and don't realize that they are making unnecessary work for themselves and possibly limiting the potential acceptance of the manuscript."

- **What else have you realized about the author/illustrator relationship?** "I've also learned an awful lot about the legal relationship between authors and illustrators [who pair themselves up prior to submission] that most people don't realize — why, for instance, if you insist on submitting art with your story that you might want to simply contract an illustrator with a flat fee rather than offer them a percentage. And I've met a few other children's authors who've had hassles later on from contractual arrangements they made early on with wide-open but ill-informed eyes. On the other hand, there are some author/illustrator partnerships that bring themselves together before submission that last happily for decades. So go figure."

- **What would you tell a writer if they're considering finding an illustrator prior to submission?** "You just need to write a good story and get that story to an editor to read. If the editor likes it, she'll know what to do with it."

You, the writer, probably never even meet the illustrator during the publishing process, unless you two decide to reach out and make the effort to communicate on your own. After you and your editor have worked together to make your words the best they can be, your manuscript goes to a publishing house to begin the process of being turned into a book, and you most likely don't see your words again until they appear in print. We discuss more about this process in Chapter 16. But suffice to say that editors tend to keep their authors separate from their illustrators.

WARNING

We know you have images in your mind of how to bring your characters to life. Unless you're a professional illustrator, though, keep them to yourself. Board books and picture books (formats that always come with pictures) are really half the job of the author and half that of the illustrator. The author can't restrict an illustrator with ideas of what they think the pictures should be. You may be surprised by what professional artists come up with.

REMEMBER

Word people (as opposed to picture people) often assume no one could ever create images as unique and creative as the stories they've written. But artists often see the world in a slightly different way (how could they not — they even favor the opposite side of the brain from word people). These differences often interpret words in the most astonishing and gorgeous manner — a manner that a word person might never have envisioned.

Following the Hand-Drawn Illustration Process with Artist Tim Bowers

So, the publisher has accepted your manuscript for publication. Congratulations! Your picture book is slated for publication at least 18 months in the future. Why so far out? Because it needs illustrations, design, and pre-production work — all before it goes to the printer, gets checked and corrected a few times, and makes its way back as a bound book.

After your manuscript goes in-house at the publishing company, and the in-house editor is one with it, the art director takes over. They and the editor in charge of the project get together and discuss possible directions for the art. They consider artists, contact agents for the shortlist of preferred illustrators, and make a final decision. After the publishing house hires an illustrator, that artist follows a specific process to deliver the art to the publisher. First, if the art director asks, the illustrator draws some concept sketches or thumbnails — quick drawings that demonstrate where the illustrator sees the project going. Next come the black-and-white pencil drawings, followed by the finished color art, completing the various bits and pieces the publisher might require. Often, the illustrator creates the cover last.

Tim Bowers is a multitalented, award-winning, *New York Times* and *Publishers Weekly* bestselling illustrator who has more than 30 children's books to his name. Illustrating in styles as diverse as those found in *Memoirs of a Goldfish*, written by Devin Scillian (Sleeping Bear Press), to *Fun Dog, Sun Dog*, written by Deborah Heiligman (Amazon Children's Books), Tim Bowers agreed to share with us his particular process for illustrating the picture book *It's a Big World, Little Pig*, written by Kristi Yamaguchi (Sourcebooks Jabberwocky).

Tim Bowers, like many illustrators, has a three-pronged process when he's working with pencil sketches, which you can see in the following sections.

Starting with black-and-white pencil sketches

When he's illustrating, Tim Bowers starts with black-and-white pencil sketches. Figure 15-1 shows a spread in *It's a Big World, Little Pig*, in which the main character, Poppy, has just arrived at a new place and is feeling very nervous.

FIGURE 15-1:
Sketch from *It's a Big World, Little Pig.*

Written by Kristi Yamaguchi, illustrated by Tim Bowers. Reprinted courtesy of the illustrator © 2012 Tim Bowers.

Depending on the art director and editor's reaction to the sketch, Tim may get the go-ahead, or he may be get some change notes and then proceed to step two: pencils (see the following section).

On the publisher's end, after the artist has started sketches, the book designer usually starts putting together a preliminary design of the book's pages. They lay down the text for each page in a particular size and font and with *leading* (space between the lines) appropriate to the readership (although it might change, this initial layout serves as a space holder for now). Then they place the sketches on the pages while those sketches come in so that the editor can start to envision what the final book might look like when they include the final color art. By starting page design early, if the illustrator needs to make changes to the images, everyone realizes it right away, before the illustrator creates the more labor-intensive color art, saving everyone time, money, and the inevitable headache of crunching right up to the edge of a deadline — or missing it altogether.

Moving on to finished pencils

After he completes sketching out the entire book, Tim proceeds to the second step: pencil drawings, also known as *pencils.* Although he prefers to create one, cohesive piece of art at every stage, his publisher with *It's a Big World, Little Pig* asked that he create the foregrounds and backgrounds separately at both the pencils and final art stages in order to allow for repurposing and splicing of the illustrations in animation sequences and apps for tablets and smartphones. Figures 15-2 and 15-3 show the background and foreground of one spread in *It's a Big World, Little Pig.*

FIGURE 15-2:
Background finished pencil from *It's a Big World, Little Pig.*

Creating color art

The final prong of the illustration process (after the initial black-and-white sketches and the color sketches, discussed in the preceding sections) involves creating the color art. In *It's a Big World, Little Pig*, Tim works with acrylic washes on Bristol board. In other words, he paints with very thin washes of acrylic paint, adding layers of color and saturation while he goes, leaving the opaque areas last. While he renders with more layers and more color, the object that he's illustrating gets more dimension and depth.

FIGURE 15-3: Foreground finished pencil from *It's a Big World, Little Pig.*

Written by Kristi Yamaguchi, illustrated by Tim Bowers. Reprinted courtesy of the illustrator © 2012 Tim Bowers.

Tim creates distance and contrast between the foreground and the background in his drawings by muting the value contrast of the background (lighter lines, less saturated color, less definition) to allow the foreground to take center stage.

Capturing the right cover image

If a picture is worth a thousand words, then a cover is worth all your advance and royalty money put together and multiplied — if you do it right. We don't care what anyone says: Everyone judges books by their covers and makes their buying choices accordingly.

The cover of a picture book has the most important job of all: selling the book in the space of a nanosecond. Sometimes, an illustrator hand-draws some portion of the lettering on the cover to marvelous effect. Text can swirl or curve, animate or morph. It can set the tone for the whole book. In the first book in the series created by Kristi Yamaguchi and Tim Bowers, *Dream Big, Little Pig*, the publisher (Sourcebooks Jabberwocky) created hand-drawn lettering for the final cover instead of choosing a pre-existing font.

REMEMBER

If a children's book cover doesn't grab a customer's attention in a microsecond and hold onto it long enough for them to pick up the book, then it has failed in its job. A good cover is

>> Full of personality — especially of its main character, if shown

>> Representative of the interior, both visually and emotionally

>> Surprising

>> A teaser, making you want to either open the book or at least turn it over to read the *sell copy* (an incredibly seductive paragraph, usually on the back cover, that captures the essence of what the book is about without giving away the ending)

>> Unusual enough to stand out from the crowd

Figure 15-4 shows Tim's final cover art, featuring the book's main character in *It's a Big World, Little Pig.* Notice how much personality, movement, and verve this one piece of spot art encapsulates. As you can see in Figure 15-5, the hand-drawn lettering, ample white space, and other elements come together to sell the book in the final cover. (And yes, the celebrity author's name is prominently placed.)

FIGURE 15-4:
Cover art prior to design from *It's a Big World, Little Pig.*

Written by Kristi Yamaguchi, illustrated by Tim Bowers. Reprinted courtesy of the illustrator © 2012 Tim Bowers.

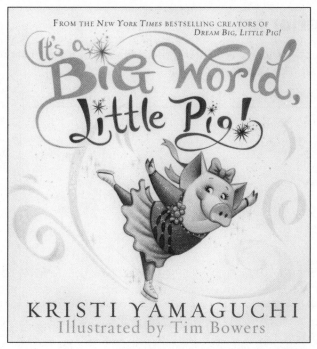

TIP

Although beginning writers almost never get cover approval written into their contracts with publishers, you may get the gift of input early on in the development of a cover. Take it if it's offered; but never insist on it unless you're contractually entitled.

Exploring the Digital Art Process with Author/Illustrator Barney Saltzberg

Although many artists and illustrators still do work by hand, creating their art on actual paper, using paint, pastel, pen and ink, charcoal, and so on, many illustrators, including award-winning children's book author and illustrator Barney Saltzberg, turn to their computers to create original digital art.

Digital illustrating follows roughly the same steps as creating hand-drawn illustrations, with a few differences that help save time.

Interior art

Figure 15-6 shows a computer-generated sketch for one of Barney's latest books, *We're All in the Same Boat!* (Creston).

FIGURE 15-6: A computer-generated sketch for interior artwork for *We're All in the Same Boat!*

The sketches then become pencils. Figure 15-7 shows an example pencil from the same book.

FIGURE 15-7: A sketch that has been digitally converted to a pencil.

Next, color is added. Figure 15-8 reflects how a pencil changes to finished art after color is added and finalized.

FIGURE 15-8:
Computer-
generated color
artwork.

From We're All in the Same Boat! *Written and illustrated by Barney Saltzberg.*
Reprinted by permission. © 2021 Barney Saltzberg

Cover art

Figure 15-9 shows how the cover evolves into its final version.

FIGURE 15-9:
The final cover art
with (a) color and
(b) hand-drawn
text for *We're All
in the Same Boat!*

a

b

From We're All in the Same Boat! *Written and illustrated by Barney Saltzberg.*
Reprinted by permission. © 2021 Barney Saltzberg

As you can see, the digital-illustration process is roughly the same as creating hand-drawn illustrations, but a sketch can be turned into a pencil very quickly, and then color can be added over that easily. Computer art is a faster process but no less lovely in its results!

DISCUSSING COMPUTER ARTISTRY WITH A PRO

Barney Saltzberg, successful children's book author/illustrator, does all his art now on the computer and has done so for years. Here's what he has to say about his process:

- **What made you start to use your computer to generate illustrations?** "I used to run an art department when the Mac first came out. I was immediately drawn to it for typesetting and design. When I sold my first tactile book for babies and toddlers, I wanted to create thick bold lines with solid color. At the time, my publisher had never received digital book art. It was so long ago that I sent the artwork on a CD. Back in those days, the technology wasn't as advanced, and I never would have attempted to make digital watercolor art. At some point, technology figured it out, and I haven't looked back."

- **How is using your computer different than working by hand?** "I use a Wacom Centiq monitor, which allows me to draw directly on the screen. I make rough sketches on one layer, and then add a transparency to that layer so I can basically redraw the artwork on another layer and then delete the rough sketch. There is no lag time when it comes to drawing. It is pretty similar to using a pen. Yet another delicious aspect of digital is that I have the Procreate app on my iPad. Using the iPad allows such flexibility since it's so portable."

- **Is digital illustration faster time-wise?** "Ultimately, much faster. Once I have my line drawings, I create layers below and do watercolor washes. They are beautiful and vibrant and because they are on a different layer than the line work, the art looks crisp and clean when reproduced."

- **How long did it take for you to master using the computer?** "I started so long ago that it's second nature to me now. There was definitely a learning curve, but I mastered it after awhile."

- **How does computer illustration change your process with the art director or designer?** "It speeds things up. I suppose with traditional art, I could scan and e-mail, but I just send whatever images I am working on."

- **What can you do on a computer that you can't do otherwise?** "In the old days, I would do a lot of random sketching and have to use a copy machine to reduce each image and create a storyboard with a lot of tiny copies from larger artwork. Now, I can literally shrink each piece by selecting the artwork and drag it into a storyboard format. Using the computer also allows a greater flexibility. I can save each storyboard and then try moving things around to see if it impacts the readability and page-turning rhythm."

- **What's better about generating art on a computer than doing it by hand?**
"That's a subjective question. For me, the colors never bleed. If I mess up a line, having the ability to hit Undo is a game changer. I once had all of the artwork for a book thrown out by accident, after the artwork had been scanned by my publisher. It was heartbreaking to lose all of that original art. I never worry about art being damaged in shipping or, God forbid, thrown away."

Getting Your Art Seen by the Right Folks

For the author/illustrators in the audience, you have the advantage of getting your foot in the publishing house door a few different ways — by showcasing your story, your artwork, or (in special situations) both. The goal is to get some feedback on your art and perhaps even find an agent through the process.

Considering some solid options

You can pretty easily get your art in front of the right people — namely, the art directors in publishing houses and the in-house book designers who actually put together all the pieces of a book — if you already have a literary agent who also represents artists or an *artist's rep* (an agent who specializes in representing illustrators). In this case, your agent or rep likely asks you early on to create samples of your work for them to send around to all their contacts.

If you don't have an agent or an artist's rep, you need to do a little more work to get your artwork seen by the children's-book-powers-that-be. Fortunately, you have a few options:

>> **Arrange face-to-face meetings.** If you happen to live in New York City, perhaps you can make appointments with every person who answers your call so that you can set up a face-to-face portfolio review. Good luck with that.

>> **Send out digital postcards.** Unlike a complete portfolio that contains everything you've ever illustrated, a full-color digital postcard can highlight a style or two at which you excel. In other words, you offer the postcard as a sample percolating with all the personality and skill you infuse into your work. You can even animate it! You can then do the research to e-mail your digital postcards directly to all the art directors and designers at publishing imprints around the world. Believe us, they want to discover new talent just as much as you want to be discovered — and hired.

>> **Provide a portfolio to art directors.** You can put your portfolio in digital form on your website. When you send out your feelers, you can include a link to your website, which features your art and all the styles in which you do illustrations. Make sure you have some examples of children and animals. If you can do different ethnicities, that's great.

TIP

Many art directors use shortcuts to determine whether an illustrator can handle the usual objects assigned to create art in a children's book. They might have the illustrator draw a child's face, a child's body, an infant (in its entirety), or a domestic animal (think puppies or kitties). Include samples of these subjects in your portfolio. And if you can send images from different perspectives (from the front, at a three-quarter angle, from the character's height-challenged perspective), you can really wow the art director. When they see your work, they focus on your skills instead of questioning whether you can deliver.

>> **Attend writers' and illustrators' conferences and sign up for portfolio reviews.** You may have to pay a small fee, but an art director or book designer sits down with you, goes over your work, and discusses it in detail with you. This kind of face-to-face feedback with a professional is absolutely worth every cent — assuming you've vetted the venue and the participants, making sure they provide the professional, experienced attendees you seek. (For pointers on picking worthwhile conferences and workshops, see Chapter 16.) Many illustrators who attended SCBWI's portfolio reviews were discovered and found representation there.

>> **Present your work on Pinterest, Instagram, TikTok, and Facebook.** But always have a printed portfolio ready and available for in-person conferences and reviews (include about 15 pieces of art).

TIP

In any meeting with someone who wants to give you specific feedback on your work, you really have to listen. Figure out which pieces of your work stand out (and consider them like calling cards). Listen when an art director suggests you can make your work less derivative if you go in this direction or more on trend if you go in that direction. Listen to the criticisms that can constructively aid you in bettering your work and your chances of being hired.

>> **Add some additional information about you as an artist to your query letter.** We explain how to craft a creative query letter in Chapter 17. But here's what you can include about yourself:

- Have you ever had your art published? Where?

- Do you have a formal art background? From which school(s) or super-famous mentor(s)? If you mention someplace or someone that non-artsy types may not know, supply enough information so that people can research the unknown schools or mentors online. Use name dropping judiciously.

THIS LLAMA WAS NO BOOK DUMMY

One famous author/illustrator got her start because a literary agent saw her hand-designed card. The artist sent a handmade New Year's card to the agent. The agent contacted her and asked for samples in a particular style for a chapter book. The agent never ended up using those samples. But after they got to know each other better, the author/illustrator prepared a book dummy and presented it to the agent. The agent took it to New York and presented it to several publishers.

The agent? Deborah Warren. The title? *Llama Llama Red Pajama,* by Anna Dewdney (Viking Books for Young Readers). Now, you can find close to 50 Llama Llama titles. Sadly, Anna Dewdney passed away in 2016, but her legacy continues.

- Are you flexible and open to art and text suggestions, both minor and major? Meaning do you take art direction well?

- Are you open to having someone else illustrate your text or to illustrating someone else's words? This can double your chances of getting a contract from a publisher who likes your art but not your text or vice versa.

TIP

Try your best to keep your query letter to one page. Sometimes, however, you have to exceed that limit by an extra sentence or two, listing your illustrating credentials. But like with writing well, showing is always more effective than telling. Maybe leave out some of the verbiage and instead show your talent by offering up fabulous portfolio pieces or postcards.

Preparing a book dummy

A *book dummy* is a book–like digital sample of what your book pages look like with text and illustrations in place. It has a threefold purpose:

>> To showcase both your story and your art

>> To demonstrate that your text can support different illustrations on each page or spread

>> To pull together the entire vision you have for your book

Although art directors generally find book dummies overkill (color art samples from the artist's portfolio normally suffice to represent the artist's style or styles), sometimes an editor may ask for a book dummy if they think the manuscript and illustration samples together show promise.

Just in case someone asks you to provide a book dummy, we don't want to leave you hanging. A complete picture book dummy would consist of all 28 pages and a front cover suggestion — or if you're good at designing all the parts of the book, include endpapers and the titles and copyright pages, too, to take it up to 32 pages. You don't have to make all pages full color; you can make some just black-and-white pencils or sketches to show what you have in mind. Make sure to include your contact information on the dummy itself, in case the query letter gets lost or misplaced. And *paginate* (put page numbers somewhere on each page).

The cleaner and more professional your work looks, the more likely a publishing professional will take you seriously. Make sure you have a dummy that doesn't look rushed — even pencil illustrations can look finished and well thought-out. If you can put together a book dummy on your computer, great — you can make multiple submissions.

If you're an illustrator only, you can have a dummy at the ready by illustrating a fairy tale or folktale, or even illustrating a book already published to show how you would have done it differently. (Make sure you give credit where it's due if you sample-illustrate a published book.)

Handling Art When You're Self-Publishing (and Not an Artist)

A lot of writers and writer/illustrators these days opt to self-publish instead of going the traditional route of submitting directly to agents, publishers, or art directors. Although we cover the ins and outs of self-publishing in Chapter 19, you have some special considerations when it comes to self-publishing an illustrated book. If you want to self-publish an illustrated children's book, consider the following tips:

>> **Find an illustration style to match your story.** You can illustrate a book in as many ways as you can write it. Look at already published books and see how various illustrators realize their styles. Decide on a few that you like.

>> **Find an illustrator.** If you have ample resources, you can track down the exact illustrator whose style you like and inquire as to their interest, price, and availability. In the event your funds aren't overflowing, you can take the example of a style you love and use it to find other, hungrier illustrators who create art in a similar style.

>> **Research.** Go to both online and real-world venues where children's book artists hang out and promote their wares. If you can't find anyone through SCBWI (www.scbwi.org), you can check out art colleges, book conferences, or comic book conventions that occur all across the country every year. In addition, artists' reps appear in sources such as *Children's Writer's and Illustrator's Market,* by Alice Pope (Writer's Digest Books), and *Literary Market Place* (Information Today), which you can access online by creating an account at LiteraryMarketPlace.com. Also, most artist reps have online artist portfolios that you can peruse.

>> **Put together a written agreement.** Before you contact an illustrator, decide whether you want to pay them a flat fee or partner with them, sharing in the proceeds (and hope that they're amenable or willing to negotiate). After you agree on fees and basic scheduling, you both should sign and date a contract, which usually involves hiring an entertainment or publishing attorney.

Your contract should cover, at minimum, the scope and quantity of illustrations you need produced (how many sketches, pencils, pieces of color art, and corrections); formatting instructions, including size, black-and-white versus color, and so on; any pre-production preparation of art; the book design and layout fee (this applies only if both parties are splitting the cost); the total amount the illustrator will receive (for example, a flat fee or an advance against a portion of the book's royalties); a schedule for payment; whether the illustrator will transfer or retain rights to the illustrations (be specific regarding which rights); and a schedule for delivery of sketches, pencil illustrations, final color art, and any corrections. If you're a member of The Authors Guild (www.authorsguild.org), they can do a free contract evaluation for you.

TIP

Although we don't really know what to call it, an element that's just as important as a contractual agreement is the feel-good mojo between you and anyone you work with — especially someone with whom you partner so that you (both) realize your lifelong dream in book form. We have heard too many nightmare stories of authors and illustrators partnering with each other in the heat of the moment without getting a feel for each other, establishing clarity on their relationship, or really taking the time to consider a project before jumping in. Get references and ask pertinent questions about working with that person before you hire them.

>> **Establish open communication.** Open communication between the two of you about what you both expect in terms of your involvement in the illustration process and its details ensures you start off on the right foot — and stay there. One way to make sure you're on the same page is to create a sample page together — another reason spending time on sketches up front can save time and heartache later in the illustrating process.

>> **Pay attention to the details.** Here's a checklist for what makes good art great:

- *The images not only complement the text, but also provide spark and personality.* Some illustrations may replace text; others may add an all-important layer of deeper meaning. Regardless, each page or spread has to come alive with an exceptional interpretation of an active part of the story.

- *The images employ different perspectives from page to page.* They focus on different aspects of the main character and take place in different parts of the scene or context of the story.

- *The illustrations provide consistency from page to page, spread to spread.* This consistency relates to both characters and backgrounds. For example, if a shoelace is untied on the first page, it should remain so throughout (unless you see a character tying it). If your main character's eyes are hazel, better make sure they don't turn blue all of a sudden.

- *The images incorporate variety.* You'd be bored out of your mind viewing inherently the same illustrations throughout an entire book. Intersperse *spot art* (smaller pieces of art, sometimes more than one on a page) against a white background with a spread of *full-bleed art* (full-color art from edge to edge) here and there. Give us the world as it appears from a short person's point of view (POV); make the reader look up into the scene, becoming a participant, instead of always viewing it from afar. Give us three-quarter views and aerial perspectives instead of just front and side views.

REMEMBER

Although different illustration styles require different focal characteristics, all must have that little something that appeals to children — be it charm, personality, simplicity, sweetness, humor, quirkiness, or plain old goofiness. Good illustrators (and good publishers) pay attention to all of these issues, as well as to each and every minuscule detail.

DIRECTING A CHILDREN'S BOOK'S DESIGN

Allison Higa was an art director and designer of children's books who has experience in novelty books, as well. She has worked in-house at Intervisual Books/Piggy Toes Press and Golden Books, and she also managed a flourishing freelance business at Allison Higa Design for over a decade. Here's her perspective on putting children's books together:

- **When does an art designer come into the book production process?** "For a printed publication, the editor would contact me with a brief description of the project and a timeline to determine my availability. In many cases, the projected release date is barely a year from the current publishing season (either fall or spring), which means turnaround times for the design stages are fast and furious!"

- **What does the designer do, exactly?** "If you look at any book, even a traditional, flat children's book, you'll be amazed to discover any number of elements which neither the writer nor the illustrator wants or needs to deal with. Take the front cover, spine, and back cover. They often require elements such as a series title, a burst treatment (such as, 'Over 10 Million Sold Worldwide!'), the age suggestion, credits, and sell copy, not to mention the very important publisher's logo, price, and ISBN numbers and barcodes."

- **Does the editor supply this information to you?** "Yes. But one element the illustrator might have a hand in (with the editor's direction) is the title type treatment. The editor might decide the title would be fabulous in a hand-drawn style unique to the book or series. All of these elements, whether hand-drawn or not, must be designed into an eye-catching cover to stand out among hundreds of others in the racks of bookstores or online."

- **What about the interior pages?** "A designer does all that. They may also need to lay out the endpapers, if there are any, and compile all of the pages into a digital paste-up for the printer, using consistent fonts, page numbers, spot art, and so on. In these days of digital paste-up, it's often the designer who doubles as the production artist, spending long hours at crunch time — when the files are due at the printer — checking art file placements, making any last-minute copy revisions, and uploading the files to the printer's server. The designer is usually involved at the proof stages as well, as they can spot technical or artistic issues."

- **Is that process any different for a novelty book?** "I would estimate, from my experience, that as much as a designer is involved in a flat book, their involvement is doubled for a novelty book. This is because a novelty book generally has 3-D elements. And that box template needs art and text, even if it's just a flat color picked by the designer. If it's art the illustrator will do, then they need that template sent to them with art direction. Novelty books are definitely a collaborative effort among art director, and designer, and illustrator!"

(continued)

(continued)

- **What's the process for a client who comes to you for art direction and design with a manuscript for self-publication?** "If the client does not have an illustrator in mind, or even if they do but don't know how to go about hiring this person, then I would also take on the role of art director. I would try to source that illustrator or one with a similar style, working within the client's budget and the illustrator's output schedule.

  For me the design process is not really different between a self-published project and a publisher-backed one. But the work ethic is. I would say, if you're going to be a publisher, then act like one. Have a budget in mind to offer to your designer and illustrator. If you're thinking of offering a percentage of sales (just like a publisher would offer a royalty), then outline this clearly in your signed agreement. Have a timeline with defined endpoints, so that everyone can collaborate on their schedules."

Chapter **16**

Finding and Incorporating Feedback

Although the words "practice makes perfect" certainly ring true in the writing profession, every writer can also benefit from candid feedback and constructive criticism from others. Most writers do plenty of rewriting and editing before their stories ever make it to an agent or an editor at a publishing company. (Chapter 14 discusses the revising and editing processes in detail.)

But even producing multiple manuscripts doesn't change the fact that having someone else take a look at your work brings a fresh perspective that can lead to invaluable improvements in the manuscript. And guess what? Good feedback can make the difference in whether your children's book ever finds its way to a bookstore shelf.

So where's the best place to get feedback? When should you get it? And from whom? In this chapter, we answer all these questions and more by focusing first on the most common source of outside feedback — friends and relatives — and then moving on to writing conferences, workshops, and writing groups.

Deciding When to Seek Feedback

We writers get very close to our work. How can we not? We become enamored with the words we write. We pour our feelings, research, desires, and dreams (not to mention our neuroses and ignorance) into our work. And after the manuscript is printed out, it just feels so final, so hard-copied, so finished. But it's not. Skipping out on feedback can mislead you into thinking that a less-than-perfect manuscript is ready when it's not.

REMEMBER

Because feedback introduces the possibility of receiving criticism for personal failings or shortcomings in the writing-skills department, many people do everything they can to avoid it. Keep in mind that criticism, when given constructively, can help you hone your story, making it more compelling and powerful (and sellable) in the process.

Using different sources for feedback while you revise exposes you to a variety of perspectives. We suggest where to go for feedback throughout the rest of this chapter. Here are our suggestions for when to get feedback throughout the writing process:

>> **In the beginning:** You may not have any words down on paper, but in the beginning, you have an idea — an idea of what your story is about, where it takes place, who (or what) plays a part in it, how it progresses, and how it ends. Before you even write a word, you can get feedback on your idea from others to find out whether it's derivative or novel, intriguing or limp. This early feedback lets you know whether you need to develop your idea further — or toss it aside and move on.

>> **After you write a few pages:** Getting feedback after you write a chapter or five can help you identify major story flaws before you go too far down the wrong path. Trust us. You don't want to be that writer who's so turned on by a particular idea, so convinced of its inherent greatness, that they huff, and they puff, and they knock out a complete book manuscript in several days or weeks of nonstop, caffeine-fueled laptop love — only to receive a response that's on the low end of the Richter scale after showing their manuscript to their agent.

As an alternative to getting feedback on your first few chapters, you can take your outline and character bibles to a group feedback session and spend some time discussing their merits. You can find pointers on finding and working with writing groups in the section "Working with a Writing (or Illustrating) Group," later in this chapter.

» **When you're stuck or uncertain:** If you don't know whether a particular scene, dialogue, and so on really works, get some feedback on it. If something doesn't feel right to you, it probably doesn't feel right to others, and getting that confirmation allows you to find out what might be off or not working. Then again, you may just be overthinking the matter. The only way to get some perspective is to ask for it.

» **After you complete the manuscript:** Before you send your manuscript to an agent or publisher, get it critiqued. Like the other old saying goes, you only have one chance to make a first impression; getting feedback on your manuscript before it gets to an agent or publisher helps you ensure that the first impression you make with them is the best one.

What questions should you ask to get the feedback you need? If you have a complete manuscript, check out Chapter 14, where we talk about the most important issues to check on while revising and editing. And even if you're just at the idea stage, you might still ask questions, such as

» Do I have an interesting idea, or has it been done to death recently? If so, how can I develop a hook and take a fresh approach?

» Can children relate to it, or is this an idea only grown-ups find interesting? How can I make it relevant to kids and not preachy or didactic?

» Is my idea a current or timeless topic? If it's current, how do I make sure I don't build it on a trend that's on its way out or that will disappear soon from pop culture?

REMEMBER

Tell the person you seek feedback from exactly what kind of feedback you're looking for before they provide you with the feedback, not after. For instance, if you want your chosen feedback provider to critique only your dialogue, don't wait until they've line edited your entire manuscript to tell them so. Your guidance helps them focus their efforts in the direction that provides you with the specific input you're looking for. You have no reason to play hit-and-miss when you can clearly describe the target to the other party.

WARNING

If you're the type of creator who can get thrown off track if you receive feedback before you have a chance to really develop your story, go ahead and use those character bibles (described in Chapter 8), develop your action outline (see Chapter 9 for guidance), write out a complete draft, and then reach out for feedback. No particular process is inherently right or wrong. Just never skip the feedback part of the creative process. And we mean never. (Did we emphasize never?)

THE PITFALLS OF WRITING TO TRENDS

Trends in publishing are predictable and common. Say that a book or series of books hits at the right time and the right place; it's written well and tightly polished, and it soars to the top of the bestseller charts. That book has a 95 percent chance of having an unoriginal idea, topic, or theme. Instead, this particular author managed to package and present their idea in a fresh manner and hit a vein in their target audience. (Need we remind you what the Harry Potter series did for upper-middle-grade and YA fantasy, or what the Twilight series did for the YA vampire and paranormal fantasy genres? A flood of riding-in-your-wake titles, that's what.)

After a book's big success, every publisher dives headfirst into their pile of hidden manuscripts, contacts all the agents with whom they have a close relationship, or calls up every reliable author they've worked with in this general genre to find the next big seller just like *Bestseller X* or *Bestseller X Meets Something Slightly New*. And then we're off to the races to see who else can jump on that bandwagon and share in the bounty while the public is still eating up the subject. This approach works for publishers for a while — until the next big thing hits. Then the cycle begins anew.

What this means for you as a writer is — precisely nothing. If you try to write to a super-hot trend, you probably aren't sufficiently inspired by it to do a good job (unless you're already happily and coincidentally finishing one). Even if you do churn one out, by that time, the wave is over. The market is suffering from a glut and readers are exhausted from overexposure.

The moral of the story? Be true to yourself, your interests, your creativity, and your passions. Write what you love to immerse yourself in for months or even years, and ignore the trends. They flit away as quickly as they came.

Getting Help from Friends and Relatives (or Not)

Many writers feel most comfortable testing their work on the people closest to them. They sit down with their children, their significant other, or their best friend's dog, and they read their manuscript aloud. And — almost invariably — they're showered with kudos and accolades (or dog licks).

After a response filled with praise, how could a writer not believe that they're destined for great things? But getting help from friends and relatives has its pluses and its minuses. Do the most honest critiques really come from the people who know you and care about your success or failure as a writer? Well, not really — unless these people are professional, published children's book writers who have experience in the genre you choose to tackle. The following sections discuss what to take away from family and friends' reviews, and answer the age-old question, "Should I send this manuscript to my old college pal who's now a big name in the children's book biz?"

Delving into the pros and cons of friendly advice

When you have friends and relatives read or listen to your manuscript, you probably get some initial feedback that's very enthusiastic. As an author, you definitely need to feel appreciated and that you're doing a good job. Friends and family can happily provide that kind of support. Also, if someone within that close circle is an avid enthusiast of children's literature (or has children they read to a lot), then you may get some helpful criticism, as well.

WARNING

But when you solicit help from friends and family, although they usually provide you with a willing audience, they aren't always the most discriminating. Or objective. Or professional. Or knowledgeable. According to editors we've interviewed, the one thing that leads to an almost immediate rejection of a submission is hearing the writer gush about how much the spouse, grandkids, students, or very own children loved it. Of course they did! Would any kid say they didn't like what Mom or Dad wrote?

TIP

Truth be told, pretty much every editor in the universe feels this way about an author's family accolades. Do yourself a favor: Get your material in front of a real writing group — which we talk about in the section "Working with a Writing (or Illustrating) Group," later in this chapter — where you can receive some honest and pointed criticism, or find a professional editor who can do the job (discussed in Chapter 14). You can have fun giving your work to a familiar audience, and children can give you some great initial feedback regarding certain parts of your story, but neither audience can give you a critique that you can feel confident will pass muster at a publishing house. When in doubt, farm it out.

Having a friend in the business

If you have a friend in the children's book business, do you approach them with your manuscript? Do you take advantage of this connection for yourself or your other writer friends?

The simple answer is: Of course you do! But if you want that person to respect you, show them respect by doing a few things before you go to them for feedback:

>> **Have your manuscript carefully (perhaps professionally) edited before-hand.** Yes, we know this person is your friend; but that doesn't mean you don't need to put forth your very best effort to impress them. Although you have to shell out some dough if you choose to hire an editorial service (see Chapter 14), you need to make a positive first impression by presenting professionalism in your work, especially at this stage of the game. You wouldn't show up at a job interview unwashed and wrinkled. Your manuscript shouldn't, either.

>> **Do your homework.** Research what *imprint* (publishing division) in the company your manuscript fits best with, plus the name of the editor in charge of that unit.

>> **Ask whether you can submit a query letter and/or manuscript to the editor.** Let your friend know that you've done some research and think your work may prove a good fit with that editor's imprint. When your friend suddenly seems willing to consider your idea — not to mention seems to have a newfound respect for your brilliant sleuthing — you know you're halfway there.

Then e-mail the manuscript and the query letter to your friend (if you have a hard copy, submit it complete with self-addressed, stamped envelope, of course). You can then turn tail and run like heck, yelling out thank-you's over your shoulder before they change their mind. If you're super-super lucky, the stars are aligned in your favor, Mercury retrograde is not in force, Murphy's Law has failed to pass your state legislature, and your horoscope doesn't warn you to shut down all communications before self-immolating, then your friend may even offer to present your material to the editor.

Granted, this approach assumes your friend in the children's book business has a few years under their belt and isn't the newly hired editorial assistant. (Yes, publishing houses most definitely have a hierarchy.) And even if your friend is new to the company, you owe them as much respect as you owe the veteran.

Calling on Topic Experts: Beta and Sensitivity Readers

What if your manuscript needs a general read-through? Or say your manuscript deals with a culture that you're not a part of, or it deals with a hot-button issue of a sensitive nature. What if you're writing about mental illness but have never experienced it? Or you have, but you're not sure if you have it all correct and portrayed it in a sensitive manner.

To get perspective, you can turn to beta readers and sensitivity readers:

» **Beta readers:** Have familiarity with the genre and format you've written in. They give their feedback after carefully considering everything in your manuscript, from characterization to plot, from dialogue to pacing. They don't edit your manuscript, they just give it a general read. Most agents have beta readers take a look at longer works to confirm whether a book is really on target and doesn't have issues that could prevent publication.

» **Sensitivity readers:** Experts in their field. They come into the picture when your manuscript deals with a sensitive topic. Sensitivity readers give their perspective on any issue that your story delves into that readers might construe in a negative way, depending on how you present it. Sensitivity readers make sure that you don't offend, misrepresent, or otherwise inappropriately cover a subject — a must if you don't want critics and angry readers chasing after you with pitchforks.

Attending Conferences or Retreats

At writing conferences and retreats, you can find support from fellow writers and immerse yourself in the world of children's publishing. You can find out so much about writing and publishing just by listening to the speakers, attending the gatherings, even lunching next to someone new. Writers, editors, illustrators, librarians, agents — you get to surround yourself with a lot of people who all share a love and respect for children's books. But first, you need to figure out what kind of feedback you want and then choose a conference or workshop that can deliver just that. We help you determine what to get feedback on and when in the section "Deciding When to Seek Feedback," earlier in this chapter. The following sections get you acquainted with the world of writing conferences and retreats.

Exploring the conference scene

If you love the idea of writing children's books now, you can't imagine how pumped up you'll feel after you attend a well-run conference. Particularly for an aspiring author, being immersed in a total children's book writing experience for one exhilaratingly packed day (or several days and nights) can be a very heady brew, indeed. We highly recommend taking a gulp or three.

Although different conferences have different aims, most children's book conferences have a similar structure in that they usually

>> Offer presentations and workshops conducted by published authors, illustrators, or industry professionals (such as editors, art directors, public relations experts, or literary agents)

>> Have cocktail parties and group luncheons or dinners to allow attendees to meet and network with other writers and industry professionals

>> Offer critique groups, portfolio reviews, or manuscript reading services — usually for a nominal fee and usually requiring submission well ahead of the conference date

WARNING

If a conference doesn't offer specific workshop sessions, manuscript reviews, or individual face-to-face critiques, you won't get specific feedback at the venue.

The Society of Children's Book Writers and Illustrators (SCBWI; www.scbwi.org) is the largest organization of its kind, so you can find chapters of it almost anywhere in the world. SCBWI puts on a couple different kinds of conferences:

>> **Large-scale biannual conferences in Los Angeles and New York City:** The summer conference in L.A. and the winter conference in New York are chock-full of presentations and workshops (including sessions such as "Bunny Eat Bunny: Surviving the Kid-Lit Jungle," "Drawing Words and Writing Pictures: The Art and Craft of Picture Books," and "Creating Your Author Platform Through Social Networking" — all led by top industry pros). Critique groups and opportunities for individual manuscript readings, portfolio reviews, and consultation services are a very popular part of SCBWI conferences. You can sign up for early registration if you're an SCBWI member.

>> **Smaller-scale regional conferences:** Each regional area of SCBWI hosts at least one major annual event. Usually, these chapters cover a certain geographical area (say, Ventura and Santa Barbara, adjacent areas in Southern California). Both members and nonmembers can attend these conferences — the latter may just have to pay a nominally higher entry fee. Often, these day-long or afternoon events focus on a single aspect of children's book writing and publishing, such as "Illustrators' Day" or "The Art of the Picture Book."

CONFERENCES AND WEBSITES FOR THE MORE EXPERIENCED WRITER

While you advance in your children's book writing career, you might want to attend industry conferences so that you keep on top of what's happening in publishing. Sometimes websites offer a similar experience to an on-site conference. Although not all the conferences in this list are specifically aimed at children's book writers, they do all provide the ideal environments to write and meet up with other writers:

- **Big Sur Children's Writers Workshop** (www.bigsurchildrenswriters.com): Brings top professionals together for an all-inclusive weekend, where both seasoned and newer writers can mingle and discuss their work. Held annually in December in Monterey, California, and in May on Cape Cod.

- **NaNoWriMo (https://nanowrimo.org)** stands for National Novel Writing Month. It is held annually starting on November 1. Started in 1999, this nonprofit organization encourages writers to finish a novel of 50,000 words in one month. Anyone can enter. Many published novels come out of this month-long challenge.

- **12 x 12** (https://www.12x12challenge.com) is a site that encourages writers to write 12 picture books in 12 months. Members enjoy a tight-knit network of peers and colleagues for support, advice, and experience. They also have featured agents willing to look at members' work, and they offer scholarships.

- **WriteOnCon** (www.writeoncon.org): Held annually online in February, specifically for children's book writers. You can access keynote events and critique forums for free, and you can get the rest of the conference content for a fee starting at $10. This virtual conference also offers (and encourages) critique partnerships, where writers get together to critique each other's work.

- **The American Library Association Annual Conference** (www.ala.org/conferencesevents): Although authors and illustrators attend this conference and even have events such as book signings or presentations, it's really a trade conference in the purest sense. Its primary purpose is to give publishers and librarians an environment in which to connect.

WARNING

You can find conferences by asking around for recommendations or by typing "children's book conferences" into an Internet search engine. Just be sure to check out any conference thoroughly before you spend your hard-earned money on a registration fee. Find out the answers to these questions before committing to attend any conference:

» What are the credentials of the people running it?

» Why are they qualified to put it on?

>> Do they also have events for children's book writers, specifically?

>> Does it offer an opportunity to workshop my work?

>> Can I participate in one-on-one critiques with editors or agents?

>> Are the headlining presenters noteworthy?

>> Has the conference garnered a lot of positive reviews?

>> Can I contact past attendees for their candid feedback?

Getting away with retreats

Writers' or illustrators' retreats offer an incredibly satisfying opportunity for children's book creators. Imagine spending a weekend, a week, or even a month or more away from your day job, focusing on just your craft. Nirvana? To many, a writers' or illustrators' retreat can provide a setting in which creativity can absolutely flourish. Whether stimulatingly urban, country idyllic, or somewhere in between, writers' retreats offer a place and time for the children's book creator to hone in on manifesting the passion you have for children's books in a meaningful and productive fashion.

As opposed to providing a zillion interesting events all competing for your attention (like at a conference, which we talk about in the preceding section), a retreat provides a welcoming space conducive to creativity. As such, a retreat has a calm atmosphere and allows for hours of writing, contemplation, or group readings. In a retreat, you literally and figuratively move away from your usual life to focus on your craft. Because everyone else is doing the same thing, retreat organizers often set up times in which you can choose to get feedback from those willing to give it. Consult the ShawGuides (http://writing.shawguides.com) to find a writer's retreat that suits your tastes, budget, and time constraints.

TIP

You might also consider a retreat that focuses on yoga, personal growth, spa services, or any number of themes. As long as you get time and space set aside for writing, illustrating, or both, you can make something as simple as going away for the weekend into a retreat. You can lock yourself up in a hotel room somewhere pleasant (and order room service), or maybe you can borrow a friend's beach house for an extended weekend, clearing your mind of clutter and focusing on your craft without interruption.

Participating in a Workshop

A *workshop* is just a fancy name for a class or course about some aspect of the children's book writing process, usually led by a writing teacher or publishing pro. Depending on the particular workshop you enroll in and the way it's structured, you may (or may not) get good feedback from a workshop.

To ensure that you get the feedback you seek, consider the following when signing up for a workshop:

>> **Quality of workshop leader(s):** Who's leading the workshop? If your instructor is someone like a current bestselling children's book author, an acquisitions editor at the children's book imprint of a publishing house, or an art director who has dozens of books under their belt, you probably get much better feedback in their workshop than if your instructor has only shopped around a couple of book proposals and has yet to be published.

>> **Quality of presenters:** Many workshops offer informational or inspirational speakers. Do the workshop's speakers have enough experience as an author and professional for you to spend time on your butt listening when you could be writing? If the speaker is a current bestselling children's book author or the acquisitions editor at a vibrant children's book imprint, listening to them is probably worth your time.

>> **Length:** You're much more likely to get the quality feedback you seek in a workshop that lasts at least a day or more.

>> **Number of attendees:** If you're jockeying for your instructor's attention along with 100 other eager children's book writers- and illustrators-to-be, you have a greatly limited chance of getting any sort of useful feedback. Small workshops of, say, five to ten people provide an environment in which you can get the feedback you seek, unlike the let's-see-how-many-people-we-can-pack-into-this-room variety.

>> **Structure:** Some workshops specifically set aside time for critique and feedback of attendees' work; some don't. Be sure to take a look at the workshop schedule to find out whether feedback is a part of the plan. If it's not, you should pass.

With a plethora of workshops available around the country, we don't list any specific ones. Ask other children's book writers for their recommendations or type "children's book workshops" into any search engine to find your options.

REMEMBER

In general, workshops are smaller and more intimate than the large national or regional writing conferences (see the section "Exploring the conference scene," earlier in this chapter). Consequently, they offer you a much better chance of getting direct feedback on your writing from the person(s) running the workshop.

Working with a Writing (or Illustrating) Group

Have you ever read a book by an established writer, and the story seems like a good idea, but it has poor execution or an excessive length? Although an editor is ultimately to blame (for not brandishing the editorial whip, no matter how famous and influential the writer), the writer probably failed to get adequate feedback during the writing and revising processes.

If you join or create your own writing group, your fellow members probably don't let you get away with such sins. A *writing group* is a gathering of committed writers — typically composed of at least two members, but often more — who get together on a regular basis to critique one another's work and make it the best it can be.

Some writing groups have stuck together for years with the same participants year in and year out — insular, protective, and productive for their members. Some writing groups have members joining and then quitting every few months. You probably want a group that falls somewhere in between.

So, what better way to get feedback during the writing process than by joining a weekly, biweekly, or monthly writing group? A good writing group can shave years off the time required to refine your writing skills. It can also provide you with a tremendous motivator, as well as accountability for getting those pages written. But be careful: A bad writing group can really set you back or derail your writing career altogether. The following sections help you get into a great writing group.

Finding the right group

Before you can hop into the ideal writing group, you need to find it. So then how in the heck do you go about doing that?

First, try contacting local community colleges or universities that offer writing programs. These programs often have bulletin boards that list writers who are looking for other writers interested in forming a group.

Also, check out your local chapter of the Society of Children's Book Writers and Illustrators (SCBWI). Find the chapter nearest your home through SCWBI's website (www.scbwi.org) and contact the regional advisor about joining a writing group.

Other resources that can help you find a writing group that's right for you include the following:

>> **Writing classes:** Take a class in writing and form a group with some of the people you meet in the class.

>> **Word of mouth:** If you're friendly with writers in your area, ask whether they know of any writing groups.

>> **Online writing discussion groups:** Functioning like a group chat, online discussion groups consist of writers who get together online to share ideas and offer feedback. Group members send manuscripts as e-mail attachments or post them on a website. Members read the manuscripts by a certain deadline and get together online to discuss the chosen manuscript. This is just like an in-person writing group, but it's done virtually.

Tons of online resources can help in your search for a writing group or online writing class. But again, we urge caution: Make sure the website is a reputable one before committing yourself and your precious creative energies. Talk to its members and see what they say before making a decision.

TAKE DISCRIMINATING NOTES

In my (Lisa's) very first writing class, being a diligent, apple-polishing, A+ student, I wrote down every darn thing everyone, including the teacher, said about my writing. And I didn't separate one comment from the other. I took notes this way throughout the ten-week class, even though I began to figure out about halfway through that perhaps not everyone's comments were as educated or on the mark as the teacher's.

Alas, when the class was over, and I tried to apply the feedback I received, I was extremely confused about what advice and commentary to pay attention to — and what to ignore. I had no way of distinguishing the teacher's comments from the yahoos', so I had to put aside the rewrite of my story for a good year until I forgot most of the remarks and could start from scratch. The subject matter was timely the first time around, but unfortunately, by the time I got back to my story, it was passé.

So let my mistake be a lesson for you: Always take discriminating notes when you're receiving feedback in a group setting!

Starting your own group

Having a hard time finding the right feedback group? Why not start your own? You just need one friend who wants to write (or a friend focused on children's book illustration) who's serious enough to commit to producing meaningful content and meeting on a regular basis. If you're in a class, choose a few people whose writing impresses you and who seem amenable, and ask them whether they want to join your group.

TIP

Recruit more than two members, but definitely no more than eight. In our experience, everyone eventually has something to read and wants time to share. If your group has ten members, and they each get a half-hour, your meeting lasts five hours — that's way too much time for people who are likely juggling busy careers, families, and extracurricular pursuits. A group of three to eight people ensures that enough people — and not too many — have new or revised material for consideration at every meeting.

After you select your members, establish some ground rules to help avert problems later on. Here are some good rules to consider:

>> **Size of submission:** Limit the length of submissions covered in each session to one picture book manuscript (or its equivalent of 1,000 words max), one middle-grade chapter, or a limited number of illustrations or sketches.

>> **Type of critiquing:** Does each member read aloud and get verbal feedback? Or does each member submit a written manuscript and get written feedback? Or a combination of both? If your members don't like the idea of homework, they may prefer simply to listen to the writer read aloud during the workshop while they take notes, offering a verbal critique at the end of the reading. If members like to read in peace and quiet, take notes, and then offer their critique aloud during the next workshop, you can also use that approach. Whatever you decide, all your group's members need to agree about how they want to conduct the critiques.

>> **Required critiquing:** Does each member have to critique each submission? How long do they get to critique their peers? In most groups, everyone can participate in critiquing if they have something productive to add to the discussion. And the time taken to offer a critique totally depends on what the members consider appropriate. If your group requires a written critique, everyone who gets a copy should offer at least some comments.

>> **Participant behavior:** Don't tolerate certain behaviors; some should lead to dismissal from the group. For example, if a member misses a certain number of meetings in a row, the group should require that they drop out, opening up a place for a replacement. Also, some member always tries to get more from the group than the others, which can cause resentment and, ultimately,

dissolution of the group. Speak up (nicely) if you notice this happening. Set ground rules and expectations from the start so that you have a process in place before you need it.

Mean-spirited criticism, sarcasm, and ad hominem comments don't help create a forum for open and creative discussion, so don't tolerate them. Make sure feedback stays structured in a positive, respectful, and constructive manner. Make professional, courteous delivery a basic ground rule for your group.

>> **Meeting location and provisions:** If the meetings take place at the same private home, you need to decide how to deal with refreshments. Does everyone contribute a sum of money every month toward coffee and donuts? Is it BYOM (bring your own munchies)? If the group alternates between different members' homes each week, should the weekly host provide the refreshments? (Of course, if you're meeting online, you don't have to worry about these issues.)

>> **Structure of readings and critiques:** Decide whether to time the participants' readings or critiques so that you can keep a big group from running long each week. How much time do you want to allow?

Provide a copy of the preceding rules and considerations at the first meeting. Open up the floor to discussion so that you can decide together how you want your group to work. Taking this approach allows you to get rule-making out of the way quickly so that feedback takes precedence. The group host or leader can create a member roster — always appreciated by members of any committed group so that they can easily communicate with both the group and individuals within that group.

Sifting through the feedback you receive

Writing groups give you free feedback from the many different writers participating. However, the feedback you receive comes primarily from other new writers who may not know any more than you do and may not steer you in the right direction. So how do you get the right feedback from the right people?

If you're in a writing class in which everyone takes turns reading aloud and everyone else can comment, listen carefully to the teacher's comments and take into consideration the comments from the participants in the class who consistently make solid observations. Whom you decide to listen to is a strictly subjective choice, so consider everything, but choose only what seems to make sense to you.

BUILDING YOUR WRITING AND ILLUSTRATING SKILLS

Stephen Mooser, an author who was a founder and the president of the Society of Children's Book Writers and Illustrators (SCBWI) for decades, knows a lot about how writers and illustrators obtain feedback. He ran SCBWI's biannual in-person international conferences with Lin Oliver, the other SCBWI cofounder, but he's also familiar with the online world of feedback on children's books. Here's his perspective on the best ways for writers and illustrators to hone their craft:

- **You used to have to physically meet up to get feedback and input on your writing or your illustrating. Is that still the case?** "Hardly. The Internet, of course, has made it possible to form a critique group with other writers, whether a street away or a continent. But you still need to find a group you are compatible with and whose opinions you respect. I've discovered the best groups are made of people generally at the same stage of their careers and wrestling with the same problems. Sometimes putting together a group like that takes time and comes from at least initially getting to know someone face-to-face, even if just for a few days at a conference."

- **What do you know about online writing or illustrating workshops?** "With any online commercial business, do plenty of research before handing over any money. Look for backup information online and, if possible, talk to one or more former students. When verifying a group's viability for you, I always advise people to type in the name of the business and such key words as *scam, trouble,* and *disappointed.* Finally, research any listed instructors. Well-published and respected authors are unlikely to lend their name to an institution they don't believe is honorable."

- **Can new writers get feedback through authors' or illustrators' own websites?** "It depends. Most writers and illustrators probably don't have the time to critique your manuscript. Think, instead, about attending a local workshop or conference. Ones sponsored by SCBWI often offer critiques at a reasonable price, as well as opportunities to meet fellow authors and illustrators who may be interested in participating with you in a critique group."

- **Are blogs good places to try to get feedback?** "Yes — I think blogs are excellent places to get in on the conversation. Spend a few hours checking out blogs by authors and illustrators whose work you admire. Links leading from these blogs can often take you to all kinds of places where you can learn about everything from the latest industry gossip to the hottest trends in young adult fiction."

- **What about online classes? Can they offer unique value to a newbie?** "What I like best about online classes is that they enforce discipline. Most schools, such as The Institute for Writers, which offers courses in children's literature, have top-notch faculty, but just as importantly, give out weekly or monthly assignments forcing you to sit down and write. If you want to be a success at writing or illustrating, you have to be disciplined. Going to school is a good way to get in the habit of writing every day."

- **How do you judge whether online feedback is useful?** "That's a hard question. It is why you need to find someone you respect, someone honest, but also someone who sees the positive and is constructive. It also means you may need to have more than one person (again, whose opinion you respect) look at your writing. Illustrators ought to attend events such as SCBWI portfolio displays to discern how their work stacks up — particularly against portfolios that tend to win prizes."

- **One very motivated person is self-taught in many different approaches and styles of art creation, entirely by watching YouTube videos. Do you believe that's a viable option for beginning illustrators?** "Different approaches work for different people. I do know the one thing that every illustrator says is that before you can really hope to create that unique style everyone is looking for, you must be able to draw. That probably means getting some kind of formal art education."

- **Any closing comments?** "No matter whether you are using online resources, reading books on writing and illustrating (illustrators should check out *Writing with Pictures,* by Uri Shulevitz [Watson-Guptill]), or taking classes at a university, two things matter most: (1) Come up with something unique that no one has seen before, whether a character, a plot, or an art style; and (2) Be persistent. There's generally not a lot of money in children's books, but those who work at their craft and are persistent will almost always end up selling a book to a publisher — even if that takes 5, 10, or sometimes 20 years."

Good questions for writers to ask

TIP

To ensure you get clear feedback, ask pointed questions when you finish reading your piece aloud to the members of your writing group. Here are some good questions to ask so that you get useful feedback:

>> Is my main character believable here? Why or why not?

>> How can I improve the secondary character(s)?

>> Is my story exciting or interesting to you? Do you want to find out more about the protagonist or what happens next? If not, why?

>> Is the action well paced, or did you feel the story lag?

>> Is my point of view consistent?

>> What do you think about what the characters said to one another? Does the dialogue ring true?

>> Does anything in particular bother you about my story/chapter/scene? Something you want to see improved? A place where you zoned out or got lost? (Only the brave of heart need ask these questions.)

>> Do you think the humor worked? (Usually, the audience's response during your reading lets you know whether your humor is effective, but you can ask to find out how to make something funnier if the response fell flat.)

Good questions for writer-illustrators to ask

If you're a writer–illustrator, here are some good questions for you to ask to make sure you get the type of feedback you need:

>> Do my illustrations complement the text or merely compliment it? In other words, do the images add a layer of meaning, development, or humor to the text? Or are they merely representative, failing to add my (the illustrator's) personality?

>> Are my representations of the character(s) on target?

>> Do the characters I've illustrated show personality? How exactly?

>> Are my images derivative; does my style and execution feel original?

>> Do my backgrounds add a layer of dimensionality to the book, or are they mere clutter or settings?

>> Do I offer different perspectives for the eye to feast on? For instance, would an aerial view or a different perspective or a modification in size in relation to the page add insight and excitement?

>> Are the faces of my characters — human, animal, or otherwise — expressive, and do the illustrations present their emotions subtly, or do I slam the reader over the head with a screaming termagant of a mother every time I show her?

>> Do I follow through consistently with the details of each character, place, and setting? For example, do my characters have the same color shoelaces on the same day, and do my scenes show the same color curtains in the windows of the house?

>> Are my backgrounds competing for attention with the characters?

>> Do my illustrations have enough details so that a writer can delete some descriptive parts of the textual narrative?

Questions like these and others tailored specifically to your work elicit answers that you can use, as opposed to criticisms that you can't. And although you usually don't get enough time to ask all your questions at one group meeting, asking the right ones can make all the difference when you're revising your book.

TIP

Ask people to be specific in response to your questions. When you have limited time in a group meeting, you can quickly get to the heart of what someone thinks about your work.

What Feedback Should You Expect During the Publishing Process?

After you write your book and submit it to your publisher, you can expect to receive a lot of feedback during the publishing process. Here are the people most likely to weigh in with their opinions along the way:

>> **Your editor:** You have the most contact with the editor who acquires your book at your publishing house. They make and suggest edits, minor and major, and you go back and forth with them until they think your manuscript is ready for the next step (sending it to the copy editor). You also deal with them in negotiating your contract.

>> **Your copy editor/fact checker:** After you and the editor finish the substantial editing, the manuscript goes to a copy editor, who often does fact checking, as well. The copy editor polishes your work and makes the book better in many small ways. They may ask a lot of questions and suggest changes in sentence structure, spelling, style, flow, use of capitalization, and more. You get to make revisions based on this feedback.

After these people give their feedback, the book moves into production — and it's out of your hands until the publisher generates a proof and your editor asks you to check it over one last time (which they do, as well).

5

Getting Published and Promoting Your Book

Decide what path you want to take to get published — a traditional publisher, a hybrid publisher, or self-publishing.

Work to land a traditional publisher and find an agent or attorney to help you deal with all the paperwork and legal mumbo jumbo.

Consider the role of hybrid publishers.

Explore the pros and cons of self-publishing.

Discover the most effective ways to promote your book and get it noticed, using social media to help spread the word.

Chapter **17**

The Traditional Route: Signing with an Agent or Publisher

Before you can get your children's book published, you have to find someone to publish it. In these days of self-publishing, hybrid publishing, and print-on-demand, you have more options than ever before to get your children's book into print. But you can't beat the feeling of truly getting published — to have a real, live publisher pay you an advance and royalties, promote and market your book on its own dime, distribute your book to bookstores, and hire salespeople to sell your book.

Believe it or not, children's books usually don't sell themselves to prospective publishers — you have to get your manuscript in front of the right person at the right time if you hope to sell it. You can choose from two time-honored ways to accomplish this:

>> Send off your manuscript yourself to acquisitions editors at every appropriate publisher you can find who are open to submissions

>> Engage a literary agent to sell the manuscript for you.

In this chapter, we weigh the merits of both approaches.

Identifying the Right Publisher

You can find many, many publishers out there in this wide and wonderful literary world. Some are small — publishing only a book or two a year — whereas others are relative giants — publishing houses that have many different *imprints* (smaller publishing divisions within the publishing house), each with its own publishing director, churning out catalogs full of books and other book-related products. Not only that, but each publisher and imprint has its own distinct personality. Some are buttoned-down and corporate, whereas others are impetuous and quirky. Some love to make a big splash in the marketplace; others cater to a distinct niche of readers.

TIP

Make a chart of the publishers you're considering, listing the imprint name, the acquiring editor's name, and the formats, genres, and subject matter (even comparative titles) they specialize in. You can expand this same chart when you're ready to submit to help you keep track of who has your manuscript, when you sent it, and what response you received.

Gathering information from the marketplace

Check out bookstores, libraries, and online booksellers to help you gather more information about the publishers you should pursue. Hit the stores and walk the aisles to find children's books organized by overall category — fiction and nonfiction, series and award winners. Not only that, but board books have their own area, as do chapter books, young adult novels, and everything in between. Then check out the back covers or copyright pages to see who's publishing what. Walking the shops can help you in a number of ways. You can

>> Compare your book to published books to see where yours fits. Then, when you submit, you can mention how your book trumps the recent competition.

>> Find out which publishers are publishing books like yours so that you can target them during the submission process. Write down editor names, often

found in the acknowledgments, and then hunt down their contact information online.

>> See whether any other books approach your topic in the same way you do so that you can make sure yours is different.

HOW TO WOW (OR REALLY ANNOY) A PUBLISHER

Doug Whiteman, former president of Penguin Books for Young Readers (and now founder and president of The Whiteman Agency), has some pointers for writers submitting books for consideration at any publishing house:

- **What in a submission identifies a children's book writer as a pro who knows their stuff?** "That's actually pretty simple: It's all about the homework. The writer who has gone out to the stores to see what her potential competition is and who has presented her submission in a way that distinguishes it from the rest of the field gets my attention immediately. And you really have to go to the stores; simply looking things up on Amazon or going to the library doesn't do it because you need to see the space stores are giving to the various genres; you need to see the jackets against each other; and you need to see what is drawing the customers' attention recently."

- **In your experience, what's one of the most common mistakes new writers make?** "Not listening: To your editor, your publicist, your booksellers, and your readership. It's really imperative that you soak up everything you can about our business and the way things work if you're going to succeed over the long term. And that includes advice, particularly in the editorial area."

- **Anything you'd like to rant/rave about?** "I wish you'd asked me this one first! I'm always willing to rant. I think the thing that annoys me most is the new writer (or veteran adult writer) who assumes that writing for children is easy, and gives me a half-hearted, half-baked submission that they'd never do for an adult book. One should come to children's writing with at least as much respect as you would for an adult project, and many would argue that it takes even more effort to connect with children. It's not easy for an adult to communicate with kids via the printed word, and all prospective writers need to remember that!"

- **Do you have any pet peeves when it comes to the book business?** "I'd like to leave new writers with this quote from Barbara Kingsolver: 'This manuscript of yours that has just come back from an editor is a precious package. Don't consider it rejected. Consider that you've addressed it *To the editor who can appreciate my work,* and it simply came back stamped *Not at this address.*'" While submitting your work, keeping looking for the right address — or let someone like me do it for you!"

Perusing writer's guides and directories

Writer's guides and directories — both printed and online versions — can help you identify the right publisher and give you all the information you need in order to determine what kinds of communications the publisher prefers, along with editors' names and contact information.

Here are some of our favorite writer's guides and directories:

- » **Children's Writer's & Illustrator's Market** (Writer's Digest Books): This book can guide you toward figuring out the best publishers to approach and how to reach them. It also includes lists of literary agents and art reps. **Remember:** It's updated annually, so get ahold of the latest version.

- » **The Children's Book Council** (www.cbcbooks.org): This website includes a comprehensive list of all members of the Children's Book Council, a trade group representing children's book publishers. Click the Our Members link to access publisher names, contact information, publishing interests, and brief submission guidelines.

- » **The Society of Children's Book Writers and Illustrators** (www.scbwi.org): SCBWI offers its members an annually updated market survey that lists the names of all the major acquiring editors at all the publishing houses that choose to participate, as well as all their contact information. Visit the SCBWI website for membership information.

- » **QueryTracker** (www.querytracker.net): Use this free resource to find publishers, agents, and editors who are looking for manuscripts.

- » **The Canadian Children's Book Centre** (http://bookcentre.ca): A national not-for-profit organization and registered charity, the Canadian Children's Book Centre (CCBC) was founded in 1976 to promote, support, and encourage the reading, writing, and illustrating of Canadian books for children and teens.

- » **U.K. Children's Books** (http://ukchildrensbooks.co.uk): Click the Publishers option to access a detailed listing of children's book publisher websites (with an emphasis on publishers in Great Britain).

Drafting Query Letters and Proposals

Publishers and literary agencies don't have time to review mountains of complete manuscripts. Instead, they generally require prospective authors to submit either a *query letter* (a one-page letter of introduction inviting the publisher to ask for more details about your project) or a *proposal* (a longer document that provides additional editorial and marketing information about your book).

Most publishers and agencies have guidelines for how they want your material to arrive, regardless of whether you're sending a query letter, a manuscript, a few chapters, or a full proposal. Always find out the guidelines and follow them to the letter.

Take one of these three easy routes to getting a publisher's guidelines:

>> Visit their website. (Usually the best option of the three, the website gives you up-to-date information, and you can get it quickly.)

>> Send an e-mail to the address listed on the publisher's website, requesting their submission guidelines.

>> Consult a written or online guide to children's book publishers. (We list several in the section "Perusing writer's guides and directories," earlier in this chapter.)

After you know how your chosen publisher or agency wants your materials submitted, you're ready to pull together your query letter and/or proposal. Generally, create a proposal only for longer nonfiction books. Never do a proposal for a board book, for example — unless for some strange reason that's how the publisher wants board books submitted.

After you have the submission guidelines, make sure to follow them to the letter! And illustrators: Artists' reps also have guidelines for portfolio submissions. Figure them out before sending out your materials.

Perfecting the query letter

A good query letter (usually sent via e-mail nowadays) is short and sweet; one page should do the trick. A query letter just gives the publisher or agent a quick rundown on your idea, describes how it fits into the marketplace, and shows some indication of your ability to write the book and help promote it. A query letter also gives you the first chance to wow a publisher or agent (after you complete your research and know you simply must make contact with this person or entity).

I (Lisa) have a tried-and-true approach to writing query letters, and I share this approach with everyone who asks. Here's what you need to put into your one-page query letter:

>> **Greeting:** You know, "Dear [person's full name]," then two lines down, you start. If you actually met the agent or editor at a conference, then, and only then, can you start the query letter with a more personalized, first-name-only greeting acknowledging where and when you met and reference that person's expressed desire to consider manuscripts from attendees.

Never ever send group messages with the generic "To Whom It May Concern"! You don't have the time to send a personal e-mail? We guarantee you won't get a personal reply — if any at all.

>> **Hook:** A few powerful, attention-grabbing sentences that make the reader want to read the book. For instance: "What would you do if your older sister was the famous, glamorous, legendary Tooth Fairy and you were just the pesky little sister no one cared about? Would you hang onto her coattails (or gossamer wings) hoping just a bit of attention will rub off on you? Or would you get inventive? Meet *Switch Witch*, a 500-word picture book about a little sister named Esme who decides enough is enough."

>> **Overview:** Give a bit more about the book, including audience, age, format, and word count (don't write a book report or a plot summary; just give an overview of the main character(s), setting, and dramatic conflict, written in the same style and tone as your captivating manuscript). Also briefly reference why your book is different from other similar books and the current competition (which shows you did your homework). Including a sentence that tells why you chose this particular agent or publisher might score major brownie points by showing you did your homework.

>> **Biography:** Convince the reader you're the best person to write the story you summarize in your overview. (Published writers always list their most recent books first; if you haven't been published, then relevant professional experience will do.)

>> **Closing sentence:** Brief, but powerful! Just make sure you don't plead to be published. After all, they know why you're writing them. Something along the lines of, "I'm super excited by the prospect of being published by your firm — please let me know next steps."

>> **Contact information:** Provide your phone number, e-mail, and physical mailing address.

A query letter that goes to an agent versus one that goes to a publisher differs only in the research that you indicate you did (which led you to choose to submit to this particular person).

Figure 17-1 shows what a query letter looks like, but be careful to tailor your letter to a prospective agency or publisher's guidelines. (You can find these guidelines on the agency or publisher's website or in writing if you request them from the company.) And, again, be sure to keep your query letter to just one page.

Your Name
Address
City, State Zip code
Phone
E-mail

Date

Agent's Name
Agency Name
Address
City, State Zip code

Dear Ms. _____:

What would you do if your older sister was the famous, glamorous, legendary Tooth Fairy and you were just the pesky little sister no one cared about? Would you hang onto her coattails (or gossamer wings) hoping just a bit of attention will rub off on you? Or would you get inventive?

Meet *Switch Witch*, a 500-word picture book about a little sister named Esme who decides enough is enough.

I have selected your agency because of your success in placing humorous, high concept, picture books, most notably your recent sale of *Tutusaurus Rex*, by Ima Big Author, to Chronicle Books.

Switch Witch is the story of how Esme, jobless and aimless (and not a little jealous), gets to work trying to find a purpose in life. She goes through all the other major events and holidays in a kid's life (Easter? Nope. Bunny's got that covered. Christmas? Nope. Santa and a whole lotta small guys are already up and running the toy factory.) Finally, one Halloween night, Esme realizes she could do some real good. She turns herself into the Switch Witch, the one who takes all the extra candy kids don't really need and swaps it out for an alternative after all the trick-or-treating is over. And of course she does something virtuous with all those leftover sweets!

I have been writing for 20 years. I've had three picture books published over the last five years: *Doggone!* (2022), *You Can't Pet a Pet Fish* (2020), and *Stinkerbella* (2018). All three have sold over 5,000 copies in hardcover over the first year and have been reprinted in paperback picture books for the book clubs and book fairs.

I'm a member of SCBWI, and I was a finalist this year in the SCMMWWSMW (Southern California Misguided Mommies Writing While Simultaneously Mud Wrestling) Contest.

Please let me know if you are interested in switching out this query letter for the entire, thrilling manuscript of *Switch Witch*. I will be happy to send you a copy by e-mail immediately upon your request. I would also send you a piece of leftover Halloween candy as a friendly bribe, but that's kind of difficult to do via e-mail.

Thanks for taking the time to consider this query.

Sincerely,

Your Name

FIGURE 17-1: A sample query letter.

TIP

When communicating with agents or publishers in a query letter, always make sure to identify the format of your book (we tell you all about formats in Chapter 2). The preceding query letter identifies the format as a picture book, allowing the agent or publisher to immediately understand your intended audience, as well as the approximate page count and size of the book. Identifying the format also assures that the right in-house editor receives your submission if it gets past the first reader. And perhaps most important, it illustrates that you've done your research and separates your submission from those of the wannabes who refer to their work only as a "children's book" (and who most likely receive only a rejection in return for their limited efforts).

Drafting a great book proposal

When submitting your idea for a nonfiction book, most publishers require you to send in a book proposal. This provides them all the information they need to decide whether to consider your book for publication.

REMEMBER

A nonfiction book proposal most often contains some form of the following, although many publishers and agents have specific guidelines for submitting nonfiction proposals. If a publisher or agent requests that you submit a proposal for fiction (an unusual request), you can use these same elements:

» **Contents:** A table of contents for your proposal, not your manuscript. This part lists all the other parts of your proposal — such as the marketing plan, target audience, author biography, and so on — as well as the page on which each part begins.

» **Summary:** Write the sexiest, most engaging and intriguing teaser about the book without giving away the ending, much like the copy on a hardcover book jacket or the back cover of a trade paperback. Aim for no more than two pages of summary material.

» **Author bio:** The part about you, often written in the third person, indicating why you're the best possible person to write this book. What are your special qualifications? What else have you published, and were any of these publications critical or commercial successes? Do you have your own successful podcast, a blog with tons of visitors, or a million Twitter followers? Don't be afraid to brag here — but don't do it for more than one page.

» **Audience:** Who's your target audience? (And no, "children of all ages" is not a target audience — see formats and ages in Chapter 2.) Why will your audience buy, keep, download, talk about, and share your book with others? What does your book offer that others of its specific ilk don't? What about it can get the Twitterverse tweeting like mad on the day of its release? Describe your audience as specifically as possible — in one page.

- » **Competition:** What other recently published books like yours have been successful? How is your book different from the competition and unique? Identify the exact title, author, publisher, and year of release for all competitive titles you list. You can make this part up to two pages long.

- » **Marketing plan:** Every agent and publisher wants to make money, but they can do that only if your book sells. How do you plan to sell copies of your books? How does your standing — in the universe, your profession, or your social life — afford you (and thus your publisher) any advantages when it comes to advertising, promoting, or marketing your book? Do you have a blog with 10,000 hits a day? A contact in the Department of Education who can get your book in front of book adoption committees for school curricula in various states? Be specific and realistic. Don't overpromise and therefore underdeliver when the publisher or agent follows up. And keep this section of your proposal to no more than a few pages. (See Chapters 20 and 21 for more about marketing.)

- » **Manuscript specifications:** Note the nitty-gritty details of your proposed book in a paragraph or two: Word count or number of pages based on a specific existing format and the number of illustrations, photographs, images, charts, and so on. Do you plan to obtain images for your book yourself, in the proper form and including legal permissions? (The answer is usually yes.) Does anything about the format you're proposing make it out of the ordinary? (For example, say you're writing a nonfiction book about how to build Victorian dollhouses, and you want to include the materials to make a miniature rag doll.) Finally, do you already have a complete manuscript?

- » **Outline:** Tell the publisher or agent what they can expect to find in the guts of your book, starting with the book's table of contents and adding a paragraph about each specific chapter's contents. Imagine a screenshot of how you organize the entire book. You don't have to be married to this outline forever — often, content and plans change — but make your outline as thorough as you plan to make your book. Include section and chapter headings; below each heading, write one to three paragraphs explaining what the chapter contains and how the content moves the book forward.

- » **Sample chapter(s):** One great chapter (usually the first), well representative of your style, approach, voice, and ability to deliver what your proposal offers. If your chapters are short, (fewer than 10 pages or so) then you should include more than just one.

TIP

A proposal typically runs anywhere from 25 to 50 pages, double-spaced throughout with 1-inch margins all around. The publisher or agency likely wants you to e-mail a copy to them, in which case, send a PDF. If they ask you to mail a hard copy, leave it unbound and include a cover letter that introduces yourself and the book.

Joining Forces: Working with an Agent

An *agent* (or an *artist's rep* for illustrators) is someone who works to sell your work to a publisher. Agents may own their own businesses — working solo, or perhaps with another agent or two — or they may work for a larger agency, one among many other agents. Regardless of the size of their business, agents work on commission. They receive a percentage of the advances and royalties stipulated in your publishing contract (usually a flat 15 percent). If the agent has to engage the services of a subagent in order to sell foreign or other specialized rights, sometimes the commission percentage is increased up to 25 percent.

Although you might not be too happy about giving away 15 percent or more of your hard-won publishing deal to someone else, many authors consider the price to be well worth it. First, many publishers refuse to accept unagented book manuscripts, queries, or proposals. Second, agents can work magic because they're in much better contact with publishing companies than unpublished authors are. The best agents know exactly what children's book editors at different publishing houses are looking for, and they do their best to provide it.

REMEMBER

Keep in mind that agents are in business to make money. For that reason, they're very selective about the authors they choose to work with. Many agencies receive thousands of queries, proposals, and manuscripts from prospective authors each year; out of necessity, they reject far more authors than they accept. If an agent turns you down, don't let that rejection slow you down, too — submit to another agent or consider submitting directly to a publisher.

Finding and approaching your ideal agent

Here are some tried-and-true approaches for finding your ideal agent.

Obtaining referrals

Authors who are happy with their agents will usually refer you to them. So the next time you're chatting with a children's book author, be sure to ask them who their agent is, whether they're happy with that agent, and whether they can make an introduction for you. If you don't personally know any children's book authors, consider reaching out to some of your favorites online through their websites or social media.

Researching your heart out

If you don't know any agents personally, or if you can't get referrals to agents, then do some research, using online agency listings or print resources. Check out the section "Perusing writer's guides and directories," earlier in this chapter. These directories provide you with agent and agency names, addresses, phone numbers, and detailed information about what kinds of books the agency specializes in representing. Find an agency that looks like it meets your criteria, get the contact information, check the listing to make sure they're accepting unsolicited (unrequested) submissions; if they are, get in touch.

While you look through agent directories, be sure to focus only on agencies that specialize in children's books.

Attending conferences

Agents sometimes participate in conferences and workshops to find promising new talent — some agencies even sponsor those conferences and workshops. Because the promising new talent may very well be you, you should consider attending writers' conferences for the express purpose of hooking up with an agent.

Here's how to increase your chances of finding a great agent at a conference:

>> Check out writers' conference or workshop agendas and participant lists to see whether any agents plan to attend.

>> Memorize your pitch and bring a few copies of your manuscript. Although an agent at the conference or workshop most likely won't ask for a copy then and there (unless you paid for a manuscript or portfolio consultation in advance), you never know.

Agents attending conferences and workshops are often very popular people, so you might have difficulty cornering one to make your pitch. They may be leading roundtable discussions or making presentations, plus getting pitched by other prospective authors. Get a jump on the competition by making contact with the agent via e-mail before the conference to let them know you're hoping for a minute of their time to introduce yourself. Be patient, be polite, but be persistent — eventually, you'll have an opportunity to make your pitch.

Managing multiple agent submissions

When you're first looking for an agent, you can send your query letter or proposal to multiple agents all at the same time. Just check the agents' policies if you decide to take this course. Some agents get touchy when they find out they're competing against other agents.

PITCH WARS AND #PitMad

Writing contests, where you submit your query, manuscript, or short pitch with the promise that the winner or winners get published — or at least submitted to a receptive agent or publisher — aren't new. Many have gone the way of the brontosaurus, but some have stood the test of time. One such survivor is Pitch Wars and its close relation, #PitMad.

Author Brenda Drake established the annual Pitch Wars pitching contest (http://pitchwars.org) in 2012, and the contest is still going strong today. Writers submit their un-agented, full-length fiction manuscript pitches (for unpublished middle grade, young adult, new adult [roughly ages 18-30], and adult works only) for consideration by mentors (published/agented authors, editors, or industry interns). Each mentor chooses a writer to work with — reading their manuscript and offering suggestions on how to improve it. Mentees then participate in an agent showcase (again, assisted by their mentors), where agents can view and select from posts that feature their pitches.

#PitMad is a quarterly event run by Pitch Wars. On a specific date each quarter, un-agented writers can tweet 280-character pitches for their completed, polished, unpublished manuscripts. Agents and editors can then request a copy of the manuscript by liking or favoriting the tweet. Unlike Pitch Wars, all genres and categories are eligible.

According to the Pitch Wars site, the organization has had 500 successes from its inception through 2020. If you can't seem to attract the attention of an agent, then Pitch Wars and #PitMad might be worth a try.

TIP

If you send out multiple submissions, set up a computer spreadsheet that lists the name of each agent, their contact information, exactly what you sent, and the date you sent it. While you get responses (or not), note them on your spreadsheet.

REMEMBER

If you don't hear from a particular agent after about two months, they aren't interested in your submission. Ping them one more time just in case, and if you don't hear back soon after, then go ahead and scratch that agent off your list for this project.

Understanding typical agency agreements

Depending on the literary agency you select, you may be required to sign a written agency agreement before an agent will represent your work to publishers. Although a handshake agreement may work out fine for you and your agent, we prefer agency agreements in writing because life is complicated enough; always get it in writing. The following sections describe the standard terms and conditions that go into most agency agreements and give you tips on how to negotiate your end of the deal.

Sizing up the standard terms and conditions

A variety of terms can make their way into a typical agency agreement, including some of the following:

>> **Scope of the agreement:** Spells out exactly what the agency is going to do (represent your work), where the agency is going to do the work (within your country or throughout the world), and whether the relationship with you, the writer, is exclusive or for a specific project (see the following section for more details on this distinction).

>> **Duration of the agreement:** Many agreements last for the duration of a specific project — from the initial pitch to publishers until the book eventually goes out of print. Other agreements cover a minimum of one year and apply to all projects sent out during that year; after the one year, you can assume the relationship will continue until either party decides, at will, to pull out.

WARNING

Suppose you've been with an agent for over a year and really feel they're not the right fit for you. Your contract may allow you to terminate the agreement from that point on, but any project the agent has submitted to publishers and that's accepted after you terminate the agreement is still covered under the old agreement. In other words, for any work that they've done for you on any particular book that you gave to them during the time of your agreement, your contract applies in perpetuity.

>> **Handling of funds:** Typically, the agency receives payments from publishers, disburses your portion to you within a certain amount of time, and keeps an accurate accounting of all financial transactions.

>> **Commission rate:** The agency gets to keep typically 15 percent (or 20 to 25 percent for sales of foreign and other rights involving subagents) off the top of each publisher's check before any monies get to you.

>> **Expenses:** The agreement may spell out exactly what expenses the agency bears as a part of its standard commission (typically, routine overhead items such as domestic phone calls, small copying jobs, computer, employee time spent editing your manuscript and presenting it to publishers, and so forth) and what expenses they plan to bill against the author's royalties (typically extraordinary expenses such as overnight shipping, messengers, large copying jobs, international phone calls, and the like). Avoid agents that charge reading fees. These fees border on being unethical and are expressly prohibited by the Association of Authors' Representatives' Canon of Ethics.

- » **Indemnification:** Some agencies may want the author to *indemnify* (protect) them against legal claims resulting from acts or omissions on the part of the author that exposes the agency to legal claims. Such provisions are generally not in your interest, so consider trying to negotiate them out.

- » **Termination:** This part of the agreement spells out the conditions that each party must undertake to end the agreement. It usually involves waiting a specific amount of time from signing, typically a year, and then allows either party to bow out, at will, in writing.

TIP

Make sure your agency agreements contain a specific mechanism for termination. If you spell out these understandings in advance — when you and your agent are cool, calm, and collected — you don't have to try to sort out a big mess when emotions are running high.

If you don't know what terms and conditions you should accept or reject, or if you're uncomfortable negotiating the agreement yourself, seriously consider engaging the services of an attorney who specializes in the practice of publishing law. Alternatively, the legal team at the Author's Guild (www. authorsguild.org) reviews agency agreements for its members at no additional cost.

Distinguishing between exclusive and by-project services

When you work with an agency, you may face the issue of whether your relationship is going to be exclusive or by project. The difference between the two is major and can have a significant effect on your writing career:

- » **Exclusive agreement:** When you enter into an exclusive agreement with an agent or literary agency, you're turning over representation for all of your work for as long as the agreement is in effect. Although this arrangement may make your life easier because someone else is worrying about placing your projects with publishers, on the other hand, you greatly reduce your flexibility to try different avenues to get published — perhaps for many, many years. On the other hand, an agent who handles all your creative work is more likely to be invested in your career in the long run and has more incentive to sell all your projects, as opposed to just one.

- » **By-project agreement:** This kind of agreement is for one project only, including any sequels or derivative works that may spin off of the original work. Although your agent takes full responsibility for selling a particular work to publishers, you can take your other projects to other agents, or submit them directly to publishers yourself — whichever approach makes the most sense to you.

TIP

You can look at a by-project agreement as kind of like going steady or getting engaged before you tie the knot. But to make the up-front investment in building your career from the ground up and then keeping it simmering between sales, most agents don't even offer this option. Mostly, already-published writers can work with a by-project agreement for a number of reasons:

>> They're changing directions in their writing and may not have contacts in this new area,

>> They have publishing agreements they already set up on their own and just want an agent to handle all the negotiations so that they can get back to writing.

>> They're already active in the industry and for some reason have gotten to the point at which they need an agent to step in and take over the selling portion of the job.

Terminating your agency relationship

Entering into a long-term relationship with an agent can be like getting married — both sides of the aisle have a lot of expectations, and when things go wrong, breaking up can be rather like getting a divorce. But sometimes you have no choice, and breaking up isn't just the right thing to do — it's the only thing you can do.

When things go from bad to worse, don't hesitate to terminate your relationship, invoking the termination provisions in your agency agreement. Typically, you simply need to mail a letter (or send an e-mail) to the agency stating that you're terminating the agreement (make sure you get a reply that indicates the agent has received and accepted the termination). Your particular agreement may or may not require a certain number of days' prior notice before the termination becomes effective (usually 30 to 60 days), so be careful not to enter into an agreement with a new agent before the agreement with your current agent is officially dead. Send the letter via certified mail, return receipt requested, so that you have a record of the mailing.

REMEMBER

Before you break up with your agent, make sure both of you have been on the same page about the particular problem. If you have an issue that you need to address with your agent, always try talking about it first, hammering out the details between the both of you. But if you try to work through whatever your issues are and truly have reached the end of your rope, then take the high road and behave like a perfect gentleperson. Get your divorce agreement in writing and then move on. Above all, be professional, be polite, and do whatever you can to avoid burning bridges along the way. The children's book industry really is a small world, and the relationship you save today may be one that will serve you well years down the road.

DRAWING INSPIRATION FROM PUBLIC DOMAIN WORKS

A story falls into public domain if it's a creative work or intellectual property that copyright no longer protects (generally, a copyright lasts for the life of the author, plus 70 years), so anyone can use it. Stories in the public domain include many fairy tales, as well as works such as *Alice's Adventures in Wonderland,* by Lewis Carroll (Macmillan), or *A Little Princess,* by Frances Hodgson Burnett (Charles Scribner's Sons). What do you do if you want to use a story that's in the public domain as a starting point for your own story? You first have to find out if you can.

To find out whether anyone owns a story and whether you can retell it in your words without getting in trouble, use this fairly reliable test: If you can find at least three different and separately copyrighted and recent adaptations or retellings, then you can comfortably assume the story is up for grabs. For instance, the Old Testament Bible and the musical works of Beethoven are in the public domain, but someone could have translations of, adaptations of, or performances of these works copyright protected. Actually get your hands on the book from which the story you want to reimagine comes. Check the copyright and permissions pages, and make sure that the author didn't have to obtain permission from someone to use the story. If they did, they have to credit it in their book, and they may have had to pay for the privilege of using or adapting it — something you may not want to do.

Tip: The Public Domain Review houses collections of fairy tales and folk tales from around the world. The site's vast catalog of out-of-copyright material is free to use without restriction. They focus on "the surprising, the strange, and the beautiful." Their blog offers treasures like a Countdown Calendar that announces when new works will enter the public domain. Check out their site at `https://publicdomainreview.org/tags/best-of-folk-and-fairytales`, or swing by their blog at `https://publicdomainreview.org/blog`.

A word of caution: If you choose fairy tales, go back to the originals, not the Disney adaptations. Certain additions to the Disney tales aren't public domain, such as the characters Flounder (a fish) and Sebastian (a Jamaican-accented crab) that Disney added to Hans Christian Andersen's classic tale "The Little Mermaid."

Copyright: Protecting Your Work

The most commonly used — and perhaps most commonly misunderstood — way of protecting a literary work is by a copyright. A *copyright* is simply a legal protection of an original work. You can copyright literary, dramatic, musical, artistic, and other intellectual works. Only the owner of the copyright (or someone that the copyright owner expressly authorizes) may reproduce the work, prepare derivative works based on the work, perform the work publicly, and display the copyrighted work publicly.

You're probably familiar with the famous mark that signifies an item is copyrighted: ©. The copyright symbol is one-third of a copyright notice. A complete *copyright notice* consists of the copyright symbol (©), the year of first publication of the work, and the name of the owner of the copyright, like this: © 2022 Lisa Rojany.

WARNING

Legally, you don't have to place a copyright notice on your work for copyright laws to protect it, and we advise you not to overuse it. A little © on every page or on a cover signals an amateur who doesn't know that the moment you save a file that contains your story, with that file's date and time stamp available for confirmation, copyright law protects your work. Having a dated document doesn't mean that someone else can't use the same idea — no copyright can protect you from that (besides, most stories have been told before). But a dated file does protect your unique voice and the particular way you developed the story you want to tell.

WARNING

You may have heard that sending a copy of your work to yourself (a practice known as a "poor man's copyright") provides protection. This story is nothing but a myth. According to the U.S. Copyright office, copyright law makes no provision for this.

You can't copyright ideas, procedures, methods, systems, processes, concepts, principles, discoveries, or devices (as distinguished from a description, explanation, or illustration). But, boy, you sure can patent and trademark the heck out of some of these things; visit the U.S. Patent and Trademark Office website (www.uspto.gov) for more details. So even if you have an idea, you can't protect it until you develop and write that idea into an actual story.

REMEMBER

A lot of people think that you need to fill out a form, hire an attorney, or pay a fee to copyright your work. Although any number of attorneys would love to take your money to secure a copyright for your work, you don't have to. According to U.S. copyright law, your work is automatically copyrighted the moment you create it in *fixed form* (meaning it's tangible — such as a published story, written song, or printed photograph — or can be communicated with the aid of a machine or device), and the copyright immediately becomes your property because you're the person who created the work.

Say you submit a query letter to a bunch of publishers about your idea for a story about a girl who finds a lost puppy. You get rejected everywhere. Then months (or years) after that rejection, three different books with the exact same premise are released from three different publishers. Have they stolen your idea? They can't! Ideas aren't protected; therefore, no one can steal them in the first place.

Although copyrights don't protect your work forever, they do last a pretty long time. In the United States, for works created on or after January 1, 1978, the copyright lasts for the author's entire life plus 70 years after their death. When the work is an anonymous work, a pseudonymous work, or a work made for hire, the copyright lasts for 95 years after the year of its first publication or a term of 120 years from the year of its creation — whichever of those terms first expires.

So what happens to ownership of your work after the copyright expires? When your copyright expires, your book enters the *public domain* (see the sidebar "Drawing Inspiration from Public Domain Works," in this chapter); no person or organization has an exclusive right of ownership in the work, and anyone can then use the words you wrote in any way he or she sees fit. Eventually, all copyrighted children's books meet this fate — even Mickey Mouse (*Steamboat Willie*) will enter the public domain in 2024!

Success! Reviewing Your Publishing Contract

One of the greatest moments of a writer's life comes when you get the news that a publishing company wants to publish your book. Quite quickly following that wonderful moment comes the (very) scary part: signing the *publishing agreement* — the legal contract that spells out the terms and conditions under which the publisher can publish your book, including important considerations such as payment, schedule, and copyright. Never fear. In the following sections, we arm you with the information you need to distinguish between the types of agreements and ensure you get what you want in yours.

Surveying the two types of publishing agreements

Generally, you find two types of publishing agreements: the traditional advance-against-royalties agreement and a work-for-hire or flat-fee agreement. (For our purposes, the terms *contract* and *agreement* refer to the same thing.) Here are the two main types of agreements:

> **Royalty agreements:** The traditional form of a publishing agreement. *Royalties* are a percentage of the proceeds from the sale of each book, minus the *advance* (which is the money the publisher pays you up front).

> **Work-for-hire agreements:** When a publisher engages an author under a work-for-hire agreement, the publisher pays the author a fixed amount of money for a specific piece of work. When the author delivers the work, the publisher pays the money and takes all rights to the work with no residual payments, such as royalties, due the author.

TIP

Publishing agreements usually contain all kinds of provisions, including grant of rights, payment, reversion of rights, and more. If the entire process gives you hives, consult with an attorney who has demonstrable experience in publishing agreements.

Getting what you want in the contract

The publisher drafts publishing contracts, and they write those contracts in a way that minimizes the publisher's risk and maximizes the publisher's financial return, not the author's. Decide for yourself the degree to which you'll give up provisions (such as getting a net royalty rate versus a gross royalty rate) in order to secure the publishing contract for your book.

REMEMBER

If you engage an agent to sell your book for you, they take care of the negotiations for you — often leveraging concessions that they've earned from previous deals with the same publisher. If you're on your own, you need to review the contract in detail and negotiate terms. Don't hesitate to engage the services of a competent attorney who has experience with book contracts if you feel completely out of your element. The Author's Guild (www.authorsguild.org) offers its members free legal review of publishing, agency, and other book-related contracts — a valuable benefit.

Although new authors often give in on a lot of issues because they're so excited to have their first book published, take a look at some of the aspects of a contract about which you should try to have a say:

> **Front cover byline:** New authors, especially, should require that their name appear on the front cover and the spine of the book in a large-enough font size that an average person can read it without difficulty, and that the author's name appears as big as the illustrator's name.

>> **Digital or electronic rights:** Many agents complain that they spend the majority of their negotiations with publishers haggling over *digital rights* (rights for formats such as e-books, apps, podcasts, video trailers, and multimedia formats we haven't yet invented). Digital rights represent a lot of profit, potentially — and a lot of unknowns. If you're negotiating by yourself, do some research.

>> **Free copies:** Make sure you get enough free copies to give away to your family and friends, as well as to hand out as promotional copies to noted bloggers, reviewers, your local cozy cafe, and so on.

Many publishers send out promotional copies, including an introductory letter (at no cost to the author), to important media contacts that the author provides. Find out their publicity department's standard practice and see whether you can negotiate more free copies if you need them.

>> **Additional copies:** Make sure that you can purchase additional copies at a deep discount; typically either the publisher's cost or 50 percent of the suggested retail price (what publishers charge most retailers).

>> **Option to purchase:** Just before it goes out of print, your book may be *remaindered* (sent off to discount retailers at a price significantly lower than the suggested retail price). Make sure your contract states that the publisher has to notify you first so that you have the option to purchase those copies at a certain (low) price per unit before they're sent away.

>> **Royalty rates:** Royalties are specific to the format and geographic territory, but are generally 10 percent total on hardcover sales and 5 to 8 percent total on trade paperback sales. The royalty rates for electronic versions of your book can range from a few percentage points to 50 percent or more.

On the print version, push for a *gross royalty rate* (royalty based on the suggested retail price without the publisher's cost subtracted from the price) versus the *net royalty rate* (royalties based on the retail price minus the publisher's costs). You often can't easily quantify ahead of time what the publisher considers fair, fixed costs to charge against the royalty monies owed to you, which means you often end up with a lower net royalty rate than you expected when you negotiated your contract. Go for the gross royalties to maximize your financial return.

>> **Escalating royalty rates:** The more books you sell, the more royalties you get paid. Although first-time authors often don't get the option to push for this type of royalty rate, you can always try. You make more only if the publisher also makes more — a win-win situation as far as we're concerned. And be sure that the publisher counts in sales for a revision to your book as additional sales for the initial edition (instead of being counted as a new book for which you have to earn out the new and usually lower advance before earning royalties).

- **Royalties from other countries:** Publishing agreements get very specific about *subrights* (generally rights concerning other countries, languages, and formats). Although you can't predict what subrights will sell where, make sure you have specific negotiated royalty rates. Do you get the same amount of royalty for World Rights that you do for North American Rights and for World All Languages? For instance, do you get the same amount of royalty for books printed in the United States in English (American English) and sold in Britain (as opposed to British versions that contain British English) that you do for those same books sold in the United States? Or does your contract classify Britain and Canada as foreign sales, with applicable royalty rates?

- **Copyrights:** Make sure that the agreement provides that the copyright is in your name, not in the publisher's name. (You don't have this option in a work-for-hire agreement or an agreement in which you contribute to an already-established series, such as *For Dummies.*) For more on copyright, see the section "Copyright: Protecting Your Work," earlier in this chapter.

- **Schedule for manuscript delivery and acceptance of manuscript (timeline and format):** Give yourself a reasonable amount of time to complete the manuscript well. Don't rush to try to please the publisher; they're already pleased, that's why you're in contract negotiations. If you're so new that you don't know how to define *reasonable,* the publisher can provide a suggested date; if that date gives you hives, you're probably allergic to it and need more time.

  Also, if the publisher doesn't accept your work when you deliver the final manuscript, they should explain, in writing, why they're rejecting the work and allow for good faith changes within a designated period of time.

- **Accounting statements (annual, semiannual, or quarterly):** Make sure that the publisher doesn't use *cross accounting* (sometimes called *cross collateralization* or *joint accounting*), meaning that this agreement applies to only this book and doesn't tie into the royalty accounting for subsequent titles that may or may not pay off their advance.

- **Indemnity/insurance:** You probably can't obtain any concessions in the indemnity clause, but you should try nonetheless. If the publisher has the ability to settle claims without the prior approval of the author, make sure the clause includes a dollar amount limitation. Furthermore, legal expenses should be held in an interest-bearing account. Query as to whether the publisher's insurance policy might include the author as an additional insured.

- **Right to audit:** Every publishing contract should give the author the right to audit the publisher's accounting records for that book.

- **Publisher bankruptcy:** Some authors try to include a clause in their contract stating that if a publisher goes bankrupt, the rights to the book revert immediately to the author — regardless of whether another entity subsequently buys the publisher's assets. We think that's a fair request: If they aren't doing anything with your work, why can't you get the rights back to try to use your material, instead of letting a total stranger sit on it for the next century while they figure out what if anything to do with it?

>> **Out-of-print:** If the publisher doesn't print the book on the contractually promised date or within 18 months of it, you have a right to ask for the rights to revert back to you. Also, if no print copies remain of your book and the publisher hasn't sold one in 18 months, the publishing industry considers that book out of print, and you can ask for the rights back. But understand that a publisher only has to sell one copy for this clause to remain unenforceable.

TIP

In our experience, newbies often have to accept 90 percent of the original terms in a publishing contract — but that doesn't mean you can't get some concessions here and there. If it's your first book and you've been offered a contract with a reputable publisher, ask yourself this: Do I want to be published more than I want X? If the answer is yes, suck it up. You'll have more clout with your second book.

WARNING

Whatever you may find in your publishing contract, be sure someone on your side carefully reviews the contract before you sign it — either your agent, you (if you're sufficiently qualified), or an attorney (if you're not). And don't sign the contract until you understand exactly what you're signing and fully agree with its terms.

Dealing with Rejection

A *rejection letter* is notification from someone to whom you sent your manuscript — usually either a literary agent whom you hope can represent your work to publishers or an editor who acquires new titles for a children's book publisher — telling you that they don't want to accept your manuscript for publication.

The bad news: You're going to get a lot of rejection letters while you travel along the path to getting published — from literary agents, editors, and publishers.

So, what should you do when you receive a rejection letter? After having a quick cry (always keep a box of tissues handy when you open letters from publishers), you can do a number of things to turn this particular lemon into lemonade and grow from the experience:

>> **Take some time to cool down.** A rejection can bring your dream of getting published to a screeching halt, and you can find it a very emotional event.

If you find yourself upset by the rejection, take some time to cool down before you do anything related to your manuscript. Relax. Take a deep breath. Don't throw your manuscript in the fireplace.

>> **Look for clues.** Is the rejection letter one of those form letters where someone wrote in your name after the typed-in "Dear," or did you get an actual personal letter in which the agent or editor offers advice or encouragement? If they include advice specific to your book in the letter, read it closely! These bits of info — such as how to improve your manuscript or where you can find a more appropriate agency or publisher for your book — can help you create a better book (while giving you a greater chance for eventual publishing success).

>> **Revise your manuscript.** If the person who sent you the rejection letter took the time to give you specific advice on how to improve your manuscript, by all means, take it and revise your manuscript accordingly. (You don't need to wait to receive such a letter to improve your manuscript.) Editors and agents know what books can sell. Sure, they make mistakes from time to time — launching books that sink in the marketplace faster than you can spell *Titanic,* and rejecting books that another publisher picks up and turns into a raging success — but their advice is as straight from the horse's mouth as you can get. And most of the time, it's dead-on accurate (as painful as it may be). Also, the advice costs you nothing (except a little pride).

TIP

Someone who takes the time to write a real reply and includes suggestions on improvement may be willing to take a second look after you implement those suggestions. Consider it a slightly opened door. You may want to send the contact a revised version of your work if you agree that the suggested changes make your work better.

>> **Redo your research.** Did you send your manuscript to the right agent or publisher? Different agents and publishers specialize in different genres and types of children's books (see our extensive coverage on these topics in Chapters 2 and 3). Does your manuscript conform to the common publishing standards for that type of book? If not, then the agent or publisher may reject your manuscript for that reason alone. Do your research and double-check that you sent the right manuscript to the right agent or publisher.

>> **Remember that it's not personal; it's just business.** Book publishing is a business. If your manuscript was rejected, the editor didn't believe the book would sell enough copies to be a profitable venture for that publisher. It's that simple. Move on, and keep looking for the right publishing home for your baby.

A STORY OF PERSEVERANCE (AND FLATULENCE)

Glenn Murray, who cowrote the Walter the Farting Dog series (North Atlantic Books), with William Kotzwinkle, knows all too well what it feels like to be rejected. No one wanted Murray and Kotzwinkle's first story of a farting dog. Until one dark and windy night:

- **Tell that great story about how your book finally came to be published after ten years of solid rejection.** "I've had a lot of requests to read manuscripts since Walter's rise to success — as if I have anything to offer! My co-author was the guy who wrote the novel *ET: The Extra-Terrestrial* (Putnam), and that still wasn't enough to get our book published. Walter's story of getting published shows that even when you try to cover all the bases, and you have an agent, it's not always enough. There's a certain amount of luck, of being in the right place, and of timing. It's amazing the difference a little time can make, especially in matters of taste or propriety. The problem was that we used the F-word [farting] in the title and throughout the book. We went out on the edge a little before the publishing world was ready for us. What's acceptable today was not acceptable then."

- **Where did the idea for *Walter the Farting Dog* come from?** "One night, when we were working on this kids' adventure screenplay, my co-author, Bill Kotzwinkle, was reminiscing about this dog he had met in an office supply store in town. This dog had a prodigious capacity to produce gaseous emissions. The dog was famous for this. When he let go, the entire store would clear out, it was that bad. I asked Bill if he remembered the dog's name and he said, 'Yeah, it was Walter.' Immediately, I could see it, the title — *Walter the Farting Dog* — blazing across the skies. 'Gee, that would be a great title for a children's book!' And we sort of let it go, like a joke. Then circumstances changed, and we had to put our children's adventure screenplay away for a while. As a consolation to ourselves, I said, 'Let's write that farting dog story.' And we did. We laughed all day long and had a pretty good time. We wrote about a dog who was making the best of a bad situation, turning his liabilities into assets, which was what we, as writers, were trying to do, as well. It was a simple, but satisfying, story, and I knew, having spent a great deal of time reading to kids in the school system, what kids like and what would grab their attention. Little did we know that we would have such a hard time selling it."

- **So what happened next?** "Bill has been published a bunch of times, so we sent it to his longtime agent, as well as to the illustrator he had been paired with on previous books. And before we even got the agent's reaction, we got rejected by the illustrator, who was not interested. But we still had high hopes. And it didn't take long before a lot of responses came in."

- **What were those responses?** "'We laughed and laughed, but we cannot publish this.' No one wanted poor Walter. Then after five years had gone by, we sat down again and tried to soften up the manuscript a little by changing a bunch of F-words to "and he did it" and the title to *Get That Dog Outta Here!* — a change that made me pretty unhappy. But we wanted to get published, and we thought it would help. It didn't; the rejections kept coming. Then, in 2001, Bill was at a dinner party, and the host asked him to get the dog story out and read it to everyone as sort of an after-dinner mint. So he did, and the entire room fell off their seats roaring with laughter. One of the guests was a publisher who said he had to publish it, even though he didn't publish children's books. That's how it all started."

- **What advice would you give fledgling writers regarding rejection?** "You can't be too sensitive at the beginning. The people at the other end have their guidelines about what their company wants to publish, and they have their own idea of what they are looking for. There is not much that we can do about it. But they are not out to get us. So as soon as the manuscript comes back, send it out again. If you have a manuscript in the mail, you have hope. If you don't, you are just sitting around kicking yourself in the head and no way anything will ever happen. Remember Ted Geisel. His first manuscript was rejected 26 times. That was *To Think That I Saw It on Mulberry Street*. And he, as Dr. Seuss, is the most loved children's book writer in America today. Do you think we would know about him if he were easily discouraged? Rejection is all about tenacity. As I tell the children I speak with: If you are gonna give up the second time you fall off a bicycle, you are never going to learn to ride a bicycle."

Chapter **18**

Considering Hybrid Publishing

As you may know from personal experience, getting published by a traditional publisher is no easy feat (see Chapter 18). Here's a little secret: it's not getting any easier.

First, a rising flood of authors who have manuscripts for children's books — some good, some not so much — are looking for traditional publishing deals. Not only that, but many of the top traditional children's book publishers don't accept unsolicited queries or manuscripts. To get their attention, you need to enlist the services of a literary agent, and these professionals are becoming ever more selective in the clients they take on.

Self-publishing has become easier, more accessible, and less expensive than it was even just a few years ago (see Chapter 19), but it's still not exactly a piece of cake with rainbow sprinkles on top. Self-publishing involves a lot of work, trial and error, and figuring things out. But if you have some spare time on your hands and want to understand the ins and outs of the publishing process, then self-publishing might be the perfect path for you.

Fortunately, you can take another path to get your book into print. If you can't gain the interest of a traditional publisher and don't want to become your own publisher, then hybrid publishing may provide the answer to all your children's book publishing prayers.

The Good and the Bad about Hybrid Publishing

Hybrid publishing is a mashup of traditional publishing (where you get paid to be published) and self-publishing (where you pay to be published), combining elements of both. You can take a variety of approaches to hybrid publishing, and it goes by different names, depending on who's doing the talking: co-publishing, subsidy publishing, author-assisted publishing, fee-based publishing, partnership publishing, and more.

Regardless of what you call it, when you work with a hybrid publisher, you most likely earn royalties — usually at higher rates than traditional publishers — but you also take on the responsibility of contributing toward the costs of publishing your book. For example, you may need to pay fees for editing, cover design, interior layout, and distribution of your book, and if you want the publisher to help you do marketing and PR, you likely have to pay a fee for that, too. The publisher may sell these services separately (à la carte) or in bundled packages.

The good about hybrid publishing

Many people find that the hybrid publishing route works for them. Here are some of the advantages that hybrid publishers offer:

>> Good hybrid publishers have quality standards at the same level as traditional publishers. You might not see any difference between a traditional and hybrid publisher's finished book, other than the name of the publisher on the spine.

>> Most hybrid publishers don't require you to submit your query or manuscript via a literary agent (though some agents include hybrid publishers in their submissions). You can make the submission yourself, significantly shortening the amount of time it takes to get your book into print.

>> The best hybrid publishers are very selective about the books they agree to publish. They don't accept a book that they see as subpar. That said, most hybrids have editors available who can help you bring your manuscript up to snuff — for a price.

>> Even though you pay some portion of the cost to produce and publish your book, hybrid publishers often pay higher royalty rates on sold books than traditional publishers. So, in the end, you may come out ahead financially if your book sells.

>> With a hybrid publisher, you probably have a higher degree of control over the final product than if you work with a traditional publisher. Because you pay much of the costs of production, hybrid publishers often allow you to make more decisions along the way.

>> When you work with a hybrid publisher, you're the customer, and they treat you as such. (A traditional publisher has booksellers as their customers. The author is not their primary concern.)

>> Hybrid publishers both print your book and also create your e-book.

>> Hybrid publishers use many of the same book distribution channels as traditional publishers, so they can place your book with wholesalers, bookstores, airport retailers, and online booksellers such as Amazon and Barnes & Noble. They often distribute your books to libraries, as well.

>> Most hybrid publishers will market your book for an additional fee, often assigning book PR people to the task. They may also create advance reader copies of your book to send out to reviewers, podcasters, bloggers, and others.

>> If you're concerned about retaining the rights to your intellectual property — the contents of your book — hybrid publishers generally grant these rights to you, ensuring that you can use it in any way you like after they publish your book.

WARNING

For many authors, good news like the points in the preceding list makes hybrid publishing the best option for them. However, before you sign on the dotted line, do plenty of research into whichever publishing option you choose. And if in doubt, enlist the services of an attorney who knows publishing agreements, or join the Author's Guild (www.authorsguild.org) and enlist their legal team to review your agreement — a service provided to members for no additional cost.

The bad about hybrid publishers

Of course, not everything in the wide world of hybrid publishing is magical flying unicorns, sweetness, and light. Although you can find plenty of good news when it comes to publishing your book with a hybrid publisher (as we discuss in the preceding section), you can also find some bad news. While you make your decision about which route to take to get your children's book published, consider these negative aspects of hybrid publishing:

>> You have to pay to play. Although you don't pay a traditional publisher a dime to get your book published, with hybrid publishers, you need to pay for many of the services they provide — sometimes, you have to shell out many thousands of dollars.

>> You may not receive a royalty advance from a hybrid publisher. If you do, it's probably relatively small — no more than a few thousand dollars.

>> You may have to commit to buying a certain number of copies of your book — sometimes in the thousands of copies — for the duration of your publishing agreement. That way, the publisher ensures that they make money on your book. (**Note:** Some traditional publishers also make this a requirement for publishing books.)

>> Although you can get your book published faster using a hybrid publisher than if you work with a traditional publisher, hybrid publishing still takes considerably longer than if you self-publish your own book.

>> Some hybrid publishers will publish any manuscript, regardless of quality. These vanity presses do a disservice, both to authors and to the book industry, in general. (See our warnings about vanity presses in the following section.)

REMEMBER

The Society of Children's Book Writers and Illustrators (SCBWI) maintains a list of Published and Listed (PAL) publishers (www.scbwi.org/list-of-pal-publishers) that meet a set of six different criteria. The first PAL criterion precludes authors or illustrators from paying money to the publisher for the publication, marketing, editing, and/or distribution of their books, which automatically disqualifies hybrid publishers from SCBWI's PAL list. Regardless, most in the publishing industry consider hybrid publishing a legitimate — and sometimes even preferable — way to get books into print.

Vanity presses: Don't say we didn't warn you

When an author can't get a traditional publisher to publish their book, they might turn to *vanity presses* — publishers that publish any manuscript for a price. The author pays all the costs of publication — plus a little (or a lot) something extra — and the vanity press takes no risk at all. Sometimes, vanity publishers ghost authors after accepting their money, producing substandard books (or in some cases, no books at all), giving vanity presses and the authors who use them a very bad reputation.

WARNING

Truth be told, you might find it difficult to figure out whether the publisher you just selected to publish your children's book is a vanity press. Many try to pass themselves off as legitimate hybrid publishers. Here are some clear warning signs:

>> You find yourself in a high-pressure sales situation, not unlike with a used-car salesperson.

>> An online search of the publisher's name leads you to numerous reports of authors who were disappointed or even ripped off by the company. Complaints often include:

- The publisher overstates promises and underdelivers them (or sometimes doesn't deliver at all).

- The production process is opaque and costs are deliberately misrepresented.

>> The publisher pressures you to pay for services that clearly don't improve the quality or salability of your book. For example, using a contest as a front. The writer pays a fee to submit their story to a contest. The "top" entries will be published in an anthology which the entrants themselves will have to foot the bill for and also must buy the copies that are printed depending on the number of "winners."

>> The publisher strokes your ego or takes advantage of your desperation to get your book published.

>> The publishing agreement requires you to pay a substantial fee to get back the rights to your book.

>> The company publishes books of low quality, poorly printed and containing typos and other issues.

TIP

Although pure vanity presses still exist, legitimate hybrid publishers have, for the most part, taken over the space formerly occupied by them, publishing high-quality books and paying royalties to authors. Writer Beware (`http://sfwa.org/other-resources/for-authors/writer-beware`), a website maintained by the Science Fiction & Fantasy Writers of America, keeps up-to-date descriptions and lists of literary scams of all sorts, including vanity presses, predatory contests and awards, dishonest literary agents, and more. Study it before you sign a publishing agreement or write a check.

Identifying the Right Hybrid Publisher for Your Book

If you decide to take the hybrid publishing path, you need to find one that can deliver a quality product at a price that makes sense for your budget. This is a tall order, especially for the new author who doesn't yet know the lay of the publishing land or what return on their investment they might see. However, you can separate the best hybrid publishers from those that aren't so great. We explore how in the following sections.

REMEMBER

You can find a lot of great hybrid publishers out there. Be sure, however, that the publisher you choose has published more than just a few children's books and has experience in your format. The best publisher for a children's book is one that either fully focuses on the genre or has a significant number of children's titles in print. Don't leave your manuscript — the labor of your love — in the hands of a beginner.

Doing your research and asking around

TIP

When you begin your search for a hybrid publisher, you can vet potential companies in several different ways. Be thorough in your research. Get all the information you need so that you can choose the very best publisher for you, one that produces a quality product at a price you can afford:

» **Ask around.** One of the very best ways to find a great hybrid publisher is to get a referral from someone who's happy with the book that their hybrid publisher produced for them. Ask other children's book writers — in person or via e-mail or social media — which publisher they used and if they're happy with the service they received.

» **Conduct online searches for hybrid publishers.** The results of your searches turn up plenty of quality hybrids, along with articles or posts by authors who have something to say about their hybrid publishing experience — sometimes good, sometimes bad, rarely indifferent. After you get a list of potential, seemingly reputable, hybrid publishers, do another round of searches, coupling the publisher's name with words such as *scam*, *avoid*, or *beware*, to see if any red flags pop up.

» **Check out writer's guides and directories.** You have a number of writer's guides and directories available to you, both in print and online form, that contain listings of reputable publishers of all sorts.

Confirming some important criteria

With so many hybrid publishers out there, all making so many promises, how do you know which one to choose? Fortunately, the Independent Book Publishers Association (IBPA; www.ibpa-online.org) has an answer to that question. Although the IBPA can't tell you exactly which hybrid publisher you should pick — that's your job to figure out — the organization has created a list of nine criteria that they feel reputable hybrid publishers should adhere to:

>> **Define a mission and vision for its publishing program.** Traditional publishers have distinct personalities, interests, and values. They don't claim to be one size fits all. Neither should quality hybrid publishers.

>> **Vet submissions.** Good hybrid publishers don't publish every manuscript they receive. They reject those that don't have sufficient quality or that don't fit the mission and vision of their publishing program.

>> **Publish under its own imprint(s) and ISBNs.** The hybrid is a real publisher that publishes real (quality) books, not a fly-by-night operation created solely to extract money from authors' bank accounts.

>> **Publish to industry standards.** The book you receive from a hybrid publisher should have the same basic elements as books published by a traditional publisher. These elements include such things as a title page, a copyright page, quality writing, professional interior design, and more.

>> **Ensure editorial, design, and production quality.** Hybrid publishers produce professionally edited and designed books that have a high level of quality.

>> **Pursue and manage a range of publishing rights.** At minimum, hybrid publishers generally publish print and digital books, but they may also pursue audiobooks, foreign editions, and more.

>> **Provide distribution services.** The hybrid publisher does more than just listing your book on Amazon. Good hybrids have their own well-developed distribution channels, or they partner with large, established book distributors (such as Ingram Content Group [simply, Ingram] and Baker & Taylor). In addition, they work with their authors to develop sales and marketing strategies that can get their books in front of the target audience.

>> **Demonstrate respectable sales.** Reputable hybrid publishers don't just print books, they also sell books — and not just to their authors. They can show that books they've published have sold in significant numbers for the particular genre.

>> **Pay authors a higher-than-standard royalty.** According to the IBPA, the author's royalty in a hybrid publishing agreement should exceed 50 percent of net for both print and digital books.

Does the hybrid publisher you're considering meet all nine of these criteria? If not, move on to another. You have plenty of reputable hybrids to choose from. (You can figure out how to find a reputable one in the preceding section.)

Approaching a hybrid publisher

TIP

Once you've decided that you want to pursue working with a particular hybrid publisher, you'll need to get your book idea in front of them for consideration. Here are a few tips for doing just that:

» **Check their submission requirements.** Go to the publisher's website to check their submission requirements, then follow them to the letter. This may be as simple as filling out a submission form on the website or you may need to send a query or proposal.

» **Send a query or proposal.** If the publisher requests that you send a query or proposal for your book, refer to Chapter 17 for advice on how to do that.

» **Be prepared to discuss your vision for the book.** Expect to get on a call with the prospective publisher so they can dig deeper into your vision for your book and how they can help you achieve it. If there's a fit, then you can move forward. If not, then you'll need to try a different publisher.

Getting the Biggest Bang for Your Hybrid Buck

If you've never worked with a hybrid publisher before, you probably have a lot of questions about what they can do for you and how much you have to pay for their services.

The best hybrid publishers today produce books that are indistinguishable from those produced by the best traditional publishers. In addition, they can provide all the same services that traditional publishers do, including distribution, marketing, and PR, but you have to pay some amount of your own money (maybe a lot of it) to get these services. The following sections take a closer look at what you can expect when working with a hybrid publisher.

Fees and payments

A hybrid publisher may adeptly and professionally deliver all the publishing services you want, but they don't provide them for free. Evaluate your goals for your manuscript and how much value you can get from each step of the publication process.

The contribution that a hybrid publisher expects you to make toward publishing your book varies considerably from publisher to publisher. As a result, we can't give you a single price range that covers all these different publishers and situations. Suffice it to say that you have to pay anywhere from the low four figures, well into the five figures, and maybe even higher, depending on the publisher and the choices you make.

REMEMBER

Some hybrid publishers want you to pay some or all of these fees up front, while others divide up the payments over the course of production of your book. Know up front what your costs will be and make sure that you can afford them before you sign on the dotted line. You don't want turning your manuscript into a beautiful book to bankrupt you in the process.

What about distribution and marketing?

Most hybrid publishers provide distribution and marketing for your book. Like with most everything else when it comes to hybrids, you have a lot of choices to make, and these choices drive up the price you ultimately pay to get your book into print.

When it comes to distribution, some of the large hybrid publishers have the ability to distribute the books they publish directly to booksellers themselves, sometimes even retaining their own salespeople. Others partner with established book distribution companies to get their books out into the world. Your publisher might offer you the option to conduct a co-op promotion, which gets your book prominent placement in bookstores. This option doesn't come cheap — it often costs between $5,000 and $30,000.

Your hybrid publisher can also offer you many different marketing and PR options: everything from conducting targeted advertising on Amazon to creating digital press kits, distributing a press release, conducting book giveaways, reaching out to podcasters, submitting your title for book awards, and much more. Because you have just so many options to evaluate, think critically about the effectiveness of each option and the potential it can deliver for your publishing goals.

ASKING AN EXPERT ABOUT HYBRID PUBLISHING

Tanya Hall is CEO of Greenleaf Book Group (www.greenleafbookgroup.com), a leading hybrid publisher and distributor based in Austin, Texas. The company recently celebrated its 25th birthday and has close to 300 children's books in the nearly 2,500 titles on its active list, with numerous bestsellers to its credit. Tanya explains the ins and outs of hybrid publishing:

- **Why should a children's book author consider a hybrid publisher?** "It's always a good idea for authors to explore the various publishing options available to them in order to find the best possible fit for their unique goals and resources.

  "Hybrid publishing is a good choice for authors who want to maintain creative control and a larger share of the royalties while also having access to a proactive distribution (sales) program and a team of experts who can create a quality product."

- **What can an author expect a typical (if there is such a thing) hybrid publishing deal to look like?** "Hybrid publishers vary by range of services and financial terms, but they all borrow elements from both traditional and self-publishing models. Each deal looks different, depending on whether illustrations are needed, scope of editorial work, cover design, how aggressive the marketing plan is, and print quantities and specs.

  "In general, an author can expect to contribute toward some or all of these production costs in exchange for control of their rights and a larger share of royalties on the back end — usually somewhere between 50 to 70 percent of net. That can be five to ten times more than a traditional royalty rate, but there is generally no upfront advance paid."

- **What does the publishing process look like on the author's side?** "Hybrid publishing is typically very collaborative since the author ultimately controls creative decisions. A smart author will trust the recommendations the expert publishing team provides concerning illustrations, design, pricing, print quantity, and so on but will have final say on these matters, unlike in a traditional publishing arrangement.

  "Typical children's book authors in the hybrid model will hire illustrators in a flat-fee, work-for-hire arrangement, as opposed to sharing royalties with them, as a traditional house might do. Otherwise, the publishing process with a legitimate hybrid publisher is not much different than with a traditional publisher.

  "Compared to self-publishing, the hybrid process will allow the author to avoid working 'in a vacuum' on their own, and instead provides support and experience to avoid critical mistakes."

- **When considering hybrid publishers, what should authors be looking for — good and bad?** "A legitimate hybrid publisher places a strong emphasis on book sales and the quality of the titles they represent. In order to vet a hybrid publisher, start with their website. Is the emphasis on selling service packages or books? If it's services, they may be more of a book packager masquerading as a publisher. Do they have a proactive sales force including in-house and field sales reps who champion their title list? Do they have experience with books like yours? Do they have bestsellers to their credit? How long have they been in business, and how experienced is their staff?

  "If retail distribution is a priority in your publisher decision, dig deep into the structure of their book sales team. Some publishers will advertise distribution services when, in fact, they only upload metadata to wholesale accounts so that the book shows up online and is available should someone order it. This is very different than the impact a dedicated retail sales force can have on book sales, especially if it is an in-house sales force with book sales accountability."

  "It's also important to look for transparency. Does the publisher dance around their business model, or are they forthcoming in how they work with authors? Are they clear about how they distribute their titles, or are you left guessing about whether or not they have any distribution muscle?

  "It's always a good idea to ask to speak with a few of the publisher's authors about their experience.

  "Finally, publishing contracts can be complex. Make the investment to have a good intellectual property lawyer with book publishing experience review any contract you're considering entering to ensure you fully understand the arrangement and your rights."

» Exploring your self-publishing options

» Pricing your self-published book

» Getting your book into the hands of your readers

Chapter **19**

So You Want to Self-Publish?

N ot too many years ago — before the proliferation of blogs, e-books, print-on-demand (POD), Kindles, iPads, and all the rest — many considered self-publishing the province of losers, the last resort of those rejected by traditional publishing houses. Well, times have changed. For an increasing number of people, self-publishing isn't the only way for them to get their books into print — it's the preferred way.

You can find a lot of good reasons to self-publish your children's book, as well as more than a few reasons you might want to avoid it. In this chapter, we explore both the good and the bad, and we consider the best options for becoming your own publisher. In addition, we take a look at what price to set for your book and then how to get it into the hands of children.

Weighing the Pros and Cons of Self-Publishing

So why self-publish? Maybe you've huffed and you've puffed, and you still can't get an agent or publisher interested in your book. Maybe you want complete creative control, and you can get that control only by doing everything yourself. Or maybe you just want to keep as much of the proceeds as possible from selling your printed book. Here are some of the best reasons for taking the self-publishing road in print:

>> **You get a viable (and perhaps the only) option for getting your book into print.** Most children's book publishers reject 95 percent or more of the manuscripts they receive. Self-publishing offers rejected authors a path to publication that traditional publishers may not be willing to provide, for any number of reasons. (We talk about the ins and outs of traditional publishing in Chapter 17.)

>> **Self-publishing is way faster than the traditional route.** It can take 18 months or more to go from pitching your idea to an agent or traditional publisher to finally seeing your book in print. With self-publishing, you can go from final, edited manuscript to e-book (or even hard copy) in just a few weeks (maybe a few months if you have illustrations). And with the advent of online self-publishing platforms such as Amazon's Kindle Direct Publishing (http://kdp.amazon.com), you can reduce this time to just hours.

>> **You're the boss!** When you print and publish your own book, you keep the rights to your work, you decide what goes between the front and back covers, and you set your own writing and production schedule.

>> **You get to keep most of the profits.** Traditional publishers and agents take a big cut of the proceeds from your book sales. If you're organized, determined, and have a knack for marketing, you can make just as much money — or more! — by self-publishing as you would if a traditional publisher produced your book.

>> **Some books actually are better off self-published.** If you write something for a small, niche audience that you have direct access to, self-publishing may give you the best way to get your book to that audience and keep the largest portion of profits.

>> **Your self-published book may draw the attention — and publishing power — of a traditional publisher.** Sometimes, self-published books that sell a lot of copies attract the interest of a traditional publisher, which can give you a golden ticket to success as a children's book author.

Although you may have plenty of good reasons to put your own printed book on the market, keep in mind a number of reasons to pass on this option:

>> **The publishing industry still takes self-published books less seriously than traditionally published books.** Unfortunately, relatively few legitimate and credentialed reviewers or reviewing sites bother reviewing self-published books (although this perspective is changing because the industry is changing), and few bricks-and-mortar bookstores carry them.

>> **Self-publishing takes a lot of work.** Writing, illustrating, laying out text and art, and arranging for printing, distribution, and promotion of a print book is no small task. Online self-publishing platforms and self-publishing consulting firms make this daunting process much easier, but you still need to put some time and effort into it.

>> **Self-publishing doesn't necessarily come cheap.** While self-publishing doesn't always have to cost a lot, some authors who select the self-publishing path spend upward of $10,000 or more to write, illustrate, print, and bind a couple hundred copies of their book to hand out to family, friends, clients, and associates.

>> **You don't get to keep all the money.** Most print-on-demand (POD) publishing platform providers want a piece of your proceeds, as do your distributors (Amazon, Barnes & Noble, and so on). If you hire a book marketer and others to help, you need to pay those fees, too.

>> **You can get scammed.** A number of shady operators know that some people will do most anything to get their books into print. Beware self-publishing promises that seem too good to be true.

Ready to give self–publishing a try? Then check out the rest of the sections in this chapter, which serve as your primer.

AMANDA HOCKING'S INSPIRING PATH TO SELF-PUBLISHING SUCCESS

So can you really find success through self-publishing — enough to create a sizable fan following and maybe even make some serious money in the process? Ultimately, it depends on the quality of your work and whether you can get the word out effectively to your waiting horde of potential fanboys and fangirls; however, a number of talented writers have done quite well without traditional publishers, and that number is growing every day.

(continued)

(continued)

Consider the example of Amanda Hocking (http://hockingbooks.com), who decided to self-publish her young adult paranormal novels after being turned down by numerous traditional publishers. Amanda started selling digital downloads of her self-published novels through Amazon and Barnes & Noble at prices ranging from 99¢ to $2.99. Within a few months, she was selling hundreds, and then thousands of copies of her books. Just nine months later, Amanda had sold a total of 164,000 books.

But that was just the beginning. In January of the following year — a one-month period of time — she sold 450,000 copies of her various books, 99 percent of them in the form of e-books. Although we don't have access to Amanda's accounting spreadsheets, we can take a wild guess (based on the typical cut of proceeds that Amazon and Barnes & Noble take from e-book sales through their sites) that she cleared hundreds of thousands, maybe even more than a million, dollars.

The publishing house St. Martin's found out about Amanda's *Trylie Trilogy* and re-released the books in traditional print. All her efforts resulted in enough sales to land her on *The New York Times* Best Sellers list. Amanda has other series in the works as of this printing, and she sells tons of her more than 30 existing books.

So we'll ask the question one more time: Can you really find success through self-publishing? In a word, the answer is, "Yes."

Exploring Your Self-Publishing Options

When it comes to self-publishing, you have an almost unlimited number of options for creating your book. You can make your self-published book anything from a stapled copy of your manuscript (produced on the printer in your home office or at a local copy shop), to an interactive e-book app that you can read on an iPad or Kindle, to a top-quality hardcover that no one can distinguish from the best book produced by a traditional publisher or independent press.

REMEMBER

Although you can choose from many different self-publishing options, they generally fall into one of two categories: print and digital. Sure, you find some overlap in the way you create, promote, and distribute these two categories of books, but ultimately they're completely different animals.

In the sections that follow, we closely examine each of these beasts and provide you with the information you need to make an informed choice about which route — print, digital, or both — works best for you and your book.

The print route

Although the world of digital books is expanding rapidly, a lot of people still buy — and prefer to read — good, old-fashioned printed books. Despite the proliferation of e-books, printed books are nowhere near extinct, and they aren't on anyone's endangered species lists — at least, not yet.

The following sections consider two of the most common approaches to getting your self-published book into print: working with an offset printer and taking the leap into print-on-demand.

Working with an offset printer

Offset printers truly just do what their name suggests: They print. You provide a file, and they print it to certain specifications. Even when a traditional publisher prints copies of a book, they use offset printing. Nearly every city has one or more printing companies (as do many small towns) that use the offset printing process to create a wide variety of different products, including flyers, business cards, brochures, restaurant menus, envelopes, sales sheets — and books.

For years, offset printing was the first choice in self-publishing methods. It's fast and relatively affordable, and you can get a finished product of quite good quality; however, because a printing company does just that — printing — you personally have to take on many of the tasks a typical traditional publisher completes. (*Remember:* Publishing is not the same as printing.) Tasks that a printer typically doesn't do include

>> Editing and formatting your manuscript

>> Designing a cover (plus or minus an image) and interior page layout

>> Creating or obtaining illustrations

>> Proofreading the final copy to make sure it contains zero errors of any kind (copyediting, as well, if you have a nonfiction work)

>> Deciding on a trim size and binding type

>> Choosing paper and other materials

>> Obtaining an ISBN (the International Standard Book Number), required to sell your book commercially, and a Cataloguing in Publication Number (CIP) from the Library of Congress (LOC)

>> Warehousing your book if you handle distribution and sales by yourself or hooking up with a fulfillment and distribution house so that they can handle these functions for you

>> Marketing and promoting your book

TIP

Before settling on a particular offset printing company, first do your due diligence. Get quotes from different companies and get answers to the following questions so that you can make an informed decision:

>> Does the company have experience printing books like yours?

>> Do samples of their work look well done and professional? Does the company guarantee your book will end up the same?

>> Does the company do its printing in-house, or do they outsource the work to other companies — or even other countries?

>> Can the company accommodate your schedule?

>> Do they offer reasonable prices and fair payment terms?

>> Can they warehouse and ship out the books per your instructions (if you need them to do so)?

Taking the print-on-demand (POD) path

Print-on-demand (POD) publishing can save you time and money when compared to working with an offset printer. With POD, instead of ordering a set print run through an offset printer, the POD service prints copies of your book when they receive an order. The POD process works like this:

1. **Set up an account with a POD service.**

2. **Upload your completed manuscript and cover files.**

3. **Review the proof file that the service generates.**

    Order a physical proof if you want to see it in hand.

4. **Approve the file and indicate that the service can publish/release it.**

    When someone orders a copy, the POD service prints it, packages it, and mails it out. The service also keeps track of sales.

Within these steps there are options to consider. For instance, if you don't have print-ready manuscript and cover files, you can pay for this service because most PODs will offer this as an option. If you want more targeted advertising and marketing, if you want to order a bulk amount, if you want foreign rates, PODs will offer these options as well, and some have packages if you need more help with a certain step in the process.

Each POD publisher offers a wide variety of publishing packages and services. In some cases, the POD publisher's website clearly presents these packages; in others, you need to schedule a personal consultation. Figure out which level of POD processes works for you:

>> **Basic, bare-bones service:** This level of service puts most of the work in your hands. You can choose from some basic cover and interior templates; you need to edit, format, and proofread your own manuscript. Potential buyers can get your book in a trade paperback edition. (At this price level, you probably can't include illustrations.) This service starts at around $50 and goes up from there. Although Kindle Direct Publishing (http://kdp.amazon.com) and Blurb (www.blurb.com) set you up with this basic level of service for free — you pay only for the books you order.

>> **Mid-level service:** You have even more templates to choose from than with the basic service, and you get to customize your book's look, as well as its cover. You can also add illustrations, tables, and an index, and you have the option of a trade hardcover or paperback edition. At this level of service, your manuscript may receive a basic edit, you can expect the paper and materials to be of a higher quality than the basic level of service, and you probably receive a nominal number of copies of your book for no additional charge. This level costs you from $750 to $1,250 and up.

>> **Deluxe, top-of-the-line service:** This service offers the highest possible control over your book's design, along with the best materials and finishes. Deluxe includes all features of mid-level service, as well as a higher level of editing. It allows you to talk to a designer, combining your creative input and their expertise to achieve the personalized page design and cover look that you want. This level also includes even more copies of your book at no additional cost — likely in hardcover format. This service costs from about $1,500 on the low end, all the way up to many thousands of dollars.

In addition to these up-front fees, you pay every time you order a copy of your book (beyond the author copies included in your plan, if any). Print-on-demand books vary widely in price, depending on the publisher — anywhere from $3 to $50 or more per copy for a trade paperback.

The print-on-demand scene is in a constant state of flux, and a company that's hot one year may be dead and gone the next. Currently, some of the top print-on-demand companies include Kindle Direct Publishing (http://kdp.amazon.com), owned by Amazon and therefore designed to play well with the Amazon website; IngramSpark (www.ingramspark.com), known for its strong distribution channels; Blurb (www.blurb.com), which specializes in books with a lot of illustrations or photos; and BookBaby (www.bookbaby.com). Any of these companies can easily meet your print edition self-publishing needs — you just have to weigh the costs.

REMEMBER

Make sure you closely examine exactly what you need and compare it to exactly what you can get before you commit to any POD publisher. Some of the tasks that they charge for are super easy to DIY (do it yourself), so make sure you're not paying for something as simple as clicking a button that you can press all on your own. In some aspects of publishing, you don't face a very steep learning curve. If you plan to publish more than one book, you might want to familiarize yourself with the steps.

The digital route

You can find most books published today also available as *e-books*, or electronic books, published in the form of a digital file that you can read on a variety of electronic platforms, including smartphones, tablets, dedicated e-readers (such as Kobo and Kindle), and good old-fashioned laptops and desktops. As a self-published author, you have the option to forego a print book and create an exclusively digital e-book. If the digital route sounds right for you, ask yourself these questions — your answers determine the approach you should take to publishing your e-book:

>> For what platform(s) do I want to publish my e-book?

>> What do I want to do with my e-book after I publish it?

To create a professional-looking e-book that has all the bells and whistles that you want to offer for sale on Amazon or Barnes & Noble in significant quantities — while making some money in the process — you can take your e-book to one of the POD publishers described in the preceding section. Many of these companies also offer e-book publication services that can set you up on Amazon or other websites.

If you want to create a professional looking e-book that you can sell on Amazon and other websites, but you don't want to spend a lot of money (and you're willing to do more of the work yourself), we suggest you consider an e-book publishing platform. Each platform offers pluses and minuses. Closely compare the offerings to see which one is best for you:

>> **Smashwords** (www.smashwords.com): Using its proprietary e-book publishing and distribution platform for e-book authors, publishers, agents, and readers, Smashwords offers multiformat e-books through its website, which visitors can browse, buy, and then read on most e-readers including Kindle. Smashwords can also distribute your e-book through Apple Books, Barnes & Noble, and Kobo.

- **Kindle Direct Publishing** (http://kdp.amazon.com): If you want to sell your e-book solely on Amazon for the Kindle e-reader, then consider using the Kindle Direct Publishing service. You can create Kindle books for free, use your Microsoft Word manuscript files to create your e-book, and make your finished product available on Amazon, which sells far more e-books than any other website.

- **Apple Books for Authors** (http://authors.apple.com): By using this Apple word-processing application and its included book templates, you can easily create your own e-book that incorporates text, photos, image galleries, videos, audio, shapes, and much more. After you complete your book, you can publish it directly to the Apple Books site at whatever price you decide.

TIP

If you simply want to create a casual e-book to send to friends and relatives, and you have no intention of selling the book commercially (at least, not now), then you can easily produce it yourself by using standard word-processing software (such as Microsoft Word or Apple Pages) and saving your file as a PDF that readers can view on computers, tablets, smartphones, and other digital devices.

Setting a Price for Your Publication

No matter which format you chose to publish in, setting a price for a self-published book is the subject of much debate — and sometimes anguish. In our experience, you have three key choices:

- **Emulate the traditional publishers with your printed book.** You can price your printed book to make it consistent with comparable traditionally published books. So if you have a hardcover book similar in size and page count to most 32-page hardcover picture books, you can price your book anywhere from $14.99 to $24.99, like a traditional publisher would.

- **Charge just a little bit of money.** A low price of between 99¢ and $4.99 can help you generate sales, which can lead to positive word-of-mouth recommendations from readers — and more sales. Successful YA author Amanda Hocking took this path (see the sidebar "Amanda Hocking's inspiring path to self-publishing success," in this chapter).

- **Give it away for free.** Perhaps the most controversial approach to pricing your self-published book, although in some cases, you may find it the most rewarding option. Many new authors use this strategy, offering their self-published e-books online for free in hopes of generating huge reader interest and buzz in the process.

TIP

Alternatively, you can use a combination of pricing approaches. For instance, when you first launch your e-book, you can give it away for free for a certain period of time — perhaps for a week or even a month — to gain audience traction (while social networking, marketing, and promoting it like mad). Then, after you have enough people downloading your book for free, you can change the cost to 99¢. Then, when you really have a solid readership and feel your book can sustain the increased price tag, move it on up from there. If you write more than one title in a series, perhaps you give away the first title until you publish the second title; at that point, your first title goes up to 99¢ or more, and the new title sells at $4.99. You can choose from a lot of creative pricing structures. Find out more about promoting and marketing your books in Chapters 20 and 21.

REMEMBER

You get to make the decision about how to price your self-published book; make sure it fits in with your overall marketing strategy. Just keep in mind that if you make the price high, fewer people probably purchase it; alternatively, if you make the price low, more people probably purchase it. The amount you make may be about the same, whichever way you go.

Distributing Your Self-Published Book

One of your greatest challenges as a self-published author involves getting your books into the hands of potential readers. Although traditional publishers can easily get their books into bookstores, self-published authors don't have the same ability. The following sections give you the scoop on getting your self-published book out into the world.

Getting in the door at traditional bookstores

Self-published authors can't easily get their books into traditional bookstores. Traditional bookstores work directly with established traditional publishers, small and independent presses that have track records of successful publishing.

This is one of the great trade-offs of every author's publishing endeavor. An author either faces barriers to entry, getting an in with a traditional publisher on the front end of this process, or facing the barrier to entry on the distribution end of the process. Traditional bookstores, well, you guessed it, they work with the world of traditional publishers. Don't be discouraged by this because there is just as much a self-publishing distribution world as there is a traditional distribution world. This is an opportunity for you to be creative with reaching your audience. The self-publishing distribution process can be a rewarding adventure.

Of course, self-published authors can get in the door at traditional bookstores. You may have an in if you're a local author (many bookstores have shelves devoted to books of local interest) and you develop a good working relationship with the bookstore owner or manager. To get your book into a real, live bookstore, make an appointment with the store's manager or book buyer, and bring along the following:

>> A sample copy of your book

>> A one-page sell sheet that provides

- Details about your book (author, publisher, ISBNs, cover price, page count, and trim size)

- A short description of the book and its intended audience

- Photos of the book cover and the author (you!)

- A brief author bio (and illustrator bio, if applicable)

- Information about where the bookstore can order your book (whether through a distributor or through you directly)

>> A *pitch* — the story you tell to convince the bookstore owner, manager, or book buyer to carry your book. This pitch shares a lot of qualities with the query letter that you send to traditional publishers, described in Chapter 17.

Persuading online booksellers

You can convince online booksellers — even the big ones such as Amazon and Barnes & Noble — to sell your self-published book pretty easily, whether your book comes in hard-copy or digital form (or both). We both personally know numerous authors who sell their self-published books through these sites and others like them. You just need to follow the instructions on their website about how to format the book for uploading, establish a business relationship, and then supply copies of your book.

If you choose to print actual copies of your book and sell a certain quantity directly to an online bookseller (yay!), then you need to periodically ship more books to them on an as-requested or as-sold basis. If you have an e-book, you don't have to worry about shipping books at all after you send your online bookseller the e-book file.

Decide which online booksellers you want to approach, then visit their websites and follow their procedures for getting your book into their systems. Here are two of the best:

>> AbeBooks (www.abebooks.com)

>> Powells (www.powells.com)

You can sell your book at as many online bookstores as you like — even creating different versions of your book for each.

Considering other places to sell your book

Many self-published authors have found success selling their books outside of the traditional bookselling channels.

You might consider selling your self-published children's book at some of these places:

>> Facebook fan page or website created just for your book

>> Discount link on Twitter

>> School or library readings

>> Your personal blog

>> Instagram, TikTok, or YouTube (or whatever the media-of-the-moment might be)

>> Book fairs

>> Trade, literary, or publishing magazines

>> Gas stations, convenience stores, gift shops, car washes, local restaurants, antique dealers — most anyplace (just make sure you can tie it into their theme or other merchandise in a logical, sales-oriented pitch)

>> Local crafts fairs or farmer's markets

In addition, since you become an independent book publisher when you self-publish your book, be sure to check out the website for the Independent Book Publishers Association (https://www.ibpa-online.org/page/booksellers), where you'll find all sorts of resources that can be helpful in marketing your book.

Chapter **20**

Donning Your Publicity Cap

Getting your book onto a bookstore shelf is only one part of the thrill of being a published children's book author. The other part — which is just as important — is getting your book off the bookstore shelf and into the hands of a child. And you must play a big part in making that happen.

In this chapter, we present the basics of publicizing and promoting your books. Not only do we address some of the tried-and-true techniques for building a buzz around your books, but we also take a good look at the pros and cons of hiring a professional publicist and doing book tours and readings.

REMEMBER

Keep in mind that publicity is not a one-size-fits-all kind of thing. Each author and each book will have some tools and techniques that are a better fit than others. Pick and choose what makes sense to you and have fun with it.

Understanding How Your Publisher Promotes Your Book

Most authors we know expect their publishers to roll out a multimedia marketing blitz that can make their books household names — and *New York Times* bestsellers — overnight. Unless your name is J. K. Rowling, Sandra Boynton, Stephenie Meyer, Jeff Kinney, or any number of other bestselling authors, you probably don't get this kind of treatment.

REMEMBER

At a minimum, your publisher should engage in the following promotional efforts:

>> Send out press releases.

>> Mail copies (or e-mail PDFs) of your book to key reviewers and review sites.

>> List your book in its sales catalog and on its website.

>> Create *sales copy* (sales-y summaries of your book) for Amazon and Barnes & Noble listings.

>> Support book signings.

This limited amount of publicity gives your book a good start, but you can do much more — either by yourself or with the help of a professional book publicist whom you hire (see the section "Hiring a Publicist," later in this chapter) — to get the word out about your book. This chapter gives you the tools you need to help promote the result of your hard work.

TIP

Regardless of what your publisher ultimately agrees to do, make sure you closely coordinate your own publicity efforts with theirs. You definitely don't want to duplicate (or leave significant gaps in) your efforts.

Publicizing Your Own Book

The thought of doing your own book publicity can be both exciting and overwhelming, thanks to the almost unlimited number of potential tools available, such as websites, blogs, videos, radio and television interviews, press releases, podcasts, and social media. Ultimately, though, taking a two-pronged approach to publicity can get more eyeballs for your book by embracing both the digital and traditional components of publicity campaigns. We outline some of these components in the following sections; for a crash course in using social media to spread awareness of your book, head to Chapter 21.

Focusing on the digital components

When we wrote the first edition of this book back in 2005, you accomplished most book publicity efforts through good old-fashioned in-person meetings, phone calls, faxes (remember those?), and snail-mailed letters and promotional copies. Today, you accomplish most book publicity efforts digitally (and inexpensively) by way of e-mail, websites, blogs, and social media. So focus your initial publicity efforts on the digital world. You can start by creating an online presence for your book and e-mailing your very own press release.

Building an online presence for your book

Nowadays, every effective publicity campaign needs to build an online marketing platform to display, promote, and sell your book. Here are the most effective online marketing platforms (for detailed advice on using social media to market your book, see Chapter 21):

- **Website:** Feature your book on your own existing website or create a new website dedicated to your book. You can also try to get other website owners to feature your book and link to your site.

- **Blog:** Feature your book on an existing blog or create a new blog dedicated to your book. Like with websites, you can try to get other bloggers to talk about and link to your book's site.

- **Podcasts:** You can start your own podcast or get booked for interviews on already existing podcasts. If you retain the audio rights to your book in your traditional publishing contract (or for promotional purposes), you might want to create a series of podcasts of you, the author, reading chapters of your book aloud.

- **YouTube or TikTok videos:** You can create videos based on your book and post them to YouTube or TikTok. (If you post to TikTok, use the #BookTok hashtag, which we talk more about in Chapter 21.) If you want to earn some bonus points, consider creating a series of videos based on your book, setting up a YouTube channel for potential readers that they can visit, and then subscribe and watch your videos.

- **Book trailer:** Back in the day, only movies got trailers, but now many books do, as well. Publishers and authors can go all out with animation or use a quality smartphone or a digital camera to create a catchy trailer to post on YouTube, TikTok, your website, your friends' websites — anywhere. If you want to take it to a higher level, then consider enlisting the services of a professional video production company.

- **Facebook:** You can create a *Facebook author page* (a Facebook page just for your book), make your book a part of your existing Facebook page, or even buy an ad — or two or three.

- >> If you have your book listed on Amazon, you can buy ads on Amazon to promote your book. Be sure to keep track of your ad's stats to figure out what PR approach leads to the most sales for your book.

- >> **Twitter, Instagram, and other social media:** If you have a Twitter, Instagram, or other social media account, then you can send out a steady stream of notices about your book, as well as about other books and authors that you love. Engage with your audience, don't just sell your book. And if you don't have a social media account? Get one.

REMEMBER

A well-designed online marketing platform can give you a powerful advertisement for your book. And — best of all — it's available 24 hours a day, seven days a week, and potential book buyers can view it anywhere in the world.

Sending out press releases

A *press release* (also known as a *media release* or *news release*) is simply a brief, written notice of some newsworthy event — in this case, the publication of your book. You generally send out press releases via e-mail or by way of an online press release service.

REMEMBER

A press release is most often one — and never more than two — pages in length. Work hard to keep it to only one page. Here are the key parts of a well-written press release:

- >> **Release date:** Unless you want the end recipient to hold off on using the information for some reason, the release date for your press release should read FOR IMMEDIATE RELEASE (and yes, use all caps).

- >> **Headline:** Write a punchy, one-sentence hook that makes your audience want to read more. Be creative and have fun. Capitalize the first letter of all the words in your headline except articles (*a, an, to,* and *the*).

- >> **City, state, date (when you're sending out the release):** Your reader wants to know where you are and how timely the press release is.

- >> **Introductory paragraph:** Write a strong introductory paragraph that includes who, what, when, where, why, and how about your book — as concisely as possible.

- >> **Body:** The heart of your press release. It should be at least two paragraphs long (but remember — keep your press release to no more than a page).

- >> **Biography:** A brief biography of the book's author — you.

- >> **Detailed contact information:** The name, address, phone number, website address, and e-mail of the person to contact for more information about the book.

Figure 20-1 shows what a press release that uses the preceding elements might look like.

FOR IMMEDIATE RELEASE

New Kid's Book Digs Deep Into the Past

Chicago, IL, January 5, 2027 — Bestselling children's book author Divvy Bobivy digs deep into the Egyptian pyramids in her new book *Who Built the Pyramids*? published by Acme Press in January 2027 and available now for $19.99 at Barnes & Noble, Amazon, and other fine book retailers nationwide.

In what promises to be her next blockbuster children's book, Divvy Bobivy blows the lid off centuries of myths and misinformation surrounding the mysterious Egyptian pyramids. An amateur student of archaeology, Bobivy has long wanted to write a book bringing ancient history to life for its young readers, while finding the truth behind these mysterious structures. Says Bobivy, "I've long had a fascination with the pyramids — where they came from, who built them, how they were built. This book brings it all together for me in a fun and fact-filled way."

Author Bobivy has tapped into a huge potential audience with her latest book. A recent study by researchers at Techmasters shows that 79 percent of all readers age 8 to 12 years are interested in learning more about the ancient pyramids. This group of influential potential readers numbers in the millions.

For additional information, contact ChloBo Boochee at 312-555-1212 or chlobo@bestbookpromoters.com.

About Divvy Bobivy: Divvy Bobivy is a bestselling children's book author who has written or co-written more than 25 titles, including the blockbusters *What's That Smell?* and *Baby, You Can Drive My Go-Kart*.

CONTACT INFORMATION:

ChloBo Boochee

Best Book Promoters

312-555-1212 (voice)

chlobo@bestbookpromoters.com

www.bestbookpromoters.com

FIGURE 20-1:
A sample press release for a children's book.

Who should you target with your press release? Anyone you think may have an interest in reading it, including newspaper reporters, radio and television talk show hosts and producers, children's book bloggers and website operators, podcasters, magazine editors, bookstore owners, and librarians.

TIP

Whenever possible, address your press release to a specific individual in an organization. A press release addressed to a specific person has a much better chance of getting read, which means you have a much better chance of getting the media attention you seek.

In addition to your own list of places to send your press release, you may also consider sending it out using an online press release service, such as

>> Business Wire (www.businesswire.com)

>> Cision PR Newswire (www.prnewswire.com)

Getting reviews

If you want to get your book reviewed, you need to find someone to review it. In some cases, your publisher needs to submit your book to the reviewer for consideration; in others, you can submit your book yourself. Check the submission guidelines for direction.

Here are some tried-and-true places to get your book reviewed:

>> *The Horn Book* (www.hbook.com): *Horn Book* reviews only children's and young adult books. The magazine is published six times a year.

>> *School Library Journal* (www.slj.com): This publication focuses on reviews of books for children and teens.

>> *Goodreads* (www.goodreads.com): According to Goodreads (owned by Amazon), it's the world's largest site for readers and book recommendations. You can join the Goodreads Author Program for free, which allows you to manage your profile, promote your books, and interact with readers.

>> *Publishers Weekly* (www.publishersweekly.com): *Publishers Weekly* is the bible of the publishing industry, and they invite you to submit your book for review at no cost. Reviews are very competitive, however, so many books never actually get reviewed.

Publishers Weekly also offers a paid review service called Booklife Review that you may want to check out if you can't seem to round up any unpaid reviews. You can find the submission guidelines at http://booklife.com/about-us/review-submission-guidelines.html.

- » ***Booklist*** (www.booklistonline.com): A publication of the American Library Association (ALA), *Booklist* naturally targets librarians, and its reviews cover every possible genre, not just children's books.

- » **Amazon** (www.amazon.com): Customers leave reviews for many books listed for sale on Amazon. Some books have thousands of these reviews. If your book is available on Amazon, encourage your readers to leave their own honest reviews.

- » **Barnes & Noble Review** (www.barnesandnoble.com/review): Reviews fiction and nonfiction books, as well as essays, interviews, and other features.

- » **Bloggers/#BookTok:** Get your book in front of bloggers and TikTok users who do children's book reviews (using the hashtag #BookTok). See Chapter 21 for more information on promoting your book through social media, including how to use #BookTok.

TIP

If you decide to send your book to a reviewer for consideration, carefully follow their submission guidelines. At minimum, expect to send reviewers a free digital copy of your book — some reviewers may prefer an actual book. And keep in mind that reviewers receive many requests for book reviews, so you need to be patient. If you haven't heard back within a month or so, send them a gentle status request.

Touching on the traditional components

You have publicity options outside of the Internet and social media. More traditional approaches to getting your book noticed still work. Consider putting together a press kit and arranging promotional radio and television interviews.

Putting together a press kit

REMEMBER

A *press kit* is a collection of press materials that an author or publisher sends to the media (radio, television, newspapers, magazines, blogs, podcasts, websites) to get them interested in covering your book. Although everyone used to send out hard-copy press kits, digital press kits are more commonly used today. They're less expensive than hard copies and faster to produce and distribute. Either way, the best press kits contain the following:

- » **One-page press release:** Describes your book as breaking news. (We tell you how to craft a press release in the section "Sending out press releases," earlier in this chapter.)

- » **Two-paragraph bio:** Include interesting tidbits describing you and your background. For example, "As a nationally syndicated columnist, Genny has been interviewed on NPR and CNN."

- **Bulleted fact sheet or essay-style background:** Give some info about your book. For example, "Two years of research showed that pandas don't actually prefer bamboo leaves."

- **FAQ (frequently asked questions):** Eight to ten suggested questions that the reporter might want to ask you during an interview. For example, "How did bells become so important to the story?" or "As a full-time amateur archaeologist, how do you find time to write?"

- **Copies of past press clippings:** To show that you're newsworthy.

- **List of past and future signings or events:** Shows relevance, competence, and experience.

- **A sample article:** Basically, create a short version of your press release that a busy media professional can print verbatim if they want (make sure you include a copyright release at the bottom of this sheet).

- **Photos:** A picture of the book cover and headshots of the author and/or illustrator.

- **A copy of your book:** Depending on how many free books you negotiated for in your contract, which we explain how to do in Chapter 17, you can give them a hard copy of your book. Otherwise, sending them a PDF works, too.

- **Giveaways:** Such as bookmarks, posters, or pencils that your publisher may produce to garner word-of-mouth advertising.

TIP

You can drastically reduce the cost of hard-copy press kits by writing the material yourself and printing it from your home office. Target your recipients carefully, and create a downloadable PDF version of your press kit for your blog, Facebook author or book page, or website.

Booking radio and television spots

In the bang-for-the-buck department, you can't beat getting interviewed on a radio or television show. In particular, shows on major network radio and television stations reach a very large audience; so do some cable shows. If you get the call for an interview on *Today* or *Good Morning, America*, you may think you've died and gone to heaven.

You simply can't buy this kind of exposure for your book, but you can get your book in front of the producers or hosts — national and local — who are constantly on the lookout for interesting people with fascinating stories.

Here are some tips for getting booked for radio or television interviews:

>> **Understand your market.** Research your local stations, the networks, and the TV shows you're interested in. Get their schedules, check out their websites, and tune in. Don't even think about pitching yourself before you've done your research.

>> **Have a hook.** Why should the radio or television producer or radio host book you for this show? If you want to be booked, you need a hook — the aspect of your story that's going to rivet viewers and listeners, preventing them from changing the station.

>> **Be selective.** Don't send your press release out to 1,000 random radio and TV stations — instead, pick out the 15 to 25 that might actually be interested in you and your book. Start with local stations. Work those prospects thoroughly, and then select another batch of stations.

>> **Target a live human.** Target a specific show, get the name and e-mail address for whoever books guests (usually a producer, program director, or booker — sometimes the host), and send your press release to that person directly.

>> **Be persistent, accessible, and flexible.** You never know when you'll get the call for an interview or appearance. Be persistent — stay in the minds of those doing the booking for your targeted show by sending a press release every once in a while — and be accessible and flexible if the show needs someone to fill in unexpectedly.

THE WONDERFUL WORLD OF BOOK REVIEWS

Rhonda Sturtz is the marketing and social media director of New York Journal of Books (NYJB; www.nyjournalofbooks.com), an influential online book review site. Here, Rhonda goes into the whys and wherefores of book reviews:

- **Why should children's book authors care about reviews of their books?**
  "A review guides the potential reader inside the cover, beyond the first impressions, into the guts. A review introduces your book and reveals something about what's inside so the reader can make an informed decision about whether or not to spend the money to buy it or the time reading. A review opens the door, inviting the reader inside."

(continued)

(continued)

- **How should authors attract the attention of reviewers?** "With professional reviews like NYJB, typically you must go through administrative channels to get your title assigned to a reviewer. Starting your campaign for a review early is important, at least four months before release date. The more lead time you provide, the better chance of getting your book on a reviewer's schedule. You can reach out by e-mail. Some authors or publishers mail advance copies, but this is costly and doesn't always work. You can also try to reach out personally and attempt to set up appointments with publishers of book reviews. Emphasize a hook, what's important or timely about your book, and how it impacts the cultural or literary dialogue."

- **Do book reviewers really ignore self-published books?** "There is a great deal of worthwhile work being self-published today. At NYJB, we don't cover self-published titles only because the universe is so large, we would be inundated with requests and do not have the staff to cover that tsunami. There are, however, some review sources today focusing on self-published works."

- **What can authors do to facilitate the process of getting reviews?** "It takes time and effort, but these days, you can use social networking websites and online press releases to promote your book, as well as develop a list of contacts. You can also hire a publicist to do this work for you."

- **What are some good ways to leverage reviews for publicity?** "Network, network — and network some more. Link to them on your website and Facebook; send out (free) e-press releases with compelling review blurbs; post on Amazon (don't forget to fill in your Amazon author page); and do e-mail blasts with relevant updates."

- **If an author gets a bad review, can they do something about it?** "If you're an author, you must have thick skin and understand that not everyone will love your work. I don't like to use the word *bad*. I distinguish between favorable and unfavorable reviews. The best you can hope for is a solid review that reflects an understanding of your work. If certain negatives are noted, well, nothing is perfect. A rave review is a gift, but overall, you hope that the reviewer will connect with your work and offer constructive commentary. Many authors have contacted NYJB about the reviews of their work, and what they appreciate most is that our reviewers seem to 'get it.'"

- **Should authors consider paying for reviews of their books?** "We at NYJB feel a paid-for book review is compromised and lacks integrity. How can a reviewer be objective if the opinion they are writing is purchased by the author? At NYJB, we feel it is essential to maintain credibility and complete objectivity by keeping an appropriate separation between authors and reviewers. All review requests and scheduling is done through admin. And we do not accept any payment for reviews."

Promoting Your Work in Person

Sometimes, you just need to give your book's publicity a personal touch, putting yourself out in the world and mingling with your readers and the people who are often in charge of your readers' literary choices — namely, parents, retailers, teachers, and librarians. Whether you want to hit the road for a full-fledged publicity tour or stay closer to home and conduct book signings or readings or targeted workshops, the following sections have you covered.

Planning a publicity tour

Many new book authors think that after their publisher releases their book, the author goes out on a multi-city publicity tour, complete with media handlers, tour guides, limousines, and travel expenses paid in full. Unless you're a celebrity or an established bestselling book author, you probably don't get this treatment.

TIP

You can, however, create your own publicity tour. When you're planning to visit another town or city, line up some publicity while you're there. You can do a little or a lot; it's up to you. Here are some ideas:

>> Drop by some bookstores and offer to sign some copies of your book.

>> Offer to read at local schools and libraries.

>> Schedule a local radio or television interview or two.

>> Make yourself available to local print media.

With a little advance planning, you can accomplish a lot — all on your own schedule.

Joining the signing and reading circuit

One of the key ways that children's book authors get publicity is to do book signings and readings:

>> **Book signings:** Either informal, where you drop in unannounced and sign however many books of yours happen to be in stock; or formal, where you and the bookstore set up a signing event on a specific date for you to chat with customers and sign books.

TIP

Be sure to bring a couple of fresh, fine-point, permanent markers in whatever color you like — they're great for signing books.

>> **Book readings:** Generally scheduled well in advance so that the organization can fit it into their routines, and announced far enough in advance to generate interest in the event — and attendees.

Whether you decide to pursue a book signing or a reading, simply call the organization that you want to work with and ask for the person in charge of arranging author events. You'll soon be on your way to getting the word out about your book.

Hiring a Publicist

Authors love to write books, but many authors don't feel the same way about publicizing and marketing them. Maybe you don't feel comfortable selling books, or maybe you just don't know anything about the process. For these reasons and more, consider hiring a professional book publicist. A good publicist isn't cheap, but they can make the difference between a book that sells a few copies and a book that sells a few hundred thousand copies. The following sections explain exactly what a good book publicist can do for you, how to find one, and how to get your money's worth.

Discovering what a publicist can do

The most important thing a publicist can do for you is get your foot in the door at a media outlet, generating enough interest to get you scheduled for an interview, profile, or other article. Specifically, a good book publicist can

>> Draft and distribute digital press releases, press kits, and brochures.

>> Set up interviews with print journalists.

>> Schedule live and phone-in radio and television interviews.

>> Build buzz through their network of traditional and social media contacts.

>> Arrange book signings and readings.

>> Place articles and book excerpts in publications — both print and online.

>> Submit your book to reviewers.

>> Schedule appearances at conferences and seminars.

>> Submit your book for consideration for awards and prizes.

When it comes to publicity, a publicist can do just about anything you'd ever need this side of writing your book. What you have your publicist do for you is limited only by the size of your bank account.

INSIDER TIPS FOR PUBLICIZING YOUR CHILDREN'S BOOK

When it comes to publicizing your new labor of love, you need to make a big splash and get noticed in a sea of competing titles. We asked children's book PR professionals Barbara Fisch and Sarah Shealy, of Blue Slip Media (www.blueslipmedia.com), and social media marketing maven Megan Barlog, of Purple Shelf Media (www.purpleshelfmedia.com), for the inside scoop on how to do just that:

- **What publicity should authors expect from their publishers?** "We would answer that by saying authors need to change their expectations. Publishers do quite a bit overall — from making sure the metadata is correct on a book when it appears on booksellers' websites, to ensuring books are presented to the appropriate audiences (librarians, teachers, booksellers) throughout the year, to sending out to award committees, and more. But in-house publicists can be juggling as many as 20 to 30 books a season, so it's true that many authors don't receive as much individual attention for their books as they might like. That's where authors need to educate themselves on publicity and promotion, and explore what kinds of extra publicity and promotions might benefit their book.

  "Here are areas that the major children's book publishers will cover as a matter of course:

  "Send review copies to the top trade reviewers (*Publishers Weekly, School Library Journal, Kirkus Reviews*, etc.).

  "Ensure books are sent to key influencers in the education market.

  "Send digital seasonal catalog outreach to a larger list of media and educators.

  "Include the book on their website and social media channels.

  "Reach out to general interest/consumer media, such as *The Wall Street Journal, Parents* magazine, etc.

  "Reach out to social media influencers.

  "Work with Amazon, BN.com, Indiebound, Books-A-Million, and other online retailers.

  "Present the book to indie booksellers and the big chain bricks-and-mortar stores.

  "Submit for the big awards, as appropriate (Newbery, Caldecott, etc.).

  "Display at the major conferences such as American Library Association (ALA) and National Council of Teachers of English (NCTE)."

(continued)

(continued)

- **Despite social media's importance in publicizing books, should authors still pursue traditional print and broadcast media for publicity?** "This largely depends on the audience you are trying to reach. If your audience is retirees who still read the newspaper every morning and have no idea what TikTok is, you'll still want to pursue traditional print and broadcast media in order to reach them. However, just about every other age demographic is on some form of social media:

  "You want to cast a wide net in your publicity efforts, so while more traditional media might not be a huge part of your plan, you should still include local and key outlets."

- **What are the three most effective things authors can do themselves to publicize their books?** "First and foremost — authors need to have a website and keep it up to date; ideally, a website should be ready at least 12 to 18 months before a book releases.

  "At the bare minimum, your website should have your author bio, your book cover and description with pre-order or purchase links/buttons, links to all your author social media accounts, and a contact page.

  "Second, have an active social media presence on at least one platform. Pick the platform you are most comfortable with to start rather than trying to be on all the platforms at once.

  "Third, reach out to your local media — your town's weekly paper, your library's newsletter to patrons, the daily newspaper in your region, your local morning weekend news shows."

- **What are the three biggest publicity mistakes authors should avoid at all costs?** "On social media, avoid being baited into a public verbal sparring match. Too many authors have found themselves in heated Twitter wars that made their publicists cringe. If someone is trolling you online, don't engage.

  "Don't be a diva. Booksellers, teachers, and librarians all need your respect and appreciation, and if they see you as a respectful, supportive customer or patron, it will pay off in myriad ways.

  "Manage your expectations. It's extremely difficult to be interviewed on *Today* or have Oprah rave about your children's book. Be happy and appreciative of any coverage you receive, be it a lovely blog review or a photo of your jacket in your local bookstore's monthly newsletter. Be mindful that you are building a career, and that each review and article is a step on that path."

- **What should children's book authors look for in a good book publicist?** "There are a lot of good book publicists, but the first thing we'd recommend is to look for someone with expertise in children's books. Look at the books they've worked on. Are they similar in age range/genre to your book?

"A children's book publicist will know the media landscape and where best to focus your and their efforts. Ideally, this publicist will want to be collaborative with your publisher — that way, they can dovetail efforts. It's also important to feel that this publicist will communicate with you well and be open to your ideas — and also honest when they know certain types of activities or outreach won't benefit you or your book."

Finding the right publicist

Hooking up with the right publicist is a little like dating — you really don't know how things are going to work out until you spend a little time together. If you decide to hire your own publicist, be sure they have the following:

>> **Significant experience promoting children's books:** Few publicists have specific experience in publicizing books, and even fewer have experience publicizing children's books. Don't fool around; hire publicists who have a solid track record of experience successfully publicizing children's books.

>> **Established media contacts:** In the publicity business, the *Golden Address Book* — your extensive network of traditional and social media contacts — is everything. Your ideal publicist has a well-developed list of contacts to whom they can take your book — contacts who will give it serious consideration.

>> **Creativity:** The best publicists are always trying out new and creative ways to get the media's attention — and to draw attention to you and your book, while also covering the basics.

>> **An assertive but pleasant manner:** Assertive is good; aggressive is bad. Someone who's pleasant to work with can get you a lot more interviews than someone your media contacts try to hide from.

>> **Time for you:** When you're paying someone your hard-earned money, they should answer your phone calls, respond promptly to your e-mail messages, and always treat you professionally — with dignity and respect.

>> **A personality that meshes with your own:** You not only need to trust this person implicitly, you need to get along with them. Spend some time with your prospective publicist (on the phone, Zoom, or over lunch) before you sign on the dotted line.

>> **A knowledge of industry trends:** Books are a business, and the business of books is in constant flux. Your publicist should be up to date on the latest trends and constantly adjusting their approach to respond to those changes.

To find a publicist, ask other children's book authors for referrals. If you belong to a group such as the Society for Children's Book Writers and Illustrators (www.scbwi.org), ask around. See whether you can get referrals from your literary agent, your editor, a friend or relative, or someone else you trust who's connected to the business.

Getting the most for your money

You don't want to shell out a ton of money to a publicist without getting results in return. After you make the decision to engage a publicist, and after you find a good one, you need to ensure you get your money's worth. Here are a few tips for doing just that:

» **Don't wait until the last minute.** Ideally, engage a publicist at least four months before your book is published. Six months is better.

» **Get a proposal.** Get a written proposal from your publicist-to-be that details exactly what services they provide and exactly when they'll provide those services.

» **Set a fixed price and ceiling.** Publicists usually work in one of two ways: a fixed price for an entire marketing campaign or a fixed hourly rate. If you go with the latter, set an overall ceiling price that your publicist can't exceed without first obtaining your written approval.

» **Put it in writing.** Get all agreements with your publicist in writing and signed.

» **Get reports.** Require your publicist to provide regular (weekly or monthly) reports of what they've done on behalf of your book — phone calls made, press releases sent, producers contacted, and so forth.

» **Meet regularly.** Start with monthly status update meetings, and ramp them up to weekly meetings within a month or two before and after publication. Don't just listen to what your publicist has to say — engage and push for more and better opportunities to publicize your book. Make it a partnership, not a solo performance.

» **Assess and reengage (or say good-bye).** Take time to periodically take stock of where you are: Has the publicist done what they promised? What are the results? If you're happy, continue the relationship. If not, don't hesitate to fire your publicist and find a new one.

A good publicist can be your best friend. By taking care of the business side of things up front, your relationship can proceed on a firm foundation of trust. And that's good for you — and for your book.

Chapter **21**

Getting Savvy with Social Media

Unless you've been living under a rock for the past 10 years or so, you've probably noticed that apps such as Instagram, Facebook, TikTok, YouTube, and others like them that feature content created by everyday Joes and Janes — collectively known as *social media* — have taken the world by storm. The result has been a gold rush of people, companies, and other organizations eager to establish social media platforms.

Although the jury is still out about whether having a social media platform is the end-all-be-all for the average children's book author, we personally believe it's a key element in any effective book marketing effort. So, in this chapter, we look at exactly who to influence, the best places to establish your social media platform, and how to launch a successful social media campaign. If all of this is new to you, don't worry. Take your time figuring out the different options and allow yourself plenty of space for trial and error. In addition to the material in this chapter, consider checking out *Social Media Marketing For Dummies* by Shiv Singh and Stephanie Diamond (Wiley).

Influencing the Influencers

When you market your book via social media, you don't want to do all the talking yourself — get other people talking about you. In our experience, you especially want to get people who can influence others to talk about you.

When the first edition of this book was originally published in 2005, we made a special effort to mail free copies to as many established online children's book bloggers and reviewers as we could find. The hope was that they would talk about this book on their blogs or write book reviews that would appear on influential websites. They did. Our strategy worked, and it helped make this book the #1 book about writing children's books on Amazon.

Little did we know back then that we were practicing a kind of marketing that was relatively new: *social influence marketing*. This kind of marketing simply involves employing social media to gain the attention — and mentions — of *social influencers* (people who have achieved a large social-media presence, often in the tens or hundreds of thousands of followers, possibly even more).

We have no doubt that social influence marketing should constitute a key part of your book marketing efforts. So where do you start? You start by understanding the basics of influencing others.

The basics of influencing others

Although using social media to influence others is a relatively recent phenomenon (Instagram was launched in 2010, TikTok in 2016), social influence itself isn't. People have long sought out the advice of trusted others — friends, relatives, neighbors, colleagues, experts — when they make decisions of all sorts. These decisions can range from something as simple as where to stop for lunch to something much more complex — and potentially risky — as whether to buy a house in a particular neighborhood for a particular price by using a mortgage with specific terms and conditions. Reviews and references have inundated our lives, and they can greatly affect decision-making. (Some people won't even go to a restaurant or book a hotel unless it has five-star reviews. Your book is no different: Reviews matter.)

We influence others every day, and others influence us. We are social creatures, and influencing and being influenced is a perfectly normal and often quite welcome occurrence. We want to know whether a decision we're about to make is going to be a good one or a bad one — especially if the decision has the potential to significantly affect our lives. In the same way, we want to let our friends and significant others (heck, the whole world!) know when a decision we made worked out in our favor (or not, because that information can serve as a cautionary note to others that we care about).

When you think about buying something, you can buy two kinds of products or services:

>> **Low-consideration purchases:** These items generally don't cost much, and one product is pretty much like another. Purchasing them is a low-risk proposition for the buyer. Examples include a pack of chewing gum at a convenience store or a hot dog at a baseball game. If you don't like the gum or the hot dog, you can toss it out with just a small financial loss. You're probably not going to ask your friends whether you should buy a particular brand of gum. The opinions of others probably don't influence you much one way or the other.

>> **High-consideration purchases:** Usually expensive and highly differentiated. After you buy them, you're pretty much stuck with them. Think about the process you go through when you buy a car. You ask friends and work associates how they like their cars, you read reviews, you comparison shop and take test drives. You know if you make the right decision, you'll be a happy driver for the next five years or more. Make the wrong decision, however, and you could be stuck with a very costly lemon.

Although a children's book is certainly not at the same price level as a new car, most cost far more than a pack of gum. Readers want results from their book purchases. As such, people often seek out the advice of others when they buy children's books, a behavior that provides children's book authors (like you) the opportunity to apply the principles of social influence marketing when selling your book.

Understanding the different kinds of online influencers

REMEMBER

When it comes to influencing others online, three major kinds of influencers exist — each of whom exerts influence on you in a particular way:

>> **Positional influencer:** Influencers who are socially (and often physically) close to you in some way — relatives, spouses or partners, boyfriends, girlfriends, bosses, co-workers. You get the picture. Because these people are closest to your purchasing decision, they have the most influence.

>> **Referent influencer:** Influencers with whom you hang out (and trust) on social media platforms such as Instagram and Facebook. If someone you

follow on Instagram mentions that they love their new Apple MacBook, then you probably take note. And if you're in the market for a laptop, then you probably automatically include the MacBook on your short list.

>> **Expert influencer:** Expert influencers are, well, experts — the people you consult when you're planning to make a high-consideration purchase and you want to make sure you don't make a costly mistake. They may regularly write or record reviews for their personal websites, social media platforms, or traditional media outlets (newspapers, magazines, television, radio, and so on). You probably don't personally know expert influencers (they often have huge followings in social and traditional media), but because of their demonstrated knowledge and expertise, you trust their opinions and give high consideration to their advice.

By understanding how each of these three major kinds of influencers exert their power over others, you can better determine where best to focus your own social influence marketing efforts.

Figuring out where online your influencers live

You have to make a crucial decision: where to target your social influence marketing efforts. You can't possibly get your message on all the many blogs, podcasts, Facebook author and book pages, message boards, and other social media devoted to children's books. Don't even try. Be selective when it comes to deciding which influencers to approach and which ones to pass by.

REMEMBER

Although a quick Internet search reveals a near-endless list of social media devoted to children's books, not all sites are created equal. Some are probably lucky to attract one or two visitors a month, whereas others attract many thousands. Clearly, if you want to influence the influencers, it makes more sense to put your focus on the sites that get the greatest number of visitors and attract the most comments and contributions from others.

Knowing Where to Create a Social Media Presence

The world of social media is constantly evolving. The site that's big today may be old news in a matter of months, weeks, or even days. (Remember MySpace? Friendster? Google+?) Stay aware of what's going on with social media and focus your efforts accordingly.

The sections that follow clue you in to several currently popular social media platforms and offer tips for how to use them to your promotional advantage.

Blogs

Blogs are online journals that give you the opportunity to write about the process of writing, pass on tips and lessons learned, review the work of other writers and illustrators, and connect with other children's book writers and potential buyers of your books. Many children's book authors make writing a blog an essential part of their social media presence, posting at least once a week — and sometimes more often than that.

On the other hand, some children's book authors forego the time, effort, and money required to create their own blogs, instead focusing their efforts on being interviewed or getting their books reviewed by bloggers. Take a look at these children's book blogs to get a feel for the kinds of sites that have gained strong followings over the years:

» Here Wee Read (`www.hereweeread.com`), by Charnaie Gordon

» Seven Impossible Things Before Breakfast (`www.blaine.org/sevenimpossiblethings`), by Julie Danielson

» Cynsations (`www.cynthialeitichsmith.com/cynsations`), by Cynthia Leitich Smith

» SCBWI: The Official Blog (`http://scwbi.blogspot.com`), by Lee Wind

» A Fuse #8 Production (`http://blogs.slj.com/afuse8production`), by Elizabeth Bird

Podcasts

Podcasts (talk or music audio programs that listeners can download or stream online) have opened up an entirely new avenue for promoting children's books — or any book, for that matter. Like with blogs, you can choose to create your own podcast, appear on someone else's podcast, or do both. If you decide to create your own podcast, know that it takes a lot of work and time to build a following, but after you get it going, you can use it to build your social media presence.

Instead of creating their own podcasts, many children's book authors put their focus on booking interviews on existing podcasts. Keep in mind that podcasts need a steady stream of content to stay afloat, so podcasters are always looking for people to interview. Check out these podcasts about children's book topics — whether you're looking for ideas to start your own or to book an interview on an existing podcast:

» Picturebooking (www.picturebooking.com), with host Nick Patton

» The Yarn (http://blogs.slj.com/theyarn), with hosts Travis Jonker and Colby Sharp

» First Draft (www.firstdraftpod.com), with host Sarah Enni

» Julie's Library (www.julieslibraryshow.org/episodes), with hosts Julie Andrews and Emma Walton Hamilton

» 3 Point Perspective (www.svslearn.com/3pointperspective), with hosts Will Terry, Lee White, and Jake Parker

Goodreads website

According to the company's website, Goodreads (www.goodreads.com) is "the world's largest site for readers and book recommendations." Goodreads certainly carries a lot of weight in the publishing industry: The site has somewhere in the neighborhood of 90 million registered users, many of whom post reviews of books they've read — good, bad, and indifferent.

And although you can't control what those people post about your books, you can join the Goodreads Author Program (www.goodreads.com/author/program). If you join, you can claim and manage your author profile page, promote your books, and engage with Goodreads members; and you earn an official Goodreads Author badge to use in your promotional efforts.

Facebook

Facebook (www.facebook.com) is currently the 3-billion-pound gorilla of social media (that's about how many monthly active users the site currently has worldwide), and most every children's book author has by now established a presence there. While you consider how exactly you want to put Facebook to work promoting you and your books, keep in mind that you can create a variety of different kinds of pages on Facebook, each of which has its pluses and minuses. Page categories include Author, Book, Publisher, Independent Bookstore, Book Series, Education, and many others.

At minimum, we suggest you create an Author page. You can then customize this page any way you like, including publishing posts, photos, videos, excerpts and illustrations from your books, event invitations, your biography, and much more. Visitors can simply Like the page to follow you, and you don't have to do a thing.

Twitter

Although many people wondered for some time whether a microblogging site that limited posts to no more than 140 characters (increased to 280 characters a few years ago) really had much use, Twitter (www.twitter.com) looks like it's here to stay. That being the case, many children's book authors create a Twitter feed to keep their followers up to date (by the nanosecond) on their goings on.

Instagram

Instagram (www.instagram.com) started out as a place where people could post favorite photos. What made it unique was the availability of filters that users could select to give their photos a different look (for example, the Juno filter brightens warm hues and increases color intensity). Since then, Instagram has added messaging, a feature to post a sequence of photos and videos as stories that people can see for 24 hours, *reels* (multi-clip videos of up to 30 seconds), and more.

YouTube

You may have spent too much time on YouTube (www.youtube.com) watching videos of cute cats, funny kids, aspiring singing stars, and who knows what else. Children's book authors can (and do) create short videos and book trailers based on their books as effective selling tools, and YouTube can host them.

If you decide to create promotional videos for your children's book, we suggest you set up your own author channels on YouTube. On those channels, you can host all your videos, making it easy for visitors to find, comment on, and subscribe to your updates.

TikTok

TikTok (www.tiktok.com) is a video-based social network a bit like YouTube, but with millions of videos that are usually much shorter in length — from a few seconds to a few minutes. TikTok is all the rage right now, especially with young viewers who post (and watch) videos in a variety of categories, including comedy, gaming, food, dance, beauty, animals, sports, and more.

TIP

The key to success in promoting your book on TikTok? See what other successful authors are doing on the site and keep a close eye on fast-changing TikTok trends. Oh, and create engaging videos that get people to watch them, share them with others, and then follow you on the site.

#BookTok

We can't mention TikTok (see the preceding section) and not bring up a phenomenon that's having a significant effect on book sales: #BookTok. #BookTok is a TikTok user community whose members post videos of their book reviews and recommendations by using the #BookTok hashtag. As an author, you can post #BookTok-focused videos on TikTok, building connections with your followers and adding to your sales.

They Both Die at the End (Quill Tree Books), a young adult science fiction novel written by Adam Silvera, experienced a big sales bump after becoming a darling of the #BookTok community. Videos using the hashtag #TheyBothDieAtTheEnd attracted over 37 million views as of mid-2021.

Pinterest

Pinterest (www.pinterest.com) allows users to bookmark inspirational images that they find during their travels around the web. Children's book authors can use it to promote their own personal brands and books. Check out these authors' Pinterest pages to find inspiration for how you can use Pinterest to promote yourself and your work:

>> Kami Garcia (www.pinterest.com/kamigarcia)

>> Mike Mullin (www.pinterest.com/mikemullin)

>> Debbie Ohi (www.pinterest.com/inkyelbows)

If you have a blog or website, include that address on your Pinterest home page, along with your handles on Twitter, Instagram, YouTube, and other social media. Oh, and include a fun description about yourself that makes it clear you're a children's book author worth checking out.

EXPERT EMMA WALTON HAMILTON ON EMBRACING SOCIAL MEDIA FOR YOUR CHILDREN'S BOOK

Emma Walton Hamilton (www.emmawaltonhamilton.com) is a bestselling children's book author, editor, educator, and arts and literacy advocate. She has co-authored more than 30 children's books with her mother, the actress Julie Andrews, nine of which have been on the New York Times bestseller list. Emma is also an independent children's book editor; a faculty member of Stony Brook Southampton's MFA program in Creative Writing, where she teaches all forms of children's literature; and a co-founder of the annual online conference Picture Book Summit. She has established a particularly strong social media platform and presence, and here's her perspective on the role of social media in the children's book world:

- **Which social media platforms, if any, do you consider musts for children's book authors?** Facebook and Twitter continue to be essential, as are Instagram, YouTube, and TikTok.

  "On Facebook, it's very important to have an author page as well as a profile. This allows your readers (or their parents, caregivers, librarians, or teachers) to find the information they are looking for without having to wade through personal posts — and it also allows them to follow you without your having to "friend" them. Facebook is most important for picture book authors and illustrators, since books for that age group are purchased by adults.

  "Twitter is important not just for promotional purposes but because that's where agents and editors are, which makes it a great resource for researching wish-lists. Twitter also offers pitch-parties, such as #PBPitch and #PitMad, among many others.

  "YouTube is important for book trailers and author videos; and for middle grade and young adult authors, it's also where *BookTubers* — passionate readers who share video reviews of their favorite books — hang out.

  "Also important for middle grade and young adult authors is TikTok, since most teens these days gravitate to that platform over the others.

  "And of course, one of the best ways to build a following is via an author website."

- **What's your own approach to social media?** "I maintain an author website, a Facebook profile and author page, an Instagram account, a Twitter feed, a profile on LinkedIn, and a YouTube channel. That said, I'm not great about keeping them all updated. I tend to focus most on Facebook and Instagram. The key for me lies in linking as much of it together as possible. For instance, everything I post on Twitter

(continued)

(continued)

or Instagram also goes to Facebook, and so forth. It's fairly easy to connect everything these days."

- **What are the best ways to build a following?** "I think the first question to ask yourself is, 'Who is my audience?' Who are you trying to reach? For instance, YA authors are likely to be reaching out directly to their readers, since so many teens use the Internet as their primary source of information. But picture book authors really need to reach out to parents, booksellers, librarians, teachers, and others who put books in the hands of young children. Obviously there's some overlap, but it's important to consider whom you're talking to before you start putting yourself out there.

  "It's also important to think about what you're going to offer them. The authors who are most successful at using social media provide their readers and followers with added value, something that goes beyond just promoting books and appearances. Perhaps they are encouraging young writers, or expanding upon a specific subject they write about. They might offer links to support materials, such as coloring pages or quizzes, or host giveaways or contests. But they are doing more than just self-promotion, which is essential these days to break through the noise.

  "For those who have a new book coming out, virtual book tours are a great way to build a following. Rather than (or in addition to) touring cities, stores, or other real-life venues, authors can connect with readers online, via websites, social media, blogs, podcasts, digital conferences, web-based articles and reviews, YouTube and TikTok videos, etc. The key is to ensure that the effort is as structured and coordinated as it would be if you were on a 'real' book tour, and that it unfolds over a similar period of days or weeks.

  "Finally, and perhaps most importantly, the buzzword when it comes to using social media is *reciprocity*. Authors whose posts are purely self-promotional are less likely to develop a following than those who provide the kind of added value mentioned above: who reach out and connect with their followers and industry colleagues. Taking the time to reply to comments, for instance — whether on your blog or your Facebook page — is key, as is posting your own comments on other people's pages. It's all about building, being part of, and contributing to the online community."

- **If you could do only one thing in social media to promote your books, what would you do?** "At this point, either create an author page on Facebook or an Instagram account. You can create tabs dedicated to individual titles (which become their own sub-pages), and you can post information about and invite followers to events, among many other things."

- **What fatal errors should authors avoid in social media?** "First of all, if you've been using Facebook, Instagram, or Twitter to tell friends what you had for breakfast, stop. Start viewing these sites as the powerful marketing tools that they are. Once you start using them correctly, you won't want your followers looking back at random posts or embarrassing pictures.

> "Paradoxically, it's really important not to make all your social media efforts about yourself. Again, aim for community instead of tooting your own horn. It's what you stand on, who you are. It's your value system. That's what your followers are really interested in.
>
> "Finally, don't spend so much time on social media that you stop writing! Keep working on your writing first and foremost. Without that, the rest is meaningless."

Making a Splash: Launching a Social Media Campaign

Although a key part of establishing a powerful social media platform is persistently and consistently building your online presence by using the various tools at your disposal, also plan to make a big social media splash whenever you release a new title. You can make this big splash by launching a social media campaign.

Reviewing the ABCs of a social media campaign

So you want to launch a social media campaign — great! Now what? We suggest you do the following:

1. **Clearly define your goals in advance.**

   You might, for example, want to drive people to your children's book author Twitter feed, increasing your followers from 250 to 1,000 within a two-week period of time. Make sure your goals are SMART: Specific, Measurable, Attainable, Relevant, and Timely.

2. **Pick a form of social media you want to target with your social media campaign, and then do a Google search for that form of social media in combination with the search term *children's book*.**

   For example, if you enter blog *children's book*, you get a (very) long list of children's book blogs.

3. **Decide how many social media sites you want to initially target in your campaign.**

   Maybe you want to target ten sites — or ten sites a day. It's all about the time you want to put in.

4. **Visit the sites in rank order of their listing from your Google search.**

Keep in mind that, in general, the higher the ranking in a Google search, the more visitors the site attracts and the more influence it has on others. Always keep your eye on the prize — you want to leverage your social media efforts to the largest possible audience.

5. **Consider each site in turn to determine how you might be able to have an influence on the site's visitors.**

You might, for example, send a copy of your book to get reviewed on a blog, offer a contest with a signed book as the prize, or become an active commenter on that blog — providing valuable insights and influencing other visitors.

6. **Create a list of the high-opportunity sites.**

Namely, the ones you most want to influence.

7. **Execute your social media plan.**

Visit each of the high-influence sites on your list and accomplish the actions you think will have the greatest impact.

8. **Evaluate your results.**

If your results meet or exceed your goals, then keep doing what you're doing. If not, then adjust your approach and try again. See the section "Measuring the Effectiveness of Your Campaign," later in this chapter, for detailed information on getting feedback and acting on it.

Getting noticed on social media

After you decide that you want to create and run a social media campaign, what can you do to make a splash and get noticed? You have a lot of competition out there for the hearts, minds, and eyeballs of potential buyers of children's books. You need to do something to stand out from the rest of the pack. Here are some tried–and–true ideas:

>> Do a book giveaway on Facebook, Instagram, Twitter, and your website. You can even give away e-books on Amazon or other retail sites for a specific period of time.

>> Create a fun TikTok video related to your book.

>> Get booked to do a podcast interview (the more, the better).

>> Send copies of your book to children's book influencers (bloggers, Facebook members with large followings, and so on) to encourage interviews and reviews. (Ask the influencer whether they'd like to receive a copy of your book before you waste your time and resources.)

- >> Offer special bonuses to people who buy your book on launch day (or preorder in advance). For example, include exclusive access to your private YouTube videos in which you discuss the inspiration behind your books and the writing process.

- >> Hire a book publicist who specializes in social media.

- >> Tag influencers in your posts (for example, Lisa's Twitter handle is @KidsBookWriter, and Peter's handle is @bizzwriter).

- >> Offer to do virtual book readings and discussions for schools, libraries, and youth groups. You can use Zoom, Microsoft Teams, or another virtual meeting app.

- >> Ask your friends and family to help talk up your book on social media.

- >> Use hashtags (for example, #childrensbook or #newauthor) to attract people searching for those terms, and playful emojis in your posts to entertain (just don't overdo it!).

- >> Create memes and graphics based on your books (covers are great!) and sprinkle them liberally throughout your social media platforms. If you use your cover, make sure you can clearly see the title and your name on the cover image.

- >> Do five things every day on social media to promote your book.

Surveying the unwritten rules of social media marketing

REMEMBER

Although you can structure your social media campaign in many different ways, these inviolable rules of the road ensure you get the best possible response — and results:

- >> **What goes around comes around.** Social media depends on the idea of "you scratch my back, and I'll scratch yours." If you're going to ask your prospects to take valuable time out of their day to read your blog, watch your video, or peruse your Facebook author page, you have to give them something in return. In some cases, you might just need to give them some great information that they can't get anywhere else. In others, they might want a physical reward, such as an autographed book, a free digital copy of another book, or a reading at their child's school.

- >> **Your prospects are all created equal.** When it comes to your social media campaign, you need to treat everyone equally. No one is more special than anyone else. If you decide to reward some sort of bonus — say, a free downloadable excerpt from your next book — to people who view your YouTube video on your Facebook author page, then you need to offer the bonus to everyone who watches your video. In fact, you want to encourage people to pass the link on to their friends, who in turn pass the link on to their friends, and so on. ***Beware:*** If you're really good at what you're doing, that bonus could number into the thousands, and then you have to sweat mailing costs if it's not digitally transmittable.

>> **Be real. Be authentic. Be you.** Most people ultimately sniff out a phony.

>> **Post other things besides your book promos.** Nothing gets old faster than an author who only publishes info about their own book.

>> **If you truly love your campaign, you have to let it go.** The best social media campaigns take on a life of their own, which means you may lose control of them soon after you release them into the wild. This is actually a good thing — you want your campaign to catch fire and take off. Set your goals, design a great campaign, make adjustments if you need to, and then let it go.

Applying search engine optimization

If you've been tinkering in social media for any amount of time, you've probably heard the term *search engine optimization* (SEO), which simply means designing your website, blog, or other marketing platform in a way that attracts the greatest possible interest of search engines such as Google, YouTube, Bing, DuckDuckGo, and the like.

TIP

Here's a short list of SEO to-do's:

>> Use powerful keywords on your site. (*Keywords* are simply words that stand out to search engines. Lisa's website uses *children's book writer, book editor, e-book editor, fiction editor,* and other keywords so that search engines can easily find her.)

>> Build your web pages so that search engines will love them, including optimizing header tags and meta descriptions, using internal linking, and improving page load time.

>> Encourage other sites to link to your site.

>> Keep abreast of changes in SEO and adapt your web presence accordingly.

We could write an entire book on the specifics of how to accomplish this to-do list, but Peter Kent already did in *SEO For Dummies* (Wiley). Check it out.

Measuring the Effectiveness of Your Campaign

Can you tell how effective your social media campaign was without measuring the results? In a word, no. No matter how many friends complimented you on your new book, how many comments you received on your latest Instagram post, or how many people pinned a photo of the cover of your book to their Pinterest boards, you really have no idea how effective your campaign was until you measure the results.

TIP

Here are some of the measures you should consider for some of the most common social media platforms:

» **Blog:** The number of visitors, the number of comments your visitors make, and the number of times they share links to your site with other people or other social marketing platforms (by using, for example, the Like button for Facebook or by retweeting a post of yours on Twitter)

» **Facebook:** The number of fans of your author fan page, the average growth in the number of fans, the number of page interactions generated by each post you make, the click-through rate of your stream, and much more

» **Twitter:** The number of mentions that you or whatever you're promoting receive, the number of retweets of your own tweets, the number of click-throughs, and more

» **YouTube:** The number of views that your video generates, the demographics of the viewers (say, 18- to 24-year-olds), and the number of comments and shares your video accumulates during a specific period of time

Social media measurement tools are constantly improving. Be sure to keep up with the latest offerings of whatever platforms you decide to target for your social media campaigns. If you're not getting the results you expected, make sure you use the best platform for your goals. Things change, so your audience may have moved somewhere else: Facebook and YouTube today, something else tomorrow.

REMEMBER

To properly measure the results of your social media campaign, you have to start with clearly defined SMART goals (Specific, Measurable, Attainable, Relevant, and Timely).

6

The Part of Tens

IN THIS PART . . .

Get inspired with a ton of storyline sources.

Set your sights on some of the most important and well-known children's book awards out there.

Chapter **22**

More Than Ten Great Sources for Timeless Storylines

Y ou can employ certain premises for story lines time and again. Whether your take on an existing story sounds derivative is up to you and your writing skill. But ever since we writers started scratching our stories on the walls of caves or sitting around a fire listening to a tale told with a good cup of tea, we've been sharing our experiences and imaginings with others. And some of these experiences and imaginings are more universal than others.

TIP

If a story was written prior to 1923, it's probably in the public domain. To find out whether anyone owns a story — and whether you can retell it in your words without getting in trouble, see our discussion of public domain in Chapter 17. Also, try an Internet search for the story name with key words *public domain* and see what information comes up.

In this chapter, we list some fabulous resources for story lines that you're welcome to pilfer and tinker with to your heart's content because no one — and everyone — owns them.

Tales of Yore: Fairy and Folk Tales, Fables, and the Like

Fairy tales, folk tales, and fables are all fictional stories told generation after generation (some for hundreds of generations). They're usually short (the length of short stories, as opposed to novels) and often devoid of description or context-setting narrative, focusing only on character and action. They vaguely capture a bygone period of time or history — when you read the original version. And they often embody a lesson or moral — or you can deconstruct them to reveal one. Classic tales are a subgenre of this category. They are tales that have been told again and again by different writers.

Although you can have difficulty trying to discern one of these types of tales from the other, and the subjects in one type mirror subjects in another, you can distinguish each of these categories by a few salient differences:

>> **Fairy tales:** Fanciful and imaginary stories about people, animals, things, or magical beings who have magical powers. They have satisfying themes, such as good triumphing over evil. Fairy tales follow certain conventions: You definitely know who the good guys are, magic often abounds, and the bad guys usually get their due.

WARNING

If you choose to adapt fairy tales, go back to the originals and not to the Disney adaptations. Certain additions to the Disney tales aren't public domain (and you don't want to incur the wrath of The Mouse).

>> **Fables:** Stories that have a point, a lesson, that's supposed to help the reader live better, understand something about a specific culture, or comprehend the natural world. Fables are heavy-handed morality tales in which animals and humans learn obvious little lessons. Although we don't advise preaching to children in your haste to teach them everything you know or believe (a very common mistake made by first-time writers), we do think fables provide interesting moral dilemmas and lessons that you can disguise with good writing.

>> **Folk tales:** Folk tales involve the traditional beliefs, practices, lessons, legends, and tales of a culture or a people passed down orally through stories. Folk tales have ways of explaining basic natural truths for each culture, such as where the world came from, why humans have power over animals, why animals act the way they do, why the seasons change, and so on. They mostly focus on the natural world, but like fables, they can also focus on human behavior; however, they rarely have that preachy, moralistic tone of fables. Often, folk tales require the characters to use their wits to solve a problem.

>> **Classics:** Classic tales have existed over dozens or hundreds of years. Some have gone into the public domain, meaning you can use them to retell or adapt them. *Alice's Adventures in Wonderland,* by Lewis Carroll (Macmillan), is one classic that's gone into the public domain.

Mythology and Mythological Heroes

The Greeks and Romans (and every other ancient culture) developed heroes and antiheroes that populated exciting stories of adventure, magic, and power — covering every imaginable activity, behavior, hope, and emotion that humans or immortals could conceive. These mythologies, regardless of origin, have been adopted into nearly every culture and religion in the world in some way or another, representing universal experiences.

Nursery Rhymes

Nursery rhymes — those little ditties from your childhood — are great sources for characters and story lines. Imagine "Mary, Mary Quite Contrary" as the star of her own hip-hop troupe. Or what if "Little Miss Muffet" wasn't arachnophobic and instead befriended the spider? How would Jack and Jill have approached the hill if one of them were physically challenged? Nursery rhymes are also perfect for getting you in that kid-space, rhyming, upbeat, fun-time, story line–writing mood.

Bible and Religious Stories

The Bible, both the Old Testament and the New Testament, is full of exciting stories. The Bible provides plenty of both miracles and controversy, and it can give you a great launch pad for children's stories. The Torah (Talmud), the Koran, Buddhist teachings, and Native American/indigenous stories are also great sources for stories.

Family Issues and Changes

Most children must face changes that alter the delicate balances of the family unit in subtle and not-so-subtle ways. Because children seem to thrive with structure (which ultimately allows them to fly free and experiment in the world in healthful, appropriate, and constructive ways), and because family is the most basic and important structure in their lives, any issue facing a family affects them. Some issues that you can write about include separation or divorce, remarriage, adoption, nontraditional families, moving to a new neighborhood, and abusive situations.

Sibling Issues

Certain experiences, especially involving siblings, can really alter the entire course of a child's life. What better story line for a sibling in need than one that revolves around issues facing siblings, such as when a new baby comes home, or when parents favor one sibling over another, or when a sibling becomes seriously ill?

First Experiences

Few things are more touching than thinking about a child facing an experience for the first time. For some reason, we sentimentalize (as in "How cute!") these situations, when in actuality, a child finds such experiences more often exhilarating or frightening (or something in between). In other words, anything but cute.

REMEMBER

The list of firsts is endless — and continues way past babyhood. Scour your memories for some memorable firsts in your own life or in the lives of your family members for some potent story line material.

Common Childhood Fantasies

Who hasn't longed to live in different circumstances or wished to be a different person altogether? Children move in and out of their fantasy worlds many times during a given day. More importantly, fantasies provide great starting points for interesting story lines. Consider fantasies built around astronauts, fairies, princesses, mad scientists, pirates, monsters, secret agents, wishes, and so forth.

Friendship and Social Issues

From the first time they attend a Parent and Me class to their first sleepover, children are thrust into social situations that become more and more integral to their well-being while they get older. Soon, friends supplant parents as favorite people to spend time with. You can probably come up with a ton of issues regarding friendship, such as a child trying to figure out all the ins and outs of being a friend, or navigating middle school, or dealing with mean kids. Just take yourself back to elementary school, middle school, or high school days, and it should all come rushing back to you. Some classic topics include peer pressure, cheating, smoking, drugs, religious or racial differences, and bullying.

Growing Pains (Emotional and Behavioral)

Children, even the tiniest ones, experience new and powerful emotions all the time and don't know how to handle them. Some children seem to just barely survive, whereas others make these experiences seem easy. But what if children had access to wonderful stories that star a relatable someone who has to deal with these same issues in their own lives? Then children could explore their options without leaving the comfort of their favorite secret fort. Some of our favorites include feeling shy, being left out, losing a friend to a different clique, having a disability, experiencing fears, and dealing with mean kids.

REMEMBER

Topics in this category include the simple act of growing and ongoing developmental milestones, the LGBTQIA experience, abuse — physical, psychological, verbal, and more — and addiction.

Bodies and the Brain: Their Functions and Changes

Children of all sizes and ages have to figure out how to deal with bodily functions and changes. In the last decade, quite a few books about bodily functions that polite society used to consider taboo have become raging bestsellers. Consider content, fictional or nonfiction, about body types and differences, the uses of your five senses, brain development, or potty training.

REMEMBER

Topics include eating disorders (such as anorexia and bulimia), which affect many adolescents, and sometimes even kids in their tweens; and mental illness, which affects millions of people worldwide. Because of the dark and serious nature of these topics, you probably want to cover them in middle grade or YA books.

History Makers and History in the Making

Have you ever felt captivated by a time in history or wondered what it felt like to be in the shoes of an especially fascinating contemporary or historical figure of note? You can find a lot of material for children on the usual suspects (think presidents, pilgrims, and scientists of yore), but what about today's makers of history? What about today's visionaries, such as entrepreneurs and modern-day game changers plucked from the news? Consider inventors of newer medical devices, people and cultures in developing countries, talented singers and dancers, contemporary writers and poets, and more.

REMEMBER

Teachers and librarians love books about history and historical figures because kids often have to write reports about them. Check your state's core curriculum and find out what grades explore what topics. You can probably find good subjects in those topics. And ask your local librarian or teacher about books they wish they could add to their curriculum or collection. Get ahold of a copy of any Advanced Placement course textbook, such as AP United States Government and Politics, if you really want to be in the know about what most college preparatory K–12 systems are teaching toward. It's amazing how robust the curriculums are compared with just a generation ago. Students are becoming quite savvy in many topics. If you want to contribute to the enormous body of knowledge already out there, make sure you know what they are already being exposed to.

Nature, Science, Technology

Publishers covet stories that have natural, scientific, or technological content. If you have a well-written book that covers a contemporary topic and adopts a unique approach, you have a better-than-average chance of getting published. Teachers, librarians, and parents always want new and exciting material to supplement what's taught in school — meaning material that doesn't reek of lessons to be learned or homework to be done. If you can couch finding out about photosynthesis in a story about a young boy's adventures in the Amazon, for example, or craft a biography about the scientists who created the latest Mars rover in a picture book, then you might be onto something good.

Chapter **23**

Ten Children's-Author Recognitions to Dream About

Book prizes and awards look good on your living room wall — and help you sell your book. This chapter fills you in on some of the big trophies for children's book authors, plus a couple key lists.

Newbery Medal

The Association for Library Service to Children (ALSC) of the American Library Association (ALA), awards the Newbery Medal each year to the author of the most distinguished contribution to American literature for children.

Caldecott Medal

The ALSC awards the Caldecott Medal each year to the illustrator of the most distinguished American picture book for children.

Coretta Scott King Book Award

The Ethnic & Multicultural Information Exchange (EMIERT) presents the Coretta Scott King Award each year to honor the authors and illustrators of outstanding children's books about the African-American experience.

Printz Award

The Printz Committee gives the Michael L. Printz Award for Excellence in Young Adult Literature each year to the best book written for teenage readers.

Pura Belpré Award

The ALSC gives the Pura Belpré Award each year to the Latino or Latina author and illustrator whose work of children's literature "best portrays, affirms, and celebrates the Latino cultural experience."

Theodor Seuss Geisel Award

The ALSC bestows the Theodor Seuss Geisel Award to the author(s) and illustrator(s) of "the most distinguished American book for beginning readers published in English in the United States during the preceding year."

ALA Quick Pick & ALA Notable Books for Children

The ALA Quick Pick honor highlights fiction and nonfiction books "aimed at encouraging reading among teens who dislike to read for whatever reason."

Stonewall Book Award

The Rainbow Round Table of the ALA presents the Stonewall Book Award each year to books of "exceptional merit relating to the LGBTQIA+ experience."

Robert F. Sibert Informational Book Medal

Each year, the ALSC awards the Robert F. Sibert Informational Book Medal to the author(s) and illustrator(s) of "the most distinguished informational book published in the United States in English during the preceding year."

State and Local Book Awards

Many cities and states give awards — for example, the Texas Bluebonnet Award, given by the Texas Library Association — for outstanding new books. Check your local library for listings.

Index

Y

YA (young adult) books
  age appropriateness, 37
  audience, 38
  characters, 38
  coming-of-age issues, 37–38
  language, 38
  overview, 36
  pacing, 170
  storytelling, 38
  voice, 38
YouTube, 387, 395

Z

Zack Files series (Greenburg and
  Davis), 52
Zakarin, Debra Mostow, 98–99
Zobol, Ibi, 64

About the Authors

Lisa Rojany has written over 100 children's books, including several award-winning and bestselling titles. She is also a publishing executive and editor with over 25 years of professional experience in the industry and is the lead writer for *Writing Children's Books For Dummies*. Her Young Adult (YA) title, *The Twins of Auschwitz: The Inspiring True Story of a Young Girl Surviving Mengele's Hell* (Monoray), with Eva Kor, got a stellar review by Archbishop Desmond Tutu and is an international bestseller, having been published in many languages.

As well as spearheading four publishing startups, Lisa has simultaneously run her own successful business, Editorial Services of L.A. She is also publisher and editor in chief for New York Journal of Books (www.nyjournalofbooks.com), a well-respected, online-only book review site. She has been editorial/publishing director for Golden Books, Price Stern Sloan/Penguin Group USA, Intervisual Books, Gateway Learning Corp. (Hooked on Phonics), and other established publishing houses. Lisa loves working with fiction and general nonfiction writers for all ages, helping them make their work the best it can be. She lives with her family in Los Angeles. Lisa can be contacted through the Editorial Services of L.A. website (www.editorialservicesofla.com) or by e-mail at EditorialServicesofLA@gmail.com.

Peter Economy is a bestselling author, ghostwriter, and publishing consultant with more than 125 books to his credit. Peter is author or co-author of *Writing Fiction For Dummies; Managing For Dummies; Wait, I'm the Boss?!?; User Story Mapping: Discover the Whole Story, Build the Right Product; Wait, I'm Working With Who?!?; Creating an Orange Utopia; Enterprising Nonprofits: A Toolkit for Social Entrepreneurs*; and many more books. Check out Peter's website at www.petereconomy.com.

Dedication

To writers and illustrators everywhere, aspiring and published, who use their creativity, imagination, perseverance, and courage to create children's books that make a difference.

Authors' Acknowledgments

We would like to thank Bryn Barnard, Tim Bowers, Michael Cart, David A. Carter, Jodi Feinstein, Michael Green, Emma Walton Hamilton, Allison Higa, Randy Ingermanson, Tanya Hall, Barbara Fisch, Sarah Shealy, Leslie McGuire, Erin Molta, Stephen Mooser, Glenn Murray, Don Panec, Susan Patron, Jennifer Christopher Randle, Susan Goldman Rubin, Barney Saltzberg, Andy J. Smith, Rhonda Sturtz, Ted Sturtz, Peggy Tierney, Doug Whiteman, Cynthia Willenbrock, and

Debra Mostow Zakarin. Your words of wisdom and experience are deeply appreciated — and any errors are all our fault. We are also grateful to the authors, illustrators, and publishers who gave us permission to reprint book covers and interiors. Thanks as well to the folks at Wiley who cared enough to make this third, updated edition the best it could be: Alissa Schwipps, Michelle Hacker, Elizabeth Stilwell, Laura Miller, and Cynthia Helms.

Lisa's additional thanks: Thanks to Peter Economy, again! You are the best in too many ways to count! To Ana Guadalupe Sierra de Gonzales: *Su amistad y cariño me enseñan muchissimo cada día.* To my closest girlfriends and sister Amanda for always being there to encourage and support me and all my writing. To my children, the lights of my life. And to Shane: *Enfin. Je t'ai attendu toute ma vie. Maintenant que tu es là, chaque moment est encore plus fort, plus enrichissant et magique. Aucun mot ne saurait exprimer à quel point je t'aime.*

Peter's additional thanks: A thousand thanks are not enough to acknowledge the debt of gratitude I owe my co-author Lisa Rojany for putting her heart and soul into this book — thrice! You are a joy to work with — a real pro — and I am honored to be your writing partner and friend, again and always.

Publisher's Acknowledgments

Acquisitions Editor: Elizabeth Stilwell

Managing Editor: Michelle Hacker

Project Manager & Development Editor: Alissa Schwipps

Copy Editor: Laura K. Miller

Technical Editor: Cynthia Helms

Project Editor: Mohammed Zafar Ali

Cover Image: © Stock-Photo/Shutterstock